DOWN THE HALLWAY

BY

Sherry E. Showalter, PhD, LCSW, BCD

The story of one woman's journey with
Dissociative Identity Disorder.

Dedication

This book is dedicated to all those who suffer from Dissociative Identity Disorder; those who survive and thrive with DID; those who love them as they often search for understanding, as they walk the hallways in understanding and in healing and hope.

It is also dedicated to those in the helping professions. May you look through different eyes into the life of one woman, her Alters and her therapist as you strive with the best practice using the openness of your mind, heart and spirit. May you walk in beauty with two ears, to hear what is spoken, with two eyes that see the client along with yourself fully. May you use all of your senses to understand the workings of a complex mind. You have but one mouth, to speak with understanding. Walk closely with open arms to serve as the guardian of the long and difficult journey.

As the Cherokee say, **"Listen or the tongue will make you deaf."**

A very heartfelt thanks to "Charmaine" for the gift of her story. Charmaine has allowed me to tell her story, not for personal profit but rather to help those with DID understand that they are not alone and that they can make it through the maze and live their lives to the fullest.

CONTENTS

DOWN THE HALLWAY

Introduction

"Within each of us is a light, a unique bright light. There may be a time that others may help us stir those embers to assist in the flame once again burning brightly, but it is always there. FIRE your light to outshine the sun" [DRSES]

I never dreamed I would write a book called "Down the Hallway": a book based in truth. A story gifted to me about real life between a client and her therapist, with me being that therapist. Life is like that, it happens when you make other plans. When you dream, live and work outside the box of experience, have training, and education, the newness never grows old.

Now that I think about it, I also never dreamed I had the power to clear a cocktail party when folks asked me what I do for a living as I began to talk about holding someone as they were dying on a daily basis either! Funny how that happens, many talk of the many weddings and cruises they take as I talk of the many funerals I officiate or attend, thinking my stories are just as wonderful as theirs. Life is truly interesting.

I was gifted the rights to tell this story, and I was challenged as a person, as a therapist and as a writer in the telling of it. Who would have dreamed that it would turn out this way!

I was born in a small town called Radford in Virginia, in an extended family that learned very early about devastation, heartache and loss. My personal feelings of compassion and my understanding of grief came early from a matriarch Cherokee and grew, after we moved to Northern Virginia to the big city where everything from the air to the streets were different. Vague memories of sitting on a hill at The American University years later preparing a paper in Sociology on the Psycho-dynamics of behavior would later leave me wondering about the many dimensions of people, their thoughts and ideas. Little did I know I would spend decades caring for those in hospice suffering with trauma, dying, bereavement and mental health issues.

Textbook education was no match for learning about dysfunction in families, diversity, and mental health issues in life. Every step I took along life's highway demonstrated these issues for me. From my early days on the playground, throughout my adult personal life, I had plenty of evidence that everybody has their own issues. Only later when *"Not My Family"* was published in the *American Journal of Hospice and Palliative Care* and after experiencing my own family dysfunction at its' finest did I fully understand.

My Cherokee heritage has heightened my traditional social work practice to include the teachings of broad spirituality in practice; understanding and learning from those I have been honored to provide care for along the path. My greatest teachers have been those I have stood beside, knowing they were most often experiencing their very own personal 9/11.

I have a Gestalt approach to practice and that approach has served me well in my life. Each person is so distinctly unique and significantly different from all others. Each individual perceives the world in their own unique ways. I believe that each person is valued and respected as is, and any changes for that person are dictated and limited by what that person knows and wants. The theory and practice of Gestalt therapy is adaptable as a way of life, since it describes the basic processes that are suitable for any person to live with. It offers a set of constructs that are useful but not prescriptive.

Oh, there has been much learning along the way; from old man Freud for laughs and giggles, to Erickson, Perlmann, Carl Jung, and more. I've used Cognitive Behavior techniques, EMDR from Francine Shapiro, Trauma interventions from Charles Figley, and Michel Rank, along with methodologies from many of the best teachers/mentors around the world.

Death, dying and bereavement leaders and pioneers such as Elisabeth Kubler-Ross, Dame Cicely Saunders, Jo Mango, have been close to my heart as they were rebels in their own right. They were caring leaders, teaching without boxes, making others know they mattered while using interventions and understanding that connected the body/mind/spirit of those in need.

I believe in great foundations, continued education, with experience being life's best teacher. As a clinician, I subscribe to the first rule of practice " Do No Harm."

I shall not forget those whom I adore and still look to for inspiration; Bernie Siegel, Wilma Mankiller, Maya Angelou, Einstein, the great philosophers Willie Nelson and Dr. Seuss, and funny writers Carl Hiaasen and Rita Mae Brown for balance in life, therapy or moments of wonderment and/or those of bewilderment. I can already see Whoopi Goldberg playing ME in the full feature movie of "Down The Hallway" as I do believe we are sisters of another mother, so she should be quite stunning in the role while doing this book justice in the process!

"Never use others as the mirror to judge yourselves . Their view may be distorted and things may appear smaller than they are."   *[DRSES]*

There are times when all of that training, education and exposure still leave you short; times when you think you have heard, seen, touched, smelled it all, and find yourself standing on unfamiliar turf. It was that way as a 9/11 first responder when so many of us relied on our "gut." Movement into action was spurred by our initial horror. Our "stunned into action" steps as mental health specialists is what kept us on our feet and allowed us to do what was needed. We each found some inner strength that allowed us to continue on.

Many look back now, feeling the consequences of that still today: wondering how we did it, how we stood after having absorbed so much trauma and the pain of so many others. The sights, sounds and smells   at times are still activated by triggers; by memories, by the media, by the comments of others or by a perceived threat.

Clinicians are faced with a myriad of experiences of people and their stories. Those who have worked in this field of the "helping professions" have learned it is best to learn from each of their clients and to employ not one, but all the many techniques, creativity, and prayers they can. They often find there is more than meets the eye, as the "presenting problem" can at times be more than presents initially. As I have learned through the years, even in the most horrific of times, all is kept as part of the therapy. Set yourself free. Sometimes life is just not that orderly, nor is grief by the way. Words in a book are usually linear, however that is not how things work in real life. It does not work in grief, not grieving, not living, and certainly not a person with DID.

There were many times I had to watch for counter-transference issues, for anger (on my part and Charmaine's). There were times where I wanted to scream, cuss and bang my head on the wall, but a real professional does not do that sort of thing... do they? As a person, as a therapist, I also had to wonder at times, "if I was good enough, strong enough, brave enough" to continue. During my work with Charmaine I was grateful for my training in the different modalities of therapies, in my vast experience of working with people across the life span in their varied circumstances, situations and life stages.

We utilized many different modalities in our work together once we established trust, rapport, and safety in our relationship. We took one step at a time; at times re-visiting traumas, setting off triggers but always keeping her as safe as I could as a clinician.

From art therapy, to music, guided imagery, CBT, EMDR, talk therapy, and visualization, we worked in the dirt together and utilized journaling as a major breakthrough therapy, along with photographs and videos for understanding and acceptance of her DID. The only limits of healing are our imaginations: both Charmaine and I utilized a great deal of spirituality with each leg of this journey into and out of hell that was clinical, physical, spiritual and emotional.

There were times of tears, anger, laughter, and profound silence when I could have used a quote from Dr. Seuss to calm the waters. But the waters needed to be what they were at the time, often reminding us to never turn our back to the ocean; she is always changing. The tides roll in and they roll out, on that you can count.

Every once in a great while therapists are challenged beyond traditional teachings and experiences with those we are honored to work with. It is during these moments that we find our best experience comes from those individuals and families whom we serve with our best skills and the ability to think beyond the box. There are times when the therapeutic process is painful, is strenuous, and is crucial to healing. Each person walks their own walk at their own pace.

After my book *Healing Heartaches*, I received hundreds of emails from readers asking what my voice sounded like. Readers wanted to know. They seemed to feel they were sitting at their kitchen table with a cup of coffee talking to someone who understood "What they were living through", but wished they had the voice to go with it. We always wish for a voice.

As you read this book, if I have managed to capture the "voices", I will take a bow, as they are etched in my mind. We learn as we go. We also learn from the true experts; those who are living through their experiences and find the courage to come to someone who is willing to be open, and to journey with them through their life in all its dimensions, pain, and often horror. Their desire is to come to someone who is without judgment, who allows them to tell their story in their own time and way. There are times when the challenges are more than what we think of as complex; *"Down The Hallway"* was one of those times.

Welcome inside the brilliance of the brain of one woman and her many doors down a long hallway that she allowed me access to. This is her story: a story that has been given generously and freely to me to share so that others may see that mysteries and fears can be addressed in a holistic and healing manner.

"The stones talked to me as a child. As an adult, I had forgotten to talk back to them. We must remember we are all connected to the earth."
[DRSES]

It is a journey down a long hallway that is sometimes more than the mind can absorb. It is often fraught with uncertainties through the eyes of a practitioner and a client who appeared one day asking the simple yet complex question, "Am I crazy?"

Many clients, patients and families have touched me deeply through the years. They have stayed with me in my heart and my spirit across the miles I have traveled. This woman and her many dimensions, her doors and long hallway have settled into my heart in a way that is hard to imagine. I am filled with gratitude that I was trusted with her life and her journey.

This is <u>not</u> a book of psychotherapy, nor a technical book, nor a text book to be analyzed. This is a book that has challenging parts to read. It is not for the faint of heart. It is a dramatization and a re-creation of one person and her therapist who journeyed down paths that were sometimes pleasant and sometimes dark and scary. If I have fallen short, I take full responsibility, but I hope you will find this book worthy of your time as it speaks to the brilliance of the brain, and the heart's desire to heal the spirit.

Richard P. Kluft, M.D., Ph.D., practices psychiatry, psychoanalysis, and medical hypnosis in Bala Cynwyd, Pennsylvania. His work over 40 years with those suffering from DID is landmark. For those looking for more information on DID, he would be a wonderful source. He has walked the walk, talks the talk, and has the scars to prove it! Bless you Dr. Kluft for your work, your research and your brilliance. He also joins me in the belief that you treat the person not the illness.

That includes treating the Alters with respect and accepting them as being as real as they are.

This story is one that will put another face on as well as giving life once again to DID: (Dissociative Identity Disorder) in the Diagnostic and Statistical Manual IV (DSM IV); previously known as Multiple Personality Disorder.

As the storyteller of this journey, Down *the Hallway*, I have told it like it was and how it became. There may be parts of this book that are uncomfortable or painful to read, but it is reality; it may forever change the perspective of the reader to allow hope to once again remind all of us that our brains are remarkable in their ability to allow us to survive.

Charmaine purposely asked me to refrain from making this a book about the horrors, and abuse and to concentrate on the struggles and difficulties a DID patient goes through daily. It is already established in psychiatry references that horrific abuse is usually the cause of Dissociative Identity Disorder.

Charmaine and I wanted this to be about survival and the coping skills that a DID person has. For this reason, the details of the horrific abuse are mostly at the end of the book as Charmaine and I walk out of the hallway of hell. I found it impossible to not visit the trauma, the horror, the struggle, as it is real: it is palpable in her memories, in her journals, and in the life of those who live DID; along with the helping professionals that work with them.

All names and places have been changed to protect "Charmaine", her family and others also involved. Charmaine said her desire was not to hurt loved ones but to give hope to those with DID. This is the very reason little is mentioned, or names given of her children, or other family members. She says she has no desire to embarrass or demean her family or loved ones as the perpetrators of this horror are now dead.

The story is taken from my notes, our sessions, and my encounters with her Alters. I have inserted many journal entries that are actually from her diaries that Charmaine gave me for this book. There were also interviews, conversations with others who had met Charmaine along with her Alters over time. All used with full permission from Charmaine, who wants others with DID to know they can make it down the hallway of DID and emerge whole again.

This has been a journey bred from the brilliance of the brain and a person's ability to develop creative coping strategies which saved Charmaine's life. I am honored that this person called Charmaine did come to me for help; and that she did gift me with the rights to be a storyteller of the most sacred of stories: her story *Down The Hallway* which also includes her walk out of hell.

Charmaine hopes that this story will help others in their journey with Dissociative Identity Disorder and bring them comfort knowing that someone else knows the terror that comes from lapses in time, and the shame and pain that goes along with DID. She wants her story to give hope for understanding and the comfort of the potential of healing. She knows from her own experience that there is hope for others like her.

DISCLAIMER: Although written in novel form, this is a true story. One that is intense, scary, revolting, and filled with many emotions. It is also a story of triumph after integration. There will be times that this book could be very triggering and uncomfortable.

Chapter 1- The Coming Together

Charmaine appeared after an initial phone call prompted by her physician where she had asked the same question doubting her sanity. Charmaine actually feared that she had Alzheimer's.

The Doctor had suggested therapy for unresolved grief issues and stress. Reluctantly she searched out therapists, found my name from a friend and decided to "try me." I suppose that is how many relationships with therapists begin; at the suggestion or the desperation of those thinking they are crazy or have lost their mind or someone saying this is not my area of expertise, go somewhere else.

For Charmaine, she was truly worried that her sanity was in jeopardy; and although she doubted that grief was the culprit; she was now at the point where she was desperate; so she mustered the courage to walk down the hallway and through the door to my office. It is ironic that this walk down the hallway will lead us to an even more significant walk down another hallway.

I truly believe it takes great courage to take those steps for anyone. What I discovered over time was that it took the courage similar to that of a combat warrior for Charmaine to make those steps. I found it interesting during our initial phone consult that Charmaine had a geniune frankness about her, yet a vulnerability in her words. She was honest in telling me that she did not have money to private pay and her insurance barely paid for mental health services.

She let me know up front that if that was a problem she would like to know right then as she would not be able to afford to come in for sessions. She said she did not want to begin with someone that she would not continue with if we were a good fit. I liked that about her.

Having worked with clients for a long time, I had long ago made the decision that there would be times I would determine if I would see clients on a sliding scale fee, would speak at events pro Bono and something about this woman made me know that I would deal with that issue of money as it came; so I assured her we would work within her insurance as it was, and that would not be a problem.

When the spirit speaks to me; it speaks loudly and I have learned through the years to listen to that and so far it has worked out well in the service to others. For me, being a therapist is more than just textbooks. It is about knowing the person, taking the time to see all sides of them and letting them lead me to places I might not otherwise see inside them.

Charmaine would be one of my greatest gifts, teachers and lessons to date. She has certainly been a great teacher in the world of those we learn from in my profession if we are open to learning to "journey with" versus "telling or trying to intervene" rather than be with patients and clients where they are as helping professionals to be certain.

After assuring Charmaine that I would be happy to see her; I sensed relief and dread in her voice at the same time; yet that did not really surprise me as a therapist. In the validation that cost was established and she was accepted as a client I had really given her no way out; now the only thing left was for her to get in a car and get there.

Funny how that works; she chose a therapist with certain fees and knew she could not afford to pay privately and her insurance was not very good... yet she did not choose a different therapist? Perhaps she was secretly hoping I would say no.

Having used group therapy, family therapy, one to one and in person therapy, I had long ago discovered phone therapy as well for some through the years, and not so long ago discovered that Skype sessions with clients works well for those who are often travelers or those who have heard of me from a distance. We are only limited by our imaginations and our willingness.

I like to think that when one is willing to step through their fears and into a world of therapy to seek help that I am available if at all possible. I am extremely sensitive to tones of voices and to the tearful tones, listening hard to what is both said and unsaid. I find that I am not hindered in my work by phone sessions.

I noticed through the southern drawl with the familiar "thank you" regarding the payment consideration and accommodation, the subtle hint of "Oh, no, now I have no excuse not to go" that happens when one begins a relationship with a therapist.

I engaged Charmaine on the phone as I asked her some preliminary questions to get a better feel of the situation by phone. She was nervous yet it seemed that she was also candid in her responses and it also gave an opportunity for us to chat a bit more initially before she was to walk into the office for the first time.

She did sound stress-filled as we spoke and that could have been attributed to calling a therapist for the first time, but I had suspected it was much more than that. I could tell when she had mentioned that she was calling as a result of her physician telling her she "needed a therapist" that she did not like that suggestion and had almost doubted his reasoning. Yet, I held that thought at bay for now as I listened very carefully to her worry of her sanity being on the line and her doubt of grief being her issue at hand.

I found it Interesting that she seemed to have her mind made up that her physician was off the mark, yet was taking his advice to pursue therapy anyway. She also mentioned briefly that a man of the cloth had tried to counsel her for grief after the loss of her father but felt she was too complicated and not trying hard enough for him to spend the time. My thought was this was not really his area of expertise and he was at a loss as to what to do.

She was an intelligent woman and it was easy to see that she had given a lot of thought to therapy and it's "cost/benefit" now finding that this was the avenue she was in need of pursuing for herself. She was open yet hesitant in our phone consult, and it seemed that we would be a good match once we could establish trust and rapport in our face to face sessions.

I am certain that she did not think I would be affordable for her and she would have an "out" on coming, and was still trying to wrap her thoughts around the reality that we would be meeting very soon in the near future. I asked some formal questions as a way of determining who she was currently living with, what her day to day activities were, and checking boxes on preliminary paperwork that would save us time once she arrived at the office.

More importantly I was listening so that I could better get a sense of who would be talking through the door of my office in order to make her feel comfortable from the first moment she arrived. I could not remember fully, but it seemed that the stress never left her voice in that initial call. As I recall, it seems that Charmaine was taking a chance, a large chance on herself and on me with what seemed a monumental task: her feeling that she was just losing her grip on reality.

She felt she now had to find some answers and so far those in her health care practitioner group and faith community had let her down with what they had felt about her problems and she wondered if they listened at all to her in her quest or time of need.

Those moments of stepping out of that old comfort zone that seemed to take over and that old "fight or flight" adrenaline that courses through the mind and body at once that we all experience when our safety is perceived to be threatened is scary. I too have been there.

The next step of courage was up to her now; and I recognized that as well as she did. We set the appointment, and I really gave no more thought other than to smile when thinking about sitting across from a real southern accent that made you feel like you were in the plantation era for 50 minutes each week and wondering if I would adopt her accent to some degree as I am quite malleable in the sounds or accents of clients. I knew I would look forward to meeting this woman next week. I had no idea of the journey that we would soon begin.

As I wrote my initial paperwork based on our conversation, I had put on paper some notes as reminders: "client coming in to process unresolved grief issues and concern of payment waived... southern drawl." All is good.

I do remember her voice, the kindness in her voice and the fear that kept coming through and the heartache. It somehow spoke through her words or maybe it was through her silences? I was either hearing something in her words or perhaps in her silences that seemed to let me know that we would be peeling an onion here... Or maybe it was just me and just another phone consult.

There have been many clients that walked the hallway, through and in and out the doors, and some have taken up residence in my heart, but Charmaine has stood out in a way that has made me a better therapist and a better person. With each set of footprints I hear in every hallway along my travels and in my life, I am thankful for all of their stories.

I am eternally grateful as I now share a most incredible journey that is filled with hope for those who have entered the hallways of the brain in all its dimensions along with those who find themselves standing on the side of unfamiliar roads wondering how and when did they get here.

From walking this road with Charmaine, I have come to realize just how the world is not at all what we are taught in school, nor come to think of when looking at others. It is true that unless you have walked a mile in the moccasins of the wearer, you do not know the path or their journey.

Chapter 2- The First Session

Charmaine had entered my rather eclectic office and I noticed as she took my hand in hers she was wary of me and her surroundings. I felt the trembling of her hand as I shook it and knew this was a woman in deep distress.

I smiled at her as she looked at me, and showed her a seat hoping that she would see sincerity in my face as I recognized her stress and had felt her nervousness in her hand in mine. First sessions are often that way it seemed for clients as they move from their own comfort into unknown territory of the office of a therapist. It is uncomfortable for many and Charmaine appeared nervous and as uncomfortable as a fish out of water in many ways as she looked around.

My office has a vast collection of Native American art, gifts of clients through the years along with a corner of books, a sand painting area, stuffed bears, dolls and even coloring books tucked away for play therapy. That play therapy is used for the young ones and even adults from time to time.

On the desk lay copies of my book "Healing Heartaches" along with stones that have been gifted to me over time as well. So I felt sure she might have been busy taking it all in at once. I had an overstuffed chair behind the desk where I sat to make phone calls, to make notes and very rarely where I sat to see clients.

The majority of the time, I chose to sit near the client, and just pulled up a chair on the same side of the desk as the person I was seeing to be closer rather than have a barrier between us. It feels more intimate that way, more personable and for years it served both the client and me quite well.

Looking at her, I noticed her eyes, her discomfort as she locked eyes with mine and realized at first glance that Charmaine, a woman with very long, dark hair, dressed in dark colors was not exactly what I expected. Although to be honest, I do not know exactly what I was expecting at the time. Sometimes a voice gives us a visual that does not match the person when we meet them in person and sometimes it does.

She was well groomed, wearing no jewelry except a watch with a beaded bracelet. She had penetrating, haunting eyes and a face that told a story of a life that was lived with many layers I suspected. It was not in age but in her expressions that this life was revealed. There was an air of old soul and innocence about her but I could tell right away that she was very open and direct.

It was apparent it had taken almost all of her resources to make the trip to get through this door, and in this seat of the office. I had known the look of exhaustion and she wore it as many before her. We sat down and I offered coffee for her and she hesitantly accepted. Asking if I had that "pink sugar" and wanted to know did I mind also cream in her coffee, I smiled and told her I could accommodate that request.

Another who likes a little coffee with their milk and sugar I thought to myself with a smile. I turned to go and get our coffee noticing she was looking around the room with curiosity.

When I returned with her cup, I noticed that her hands were a bit shaky as she accepted it with a smile that indicated her gratitude and nervousness at the same time. Then I sat with her while asking what had brought her to me. I was not as interested in what a physician or a religious person had thought as much as what she thought. She was careful in her speech but wanted to be clear again in telling me that she was of little financial resources and was unable to pay for sessions and that her insurance paid minimally for mental health services.

Charmaine also expressed some concern on how records were kept and how people are labeled by insurance companies as mentally ill by their diagnosis and I could tell she had given a lot of thought to those issues and concerns. She was a very intelligent woman, and one who I had to give credit to in these days and times of the "holy grail of the DSM-IV" being changed and its implications.

I answered her questions as honestly as I could and admired her knowledge of the DSM and its current revisions that were underway. Charmaine smiled an uneasy but grateful smile of acknowledgment. Charmaine went on to say that a friend had suggested me, and she felt desperate so she had decided to see if I was the person that I was "made out to be" and that could help her. She wanted to know about the paperwork, the forms that needed to be filled out before we went any further and kept eyeing what was on my lap.

I then addressed her anxiety about money, and assured her we would work with what her insurance allowed and suggested that we get the paperwork out of the way. I explained the paperwork, the places for signatures and gave her the sheet for confidentiality and all of the necessary work. I watched as she signed noting she was right handed as so many of my clients are and had a comfortable grip on the pen.

She seemed to relax a bit as we "took care of the housekeeping" that needed to be done in the beginning of this session so that it was then out of the way. I excused myself to make copies of all that she had signed with me so that she could have them for her piece of mind as well.

I also noticed she was looking around; trying to get a "sense of the surroundings" and of me I suppose, to determine if indeed this would be or was a safe place. I had a sense that she was assessing me in her own way. She was trying to determine if I was all her friend may have said about me. She also was determining if she would allow herself to trust me as the one to share her feelings, thoughts, and inner most things with. I was hoping that she did find herself wanting to stay. There was something about her that made me know that this was a life story I wanted to hear.

Later she would let me know that she felt we were both "sizing each other up" on that first session and I thought that interesting and a great statement of honesty as I wrote my initial assessment, and she was doing the same. She let me know exactly what was happening on that day, once she had established I was safe and that she felt trust in our relationship.

For that day, I was listening intently and working to make her feel comfortable in what would become a place she came to for help and for guidance. I enjoyed her naturalness and her speaking her mind and her pulling no punches, her southern drawl as we began what was to become a long walk together, sometimes comical, often hard, sometimes dark and scary to be honest. But for that initial day, I saw that she was as uncomfortable as a duck out of water; and try as I could, comfort was not to be found as I knew she would just about rather be anywhere than in that office or chair talking with me.

Several times in the session I noticed as she glanced around the office that her eyes would settle on one of the paintings or gifts of others, the random cards strewn about from previous clients. She seemed to enjoy taking in the different things that were in the office as we talked and took time to pause from time to time. It showed me she was very aware of her surroundings and alert to things. I liked that she was but I also knew that many abused children became extremely aware of their immediate surroundings because it meant life or death for them.

She inquired if I saw children in my office once she noticed the corner there. I let her know that I did but it was rare. I said that I kept things that I felt many could benefit from in therapy. That seemed to interest her at times, but she was focused yet I felt she was trying to calm her mind as she glanced around. This office hopefully would become a place she spent much time in if she felt I was safe to entrust with her issues and thoughts.

She completed all the paperwork and as I glanced to see that all the signatures were in place, she looked intently at me and around the room, and then said rather bluntly; "I want to know and I want to ask something." After setting the papers down on the desk, I said, "I like you are direct, what do you want to know?" She replied, "Am I crazy?"

She met my eyes directly with her own and I saw a woman who was desperate for an answer and did not want to beat around the bush. My answer went something like this, "We have just met... you have just walked into my office and I admire the courage it took for you to pick up that phone, to call, to get in a car, to walk down that hall and now sit in front of me, meeting my eyes with yours. Given all of that, I would say this to you. "No I do not think you are crazy. I think you are someone that is suffering greatly and scared and needs answers."

Charmaine gave a deep sigh of relief as if I had just told her that her Cancer was in remission; or that the biopsy had come back negative. It was quite remarkable actually. I believe that anyone who walks a long hallway of whatever they are going through to make a phone call and then follow through and enter a door of one who is in the helping professions is in great distress. Then to have the person ask that question shows they may be in trouble; may be in pain, but I do not believe that they are crazy in the truest sense of the word crazy. I also know that many people have a very negative connotation of the word crazy.

Her relief at my answer was obvious, and her body's response was visible as we began our work together that day. It was a fast 50 minutes of beginning to hear Charmaine speak as I listened with all my senses to a woman that was still guarded and looked to me for a reaction in each word she uttered as she tested the waters of trust.

We began with what brought her into the office initially and my usual questions, yet her eyes spoke more than her words at times, leaving me wanting to hear more, yet respecting that this would take time and much trust along the journey.

Initial sessions are filled with taking a history, with paperwork and with asking questions that seem to make a person feel that nothing really impressive is happening at the time. It is something that has to be done; those tedious aspects are actually important; are you under a physician's care; have you had therapy before, do you drink, have you done drugs, what medications are you taking, have you ever been suicidal, what are your goals, what brought you here... and on it goes. That first session goes by rather quickly when you think about it, yet it is important, and it allows you to get a sense of each other's holistic view.

I have yet to really meet someone for the first time that does not really look you over along with your surroundings during that initial session. And I could tell that Charmaine was checking me out along with each detail of the office at the same time she was answering my questions.

There were times that I could also tell she was growing impatient with the questions and wanted to get to the reason she was in the office, wanting to get past the routine and humdrum beginnings as so many before her. I could see the restlessness in her body and her face as at times she would drum her fingers on the table beside her.

My sense was right on our phone conversation: we would be peeling the onion as I believed there was much to learn and many layers beneath this woman's calm exterior that she wanted to work on in addition to the more obvious grief issues. I did believe that she had more than grief on her mind, and more stories to tell that were at the source of what led her to me; and that we would get to them as time progressed. Something told me this was going to be very intense work with Charmaine.

She had an intensity about her and her nervousness was obvious no matter how hard I tried to make her feel more comfortable with this first session with me; yet that did not surprise me as many are stressful on their initial meeting and consult. It takes great courage for someone to seek help and to meet someone in an effort to determine if they are worthy of sharing their life with in times of need, stress and vulnerability.

I noticed it was taking a lot for her to sit still, and from time to time she would rub her hands on the legs of her sweat pants as if a reminder to not have her leg in motion, as many will do when under stress or habit. It seemed to calm her or self soothe her as we continued in our first session. I was glad to see that she had seemed to have adopted some sort of self soothing techniques to help her with the stress she was under.

There were times that I could see tears well up to the edge of her eyes, yet she would not allow herself to cry in front of me. I did not address that, as I did not want to push so quickly. It is important to allow a person to be where they are at the moment.

We let whatever happens happen, and Kleenex was nearby and I was certain that she had noticed them while she was taking in her surroundings on that first day. She worked hard to keep focused and in control as we talked and as I listened to her. Her eyes were haunting.

I let Charmaine know that I would be honest with her, that we would work together and focus on the issues that she felt were important as we built trust and rapport together. Charmaine did enter into some discussion that surprised me. Once she began, I listened intently, offered Kleenex quietly in order for her to know it was safe for her to continue speaking.

Charmaine began to cry and let me know that she had been experiencing "blackouts." She went on to describe a recent outing at her local store where she had found herself in a parking lot and a stranger had approached her asking if she was alright as she appeared lost there. She was taken aback and then realized she had no idea where she had parked her car, but quickly re-oriented herself to where she was in the middle of a parking lot and had to call her son for help.

As she spoke I listened and was nodding her to continue and reflected on the history I had taken. I remembered that she was not a drinker; did not use recreational drugs and had not mentioned any physical conditions or medications that may cause such events. Charmaine pulled out a Kleenex and wiped her eyes as she talked more about that event and her ongoing fear of losing her mind. She stated it had happened on more than one occasion.

As I listened, I found that I was doing a checklist of my own, wondering if she had a recent brain scan at her physician's office to rule out any of the physical underpinnings of problems that may be causing this or was this a manifestation of complicated grief or trauma? This was not a normal reaction to grief issues to be certain.

I offered and provided support as she continued to describe what she felt was fear pulsating through her in that moment of clutching a shopping cart and not knowing where her car was, who the woman wanting to help her was, or where she was. I empathized with her vivid description of helplessness and fear that she described and the immediate relief she found when her son suggested she calm down and walk through the lot pushing the panic button on her remote of the car until she was able to hear and find her car.

She was able to smile as she shared with me her love of her children and how her oldest son had this ability to always calm her and find a creative solution when things like getting lost happened. This led me to the conclusion that her son was used to helping her find her way. This confirmed my suspicion that this had been a way of life for Charmaine without her even realizing it.

There had been more than one episode of these experiences leading my client to experience distress. The big rush of adrenaline and after effects that can be experienced by people in crisis can also render them weak and terribly exhausted in addition to even question their sanity. I could not even imagine that the physician had not checked this thoroughly as she described it in such detail that I could even visualize it. No wonder she thought herself crazy.

Charmaine let me know that she had suffered this as a little child and recalled falling asleep in front of a television and awakening to her father kicking her on the floor, but could not for the life of her remember having been asleep. She stated that for most of her life even as a young child, people had said she was a day dreamer: she had received punishment both at home and school for daydreaming but she had no recall of it. Now as an adult, she was having what she said were numerous "blackouts" and was finding this most disturbing.

Most of her descriptions I silently nodded while taking notes as she spoke, yet I was wondering again if her physician knew of this, if she had brain scans and if or why this was happening. I did not like hearing what sounded like abuse in the family system that she had perhaps just recalled with a father kicking her, if that was a memory that had just perhaps come out, or if it was a gentle nudge by a Father waking his little one. We would have to pursue this further.

I thanked Charmaine for letting me know about this in our first session as I thought that would be very helpful in our work together and I could certainly see that it would be frightening. We had a very productive first session. As I watched her, I saw that she seemed relieved to have shared that, to have gotten it out to another and did not have to carry it as a secret any longer. I asked her if her current doctor had any records and performed any tests and she replied, "He says it is all in my head and its grief Doc."

We ended the first session by giving Charmaine homework that she would do between sessions and bring with her each time. She was to keep a journal of thoughts but only share when she was ready to do so.

I had a journal ready to provide for her as we parted company. I believe that if a client has a journal more so than just a notebook, they might take ownership of it and value it. I had found from my own experience that the clients would take care of the journal and take the time to write in them. I handed her the journal and walked her out to the porch. I told her that I looked forward to our next time together and I watched her get into her car and drive away. I knew she had to be emotionally exhausted from our time together.

"Charmaine's journal is always in Italics. I am, with Charmaine's permission, sharing the contents of her journal to show her thoughts as we journey together. This journal turned out to be a great tool in our therapy sessions and her eventual healing." DRSES)

Charmaine's Journal

I found myself standing in the middle of the Wal-Mart parking lot, gripping a buggy with a death grip. All I could think was "please God, no. Not again."

The strange thing was I knew where I was. It was not as if I did not recognize our Wal-Mart. Other times, I had no idea where I was. And I even knew why I was there because I could see the two fans in the buggy and we had talked about returning the two fans and getting two more. What I did not know was how I got there and where my car was.

Sheer panic was setting in. I felt like the world was spinning around me and I gripped the buggy even harder trying to stop the spinning. I did not know at the time but I was standing there with pure terror on my face.

An old lady stopped and put her hand on my arm and said "Hon, are you ok? "Honey, can you hear me? Are you ok?" She gently shook my arm and it seemed to stop the whirling and I turned my head slowly and looked at her. She looked like a movie in slow motion as her words came out slow and dragging like a record on the wrong speed.

I managed to tell her that I had just felt a little dizzy and that is why I was just standing there. She kept patting me and told me it was ok and that I had looked "plumb terrified" and she sure was glad that I was ok.

I started walking again like I knew where I was going but I had no idea where I had parked my car. I Finally stopped a couple of aisles over and called home and told my oldest son that I had done it again and had lost my car. I cannot count the times I have had to tell a story to cover for my blank spots in life.

My son thinks I am just very absent minded and told me calmly to press the emergency button on my remote to the car and to follow the alarm. I did and soon found my car on the other side of the Wal-Mart parking lot. I guess it is a good thing that my family thinks I am just a blonde in disguise and not too bright for it helps during times like this. My youngest two just think I am fun Mama but my oldest says I am a closet blonde. He cracks me up. But I know that it is true in a way. Not that all blondes are dumb but he is referring to the cartoon blondes.

As I drive home, my mind is racing. Damn, what the hell is wrong with me that I keep losing track of time and don't remember where I have been? Surely I am not getting an early Alzheimer's. Oh please, God don't let it be that.

I knew I had to get some answers because it was happening too much lately. I had always been this way but it was sporadic I thought. Lately, it seemed to happen every day and a few times, it was not just hours I was missing, it was days. Fortunately it was during holidays where the kids were with their Dad.

I feel like I am stuck in a time warp and have no control over myself. If it were not so scary, I would think aliens had taken me over and had mind control. But, it is scary. I am afraid to sleep, afraid almost to close my eyes just to rest them because something always seems to happen.

I have tried everything to get someone to give me answers. I went to the medical Doctor and he told me I had a B-12 deficiency and put me on shots. I went to the eye Doctor and he told me my eyes were fine. I even went to my Priest and told him something was wrong and he told me he thought it was just that I was grieving the loss of my parents as my father had died three months ago and my mother had been dead for ten years. He said that I needed some grief counseling and even offered to do it.

The Pastor at another church offered to do the counseling but I think he and I both soon learned that he was ill equipped for the problems I had. We tried for months and he became more frustrated and even upset at times that "prayer" was not curing me and I became even more desolate as I felt like I was failing.

No one has any answers and yet plenty are telling me things that do not make sense. A friend of the pastor was a family counselor and I even asked him to take me as a patient but I had no insurance and he told me no. Am I going crazy? Have I always been crazy? Oh someone please give me answers.

One day a friend told me about a therapist she had heard of. This friend did not know the depth of what was going on with me but she thought the therapist might help me as I seemed to be stressed so much and she assured me that this therapist was different. She was not your by the book therapist. She really listened and used a lot of holistic methodology. And so I called this therapist.

With great anxiety, I made the big step. I am not a drinker, but I fixed myself a very strong drink and sat at my desk that I like to call my office. As I sat there sipping, I found myself trembling at the thought of *talking to a stranger about things that I feared would get me labeled crazy.*

Finally, I shut the door and dialed the number given to me. I was about to hang the phone up when I heard this deep voice say "Doc" and suddenly I could not find my words. She repeated it and I managed to stutter out that I wanted to see her. She was very calm and we got through the phone preliminaries and an appointment was made.

I sat there for a while just staring off in space. This was "make it or break it" time. I had had grief counseling with a priest, therapy with a regular therapist and now, this Doc, with her willingness to use holistic methods and willingness to try new and innovative methods was my last chance. I knew that if she could not give me answers, then I was lost forever.

Her name is Doctor Sherry E. Showalter. I call her Doc... She is the reason I am writing all of this down as she asked me to keep a journal. I have always kept a diary so doing a journal was not new to me. What was new was writing and knowing that someone I did not know was going to read it and judge me.

What can I say about her? Well, she is Native American and I love that because I am part Native American and believe in Alternative healing methods. She is small and yet walks ten feet tall. You feel her presence when she walks in the room.

She is compassionate and yet mouthy too and I love that about her for I know where I stand with her. And I feel like maybe I have found someone who can give me answers. I sure am hoping so. I cannot take this anymore for I have found myself in other towns and not known how I got there, found myself in bed with strange men and even with a woman and things have gotten too scary.

We sort of sat there the first time feeling each other out. Words were carefully spoken as it felt like both of us were edging around the room eyeballing each other to see what would fall out. She asked me why I was there and I told her "because I think I am going crazy."

She told me if I had sense enough to think I was going crazy then I definitely was not. That was a relief to hear. I do have sense enough to know I am in trouble and something is wrong but at least not what most think of as "crazy" like the crazy woman down the street.

I could feel tears welling up inside me and panic flying around inside me like someone had opened a hornet's nest because I did not want to cry. No, damn it, not now. I wanted to speak calmly and succinctly so that I did not sound as anxious as I felt trying to explain to this woman what was going on. Ok, so she says I am not crazy then what the hell is wrong with me?

I slowly told her that I was having some blackouts. The first question, which I expected, was did I drink. I told her that I had never been a drinker but that this was upsetting me so that I had taken an occasional drink just to help me sleep.

I tried to explain to her that it was not just the loss of time that scared me for I had done that for years, even as a child. I got in more trouble because I would disappear playing and then not be able to tell my parents where I had been or what I had been doing.

I remember once when I and my siblings were lying on the floor at the feet of my parents watching TV; and the next thing I knew, my father had kicked me in the head. I scrambled to get out of reach and looked at him with tears on my face and my hand to the side of my head not knowing what I had done to deserve that.

"I have told you about not answering me" he yelled at me. I tried to tell him that I did not hear him but he would not listen. I guess I was daydreaming again? Teachers wrote on my report cards that I daydreamed all the time. I figured I just got lost in thought and time flew by.

She listened quietly, nodding occasionally. I burst into tears saying over and over "I am crazy. I know I am. This is not normal. What is wrong with me?" And I sat there sobbing. She quietly pushed Kleenex into my hands and assured me again that I was not crazy. She thought perhaps the grief of my father's death had triggered a traumatic response that went all the way back to my mother's death ten years before. I just Nodded and thought maybe that the pastor was right. Maybe it was just stress. Of course, he also told me that I would be well if I prayed hard enough and for a while I believed I was a horrible Christian because I prayed and prayed and never got better.

At the end of the session, I was almost afraid to tell her that I only had mediocre insurance but she assured me that it was ok. She said she was at a place in her life where she could choose to take special clients on if she wanted to and would only charge me what the insurance company paid. I started crying again. Handing me an appointment card, she patted my hand and told me that we would figure this out together.

For the first time in a long time, I felt hope. She told me she wanted me to keep a journal of everything and to bring it to each session so that we could see where my thoughts were going. She asked me to record everything I did, every routine and what my thoughts were.

I found myself carrying that notebook everywhere I went. Writing seemed to be cathartic for me. And thus began my written journey. I realized that my memories were like a slide show with many pictures missing. It reminded me of talking on a cell phone where you miss words and sentences because of a bad connection.

All I know is that if I do not get answers and help, I fear that I will lose myself totally. How do I explain that to Doc? I feel like I have lost so much of me and where it went I do not know. I just know that I love my children more than anything and for them I need answers.

I am afraid to be friends with anyone for fear that when they find out I am so crazy that they will not come around me anymore. I actually had one person at church tell me that if I quit acting so stupid that I might get invited to more places. I came home crying horribly. So many people from that place have hurt me with their cruel comments and excluding me. I quit going to church. I don't need church. I have God and He loves me. I just pray He does not think I am bad or strange. Maybe all the things happening are cause I am so bad. I will never believe in that church again. Never ever.

I look at my kids sleeping and think about the day they were born and think how this is all I ever wanted. They grow up so fast that I want to grab them with both hands and slow it down but you can't do it. My oldest, so tall and grown acting who will be sixteen soon and my middle child who is still in the pre-puberty area and still a joy to watch. And then there is my baby girl who is 5, so beautiful and loves her mama so.

And yet there were times I missed birthdays, holidays and things at school but they always ended up getting gifts and stuff and I never knew how. They said it came from me and my bank statements showed the money came from me. I need help. Please somebody help me.

Where is family when you need them? I have none. My parents have died now thanked God. And my sister died three years ago. There is no one left that still talks to me. I am just too weird they tell me.

"The Great Spirit gave you two ears and only one mouth, so you can talk half as much as you listen." – An old Native American belief that I follow when working with clients. The more we listen, the more we understand where they are coming from." DRSES

Chapter 3- Therapy Thoughts

After our initial session; I found myself reflecting on my session with Charmaine. I was looking over my notes that I took during the session and preparing to write my notes for her chart along with the first impressions of time spent with Charmaine.

Yes, I admit I still use the old fashioned way of recording my notes with clients and not the computer generated check box type of notes being used in this day and age. While I do admit it much easier to check boxes, I prefer the old way of writing my notes in order to get a better reflection of time spent with people and it affords me the opportunity to go back and really get a feel of what work we have done together.

As I thought about our time together; I was taken by her frankness as she became almost tearful yet was able to control herself when speaking about her blackout periods. I was struck by her nervousness and her pleading eyes when asked if I thought she was crazy. She presented in great turmoil as she looked around the room and at me, and so very stressful.

I was rather surprised when she disclosed that she was having "black outs" during our initial session and suspected that it was a subconscious desire to get that out of her system quickly, and it came from a desperation mode of a need to be heard.

I had conducted a thorough history as we spoke, and inquired if she was a social drinker, casual drinker or if she was a daily drinker when she started to bring that issue up. She did not strike me as a drinker at all; and left me to wonder if the stress and issues of loss or grief were perhaps her reasoning for this.

She had told me that she had been under the care of a physician and there was no record or physical evidence or impending testing for scans regarding the history of blackouts. I made a note to ask her on the next visit if she had any scans or reports from her physician about these black outs that I needed to know about. I wondered if she had any seizure history. I made a note to inquire about that as well.

Charmaine was matter of fact when she spoke of the incident as a child on the floor of her parents' home; being kicked by her father, and episodic themes of unconscious daydreaming. In my notes I had recorded this as a "red flag" on history of abuse as a child. Could this be a reason for her having blackouts and lost time I found myself wondering? She was emphatic that the blackouts have a history since childhood; that she was punished by her parents after a school report card she daydreamed.

Note to self: Charmaine had no visible emotion when relating that she had been beaten by her father or punished by her mother as a child. She has come to therapy for grief and unresolved issues of grief as well as anxiety, yet she has indicators of abuse by her parents and speaks of it as though she were telling you good morning.

Daydreaming is a form of dissociation, which we all do at times. While driving or watching TV, we just look up and there we are, wondering how we got where we are in a plot or on a street. Charmaine was describing the event(s) to me with some intensity and attaching these happenings to punishment as a child, yet not being able to recall certain things at the same time. Had the death of her final parent triggered this again for her?

Post trauma reactions in an adult or the child that was punished so long ago, perhaps? Questions to think about in the holistic care of a client, who had disclosed just enough to make me want more and I felt certain that as she felt safer, she would dig deeper to tell me just what I needed to know along the journey in order to be of best help to her when she was ready.

I was interested in knowing her thoughts as she gazed my office seeming to take it all in, wondering what and how she used those visuals in her assessment and her ability to tell me about the black outs she was currently having. I asked her to explain in as much detail that she could.

It was hard for me to imagine having "snapped out of it" so to speak in a parking lot with a stranger asking me if I was alright and not knowing where my car was. That had to be overwhelming to the system leaving one weak in the knees as well trying to get themselves together enough to summon the courage to find the right answer and then call on their son to re-establish some balance in the process of finding their car.

My feelings on Charmaine asking so desperately of whether or not she was or is crazy demonstrated her need to feel ok about what has been happening to her more times than she liked to admit. As I pondered this; I realized she had not told me if she had a full work up by her physician or truly if she had discussed this with him/her Had she?

Fifty minutes can go by rather quickly in a session. Particularly the first session, meeting someone and looking at the reason someone has come to you, entering unfamiliar offices and a person that you are trying to determine is worthy of your trust. Along with filling out papers that you are desperately trying to understand while holding a burning question on your sanity at the same time.

Stress debilitates the brain and adds to the "fight or flight" response; and she presented in a state of very high stress along with her descriptions and angst of not knowing what is wrong with her, nor how to "fix it" seemed to heighten her arousal of stress responses.

Charmaine was working hard to maintain focus during our session; she utilized self-soothing techniques that I doubt she realized that she was doing. She finally seemed to have a need to let me know of the black-outs and to fit that information in before she left the office and for that I was more than grateful. This client has more than grief issues to process.

I also have to wonder if she is feeling some sense of guilt as a result of not feeling the typical grief of most daughters who have lost both parents over a ten year period to death, depending on the quality and kinds of relationships she had experienced during her life. This client and her tears seemed to come from a deep place of sorrow, a place that she has desperately needed to find a safe place to share without comment or thought of another.

Many adults who lose parents I have called the "forgotten mourners" over time as they find themselves without supports to talk about their feelings and thoughts as adults who come to terms with life without those who gave them birth or adopted them. These people often find that the support wanes quickly, that they are lost in a world of thoughts and wishes for more time to say goodbye or to resolve issues left unattended over time, and they are forgotten in the world of grief and mourning.

Often the grief is complicated even more particularly if they did not have the best of relationships in their parent child lives. This is a difficult subject at best and many do not have a safe place to share those stories, or the conflicting feelings that accompany them.

I felt it would benefit Charmaine to start writing in a journal; to record her thoughts, feelings, and day-to-day activities in order to assist her in seeing and feeling more control over her world. It would also prove to be a great working tool for our time together. Providing her the journal to record each thought, daily routines, and habits will give me a better insight into her life as she lives it daily and heighten our work together.

I feel strongly that there is much to learn and much that this woman wants to work on. Yet, I also know from experience that she has not had many resources or supports to trust with her fears and trials from this initial meeting. As I completed my notes; I found myself thinking she has multiple issues that she wants to address; for now I will check the code for "depression and complicated grief" on the diagnosis codes.

Stress seems to be influencing much of her movements and can be seen in her eyes and body movement as she left the office as well. I will see her next week, and look forward to seeing if she is more or less comfortable in sharing her thoughts from our first time together or her journal with me at that time. I cannot help but wonder if this woman is or has been a victim of abuse in her last marriage that now has led to divorce and perhaps as long back as a child.

I had to wonder if only for a moment if these blackouts could be the result of some type of abuse if all medical conditions have been ruled out. We will walk this path at the client's pace one step at a time. I'm sure she thinks I am one of those dolls whose heads bobble after today's session as I listened with all my senses and watched as she spoke.

I wanted her to have the space and safety to guide me as we begin our work together. Something kept telling me that we would get a lot of time to know one another and that this would not be a "few sessions" based on our first time of my hearing her speak although guarded since I had already learned much.

Charmaine's Journal

The day after the therapy session

As I drove home, I thought about all the things I wanted to ask Doc but was afraid to. I had never felt safe a day in my life and even though I liked this Doc, I still did not feel safe. I wondered how much I could tell her before she might think I was crazy for real. If my ex-husband Jeremy got to talk to her, he would convince her I was a nut case for sure.

We divorced a couple of years ago and I was raising the kids on my own. Oh sure, he had a lot to say and used the child support as leverage. And now that he had married Miss Prissy pants, they wanted to take the kids away. She wanted them to call her Mom but they all asked me if they had to and I told them no. They only had to call her what they felt comfortable calling her.

He had told me enough times I was an embarrassment to him because I was so absent minded and flighty and I did not go with the flow of the "proper woman." I hated parties and dressing up. I have one dress and that is for funerals only. I try to dress where I do not stand out because I do not like to be in the spotlight.

Jeremy wanted me to dress like the women he worked around who went to bars and stuff. I still cannot believe he married prissy pants because she did not dress provocative either. But, she did dress very prim and proper. I preferred to dress where I blended in with the background so that people did not pay attention to me. .

Suddenly a horn blared and I realize I was daydreaming again. Maybe that is all that is wrong. Maybe I just day dream my time away. I just do not know. All I know is that when that man tried to take my arm and called me Laylee the other day and acted like he knew me, it scared me half to death. I have been afraid to leave the house ever since then. He acted like he knew me but I have never seen him and I did not know who Laylee is.

I guess I better hurry as Jeremy is picking the kids up in the morning to spend the month with him for the summer break. At least the two younger ones are excited. My oldest is too much of the teen to want to go away from his girlfriend and stay at his Dad's house with his new wife.

Maybe I can get some rest while they are gone. At least I will not have to worry about the outside doors being unlocked as the kids will not be there to do it. I swear, if I find out which one keeps playing games on me they are going to be in trouble.

I just cannot stop thinking about the new therapist. I have never seen a spiritual therapist before. What am I supposed to tell her? Our first session today was kind of strange. We talked briefly about why I thought I was going crazy and I told her about the time lapses I have had since I was a young child.

I also told her everyone said I was just a day dreamer and got lost in thought. But how do I tell her that things have gotten really strange lately? I mean, *how do you tell someone who could diagnose you as crazy that you think you are doing things but you do not remember them? I mean seriously, how the hell do I tell her that sometimes I walk into a room and glance in a mirror and do not know who I am because I look like a small Rambo with a baseball cap on and black T shirt with cigarettes rolled up in the sleeve and camouflage pants on and boots? And I do not smoke...*

Or I look like Miss Homemaker in a dress with an apron and my hair looks like the 1950's? Or even worse, I am dressed like some tramp going out to a bar with a low cut top on and short skirt and makeup galore. I am none of those things.

I keep wondering am I hallucinating. And even worse, lately my hair seems to change color like the weather. It is a good thing I keep a supply of my natural color so I can change it back. She will say I am crazy for sure. I cannot do this. I just cannot.

Why can I not just always be me? I wear loose jeans and a baggy shirt and my hair hangs down my back. I guess I do look like a reject from the 60's. Maybe that is why I like being alone so much. If only my artwork would pay then I could tell Jeremy to stuff it and he might leave me alone.

I guess I better stop writing and get busy getting the kids clothes all clean and packed for in the morning. If I know Jeremy, they will be here at 8 sharp and he will be ready to go and be impatient. He drives his big fancy vehicle and wears his designer clothes but does not want to help buy the kids clothes.

I sit here and look in this car mirror and think...ok I see me so why do I see that other crap.

Maybe I am losing my mind. I am heading to bed as I am whipped. I feel so tired like my feet are dragging in the carpet. Maybe I am just run down and not eating right. I just do not know. Hell I don't know who I am anymore.

Jeremy showed up this morning at 8 and is having a fit. I get the kids all set and the suitcases out there and Jeremy tells me that he cannot keep the kids for a month as he and his new wife want to go to the beach so they are bringing them back early.

I felt so angry for the kids because I could see the look in their eyes of hurt. I started to say something and then decided not to. Next thing I realize, the kids and Jeremy are on the sidewalk heading to the car and Jeremy looks pissed.

My teenage son had come running back and hugged me and says "thanks Mom. Wow you sure told Dad. Where did you learn that walk and talk? It was like seeing Rambo? And when you put your finger up in Dad's face, I thought I was gonna bust a gut" And he laughed and ran to join the others. What was he talking about? I did not say anything to his Dad.

As they drove off, the realization hit me. I had done it again. I felt sick to my stomach and the fear hit so hard that I started shaking and before I could move, I felt the familiar warm run down my legs. I turned and started trying to run to the bathroom and by the time I got there, my bladder had totally emptied itself and my pants were drenched and smelled of urine. This is what happens when I am scared and when I do not know what I am doing, it terrifies me that Jeremy will use it to get the kids.

It hit me so hard, I found myself leaning over the toilet vomiting violently. When I finally quit throwing up, I felt such shame and embarrassment that I could not stand it. I stripped off my clothes and got into the shower and was soon in my pajamas and I went and crawled into bed and pulled Sara my dog close to me. I know it was only 9 AM but I just wanted to go to my safe place inside me. I had had accidents like this since little and suffered great humiliation from it.

Ever since I could remember, I visualized this long hallway in my head with rooms on each side and at the end of the hall was my special room. It was all white, light, soft and no corners and I would go there and feel safe.

If something scared me, I would run down that hallway and the doors on each side would slam shut as I went by them. I can hear the echo in my head. Soon I found myself drifting off to sleep. I kept picturing Doc with her black headband and long braid and wondering how I would tell her all of this about what Jeremy would do to me.

I wondered did she ever think about the people who come to her as much as they think about her and what she might say. I wonder does she realize that she is in our heads all the time even to the point as of thinking "what would Doc say?"

I felt myself drifting in and out of sleep in what I have always called delirious sleep. I could feel hands on me and I would feel pressure forced inside of me and I wake Up slinging my arms and crying out "Jeremy, stop. NO." And then I remember feeling a

pain down there only it was not vaginal and I would wake up screaming and by then I would feel the hot urine flowing and wetting me, my gown and my bed. Damn that Jeremy. He knew I hated sex with him. And I hated worse that he knew ...he knew that if he could get my body to respond, he could use it against me. And the body always betrays you. He would tell me "see, I told you that you were just a slut. You love it. Don't tell me you hate it because I will do this every time. And he would force me to tell him I loved it.

He also knew anal sex would cause me to lose bladder control and he would laugh at me and tell me I was a filthy whore. He even tried to get the kids to talk ugly to me but it did not work thankfully.

I knew that pretending to like it with him was easier than that. Anything was better than that. And when I tried to leave, that lawyer told me that it was not rape what Jeremy did to me. I would not go to the gynecologist because I could not stand to be touched. It was all Jeremy's fault.

I hate him! Ooh how I hate him!!

Last nite I laid there trying to figure out what the hell could be wrong with me. And I still come back to I am crazy. This is not normal but crazy is the only word I can think of.

I have got to have a plan. I always work better with a plan. But damn it, it is hard to have a plan when you don't know what you are fighting. Right now all I know is I feel like I have the plague or something inside me.

Maybe Jeremy has given me some awful sex disease. I just don't know.....I just don't know. He was always having affairs and there is no telling what kind of disease he brought me.

"I am a very hands-on therapist. I did not use check boxes but wanted to have as much information as possible so that when I sit down each time with my client, I know exactly where we left off and what I had discerned and discovered in our sessions. I spend hours studying and looking up information to give my clients the very best care possible." DRSES

Chapter 4- The Sessions Continue

I had a busy day today and it started with looking at the calendar seeing all the clients I would be seeing. I realized it had been one month since my first session with Charmaine and I had to pause to wonder for a moment if she would show up, as those first time clients sometimes find reasons to not make the following sessions.

After I had checked the trusty voicemail and email and was happy to not have a message of cancellation, I began my day with other clients and paperwork. As I was walking my last client out the door, I saw Charmaine sitting on the steps of the porch; just sitting there quietly seeming to enjoy the sun.

After I bid farewell to my last client and received my weekly hug, I quietly sat down on the steps next to Charmaine as it appeared she was lost in thought. To this day, I am not sure if she even noticed that I was there at first. We sat quietly for a minute or two and to be honest it was a welcome respite to just sit and feel the sun on my face and the quietness of another with no words.

The last session had been intense as had the day with back to back clients and no more than 15 minutes between all. So sitting out on the porch with an early Charmaine was a welcomed relief to me. The paperwork of the day would have to wait until the end of the day: it was good that I had taken notes during actual visits to rely upon though, as I had not taken the time to update charts between clients.

Seems they were all running early on this day of days with much to talk about and I was the recipient of their words and journals of their weeks. It is an honor to work with others, particularly when they worked on goals and plans for their own health and healing spirits.

After a couple of minutes, it was I who broke the silence with, "Charmaine?" I had to repeat myself twice before I broke her from wherever she was in her mind, as I believe she was daydreaming or just enjoying the sun. As I watched Charmaine, her face seemed to be deep in thought and she truly had no idea I was sitting beside her. I have had times like that and they are so enjoyable I hated to bring her back from it.

She seemed a bit startled, jumped slightly and then said she was sorry, but she was thinking about her children. I could not help but smile thinking it must be some fine kids to take you away from traffic on this porch and me sitting here. She did not seem stressed as she sat there, so that was good and maybe it was the kids.

I asked her if she was ready to go inside, and with that, we got up from those steps and left the sun behind. We headed into the office but for that moment in time it had been lovely. There are some days that therapists and clients need that; a moment of silence in the sun sitting on a porch.

Again she had on dark colors, her hair smelled fresh washed and was shining on this beautiful day. Yet, she moved slowly toward the office and down the hallway, and declining coffee as I led her to the office and motioned her inside.

I had moved to behind the desk to grab my pen and papers and noticed she looked at me intently: she asked me if I planned to sit behind the desk during sessions. I smiled and told her I was getting my pen and paper, but hesitated and asked if she would be more comfortable if I sat there to which she replied quickly, "NO, but I was thinking maybe that is where you sit once you have done the papers with people."

Laughing, I assured her that I enjoyed sitting on the same side of the desk as she would be, in order to be closer to her as we spent time together. I think she appreciated that reply as she laughed with me and smiled as she watched me walk to the chair nearest to her.

I do like that she is honest and speaks what is on her mind I thought as I headed around the desk and to a chair that was close to hers. I had Kleenex on the desk and some bottled water there in the case that she would want either: I let her know the water was for her if she would like it. That seemed to surprise her as she let me know she had never been to therapy before but this was nothing like she thought it would be so far, and nothing like she had been told.

My first thought was she was giving me a compliment and almost decided to just smile and go with that thought, but then the thought occurred that might just be too simple. I pursued it with some questions "Are you surprised in a good way and what did you think it was going to be like?"

Charmaine mustered a small laugh and began to tell me that she did NOT expect to be offered coffee for one and that she thought I would have a couch and expect her to lay on it. She also thought I would sit "behind" the desk to talk to her, not sit with her or offer bottled water just for her.

It seems she had her own ideas of what this therapy thing was all about. She never dreamed that I would come out and sit on the porch beside her like a real person might. My having sat with her on the porch she said was so beyond the pale in her thoughts of what to expect next.

Charmaine also wanted to let me know that she liked the office and had thought a lot about it. She thought it was nice that so many had gifted me with things because that meant in her mind I must be pretty good at what I do. Then came the long pause.

I noticed that Charmaine had brought her journal and had hoped she would allow me to view it, and during this moment of pause I browsed my notes and saw my concerns about the blackouts; thinking it a good place for us to begin.

I brought up the blackouts and asked her about whether she had seen a physician about this and if there had been scans run or testing done with follow-up. Charmaine looked at me as if I had grown three heads and looked like an alien.

She told me that the Doctor said that she needed to see a therapist and basically said there was nothing wrong with her. She had had brain scans way in the past and nothing was said to be wrong with her. She seemed almost angry that I would ask her about all this, so I explained that the reason behind it was we wanted to rule out any medical conditions or medications that may be responsible for this.

Charmaine seemed to understand the concern and accept that as a possibility yet assured me that it was not biological and every possible test she knew of had been performed on her, leaving her even more convinced she was crazy and she was certain that was what her physician thought as well.

She continually moved her hands over her journal and appeared to be nervous and wanting to talk about it, finally saying, "I wrote in the journal here like you wanted me to." I asked her if I could see it and she handed it to me while looking deeply into my eyes.

As I opened her journal, I could not help but notice a page had been ripped out of it, as I slid my fingers over the seam of the binding there, wondering what had been written and perhaps regretted afterwards. I glanced at her writing, the words she had carefully laid out for herself and I suppose for me to see, the slant of her writing and its content.

When I looked up, I was still feeling the seam of the journal and realized that Charmaine had been and still was watching me, looking from me to my hands it seemed; as if waiting for me to ask her about it or to speak. I asked Charmaine how the week had gone for her; her day to day knowing that she was now in therapy and about to embark on a different level of working on grief and issues surrounding that.

She seemed distracted and had just sat there as she glanced from me to the window. When I mentioned grief, she immediately came back to the present with a quickness that was startling and seemed to be shocked by the word GRIEF. It was not lost on me how quickly she reacted to the word nor the implication of horror that she was grieving nor her words spoken so quickly after I had her attention.

She asked me about "what grief?" almost as if she was not grieving any losses, and then went into the story of her relationship with her parents and the dysfunction of their family in a way that was blunt and significant. That one moment defined with great clarity that abuse lay at the root of Charmaine's problems.

It seems I had asked the question at just the right time, or that her journal and that page that was ripped out must have held the key to something stronger than perhaps even she was aware of. She now sat and talked with an honesty about her family system in a manner that one would have thought she had spent years in therapy to have gotten to this point. She stated that she did not think she was grieving the death of her parents as they had not been very good parents to her: they were mean and spiteful people and she had moved almost across the country to get away from them as an adult.

As I listened I nodded and she talked and I made notes. There was not much I needed to say as she was providing an oral history of remarkable depth given it was the second session with a woman who was initially seeing me for complicated grief and yet she was adamant about saying that she was not grieving. She was like a well that had been primed and was flowing freely with her memories and with her facts of a childhood and life with parents that I would not wish on anyone: yet, she insisted that there were no grief or complications of that family dynamic to talk about as an adult woman.

It sounded as though she had never grieved a childhood that was lost long ago, nor grieved the loss of an adult who had to relocate just to get away from parents who refused to allow her to live her life fully as long as they were around. When I ask again about her father only dying recently her reply was "oh yes that, but I'm over that now." She provided a litany of reasons that she was not involved in the grief process, most of which made sense from her perspective. She was a grown woman who now was expressing what I suspected: abusive parents and the death of her father had triggered her her emotional state placing her in harm's way.

As I glanced at my watch I noticed we were almost out of time, so I wanted to wind up the hour with Charmaine. I noticed that she was almost out of breath from the rapid fire of disclosing so much of her family history: she herself looked as if she wondered how she had managed to reveal so much information from the question "how was your week."

She noticed I looked at my watch and said, "Boy, we sure ran out of time quick didn't we" as she grabbed the water bottle and drank. I smiled and nodded in her direction and had a thought that I would like to make a home visit to see Charmaine in her natural surroundings the next session.

I realized that we had not discussed the journal and the missing pages and that I had not read all she had written but we could take that up at the home visit. I wanted to see her in her relaxed state; to view her in her surroundings and perhaps get a clearer picture of why and what Charmaine really wanted to work on in our times together.

I also will admit that I was curious about the page that was torn from her journal as I could see indentations of scribble on the blank page that was left behind. She definitely did not want me to see what was in there and almost acted scared about it.

As we neared the end of the session, I shared the thought with Charmaine of visiting her in her home and asked her if that would be alright with her. She looked at me intently and then said, "Well, sure, if I can get my house cleaned by then, you can." I reminded her I was not coming to inspect her cleaning but coming to see her in her home and that was the difference: I wanted to see her where she is the most comfortable and to develop the best plan of care for her for what we would be working on together.

I wanted to see her in her own surroundings: I wanted to see how she dressed, how she survived, what she liked and how she managed each day with so much going on in her life, with stressors now activated. It seemed Charmaine had a lot on her plate, trying to raise her children and deal with a very uncooperative ex-husband who seemed to like having control over her, having black outs with no idea of where or when they occur, thinking herself crazy and needing validation that she was not.

A physician and two priests/ministers who thought that she was in need of grief counseling for unresolved grief were doing only what they knew how to do. I am dealing with the reality that her parents mistreated and or abused her as a youngster and child. She will now have to come to terms that they have died and she no longer has to fear or be able to confront them and their mistreatment.

This complicated grief brought about by her parents' deaths added to the dysfunction in her family which resulted in her move to get away from them. This was a lot for her to absorb at once. It was compounded by the trauma triggered by her father's death. This seemed to be triggering so much more that stemmed from a long time ago. I do believe this is what brought her to my office in search of someone safe to talk to and work through these problems.

She needed to feel safe enough to talk things through completely while problem solving with someone she trusted in order to enhance her coping strategies. We decided that I would visit on a Thursday for our next session. I sat behind the desk and made the appointment card for Charmaine, recorded it on my calendar and handed it to her.

She looked more at ease in the office as she was leaving. As we said goodbye, I found myself reminding her to keep up the good work on that journal.

She had said her kids had messed in the pages, but I somehow doubted that had happened as much as I thought perhaps she had written something she did not like and wanted to remove it from the journal.

Journals are personal, and when reflecting on what is written, many do not want others to read what is there. There are even times that the person who owns the journal does not like an entry, does not like the truths that are written and would rather destroy the writing than deal with the ink and the feelings in the messages.

We would get to that when Charmaine was ready, not a minute later or sooner... yet, I could not help but wonder about that missing page. It may be the detective in me, or the one who just is curious, but ultimately I knew I would find out.

She hesitated at the door and looked back at me; as if she wanted either to say more or wanted me to walk her out as we had walked in together. I waited a few seconds and when I realized that we had said all that would be said, I left my chair and walked outside with her, lightly touching her arm and telling her to take best care of herself and I looked forward to seeing her on Thursday.

I watched as Charmaine made her way to her car and eased into the seat. She waved as she drove away and I had a feeling that I had much to learn about Charmaine. She told me more in this session than I had ever imagined would be shared.

Time for those notes to write, and I did have a lot of notes to decipher from our time together. As I sat down to write them, it occurred to me how she had turned from the window so suddenly and seemed aghast when I mentioned her grief of her father.

She quickly let me know that she was *"over that"* as she began to lend insight on that family system as one who had been through some type of hell that resulted in leaving one coast and moving to the other just to get rid of all traces of a mother and father. That sounds like abuse to me.

It is not often that I hear an adult use that phrase when discussing grief on any level, it does not matter if they loved or despised the one who has died. If anything, those I have seen professionally and personally hate it when someone tells them to *"just get over it"* or says *"are you not over that yet?"*

It was after 7pm when I left the office that evening and I was weary, yet Charmaine and the idea of making a home visit still was in my mind as a sound and appropriate thing to do in order to gain more insight on this client.

I have made many home visits in my life and that is where one really gets to see, hear, smell and sense the whole of a person in their own environment. Although it is frowned upon in the many therapeutic milieus, I have used great discretion in these visits and walked away with a great wealth of information to enhance my ability to work more intensely with those I have been honored to walk along with on their journeys.

I looked forward to some black coffee and all that I would learn about Charmaine in her home during our next session together. I was already learning that she was an interesting woman who had many layers yet to be seen. I still am wondering why she chose me and what her real reasons are for coming to see me.

Charmaine's Journal
The Day after therapy

I got there a few minutes early. I did not want her to think I was giving up after only a few sessions. I decided to sit on the steps outside the front door of this little building. I heard her before I saw them step out on the porch. She was walking her last client out.

I sat there quietly and she sat down beside me and leaned back on her elbows on the step above. I can see the Indian in her and she always has on that black band around her forehead. I think I like that because she seems to have a special sense many people do not have.

I brought my journal like she asked but how the hell do I tell her what happened. I cannot. The other day when I got up that morning and was getting dressed, I looked at my desk and my journal was laying out. I could have sworn I tucked it in the drawer. I opened it to start writing and what I saw brought tears to my eyes. First was the paragraph I had written about finding the therapist and that I liked her pretty well and my fears of her thinking I was crazy. And then in what I call baby writing it said: Me P and a drawing of a little girl who had had an accident. Something about it touched the very core of me and I sat there crying with no sound able to come out of my mouth.

I felt like I had been caught in a bad dream and I wanted to run away....run to my cubby. Who did this? How do I tell the Doc this? She will hate me. Oh no, I feel it coming...that warmth on my leg. I was right. Once again I ruined my clothes. I am wearing a Kotex one of the maxi ones in case it happens at the Doc's office.

Who had done this? As I kept looking, I found more and more and some were ugly and had names I did not know. I know I am crazy...oh please someone help me. I feel like I can't breathe. My heart jumped into my chest every time I thought about those ugly pages. I feel like someone is trying to drive me crazy doing all this like I am caught in some horrible horror movie and can't get out

I am beginning to wonder if I have lost all my brain cells. Jeremy has hit me enough times that could have done it. It seemed like he always had his cop buddies to cover for him. I never thought I would be free from him ....and I am not. I never will be will I? He will always be controlling my life.

I must have drifted off into la la land at the Doc's as I heard my name called and looked up and there was Doc. She asked me where I went. I told her that I must have been daydreaming about my kids and got lost in the clouds outside. Gosh I hate lying to her like that because I hate lies. Just hate them. Jeremy lied so much to me.

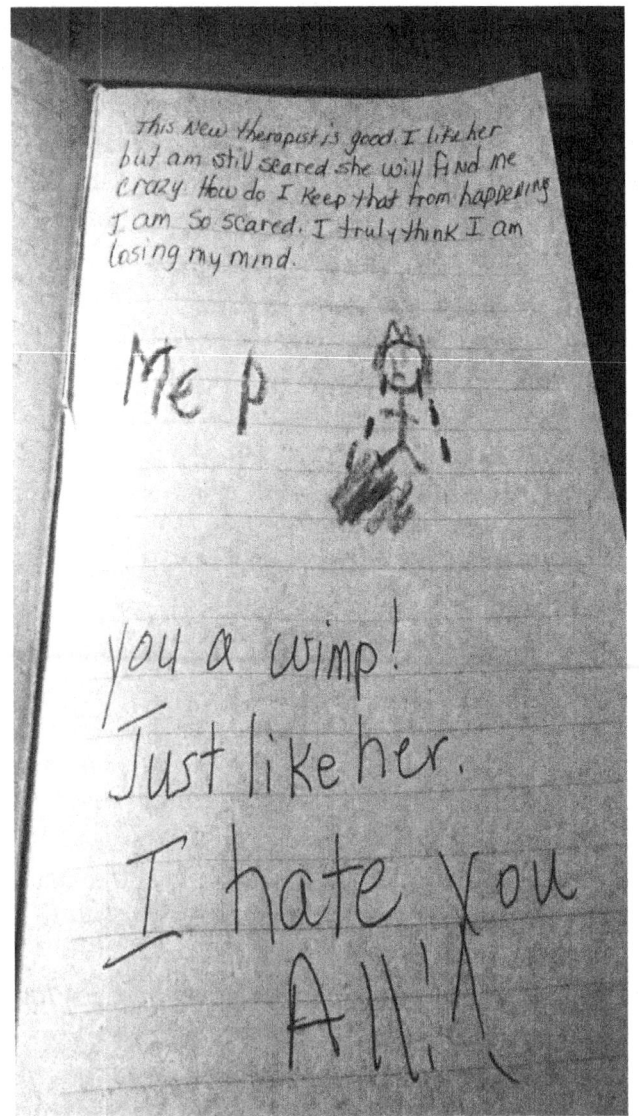

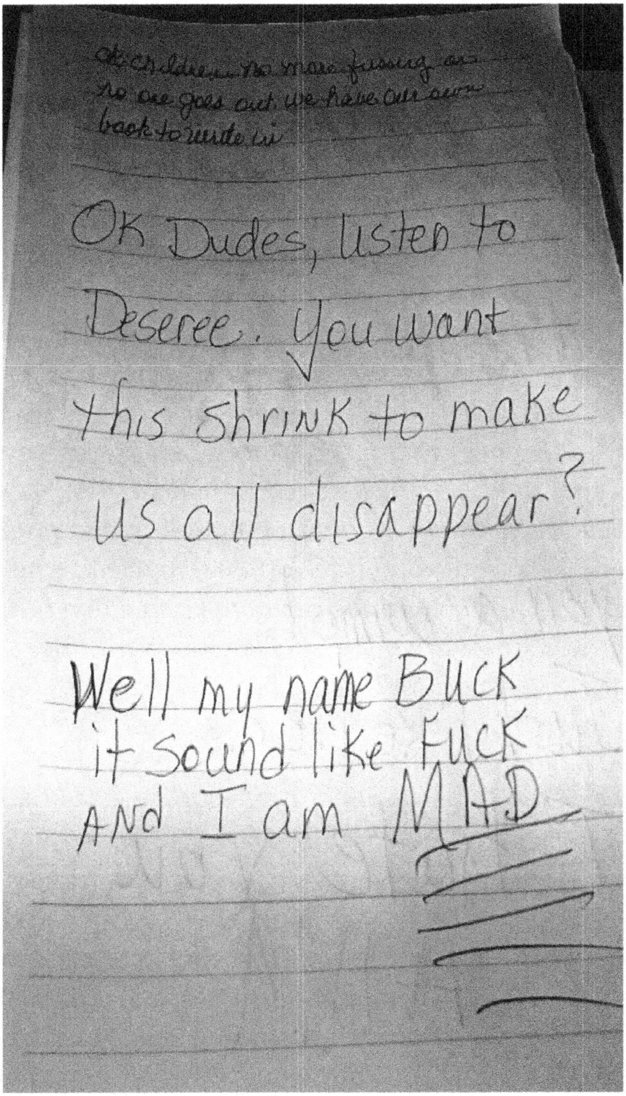

ok children no more fussing on
no one goes out. we have our own
back to write it

OK Dudes, listen to
Deseree. You want
this shrink to make
us all disappear?

Well my name BUCK
it sound like FUCK
AND I am MAD

After we sat down in the office, she asked me if I brought the journal. I said yes and I handed it to her. She opened it and propped it on her knees. I noticed she ran her hands over the blank page and down the seam in the middle but she never said a word. Whew. I was afraid she could tell I ripped out the page.

She asked me how things had gone the past couple of days. I briefly told her about Jeremy and his stunt with the kids but I left off the part about my son saying I acted like Rambo. I told her that I hoped I could get some rest while they were gone and quit having to constantly check the outside doors because one of the kids kept unlocking them. She just nodded.

When she again brought up how loss and grieving can make us lose total track of time, my head whipped around so fast I heard the vertebrae pop. I don't think I even had to say words...she knew by my face. She brought up my father dying but I let her know fast I was over that crap and was not grieving at all. I did not even go to the funeral.

I told her it was nothing to do with my dead father that she could mark that off her list. I told her we had the most dysfunctional family in history and did not even speak. I also let her know that I have moved to this coast to get away from them all. Her pencil was tapping gently on her notebook and she just nodded.

I saw her look at her watch and glanced down at mine and realized our fifty minutes were almost over. She asked me if she could come to my home since the kids were gone for the next session. She said sometimes when someone is blacking out, something is triggering it and that if she could see the home, it might give her some insight.

My mind was racing wondering if I could get the house cleaned well before she got there, but I agreed anyway. So, she wrote out the appointment card and handed to me and told me she would see me Thursday.

She again assured me that together we would figure out why I was losing time. She told me she would not abandon me and that she felt like many people had abandoned me in my lifetime and I just looked at her teary eyed and nodded yes. I got home and was so exhausted that all I wanted to do was sleep again. I seem to be doing that a lot lately. I made myself a cup of soup and was walking through the house making mental notes of what I needed to do before Thursday.

I walked into my bedroom. I loved this room because I have totally made it myself. I have always had a child's corner as I called it with dolls and books and toys. And this room was no exception. I had books ranging from The Little Engine That Could to Nancy Drew and The Hardy Boys. And I had dolls that were baby dolls, Little Lulu doll and even rag dolls. I just got great comfort in them. I called myself a collector. I also had my easel set up in there and loved to draw and pain.

When I glanced up at the easel, there was a picture on there. I thought one of the kids must have done it but I did not recognize anyone's artwork. This was a picture with a face that looked kind of like mine in the center. Whoever drew it was pretty good. And around that face were the faces of about ten people ranging from little kids to adults. It was signed Tina. Maybe it was someone my oldest son knew and he was leaving it to show me.

The strange thing was that the middle picture resembled me in some ways and had that haunting look in the eyes that I see now when I look in the mirror. Oh well, I will ask my son when they return.

The drawing left on the easel in my room found the day Doc was supposed to come and visit I keep looking at it. Who drew this? I know that looks like me in the middle but who would draw me and I not know it or who the others are. I just do not know.

Every time something like this happens, I feel this horrible knot in my stomach and want to cry and I do not know why. I just want to scream "I AM CRAZY"!!!

The one with the ponytail looks like my baby girl. Everyone always says my daughter looks just like me and that the boys look like my grandfather. Though Jeremy was not ugly, I was glad the boys did not have to carry that burden after the way he has treated them.

I finished my soup and decided to go to bed. It had been a long day. As I walked back into my bedroom from putting my soup cup in the kitchen sink, I noticed Sara was already on the bed waiting for me.

Most people that saw my room wanted to instantly rearrange it but this is how I have had my bedroom since I was a child. One side of the bed had to be touching the wall and I had to be where when I laid

down, I could look out my door. I also had to have lights on all over the house. Not bright ones but bright enough to see the whole rooms.

Pulling the covers up, I thought about what I needed to do tomorrow and then snuggled Sara up close and soon the rubbing of her fur puts me to sleep. My last thought was I hoped Ted the plumber showed up tomorrow so I could do all that laundry in the laundry room. Sometimes I am so scared that I cannot sleep. Every little sound makes me jump and I do not know why. I like being alone but sometimes I hear sounds like people talking and do not know where it comes from.

I call these the bar sounds You know the sounds like in a bar where you hear people but cannot tell a word they said. Maybe I am losing my hearing or have an inner ear thing going on. I think sometimes it is in my head and other times I fear someone is trying to break in. I will ask my Doc about it next time I do.

I think Jeremy did this to me when he used one of the kid's keys to come in one day when they were at school thinking I would go to bed with him. I was sleeping and woke up when he sat on the edge of the bed. I think Jeremy is trying to drive me crazy so he does not have to pay child support or alimony as I was never allowed to work. All I have ever done is sell a few pieces of art at yard sales.

Sometimes I feel like I am in a Sci Fi movie and someone has injected me with some kind of bug that creeps and crawls and my face falls off and I look like someone else. I know that does not make sense but that is how it feels.

She asked how I felt and my response was I felt like I had landed in a kind of hell and the hell was not knowing who I was all the time or what I was doing. This is why I never drank because I always wanted to be in control and not like when those people---those people-----who are those people? I feel so out of control.

Oh how do I explain all this to Doc? She is going to commit me, I just know it. If it were not for the kids, I would run away and start somewhere new. Maybe it would all disappear then. If I had no kids I could go to another town in another state and change my name. I hate when people look at me like here...like I am some kind of nut job.

I am starting to feel rather squirrely and I do not like the feeling. My fear is mounting and I am terrified that she will say I am nuts and recommend that I be committed. What do I do now?? Oh God, someone please help me.

The hallway...oh my hallway. To safety I will run just like Alice and the rabbit hole. I can run away to another place and live where everyone else is strange too.

The Alters

(Dramatization and a recreation of the Alters are taken from the journal and personal encounters by myself and others with Charmaine's Alters. DRSES)

"It's my turn to go out."

"No, it's my turn."

Suddenly Deseree told them all to stop fussing or no one would go out. She told them "remember what I told you? The more you fuss and no one gets to go out at all. Do you want to be put in the other room down there on the left? That is where the others are that act so ugly for now."

JR told her that he had to go out because the dryer and washer were both torn up and he was the only one that could fix them. Also the garage door was hanging. He said "come on Des, you know Charmaine cannot afford the repairman and I know how to fix them. Deseree agreed and told him that he could go out first and then gave him a stern look and said "Deseree, JR. Deseree. I hate Des."

A few were grumbling but when Deseree told them to stop, they all headed off to their rooms. All except little Charie, who turned and ran back up the hallway on baby pudgy legs holding her little hands up and opening and closing the hands saying "up pwease ..up pwease."

Deseree scooped her up and sat down in the rocker and started rocking her and singing to her. Charie had her thumb in her mouth and just smiled at her twisting one of her curls around her finger, content to be mothered.

JR slipped on his camouflage pants, wrapped his chest with the ace bandage to flatten the breasts, put on his black Tee shirt and boots and tucked his hair into his baseball cap. He gathered up the tools he needed to fix the washer and dryer and the garage door. He loved working when everyone was gone because it was so nice and quiet. He looked in the drawer for his cigarettes and rolled them in the sleeve of his shirt.

The only time he had problems was when those people came door to door handing out religious pamphlets. Now, once they saw him, they left before they reached the door. People thought he was Charmaine's brother. What a hoot. Well, at least they knew he was a guy.

It did not take long before the dryer and the washer was fixed and so was the garage door. JR pulled the cover off the motorcycle hidden in the corner of the double garage. He was ready for a ride and was going to do a little low riding out in the country and let off some energy before returning to the hallway.

Charmaine's Journal
Hours later

The doorbell started ringing. I opened my eye thinking who the hell is that now and realized it was daylight. I jump up and stagger down the hallway to answer the door. My head feels like it has become a watermelon and I am so tired. I open the door and it is Ted the repair guy.

As we headed down the hallway, Ted had teased me and said "going hunting today Char?" I turned around and looked at him quizzically and he pointed to my pants. When I looked down and saw the cammies, I almost tripped.

Damn it, this was getting beyond funny. Without looking I knew I probably had on a black tee shirt and a baseball cap. I tried to cover and said that I was doing dirty work and did not want to ruin my good clothes

When Ted checked the washer, he looked up with a strange look and told me the washer was fine. I told him "no way. Yesterday it would not let the water come out.." He said "well, it has a new filter on it. Did you have someone else fix it?" I told him that it must have been my oldest son trying to help. I thought to myself...how many times do I have to make up stories to cover what I do not know?

After Ted left, I figured I might as well get started on those piles of laundry. I grabbed the first bucket which was my teenage son's stuff. As I was sorting and putting whites in one pile, colors in another and towels in another, I picked up a hand towel and the odor hit my face and I threw up instantly. It reminded me of when I was pregnant and smells would make me vomit without any warning. I knew I was not pregnant. There was no way. That I knew for a fact.

When I threw up, I dropped the hand towel in the washer. I decided I did not want to get it again and just threw the rest of the towels in and start the washer. I might have to ask Doc about that one day. I had had this happen quite a few times and did not understand why.

I was glad the kids were gone because this was sure an off day. I hope Doc can figure out in what the hell is wrong with me because I hate this ending up looking like a stranger and not knowing why. I reached up to run my fingers through my hair and felt the cap. I started to snatch it off and decided to go look in the mirror. I think I will take a picture to show the Doc. Maybe that will help.

When I got inside, I looked in the full length mirror in my closet and looking back, had you not known I was a female, you would have sworn I was a thin, small flat chested looking male in military clothes. Who the hell is this???

Why do I keep asking that? It is me...but it is not me. I ought to dress like this when Jeremy brings the kids home next time and see what he says but I will not. I do not want Jeremy causing a stir or his bitchy ass wife. Jeremy does not want the kids, he just wants to stop paying child support and he would take the kids just to do that. And then he would let them run wild. I am starting to feel like one of those paper dolls where you have all those cut out clothes for them and different hair and stuff. I never know what I will look like when I look in the mirror. That is why I took all the mirrors down except the one in my bathroom.

I really did love Jeremy when I married him. I was trying to escape "THE FAMILY" as I call them. I hated the desert land and I hated them. And Jeremy was a good escape I thought. NOT SO

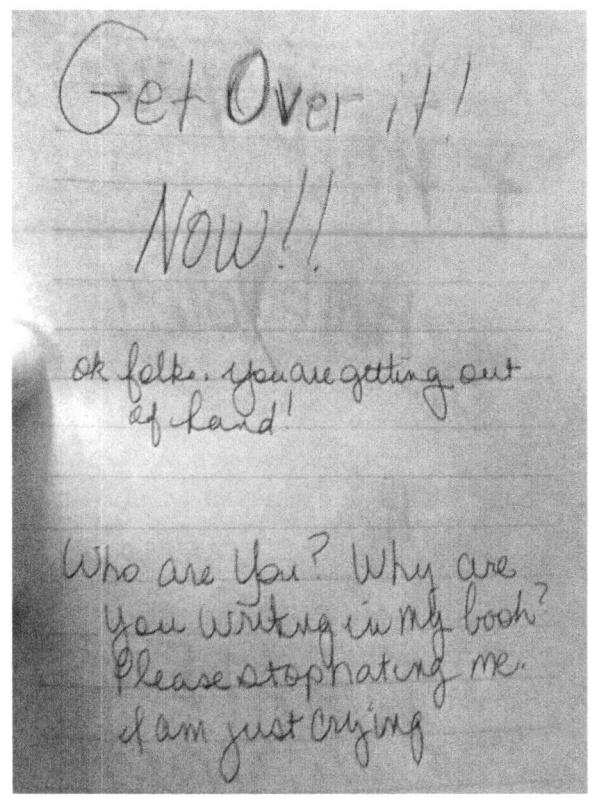

Chapter 5- The Home Visit

It was going to be a great day, that was my mantra for the day, and I planned to stick to it. After all, I get to make a home visit and get out of the office for a while and that was a great thing. I had scheduled Charmaine so that she would be my last appointment and then had plans to meet with friends for an early dinner, so it was going to be a fine day indeed in my way of thinking.

As I plugged Charmaine's address into my trusty little GPS, I found myself listening to music on my way there. I was enjoying the scenery lost in thought while reviewing the last session with Charmaine. Thinking of her journal with the missing page, I could still see the indents of writing that had been rather forcefully made leaving an imprint on the next page. It was a mystery to me.

I must have been lost in thought as I was brought out of those thoughts with the familiar voice of the GPS telling me I was one quarter mile from my destination on the right. Talk about dissociating and driving; it seems to happen all the time with these gadgets of convenience these days.

I pulled into a driveway and noticed Charmaine's car there, so was assured that I was in the right place. I noticed the flowers were blooming against the house and some toys scattered here and there: it was obvious that the house needed some work and that children were on the loose when home by the toys and balls and such in the yard.

Those flowers looked lovely though and it seemed that Charmaine has a green thumb in an area where I do notice there were no other flowers in bloom in the neighborhood. As I approach the steps to the house I ring the doorbell and catch a glimpse of someone on the other side of the door, but I am not so sure who I am looking at.

There is a hesitation in answering the door and with a second look it does seem I am seeing Charmaine, but what in the world has she done to herself? Maybe I am seeing her sister? Guess I will just have to wait and see if anyone finally answers the door as it seems I'm standing here a long time before I hear the squeak of a much needed oiling on the hinged door as it swings open, and there stands Charmaine looking quite flustered and a "red head" Charmaine at that.

She welcomes me in and immediately begins to apologize for the condition of her home, that stuff is just everywhere as she runs her fingers through her hair. She lets me know she was planning for her kids' upcoming Halloween costume with the new color, and I smile while looking at it and biting the inside of my lip wondering how could this happen. Why would Charmaine color her hair now when she knew I was coming?

Her home is strewn with all matter of things; toys, stuff everywhere, and clutter to beat the band as we meander our way to the dining room table where she offers me a cup of coffee and I gladly accept. I am taken aback by the change of hair color as it does not fit with Charmaine and her presence, her style and her simplicity in our times together to date.

She continues to talk about her home saying to please forgive her for not getting everything cleaned up and prepared for our time together. I cannot help but notice she looks exhausted. I notice heavy bags under her eyes: the darkness there led me to believe she lacked sleep. I asked her if she is sleeping at night and she lets me know that if she gets more than 2 or 3 hours she thinks herself lucky.

As I scan the room while she is pouring the coffee I am rather surprised at all I am seeing, especially knowing how much she stressed cleaning house before I arrived, yet I arrive to her looking so flustered and on top of everything else, a brilliant red-haired Charmaine. And she acts almost like she is as shocked at her hair as I am.

As I wait for coffee, I look around the living room and notice there are only a few pictures on display and they are of her sons and her daughter. Her daughter is a mini Charmaine and simply beautiful. I pick them up and look closer at them; there is a strong resemblance to Charmaine, all dark haired like her with big, blue eyes. There are no other photographs in the house of family, and the walls have a few scattered pictures placed here and there.

It looks as though someone had made quite a mess and there were things scattered, but the home had a sterile feel to it, almost as though it was devoid of character and the usual personal touches that one would expect having children in a home. It struck me that only a few photographs were placed on the table of the children, yet none of them were together. There were no other photographs of friends or family.

Charmaine offers to give me a tour of her home as she hands me my coffee, black. She makes the comment that she cannot understand how anyone can drink coffee without cream and sugar and we both laugh on that one, as we begin to walk down the hallway.

It was amazing to see her in this light, and to watch as she continually stroked her hand through her hair distracted by its new coloring as much as I found myself wondering the why of it all. I felt a little sorry for her but I knew this was meant to be for me to see this. I let the Spirit guide me when I am working.

I gaze into the children's rooms and am struck by how very neat they are: everything is in its place and clean as a whistle. She sure did put all effort into those rooms. Her kids will have a grand time once home from their Dad's with all that energy to make it shine .

There are two rooms. One is the perfect child's room and that child is a little girl. By the toys and the decorations I would say anywhere between three and six or seven. And the other room is a typical boys room though there seems to be some disparity in ages: one side had bats and balls and trucks and toys and the other side almost reminds me of a college student with the bed all neat, college banners on the wall and the desk all set up with a computer.

As we move on to her room, I still glance at Charmaine's brilliant red hair, unable to believe that she has dyed her hair like that. It is so foreign a concept to me given how quiet and simple she states that she is about things. Not liking to draw attention to herself, she has dyed her hair so that it is bound to be an attention getter when she steps outside to the world: a very contradictory move on her part.

When I tell you "brilliant red", that is not an understatement for a woman who mainly wears subdued colors and calls no attention to herself with jewelry, hairstyles or make up. It seems she was truly as shocked as I was. And not only shocked; there was something else but I could not put my finger on it yet.

I found that to be more disturbing than the color as I watched her reach up and run her fingers through it so often as she spoke to me while I was there, knowing that she could barely wait to get her hands on the right dye to restore her hair to its original color as soon as I left her home.

Now I am walking with this red haired woman, passing two bedrooms that are so clean you can white glove test them after walking into the main room that looks like a tornado went through it. My mind was moving rapidly as I tried to assimilate all this for my notes for later. As we entered Charmaine's bedroom I was in for another surprise; her bed was a mess, covered with so many things on and around it that she only has a two foot wide space the length of one person to lay on. I see that a lot with people who are trying to keep something out and feel unsafe.

There is a corner filled with dolls that look so real one would have to look twice to be sure they were not breathing, and an easel that had what appeared to be pencil drawings of people. I glanced at it and noticed that one of those people resembled Charmaine in many ways, and I could not help but wonder who the artist was.

Charmaine showed me her bathroom and it was as messy as the rest of the home, but interestingly it has a bolt lock on the inside of the door. I found myself running my finger over that lock and wondered who/what was Charmaine protecting herself from when she had to run there and used that bolt? It was not a little lock, but one of heavy metal, used to keep someone OUT and it is on the inside of a bathroom. . I was unused to seeing a bolt like that on the inside of a bathroom in someone's home.

As Charmaine was talking, I realized I was rubbing that lock with my finger as Charmaine apologized for the mess as if she were almost surprised by it. I had my finger on that lock as if it would tell me the secrets, the fears that it may know.

I nodded to acknowledge her, yet my mind was racing with wondering. How could the children's rooms be so pristine, especially the boys' room and yet the rest of the house was so untidy on a day when she knew I was to arrive? Questions kept filling my mind. I was working hard to listen to what she was telling me at the same time as I was taking in all that I was seeing and learning.

I noticed while in the bathroom that Charmaine glanced at herself in the mirror several times while she spoke. She would make an awkward disgusted face each time as she ran her fingers through her hair. Charmaine shook her head as if perplexed by the color as she continued to talk to me. I stood in the doorway with my finger on that bolt and continued to pay attention to her words.

She seemed nervous and out of sorts as I listened to her intently while I stood there and looked about. One could only stand in a bathroom and bedroom for so long before it becomes rather closed feeling and uncomfortable. I realized that at times she was so caught up in her words and explanations of things that perhaps she had forgotten that we were standing in her bedroom, among so much clutter and things in disarray. She seemed as perplexed by it as I was at the time.

"The lifelike doll that I snapped a picture of because it looked so real." DRSES

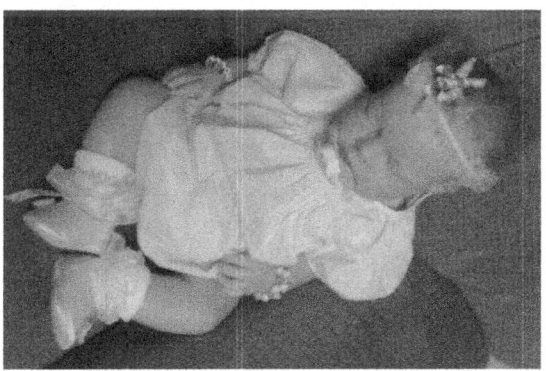

Charmaine told me about her love of dolls. How does a woman come to have dolls so life like in her bedroom? Is she a collector perhaps? Yet, she was of little means and these looked to be expensive collector dolls. I used my phone and took a picture of one of them to ask a friend who collects dolls.

Many questions continued to fill my mind; and that dye job on her beautiful dark hair was a huge puzzle piece. Charmaine told me she had always loved dolls since a wee child, and kept a little corner dedicated to them.

Charmaine loved looking at and handling her doll collection. She had a great fondness that she expressed for their expressions and for the clothing they were dressed in sitting there in the corner of her room. I could tell by the way she looked at them and spoke of them that they were special to her, and wondered if they were from her childhood or evoked tender memories for her.

My eyes kept being drawn to the sketch that sat on an easel in her room, and I found myself looking at it again and again as she spoke. Who are the ones around the center face, for I know in my heart that center picture IS Charmaine.

When she had finished telling me of the dolls, I had to ask; "Charmaine, who drew those sketches on the easel: they are quite good. Did you draw them? They are quite amazing and the eyes are haunting are they not?" Abruptly Charmaine replied that she did not know who drew them: I was stunned by that. She answered quickly and wanted to return to the kitchen after the hasty answer.

I lingered there a bit and had to shake my head on her answer. I stood and looked around her room and it was filled with such complexity. This intricate sketch of people drawn on an easel in her bedroom yet she does not know who drew it or why. That gave me more to wonder about on the list that was growing during this home visit with Charmaine as we walk through her bedroom back into the dining room and to the kitchen table.

I felt badly that she kept apologizing for the state of her home while I was there, yet it was an indicator to me that she was as shocked by it as anyone; had this occurred during one of her black outs was entering my and not told me?

Charmaine was truly out of sorts on this visit; she seemed on the verge of tears several times and not herself. She answered my questions quickly and then would look at me to see if I had reactions to her answers or so it seemed. It is almost as if Charmaine was as shocked or even more shocked than I am at her hair, her house and she is struggling to gain control of how she feels. Part of me feels sorry for her but I know that this is part of the problem and must be addressed.

I was also curious about the placement of her bed in her bedroom as it seemed to be tucked in the corner and out of sync with the room. As we sat with our coffee I casually asked about her bed placement, and if she had chosen its placement. She let me know it was the only way she could sleep, that her bed had been that way all of her life ever since a child. Yet, she still only slept a couple or three hours a night.

It seemed by her response that she felt safer with her bed tucked in the corner rather than in the middle of the room, and that she was not as concerned about fashion or bedroom style as much as she was concerned about how she had always had her bed in her room. It was her "safe place" she let me know.

Charmaine explained that the placement of her bed had to be a certain way, in a corner in order for her to feel comfortable and she usually kept a low light on all the time and quickly added that it was because of being able to see the kids should they come into her room needing her during the night. She said that her daughter was afraid of the dark.

This visit in her home had certainly opened doors for me as a therapist and it appeared I had caught her on a day of distress although it was planned for me to be there last week. She looked so fragile and tired today and so very scattered as if she were seeing each room for the first time with me.

As we walked in and out of the rooms I watched Charmaine and each reaction seemed more upsetting than the last, from the cluttered bathroom to the kitchen filled with dishes in the sink. Charmaine was appalled much more so than I was. As she spoke, I could not help but notice the amount of time she spent raking her hands through her hair as if she was really concentrating on the reality of its color now. I had asked her if she ever takes sleeping pills to help her at night and she snapped her whole body around to answer with an emphatic "NO I never want to be knocked out."

She was adamant in her answer although I had only asked casually when she spoke of not sleeping well, and it appears she caught herself as she quickly looked at me and with a soft voice explained that she could not be knocked out because the boys may need her and she had to be able to hear them and be responsive to them at all times.

It gave me the impression that Charmaine was aware of her blunt answers and was trying to reel herself in on many levels yet her distress and anxiety were apparent. I was low-keyed in listening and did not take personally her bluntness in her answers. I only made a mental note to later re-visit the questions in more detail as we continued.

It seems that Charmaine was fearful of something or has a history of something in her life that has made her afraid to be in a sound sleep or vulnerable yet today with all I have seen there seems to be more questions than I have answers for. Sleep deprivation can Alter the senses, and also leave one feeling vulnerable as I thought of her need of a night light, need for positioning of the bed in a certain way and still wondered if she needed to be semi-alert as a result of previous trauma.

After seeing her home, we return to the dining room table and I am again struck by the blazing red hair, the circles under Charmaine's eyes and by her look of a deer in the headlights as she tries to engage with me. I asked her if she had written in her journal and she let me know she had but today was not a good day to share it with me, and I told her that was fine. I could see the stress on her and did not want to cause her to run emotionally from me.

I asked her if she had anything she wanted to talk to me about, any questions for me or anything that I needed to know. I had my answer already but felt the need to try and ask. Charmaine was exhausted and had used all she had to get through this visit. She was surprised; I was surprised and knew it would soon be time for this visit to end.

I was hoping that there was something like the grief word that would spontaneously allow her to just talk to me about how the hair turned red or the house turned upside down, but that was not the case for the day. She was just drained.

As we ended our time together, I started to leave, and got to the door with Charmaine thanking me for coming. As I started to walk out the door, I thought for a moment and then came back to the table and told Charmaine I needed to spend a few more minutes with her. I wanted her to enter into a contract with me; a contract of brutal honesty of sorts and to commit to me that she would be honest at all times with me as we worked together. I knew this was essential for me to help her.

Charmaine nodded her agreement, but that was not enough for me. I wanted her to verbalize it, until she was back in the office to sign an official contract of honesty. She looked me in the eye and said that she agreed and we shook hands.

After that, I asked her point blank, "What did you rip out of your journal." Charmaine told me that her kids had written something in her journal and then Charmaine hung her head.

I just sat quietly for a bit, and then she got up and went to her room returning with a piece of paper that was wadded in a tight ball for me. I thanked her for that and asked if I might take that easel drawing with me to the office for a while and she agreed to that as well and handed it to me with her head down.

I was beginning to think we had a puzzle here that we would together figure out, and it was a very big puzzle that would require patience, honesty and honor. Again I reached over and took Charmaine's hand in mine, her eyes met mine and I repeated to her the importance of honesty in our communications.

Looking at her, I said "here's the deal Charmaine, we will find our way through this, through honesty and communication and hard work, that's the deal ok?" Charmaine had tears in her eyes and said, "Ok, you have a deal" as she nodded her head. As I was about to stand up, I stopped and sat back down and placed my hand on Charmaine's arm and said, "One more thing Charmaine, then you should probably rest. Did you color your hair red?"

Charmaine looked like she might faint and replied that she did not think so, she honestly did not think she would do something like that. I could not imagine that Charmaine would color/dye her hair either which made the puzzle even more complicated.

When I got to the door I reminded her of our deal, of our work together and thanked her for allowing me to come into her home. I soon realize the courage it must have taken once she realized that not only was her home a mess but she was a mess with bright red hair and I was standing at the other side of that door waiting for her to open it.

Driving away, I realized I had on no music, had no GPS to guide me and was re-playing each step of that home and of Charmaine. She said she is over the grief of her father, and that she did not color her hair bright red, her house has signs all over it that something is not right and she does not know who drew the pictures.

This has challenged me in ways unimagined to date as I drive past my exit and end up in the next town having to turn around and am late to dinner with friends on roads I long have known as I am trying to fit puzzle pieces together in traffic. Not the best plan and I do not recommend you try this at home or on the roads.

I had told Charmaine that we would get through this together, and I did believe that would. I was filled with questions, and wondered what "this" was we were working on: who the many faces on that easel were and who drew them. The many faces on the easel and who actually drew them had me intrigued, confused, questioning. Those haunting eyes in the sketch did show resemblances of Charmaine. When I asked her about it, she quickly let me know she had no idea in the beginning who had created the sketch.

Then, there were the fear and shock when I last asked about her hair and her response of "I don't think so and I would never do that to myself" and it was so very genuine. I am asking myself "Are blackouts responsible for this or could she have some type of amnesia? " She does not strike me as a borderline or schizophrenic: she denies hearing voices telling her what to do. I have worked with people who have suffered blackouts and amnesia for months secondary to trauma along with grief before, but it was not like this.

Charmaine is a gentle and kind woman who seemed appalled at what she observed in her own surroundings with me today. I left there suggesting we meet three times a week for now as 50 minute sessions weekly were not enough given what I was seeing. Boy was that just great given the insurance she had: they will probably stop payment in two weeks all together. This woman had keen insight for one who had not been in therapy before.

I am concerned at the notations in the journal. One was a picture, very bold and dark saying:

"I hate you and **die die."**

There was so much anger showing in these pictures and evidence of sexual abuse too.

Charmaine Drawing
left on the easel. DRSES

How has this woman endured all this time? I cannot imagine the fear she has felt, the confusion and uncertainty and yet, when she is talking, she has the very intelligent, calm and soft air. And she wants to know the answers to what is going on. She is not passive about wanting to work on herself and I am glad to see that.

The force on these pictures is so hard that the print is visible for about ten pages after. I am not talking a little mad; this is full blown rage and that concerns me greatly. And then there were the childlike drawings which at first glance appear harmless but as you take a second look, you realize what she is drawing is a penis as a seesaw or a man with a penis coming out of his pants. This perturbs me greatly.

As I look at the picture below and it makes me shudder for this is full blown rage but who does Charmaine want to die? Or does someone want Charmaine to die? That makes me even more nervous. I have not met her kids to date and do not know if the teenager is one filled with hate and anger.

And down in the corner is a child crying. This confirms my thoughts on child abuse. I am just concerned as to how Charmaine, who appears to have no knowledge of child abuse, was going to handle our discussion on these pictures. If

NOTE TO SELF: ask about all physician testing's, scans, medicines, and other therapists she has seen or had done.

Charmaine's Journal

Two days after the home visit

Well, I think I have everything clean but I need to hurry so I can change clothes. Oh damn, there is the doorbell. I better go make sure that is not Doc.

Seeing myself in the mirror, it startled me so badly that I almost fell down and when I glanced up, I could see Doc watching me through the window. My mind was screaming: **"Just what I needed today. Some way, somehow, my black hair is now bright red. Oh what am I going to do?????"**

Well, I knew one thing. I had better answer the door quickly because she was watching like a hawk. As I opened the door, my mind was racing to think of some answer for this hair color because I figured she would make a comment. But, she did not. She glanced and then walked on into the room. Quickly I told her that I was testing a new color for a Halloween Costume I was working on. She just smiled but I know that she did not believe me.

As she walked around the living room looking, I told her that I was sorry the house was not cleaned up. Inside I am screaming because the toys had been brought to the living room, the kitchen was dirty and my bed was not made and I did not know how it all had come to be. I had worked late cleaning everything up.

Doc casually said not to worry that she was not looking at my decorating or my cleaning. She only commented on the pictures of the kids. That was the only pictures I had out. She made no comment on the pictures other than that the kids were cute. I do not have any pictures of the family on the west coast and I do not intend to put any out. I have no intentions of being involved again.

We walked into the kitchen and I asked her if she would like some coffee and she said yes. While I am fixing it, she wandered around looking at the knickknacks and books and pictures on the walls. We sat at the dinner table a few minutes and then headed down the hallway to the bedrooms. She glanced into the kids rooms and both rooms were very nice and clean thank God.

She walked into my bedroom and I notice she stopped where the dolls and stuff are. Then she walked over to my easel and commented on the picture there. She asked me who they were and without thinking I said I did not know that I did not do that picture. She turned around and said "you do not know who did this picture?" I stuttered a little and said I thought it was one of the kids. Doc just nodded.

As she looked around my bedroom, she asked me why my bed was where it was when it seemed so crowded and I did explain that I had always had to have my bed that way. I did not know how to tell her that it was so I could see who came into my bedroom at night because the boogie man always came.

I told her from the time I was little, that was the only way I could sleep. She just nodded. She must get a lot of neck pain from all that nodding. She does not miss anything. She noticed the slide bolt on the inside of my bathroom door. She did not say a word to me, but I saw her trace it with her finger. She does not know but I notice things too. After she had seen the house, we went back to the kitchen and refilled our coffee cups and sat down. She told me that I did not look like I had gotten any sleep. I told her that I could not remember a time I slept more than two hours at a time.

She wanted to know had I ever taken sleeping pills and I said no, that I did not want to be knocked out where I would not wake up if something happened. I could tell she was thinking on that one so I said "you know, like if one of the kids needed me or the house was on fire." And she nodded.

But I just could not tell her yet that it was because of the liquor and pills poured down my throat when little to make me be more obedient. That is when I have those nightmares about the hands and the ugly men's breath.

She got ready to leave and told me that if it was alright with me, she thought I needed to come three times a week for now and we could see how that worked out. I nodded this time.

And she started to walk to the door and then suddenly came back to the table and sat down. She reached over and took my hand and said "This is the deal Charmaine. If we are going to make this work I need a promise of total honesty from you and no hiding things from me. A commitment? Can you do that?" And I sat and looked at her for a few more minutes and nodded yes. She said "No, I need you to say it to me because if we verbalize things then it will go in your frontal lobe and stay there." I told her that yes I agreed to be totally honest and would not hide things from her. She said "Good. Now, what did you tear out of your journal yesterday?"

I think I almost fell out of my chair on that one. I looked at her and said that the kids had gotten in my journal and written stuff and so I started it over. She asked me what it said and told me please, even if I think the kids are doing it to leave it and to never tear out anything I wrote. And again she gave me that "Deal?" and I said "deal."

I went and got the paper I had torn from my journal and brought it out to her and she asked me if she could take it for a while. I said yes. She also wanted to know if she could take the drawing on my easel and I said yes.

After we got the papers together and she was walking out the door, she stopped and turned around and said "One more question Charmaine. Did you color your hair red?" I dropped my head as tears came to my eyes and shook it no. She told me she did not think I had. And she walked back in and again told me that we were going to get to the bottom of this together. I honestly think for the first time I felt a flash of safety.

At least I did not see that look of "you are nuts" that sometimes I found myself getting. That was very reassuring and she made no mention of wanting to drop me and that also was reassuring. I truly did like *this woman since she had such a heart of compassion and understanding and she was so real.*

Although I hated the idea of doing therapy, I really was finding that a lot of my fears were getting better so maybe it was not such a bad thing after all. Anyway, if I have to act like such a blooming idiot and don't know it, might as well do it around her as she is almost as eclectic as I am.

Days Later

As I rolled over, my head felt like someone had banged a pot on top of my head. And my mouth felt like it was full of cotton. I lay there just trying to get my eyes focused and was just looking around the room. Memories of the home session with Doc came flooding back and I was afraid that she was going to decide I needed to be put in an institution or something.

It is bad enough that I must now keep two journals because of the bazaar things being written in one. If I let her see those writings I know she would have me committed. Especially the page with the blood on it.

As I lay there I felt myself getting sleepy and decided to roll over and go back to sleep. Maybe it would be just a bad dream. I just wanted to feel the comfort of my cubby. Sometimes I feel like Alice running down the rabbit hole as I run into my copy that I visualize in my head. That is my place of safety, my place of no hurts, my place of no fear and my place of no corners or hard spots. I know no one will understand that....but I do.

When I go to my cubby, I hear the doors slamming like one of those Sci Fi movies with the underground laboratory and all the hallways.

THE ALTERS

"Well, she is out again Deseree. What do we do now?" JR said as he walked down the hallway.

Deseree told JR that they would all just lay low unless Charmaine had to get up for some reason. She needed the rest and so did they. And the only way for the body to get rest is if they all would be quiet and she sleeps.

Deseree had just checked and the babies and Charie and the others were asleep and she knew that JR would keep close watch along with Bart and the older ones.

One of JR's favorite times was late at night when no one was awake. He would slip out and take a ride in the cool air. As long as he knew that Charmaine was ok, he knew he could go do what he wanted. But, tonight Deseree needed him to be on guard.

He just hoped Charmaine was back in time to go see that Doc again. She was something else coming

In here and messing with our stuff. He would love to see her.

It is the quiet times that the rowdy ones like to sneak out JR thought and knew it was better for him to stay out than any of the others.

He could hear them wandering around and talking to each other and knew they were watching for that moment when they could take over and run off and do things.

JR decided to go for a quiet ride to keep the others from coming out at least for a few hours. Then he knew he would have to let Charmaine's body rest. There were so many of them that they could her body moving twenty four seven if they all kept coming out and she would collapse again like she did a few years ago and that asshole Doctor put her in for a few days. It didn't take much to get out for Deseree became Charmaine and showed the Doctors that she was just fine.

Desire then puts Charmaine on the bed and sat guard at the door all night long. Finally she had slept. JR would come up to check on Des every so often but she told him she needed him to watch the little ones as she could not leave the post.

"Sometimes someone comes along and shows us a whole new view of an old topic. Charmaine did that for me. What I had wondered about I knew now was true. I spent many hours studying these pictures and learning as much as I could." DRSES

Chapter 6   A Surprise Visit

With all the questions and concerns I had amassed since my home visit with Charmaine, I was gathering my notes while awaiting her visit in the office and had finally gotten my thoughts and notes in order. I felt like I was working with a great jigsaw puzzle sitting in front of me, all the same color at times yet a complex pattern. We had been through weeks and weeks of therapy and more and more complex findings and pieces seemed to be appearing in her life. I needed to find the key or the reasons that these things were happening.

Some of my notes were uniting the very essence of the visit, the plan of care and the very real concerns I had for Charmaine. I had also managed to draw up our contract on honesty, and I had taken the liberty of creating a "No Harm" contract to discuss with Charmaine in the next couple of visits as well for her to sign after fully explaining why I felt it necessary. I knew that our next session would be very intense and odds were good that Charmaine would want to pick up where we left off in her home.

I had reflected again on how very out of sorts she was during our time together and the appearance of her home and her being inconsistent with her descriptions of her housekeeping and her kids' rooms along with that red hair that she was so very distressed by. Quite frankly, the most upsetting part of it all was in my asking if she had done it to herself and the reply that she did not honestly think so. That reply indicated to me that she had no recall of those events once again.

I was not prepared for who entered my doorway at the appointed time however as I had been looking at the drawing done by "who knows" according to Charmaine, and I had detected many features that certainly looked like her in the middle picture.

As I sat at my desk, I heard a car roll in from outside as I had the window open for some fresh air. It was one of those delightful days that being outside would have been the ideal places for a session, but we had too much to do and being outside to do the work of today might not be the best place for her to focus.

Thinking it was Charmaine, I got up and went to meet her at the door, and found myself a bit caught off guard to hear heavy footsteps hit the porch. As I opened the door, I was greeted by a person wearing what appeared to be black ops clothing; boots, wearing a baseball cap, who greeted me with "Afternoon Showalter", and then proceeded to walk past me into my office with a very manly stride and have a seat in the chair. I was trying desperately to understand what I was seeing.

I found myself standing still as I watched the back of this person, and my mouth was probably wide open too. A heavy scent of men's cologne wafted in the hallway filling my nostrils and jarred me into the reality that I needed to move my feet into action and that propelled me into gear as I followed behind.

My mind was reeling wondering if this was some kind of joke; if Charmaine perhaps had a twin that she had sent in her stead to play a trick of some kind as I noticed a strong resemblance in the face between and this guy dressed out and rough around the edges who referred to me as "Showalter" yet seemed to know his way around my office.

As I quickly caught up and entered my office, I noticed that he was looking around and seemed rather comfortable and for a second or two I was trying to determine whether to take my usual seat or sit behind my desk as I figured this all out. I opted to sit in my usual seat and pulled up my chair, working hard not to ask the obvious question of "what is this about?" "Who are YOU?" And "What is going on?"

However I will assure you those questions were floating by so quickly I am sure my neurotransmitters were having their own party at the time. Instead I just watched and waited for what was to come next.

Suddenly it hit me that this was no joke and I was sitting in front of an Alter and it was Charmaine that was before me. And then my mind fluctuated between thinking it was Charmaine or her brother. My brain was going off so fast that I think I could have started a fire with the neurons that were transmitting rapid fire.

I had just been with Charmaine in her home yesterday, seeing her as a red head; I was now seeing someone in camouflage looking like they were ready to drive a truck and sling back several beers in a juke joint, wearing boots and a ball cap, calling me Showalter in my office... could this be a prank and a twin brother? No, no, it must be an Alter but I was not one hundred percent sure that Charmaine was DID. I was still mulling it over in my head.

I saw no pictures of family other than the kids of Charmaine and she has indicated that the family is not in the area, so that does not really make sense. What I can see of this person's hair tucked up inside the baseball cap looks dark in color almost black, yet there is a strong eerie matter of fact eerie resemblance to Charmaine here.

I have my pad and pen and look to see that I was being watched very carefully so I asked, "How are you doing today?" I now was observing my client with legs crossed like a man with one leg propped on top of the other knee, a strong smell of men's cologne and what looks like cigarettes rolled up in the sleeve of the shirt and a "wicked grin" on the face.

I decide to continue, "What are we working on today?" While sitting close in proximity, it has definitely settled in on me that I am sitting with my client Charmaine who is dressed as a man and that long beautiful hair is pulled up and under a ball cap. OK, this is real, this is here and now and we will roll with it to see where we are headed.

Now the question is why, as I listen to and watch mannerisms that are unlike the Charmaine whom I have met and talked with in previous sessions. This person could in fact pass as a twin brother. A deep voice, playful eyes, and a comfortable in his own skin young man, all so unlike Charmaine that it is in itself remarkable.

As I sit with all that I am a part of, my mind brings up that easel drawing; I remember that the one in the top right of the easel picture looks like the person sitting here down to the cap and all. Is this a discovery brought about by my visit to her home, or is this a prank? Shall I ask who it is that has walked through my door today? Hmmm, I think perhaps I'll just go with my gut, but something tells me that I am in for a day unlike many days before. So again I ask, "How are you today?"

With that I am told that the person sitting beside me was "finer than butter on grits" I suppose it does not get any finer than that, but I cannot imagine Charmaine saying that to date; so I just go on and say these words, "I see that something triggered you today. Do you want to talk about it with me?"

As I sat and watched and listened for the reply, I find myself trying hard to suppress a grin as the person in front of me said, "Ha, ha only triggering I've done Showalter is that pretty little Glock I have and pull the trigger on when I do target practice."

I felt my body tense at the mention of a hand gun: I did not like the thought that perhaps the person in front of me was carrying a gun. The implications of that gave me pause and my mind was hyper vigilant. Inwardly I was kicking myself for not having sat behind the desk, yet grateful that I was near the door.

OK, now I had the alert button on, as I was hearing the word Glock. I had to wonder did whatever persona Charmaine was presenting as have a Glock? Interesting how I had just written up a "No harm

Harm" Contract and even more interesting the innuendo of the Glock as I was called Showalter.

As I listened carefully, I then asked about any guns in the home, the use of guns and got the reply that there are no guns in the home and they were only used as target practice. I can tell that the person in front of me did not like my questions, but answers them in an off the cuff direct manner.

This ball cap wearing, Glock talking James Dean kind of guy did not seem comfortable with my direct approach as he quickly changed the subject. I watched his leg crossings back and forth, the toothpick between his teeth and the eye contact intensify. I was still not prepared for the next statement. This person smiled at me as he said, "Mighty fine ass you got Showalter."

I thought I was going to spit my water out all over both of us but managed to remain calm and said "Thank you. Now back to the Glock. Do you all have guns in the house?" Oh, I could tell I had just pissed this person off as he gruffly answered me with a resounding NO and shifted in his seat and turned his head as if he heard something.

I was glad to know that there are no weapons in the home and the best I could assess, there were no weapons on my client sitting near me. To have worked with Charmaine who dressed in unassuming dark colors, spoke plain and clearly and quietly in her wording was one thing. And then, at the same time visiting her at her home and finding someone with brilliant red dyed hair who was very flustered and

and anxious. And now this, after our signed contract of honesty above all else, was disconcerting to say the least.

I found myself thinking that there was so much here that was about to be uncovered along with what I already suspected that I knew I would need all my wits about me and all the tools of my training to unravel this story that was unfolding before me.

If Charmaine was doing this as a prank, she was sophisticated beyond measure, and if by some chance this is another person, a twin of hers, they had me at hello on this. I found I had relaxed and was rather amused at the colorfulness of this character as he worked to get me frazzled in the ways and expressions used during our time together, but he did not like my calmness.

He did not like my asking specifics of the gun, or his abilities in using it or that I thanked him for the compliment and moved right along. He moved in his chair a few times, stretched out his legs, and then used the "Showalter" as he said colorful expressions or cursed for reactions that he did not receive. I wanted to know who this was and what made him appear today in my office at this time of Charmaine's appointment. And he acted like he had been in my office before.

As I tried to get back to the interest of Glocks, firearms and firing ranges along with target practice, what came next was astounding to me, as I witnessed something I had never seen before and like a giant pyramid that has been hit hard; things began to crumble in a hot second.

I watched as the person beside me stopped talking and became much quieter and when I asked "Is there a name you would like me to call you today"... poof gone. As I sat there I watched whoever this was that had been tough as a nail in front of me vanish: they seemed to just have just disappeared as I sat there watching and be replaced with a stunned Charmaine.

Yes, just like that, still in the same clothing, the same ball cap, sat a scared and panic filled Charmaine filling out the clothing. I felt for a moment as if I were in a Sci Fi movie or something. As I watched until I fully recognized who was in those black OPS and combat boots I said, "Welcome back Charmaine, I think you were hiding from me, inside of yourself if you know what I mean."

Charmaine looked at me quizzically and then jumped from her chair as if struck by a bolt of lightning as she glanced at the office and me as if she saw them both for the first time right at that moment. The look on face showed that she was inconsolable and unreachable. She wanted to flee, and flee she did but I was a bit quicker as I jumped up quickly and took her by the arm and tried to assure her that it was alright and she was safe.

Charmaine would have no part of it at that moment and shook my arm from her as she repeatedly shook her head back and forth crying, *"No No NO"* and left the office as fast as her feet would carry her as she cried out things like, "Where did these clothes come from, my son does not even have clothes like these. I have to get out of here. What is going on??"

She was shaking her head, trying to get past me, the furnishings, down the hall and out of the door as fast as she could. She was shaking and trembling as she made her way outside only to find herself standing stock still as she realized she did not know where her car was parked.

I was hot on her heels and felt so badly for her, the pure angst she was feeling, like a child lost in a shopping mall she seemed. I followed her outside and realized she had no idea where her car was parked, as she cried, trembled and stood there looking desperately for her vehicle and I struggled for a minute with my decision.

There comes a time when the therapist and the personal me have to make split second decisions; whether to intervene or allow a person to be where they are rather than to put my arms around them and rock them gently until they are able to regain control.

This was one of those times, I wanted to go to her, to soothe her and plead with her to return to the office. That was the personal me, yet I respected her need to do this her way, to regain her composure in a way that allowed her the needed space and ability to "re-group" on her terms, to go home, have space and to do this her way in her own time.

I spoke her name clearly, firmly to make her look at me; and then once I had her attention, I pointed to where her car was parked, and told her to call if she wanted or needed and I would see her in a few days. She saw where I had pointed and quickly headed towards her car and was gone in a fast moment it seemed without looking at me, without hesitation. She needed to get to the safety of her home.

It pained me greatly to see her so very distressed and I could not begin to fathom what she was feeling on the inside. It was as if someone had pushed her out of herself and into my office unknowingly, and she was there, just there and did not know what in the world to do next. A bird thrown from the nest, vulnerable and so sad to witness yet one must respect that this is her journey and not hold her against her will but respect where she is at the time.

My mind was still grappling with all I had witnessed from the time I heard that car screech into the parking lot, to the sound of combat boots hit the porch steps, and then the sound of "Showalter" came from the sights of what appeared to be a twin brother.

I now realized that the puzzle pieces just got more complex and as I watched Charmaine in her car, I was having my own mind race in a thousand or more directions thinking how I can best serve and care for this client who has just challenged my own sense of competence as a therapist.

I would come to realize as I had more pieces to a puzzle that was filling sheets of paper safely guarded in a locked drawer that this was a journey unlike any I had ever been on. Our work together will be stronger in time if we allow it to grow as she feels safe.

What I saw and heard and observed today had me making phone calls to colleagues, setting up meetings with those who may be able to shed light on topics that were not seen in my specialty as I gathered old books and new journal articles and went about piecing together parts of a puzzle that has boggled the brightest minds and led people to believe they have lost their minds and their way.

I was not looking for "theories": I looked for every day, in the moment collaboration that would help me to better help my client. There is a difference; I knew the theories, I had read the literature, yet what I needed was trusted and respected collaboration from those who have worked with others and had far more exposure in order for best practice to holistically take place.

I was tired after that meeting; truly exhausted, yet I could not fathom the extent of what had transpired in my office from the time I heard heavy sounds on the porch to the moments of watching Charmaine looking for and then rushing to her car, speeding off quickly to get away from what she had to in the moment as she felt so unsafe and confused.

I did believe that this person had no gun on their body when in the office; and was glad to hear that no guns were in the home because of the kids. That gave me relief but I also wanted to follow up on that with Charmaine for even though this person came across as being truthful, I needed to hear it from Charmaine that there were no guns in the house and if there were, we needed to remove them for the time being.

I stayed on the porch that evening; just sat there quietly while part of me wondered if she would get just so far and decide to return, wanting to talk about it, wanting a safe place and a familiar face to be waiting. I was glad to know she was my last client of the day in the event she had chosen to open up more. Then I would have given her more time to process what had happened, to listen to her fears, to witness the tears and the pain I knew she was feeling as she left so quickly and so confused.

As I sat, I wondered and pondered and thought about how that must feel for a person; and all of a sudden I could hear tires come to a soft stop in the parking lot, and looked up to see Charmaine sitting behind the wheel of the car, she had in fact returned. She knew not to drive in that condition and I am thankful that she did. I hoped it helped for her to look up and see that I was there; just sitting there in the event that she needed support. I knew that no one had ever been there for Charmaine and I did not want her to feel alone right now.

As I sat there, I replayed over and over the events of who would become known to me later on, and I still say that persona could have been her twin brother. She sat there for a while before opening the door and I sat quietly hoping she would not change her mind, but I was grateful that she had come back, or at least I hoped it was her who had returned.

I kept reflecting on the sound of "Showalter" and the mannerisms I had been with. Yes, there were times where that session had left me feeling extremely uncomfortable, even comical at times as I had listened to sayings and some comments meant to make me feel extremely uncomfortable but it did not work, so the ante was upped.

I am fortunate that my inside jaw did not bleed for as hard as I bit on it, and at the same time found myself going through old textbooks in my mind yearning for knowledge I had long ago tucked away thinking I would not use it.

Realizing that some suspicions were now getting some clarity, yet so much yet to know, and prayers were being said that she did not quit therapy or me although she was now so afraid of what was happening and feeling so out of control.

I was lost in thought only to look up and see she opened her car door. She started to get out of the car, but changed her mind I guess, and soon afterward she started the engine as I stood on the porch and waved. She managed to wave as well and backed out and left. I figured at least she waved, at least she seemed some calmer this time when pulling out of the driveway. So, that was good and that was enough.

As I went into the office I found myself leaving the door unlocked although she had been the last client as I worked on that dreaded paperwork; somehow I wanted to be certain that if she decided to return she would find a light on and the door unlocked.

The paperwork of the evening seemed to take forever, and before you know it, I was absorbed in a literary search on the internet finding journal articles and information, clues to what I might find helpful in the hallways that I suspected I would walk with Charmaine. This was a real puzzle and I just sat there and studied that easel picture with all those faces. My new suspicions of what I thought was wrong with Charmaine were taking root.

I had felt moments of tension during this session today; I could feel them in my chest, my shoulders and now the remains of a tension headache as I drove home. It was good to feel as a therapist but also good to know that you actually did feel and know where you were feeling as you work. I believed in letting things flow through you rather than getting stuck with you, so the Creator was letting me know that talk of guns always gave me that feeling of perceived threat until I was certain that there was no threat.

Note to self: Next session speak to Charmaine on gun knowledge/safety and if guns are in the home. Ask if she has seen other therapists.

As I wrote my notes on our session together, I realized that our contract had not been signed; my "agenda" for our session had not been touched for the session from the last notes.

There was no way to even imagine that this day would be how it turned out: no need to think that we would be able to think a routine session planned could have turned out as it did. A session that had added another dimension to the many pieces of this puzzle that now lay before me in notes; the crumpled piece from her journal page, along with the sketch that I have drawn by who knows who that she willingly gave to me to hold.

I made lengthy notes of all that I observed: Charmaine dressed as a man, the sound of the voice *wishing I had a voice recorder during that session*, his mannerisms and topics, the shift in body language and then the sudden disappearance and appearance of a distraught Charmaine. It all was stunning to observe and yet painful to see at the same time.

I found that this session would stay with me for a long time as I thought about how we would move into the next session should Charmaine return in two days to the office. I made the decision to make a call to her home after a couple of hours to let her know I was concerned and was just checking to be certain she had arrived home safely.

I had to wonder if I was making that call more for me than for her at that point, however I did want her to know about my genuine care and follow up. I heard the phone ring and ring before a weary voice came on the line with the southern drawl of "hello" and I recognized Charmaine's voice immediately.

"Charmaine, this is, Dr. Showalter, I'm calling to let you know I am thinking of you and wanted you to know." There was a long pause and then she said, "thank you Dr S., I appreciate that and I am home and about to go to bed, I am just worn out." I asked if she was o.k. and she let me know that she was confused as hell, but that she was home safe and would see me in a few days.

With that we ended the conversation, and I was glad to know that she was home safely, that she was herself and had planned to sleep in. Confused as hell? That made two of us to be honest. I had hopes that we would put this puzzle together and I also had some research to do and much to think about.

Truthfully I was still able to smile as I reflected on moments of this person that presented with such a "swagger and attitude" as I was being tested during parts of this session. Although I remained uncertain of where this was all coming from, I suspected it was a trauma that set it all off from somewhere in the past.

I finished my notes and by then it was time to move to the next client and make notes, but not before I added to those notes the following: I also made a note to ask Charmaine about the hair color, the clothing, and if she has spent time on practice ranges.

It will be interesting to see what her knowledge of guns truly was and when she had first noticed the hair color change. I wanted to talk with her about the easel faces, and delve into that more but slowly. I realized it was not good to rush this as it seems we were going into territory that was overwhelming to her senses as evidenced in the office when she saw herself in that outfit and ball cap.

I cannot imagine how drained and fear filled she must be with these episodes she is experiencing. At the end of my evening I returned home and decided to watch some mindless television and relax for a bit, ridding myself of the stories of the day while enjoying my dogs and home.

I found it interesting that the movie that aired that night was none other than "The three faces of Eve". As old a movie as it was, that was the offering and was almost perfect timing. I made myself a bowl of popcorn and settled in for the night for that classic.

It turned out to be a light bulb moment as I later realized that I had been on to something in my suspicions about Charmaine. I do not mean in a movie like way of fabrications yet in a very real way of talking with her the next session on what I felt clinically might be happening in her brilliant and creative brain as a result of a child traumatized long ago.

I had days to research, to speak with colleagues who had grand insights on what had once been called Multiple Personality Disorder (MPD) and is now known as Dissociative Identity Disorder (DID). Could this be what had been happening to Charmaine with blackouts and those times of getting lost.?

My dear friend and colleague offered great thoughts and yet let me know that he had seldom had the opportunity to do work with those suffering with DID. We both agreed it was a long process and that trust was essential along with a myriad of surprises along the way.

We both agreed that triggers of anxiety seemed to bring Alters out and that until I had a chance to really come to see and know about them my client would not accept a diagnosis of DID as she was struggling with thinking that she was just plain crazy. I feared for Charmaine as I knew that she was having these blackouts and had to wonder if she was writing in her journal and if she was safe.

The next day I phoned Charmaine to set our appointment for our next session. We spoke briefly by phone as Charmaine let me know that she felt exhausted and thought perhaps she was coming down with a bug or something. She had plans to rest until we met again, and complained of a headache that she said would not seem to go away since going to bed the night before.

I explored with Charmaine the effects of stress on the body, the mind, the spirit and she agreed that it had been a stressful week so perhaps that was the cause. She appreciated the call, yet I could tell that she was not ready to talk and wanted the call to come to closure. I looked forward to us meeting and hoped that the events of the last two days had not frightened her

The Alters

Deseree told JR and the others that Charmaine had once again run and hidden in her room at the end of the hallway and that someone needed to go to the therapy session for her. JR finally agreed to go and headed in to take a quick shower. He was damned if he was going smelling like some flower child.

JR dried off from the shower and slipped on his camouflaged pants and as always, wrapped his chest before putting on his T shirt. He sat on the toilet to tie his boots and then glancing in the mirror, he tucked his hair up in his baseball cap. He checked his pockets to make sure that he had everything and rolled his cigarettes up in his sleeve, put on his sunglasses and headed out the door.

Pulling up in front of Doc's office, he got out and headed up the steps. As he entered the front door, Doc emerged. Great timing JR said to himself...as always.

JR laughed to himself because he was here to give that ole Doc what for. He loved calling her "Showalter." That was just a man thing. He had put on his best cologne for her. He kinda liked her cause she was such a pistol rip. Laughing to himself, he thought he would pee his pants at her look when he mentioned a Glock. Hell, he bet money that she was a Glock person herself.

Sitting in the chair and propping one leg on top of the other, he looked Doc over thinking at last he gets to see this person. "Yes, Deseree, I hear you. I will not be too off the wall. I know. I know. I am supposed to be Charmaine but I ain't acting like no damn pansy. You hear me?" he hollered back down the hallway.

When I told her I was finer than butter on grits, I could see her lips twitch and knew she was trying not to smile. I said "Ok Doc. What we talking about today?"

"Yes, Des I will tell her no guns in the house. Damn woman I do have some sense." JR yelled back down the hallway. To shut Des up, when Doc casually asked if we had a gun in the house JR said "Oh hells no. Too many kids in the house; I go to the practice range."

She just nodded. JR decided to do a little playing with this Doc to see if he could rattle her cage. Pushing the black baseball cap up, he smiled at her and winked and said "mighty fine ass you got here Showalter." She just calmly said thank you and started talking about target practice again. "Well, I be hanged" JR thought. "I can't rattle her cage for nothing."

JR decided that this session thing was boring as crap and could not believe that Charmaine did this twice a week. JR hollered down the hallway to Deseree "Sorry Deseree. I am giving it back to Charmaine. I am outta here. This is boring as hell" and JR shoved Charmaine outside.

JR could hear Deseree calling to him but he pretended he did not hear her. He really knew that such a quick change would upset the whole hallway. Well, that is tough he thought. Next time Tina or Laylee can take the session.   Hell, let little Charie have it.

He knew he would hear about it but for now he was going to grab up Charie for safety from the wrath and head to his room for a while. Damn he wanted to go riding on that bike of his ...anything to get out of this office. He stood a minute and felt bad for doing that to Charmaine but enough was enough.

Charmaine's Journal

(The night after the therapy session. DRSES)

I found myself staring out the window and then heard a noise and turned my head and almost screamed "NO NO NO!" because there was Doc right beside me. There was no way I could explain this to her and so I tried to do what I normally do, which was to act like I knew where I was and what I was doing.

I just knew Doc would be too slick for me. She knew instantly. Oh dam dam, what the hell did I do while I was gone?

When Doc said "I think you were hiding inside from me" I nodded trying to act like nothing was wrong and then I looked down and saw the clothes I was in. What the hell. I really did not know what to tell her. All I wanted to do was run home and hide and get off these stupid clothes I was wearing.

Where the hell am I getting combat boots, camouflage pants and baseball caps from?. I have never seen my son wear any of this stuff. He and I are about the same size but still. And cigarettes in my sleeve?? I look like some kind of hood. I jumped up and started running out the door but Doc was quicker and grabbed me telling me it was ok but I could not face her...

I knew I raced down the hallway screaming inside NO NO NO NO but I did not even know where my car was. I was standing there in the grass looking out towards the parking area feeling panic all over me and was afraid I would have an accident. Doc watched me from the steps and then calmly said "it's down on the left Charmaine. I will see you in two days. Call me if you want to talk."

I turned and looked and ran to the car and got in and just burst into tears. I jammed the key in feeling like I bent it and started the car and took off. But I didn't know where to go. I think I drove around the block four or five times and decided I better park back at Doc's until I calmed down.

I eased back into the parking lot and sat there crying and shaking. What the hell is wrong with me? Why am I dressed in all these crazy outfits? I am crazy that is it..I am crazy. Doc may not know it but I know it. I am crazy. I laid my head on the steering wheel and then the next thing I remembered was being home in my bed.

The Alters:

Deseree raised her head and looked across the room. "Tina, it is your turn. Get out there and take care of things before she wrecks the car."

Laylee looked up and said "why does Tina always get to go when there is trouble?" Deseree replied "because I need you and the others here to help with the little ones. She is going to need me and I need you to watch the others. And I can trust Tina not to go off and do anything dumb" Laylee dropped her head and said "yes mam."

Deseree felt Charmaine fly into her arms so hard that it jolted her and wrapping her arms around her, she led her into the white room at the end of the hallway.

She and JR were going to have a talk about this because the rule was to not harm her. Sitting on the edge of the bed, she began rocking her back and forth humming softly as she did so until she began to feel Charmaine's body start to relax and laid her down on the bed. She will sleep now. If ever a person needed a mother, it was her.

After arriving home, sitting in front of the mirror, Tina fixed her hair after she colored it back blonde and thought "there, that looks better" as she sprayed hair and then sprayed one more time. Powdering her nose, she heard the doorbell ring.

She had changed into her favorite dress and was fixing her hair when she heard the doorbell. "Wonder who that is?" she thought as she stood up and smoothed her dress down and went to answer the door. She walked down the hallway in her high heels and flowered dress looking very much like someone from a commercial from the fifties. She loved shirtwaist dresses and that was just about all she wore.

Looking out, she recognized the little neighbor next door, a sweet little old lady. As she opened the door, Tina spoke in that deep southern drawl of hers *"Well, Miss Mary, how y'all doing today?"* Mary looked up and said she needed help getting her car started.

Tina smiled at Mary and said "oh my, Miss Mary, you know I know nothing about fixing vehicles. Let me see if I can get that repairman number for you" as she turned to go find the number. Mary said "but Charmaine, you got it running last time" but Tina was already inside at the phone table.

When she came back, she handed Miss Mary the phone number and a piece of cake and said that she would have to excuse her as she had work to do. As she closed the door, she could see Miss Mary still standing there with her mouth falling open.

Boy did she have work to do. The house was a mess, and laundry seemed to be everywhere. She wanted those kids rooms cleaned and crisp clean sheets on their beds when they returned.

And she hated this black hair. Tina was blonde and she got so tired of having to redo her hair over and over. So, Tina did what Tina did best. She cleaned and baked. Those kids were not there but they would be back in another week and they would want lots of goodies.

Humming to herself as she worked around the house, Tina thought about how they needed a husband in this house. There were so many things to do and the kids needed a real father. A thought entered Tina's head and that was to start checking out men that would make potential husbands. Yes, that was it. She knew what to do to make them all feel good.

Deseree peeked to make sure Tina was behaving and then went back to taking care of the little ones. She hoped that Charmaine would remain sleeping for a good while so that mentally she was refreshed.

Feeling a tug on her dress, Deseree turned and saw Charie sucking her thumb and looking at her. Slowly pulling her thumb out of her mouth, Charie said "what wong wif tharmaine?" Deseree assured her that Charmaine was ok and just needed to rest.

Charie asked could she go into Charmaine's cubby if she was quiet and Deseree told her to remember that was Charmaine's special room and no one entered it unless asked. Charie in her usually happy self replied *"otay"* and pattered off to find something to play with. Deseree just smiled but also knew that if Charie could do it, she would try to sneak into Charmaine's special cubby.

Suddenly Deseree straightens up and calls in a firm voice down the hallway "Buck! You stop that ugly talk right now. We do not use those words in this hallway." Buck muttered back an ok and then started whispering 'Fuck Fuck Fuck" and Deseree called out "I can hear that Buck." Picking up his truck, he went hunting JR. He wanted to know how Deseree could hear him whisper. Deseree just smiled to herself and went back to rocking the baby.

Chapter 7 The Double Journal

I was working at my desk when I heard a noise that was almost like a mouse sound. When I looked up, I see Charmaine sitting on the floor playing. How did she get in without my hearing her; how is it that she not only got in the door, but came down the hallway, into the office, sat on the floor and was playing so contently without a peep? I have never seen Charmaine in pigtails before.

Maybe I had the music on louder than I thought while making notes, or maybe I was so very preoccupied with what I was doing that I was completely oblivious to the world around me. Not only did she come in, but she came in and was yet someone else.

This time I would gauge her to be around 3 or so and she knew right where she was headed, and that was in the corner toy area. She seemed rather content and as I watched from the chair, she seemed happy as happy could be, saying "Hi me tome to pway wif ou toys" with a lisp to her talking.

An innocent child in a grown woman's body, and I simply do not believe someone was play acting. This was not faked; it was as real as I am. I sat memorized by her and I watched as it appeared as though someone told her that play time was over and to go and sit in the chair. Charie sat there very quietly as if she were listening to someone talking to her with her head tilted slightly and then smiled and nodded as if saying ok to someone. Only I did not see anyone sitting there.

She was most obedient, after moving those toys one last time in a way that she wanted them to be left she got up and went and sat in the chair Charmaine normally sits in. The transition from a little one to my client Charmaine happened by watching her body language change, her breathing seemed to change and when she was Charmaine again, she obviously did not know why she was there nor how she got there.

It seemed once again that she was overwhelmed that it had happened at all and needed to retreat quickly. I did not go after her this time, did not try to stop her, only letting her know I would see her at her appointment the next day at 2pm.

I found myself so frustrated I had to get up and walk around my desk, looking out the window, looking at the toy on the floor. Now this was yet another missed opportunity and it had all happened so quickly. As I sat back down at the desk I clearly brought to mind what had just transpired: my seeing what now seems to be clearly another one of her Alters that had appeared and this time Charmaine's hair was blond and in pigtails.

Now this visit, Charmaine appeared with no notice, quietly entering my office and appeared to be a small child sitting quietly on the floor playing, her that of a child, mannerisms of a little innocent child, no southern drawl, no sophistication... a child.

I found myself more intrigued at this transition, at the shifts of Charmaine, in what now appeared to be distinct Alters making their appearances in visits to my office yet I was unsure of their roles, their wants, their purpose. My regret today was that I did not grab my phone and take a picture of the little one in pigtails before she disappeared. I had to smile as Charie would hold her hands up holding and closing them when she wanted a hug. How she managed to look so small amazed me. It was almost like Charmaine folded up like an accordion.

As I was thinking, I got up to straighten the toy area and put things back to order when I found it... there on the little shelf of the toys lay a journal I suppose that the little version of Charmaine had brought in and lay down as she picked up toys. Interesting this was not the journal I had given her to write in, but it had to be hers.

I walked back to my desk and sat down wondering if this might have been the reason for the visit. Was Charmaine so overwhelmed by the last visit of an Alter in her ability to cope that now I am meeting the child that lives within her? I knew at some point, once she returned home, she would be frantic in her search for this journal. I also knew I was meant to see this. I fixed a pot of coffee and began to read. I was not prepared for what my eyes fell upon reading this journal, and I am sure that Charmaine was not quite ready for me to know of it.

This must have been Charmaine's secret journal,; but it was different in that it had different writings that appeared to belong to different writers in it. There were drawings that looked very child like with figures with appendages like the previous pictures Charmaine had torn out and given to me. These pictures were worse than the previous ones and I do not think Charie drew these.

The disturbances were many and when I looked on to a blood stained page I became increasingly concerned as I read the words "I HATE YOU!!! I HATE YOU" in thick dark penciling one again and this time I was sure it was blood. So far I could see about seven or eight different handwritings that were in this journal.

As I continue to read, I was jolted to reality by the ringing of my phone. It is a frantic Charmaine calling and stating that she thought she left her journal in my office and was on her way to get it. She sounded almost breathless as her speech was hurried and frantic.

I stopped her mid-sentence and let her know that we had an appointment for the next day at 2:00 pm and I was unable to see her until then. I had to read this journal before she got it again and destroyed it and the only way was to keep it with me until tomorrow at two.

Charmaine did not like the answer and I could hear almost anger in her voice as she wanted to come right then and right there to pick it up. I assured her that it would be safe until we saw each other, and that we had much to talk about. I then ended our call and I knew that Charmaine was not happy that she was not in control of the conversation nor the journal.

However I also knew that I was seeing disturbing entries here and that we needed that "No harm contract" signed and in place if we were to continue our work together. The journal disturbed me on many levels and it took some time to wrap my head around the many different styles of writing that now I was strongly convinced were Alters trying to talk to Charmaine and/or dictate to her and that her lack of memory and her tremendous confusion was the result of that and memory loss.

The journal that she was secretly keeping was impeding our work together and she, I am sure was probably afraid that I would think she was crazy since that was her initial fear when she came into my office the first day. I understood her reasoning behind hiding the journal and not letting me know but I also knew it was impeding our work together.

As I read more and more of the entries it seemed that she had entries asking or pleading for help and more than one that indicated self-mutilation was occurring although she had never mentioned that to me previously nor had I seen any scars on her body. As I thought more about it, I realized she seemed to always wear long sleeves with only her watch and beaded bracelet in view and when she appeared in black ops I was so taken by the outfit that I had not noticed anything else. I must be more observant.

As I read on, I was getting more and more of a picture that went hand in hand with the sketch I had pulled from my drawer in the desk as I read of times she would have outfits and hair color and experiences that she had no recall of but that were in this journal. It seemed that there was more than one life being lived within the life of Charmaine.

My phone rang again with Charmaine on the other end; "Doc, may I please come and pick up my journal; I need to write in it tonight and if you are going home you can just leave it on the porch, would that be alright with you?" I had to let Charmaine know that I would see her the next day and no, I would never leave something so very important outside and suggested she use notebook paper instead.

I knew and she knew that this was a different journal now. I would confront her about this at our session and again we would talk about the very real need for the honesty contract and the "Do No Harm" contract in order to protect both Charmaine and the Alters and to protect me. I was even more convinced that Charmaine had DID.

I read on until I finished her journal and I was worried for her. Who was this little child I could not help but wonder as I stared at the sketch... who were these people in this sketch and do they all live within Charmaine and will I meet them all? Which one is cutting her and who is it that hates her now?

I had more questions after reading this journal than I ever had before and the desire to help her was burning inside of me as a clinician. I wanted her present in the chair in order for us to begin in a way that allowed her to understand the diagnosis of DID and all its dimensions.

The next day Charmaine arrived fifteen minutes early and had a big bag in her hands. I heard her enter the building as I finished up with another client. I could hear her footsteps from time to time pacing in the outside waiting area and finally heard the door close. I guessed she had gone out to the porch where I later found her after walking my last client out, and she glanced up from where she was sitting on the steps as the door opened and we walked out.

I nodded hello to her as I walked my client to her car and then returned to find her standing in the doorway looking anxious and ready to go inside. I asked her how she was doing and she did not answer right away: she instead headed straight for the office with a bag in her hands. After the Glock talk I was a little concerned. This was not like Charmaine, and I attributed it to stress and the happenings of the last two visits at the office and our phone call of the day before. As she sat down she wanted to know about the journal, and I had to stop her there. She was not happy about that and I suggested that we start over with hello.

I let Charmaine know that I understood that she was feeling anxiety, but wanted to be clear that we had some serious talking in front of us and that it would require her to stay present with me if at all possible. It was in that instant that Charmaine began to cry and say she was afraid that I would by now just know she was crazy and tell her she had to find someone else or I was going to have her put away someplace and she just could not have that happen.

I offered Kleenex and a gentle pat on the arm to assure her that I was not abandoning her, yet we needed to discuss what had been happening to her that ended with her fleeing the office and we also needed to discuss her journals.

Charmaine looked at me with terror on her face, "Doc, did you read my journal?" I looked at her a moment and replied, "Charmaine I want to begin by telling you how your journal got to my office. And yes, I really did read it and yes, it is ok. You do not have to hold that as your secret anymore. We can work through this together now."

I then described to Charmaine how the journal was found, how I looked up from my paperwork and found Charmaine on the floor but she was a "child version" content to play and her verbiage was that of a 3 year old. She was pure, innocent and just having a good time dressed in a cute little shorts outfit and pigtails. I could see Charmaine's eyes get wider and wider as we talked and tears form as I talked about a child with pigtails.

I leaned closer to Charmaine as I watched her tension mount and continued talking. It was YOU Charmaine, but I felt perhaps you had no control, no awareness of this child within you that walked into my office carrying this journal for me to find in order to better help you. I truly believe this was left for me to help you and together we will talk about it.

I believe this journal was left for me to see and I did not find it until after this child version of you suddenly sat up straight and tilted her head like she was listening to someone tell her to go and sit in the big chair. She obeyed and did that, and not too long afterward you became aware again. It was you looking around wondering how in the world you got here. You were overwhelmed, were afraid, and you felt the need to go home to your safe place. But in the process the journal was left behind.

"Charmaine, I think that it was left for a reason, and the reason was for me to better help and to glean a much better understanding of what is going on." Charmaine continued to weep and to look down although I could tell she was listening, I just was not sure she was buying all that I was saying.

Charmaine told me that she has been a wreck and things felt out of control for her, that she was finding out things that did not make sense including what I was saying to her, that things just were scaring her to death. Charmaine was ready to speak, and once again I asked her to hold her thoughts. I needed to impress on her the importance of working hard to remain with me, to focus hard on the work we would be doing today and the things we would be talking about if at all possible.

I wanted to talk with her about fleeing the office and to stress the importance of staying with me even if she found herself here without knowing it. We talked about what appeared to be her twin brother and then finding herself in clothes that she did not recognize and her need to get away as quickly as she could, and she wept even harder and the pitch was getting higher, almost a wail.

I watched her as she took a deep breath and nodded her head, and then promised to not run again from me or the office. I was hoping that she would live up to that promise.

I asked her what it was that she was carrying in that bag and needed her to tell me, as I felt she was barely containing herself at that point. Yet, now she was quiet, almost too quiet and I had to wonder if perhaps she had found that hand gun and now was wondering if she should show it to me. I did not want to press her, yet I wondered how and why she had gotten so quiet.

We sat together in silence for a while and I asked her if she had a gun in the bag, and that got a strong reaction from her as she exclaimed, "Doc, why in the world would you ask a question like that? I would never bring a gun to your office." I smiled at her and let her know I was just curious as I had never noticed her to carry a brown bag in before and now she was very quiet. She smiled and assured me again that she would never bring a gun in a paper bag, and certainly not to my office. That seemed to offer some comic relief for the moment, and it seemed that Charmaine needed a respite from our conversation.

It may be that she was still processing the found journal and what I had let her know about and she just needed a few minutes to wrap her thoughts around that. She spent the rest of the session talking about how horrible it feels to "come to" and not know where you've been or in this case to find her in my office and be completely unaware of having gotten here, gotten out of the car, up the steps and down the hallway. I do not want you afraid for we will work on this together.

She spoke at length about the level of anxiety that she feels rushed through her head and her body in times like that and the fear that makes her want to run and hide. She seemed to forget about the brown bag sitting on the floor beside her, and needed me to hear her, to hear of the overwhelming fear that is released when the blackouts occur and the time it takes to recover from them.

I listened intently and within myself could not imagine that angst and pain that she has lived through. I could only imagine it to be very horrid. Charmaine asked if we could sign the needed papers at our next visit as she had an appointment that she had to get to and knew that we were running late and she wanted to show me something.

She did make another verbal agreement that she would never knowingly harm herself and that she would be as honest with me as she could be. She also let me know that she thought seeing me three days a week for now was a good idea, although she was concerned that I was probably not being paid by her insurance company for that.

I let her know that was not to be her concern, and that we would work as hard as we could to get answers for her, while we both had to keep in the front that honesty in our relationship was paramount. She agreed and apologized for hiding the journal from me saying she was afraid she was really crazy.

She then brought up to her lap a grocery bag, and clutching it to herself said, "Well, Doc, after what you have read, and now that you have seen some weird things, maybe you will not think this too weird... but I'm here to tell you that this is weird as all get out to me and scary too. I woke up in clothes I do not even own, looking like someone that works in the streets and did not even recognize myself in the mirror, now you just tell me WHAT IS WRONG WITH ME?"

With that Charmaine carefully opened the bag, and the look of disgust could not have been clearer as she removed clothing that she said she woke up wearing. It was a provocative outfit, with a deep V-neck top: clothes that I could not imagine Charmaine, who dressed in dark clothing, mostly jeans and denim shirts, ever putting on...not even on a dare.

She did not stop there: she removed more from the bag including high heels, jewelry, and black lace tights to go with the outfit. As she pulled them each out of the bag, she looked as disgusted as she spoke of the length of the skirt and naval observatory on the top. She referred to it all as "hooker clothing" and had no recall of where she got them or where she had gone in them.

Charmaine let them fall to the floor as she showed me one at a time and said when she awoke her head was throbbing and her stomach hurt so bad she felt like she had been run over by a truck. I listened as she described looking at herself in the mirror and wondered who she was; of hurriedly getting naked and in a scalding hot shower tried to get the filth off of her body and felt as though she had scrubbing her skin until it bled.

She said the worst part was that she had no recall of ever leaving her home the night before. The more I listened, the more I realized that it was Charmaine describing what possibly was another Alter in the sketch that was in my drawer; an Alter who liked to dress up and hit the town or perhaps the bars, but where did she go and who knew her?

I asked if she had noticed any receipts in her purse and new charges on her account anything that might account for where she had been; perhaps match books and she had nothing. We talked more and Charmaine would move into a state of quiet despair to that of emotionless monotone speech as if telling the weather, and then she would look at me and begin to sob in confusion and fear.

The interesting thing was that the focus was now off the journal and on what had just occurred, perhaps brought on by the stresses of the last two sessions and heightened by her anxiety of my having her journal that she had guarded so closely. We were making tremendous progress but at times it felt like being on a runaway train as she continued to speak and as I struggled to catch up.

I had to stop Charmaine after she showed me the outfit, had told me of her reactions and her confusion and get her back to the journal, back to the need for us to discuss the honesty contract along with the no harm contract as time was critical. It was very necessary that we used all of our time together and this was time that could easily flow into hours upon hours of revelations. She wanted me to know more about this as it was immediate; more of her being aghast at feeling these clothes on her usually well clothed body. Even in her bed asleep, she was well covered and much more so than this scantily clad outfit she discovered. She said it was important to her that I know this.

It was also important for her to let me know about her home and how beautiful everything was when she ventured out for coffee that morning; she noticed that everything seemed to be waiting for her including her coffee set up, juice in the refrigerator and coffee cake newly baked. She found that odd, yet enjoyed it immensely and now was certain she was just Looney tunes. I interrupted Charmaine, and explained that we must have these papers filled out together and it was imperative that she be honest with me at all times. And she agreed.

Very solemnly, she signed the papers and I noticed that she even wiped tears as she did so. You would have thought that she was signing a death sentence with each signature and I noticed her shoulders slump as if in defeat. This was not what I wanted and I explained to her that this was not something bad. It was good and would mean that we would each be honest with each other and that way when I say she is not crazy, she knows I am telling her the truth. She smiled a little at that and stood to leave, asking me could she leave that outfit here. I assured her that she could.

Charmaine's Journal

I cannot believe the other morning. When I rubbed my eyes, I dropped one hand back down on my chest and felt a lot of skin. I do not wear clothes, even pajamas that show my chest or up my legs. It is just part of who I am. In fact, I sleep in sweat pants and a shirt.

Looking down, I saw a shirt I had never seen before. It was very low cut and black. You also could see my belly button at the bottom of the shirt. I had on a short skirt with black lace tights. In spite of my headache, I sat up quickly and found myself doubling over from the pain in my head and the rolling in my stomach.

Finally, I stood up and walked to the mirror on the back of my closet door. I was almost afraid to open the door to look. After I opened the door, I just stood looking and all I could think was "who are you???"

I looked like a hooker. I had on a very short skirt, black lace stocking and a top that was cut so low I felt sure my navel was showing. I had on so much makeup I could have scraped it off and my hair looked like Dolly Parton's big hair. Who the hell am I???

I was so thankful that my kids were at their Dad's house. As much I could not stand him, I would rather they be there than see me like this. I went and got a cup of coffee and headed back to my bathroom, stripping off the clothes and throwing them out the door.

The hot water felt so good but for some reason I felt a need to punish my body and turned the hot water even hotter and scrubbed so hard with the loofah pad that it looked like my skin was going to bleed. No matter how much I scrubbed, I still felt dirty. I think I was actually punishing myself but for what I was not sure; for allowing this to happen? But I did not know how to stop it.

I thought to myself "I have one week to get this straightened out before the kids are home." The stress was my fear of my ex finding out and taking the children and part of me had to wonder, would they be better off without me? I felt like I had slept for days and it actually felt good. Pulling my red robe on, I wandered down the hallway looking for coffee. With only one eye open, I was still able to see that the house literally sparkled it was so clean. Guess it was the middle of the night housekeeping elf.

I opened the fridge to get creamer and saw a glass of juice already poured. My mug was sitting out by the coffee pot and on a plate was homemade coffee cake. Ok, if I am dreaming, this is one dream I want to keep.

I took my coffee and coffee cake out on the porch under the big overhanging tree. I loved sitting here. Gosh, what day is this? I do not even know what day it is. Do I have a session today? And then the memory returned. Ok, something strange is really going on because it is like I am turning into different characters just as if I were in a movie. I wonder what Doc will say about all this? Is this what crazy feels like?

I actually wondered was someone drugging me and I did not know it. When that thought hit my brain, I got up and went into the kitchen and threw away any food that was open or had been given to me to "help" while my kids were gone. I did not have much money but I would rather throw the food away than have someone messing with my head.

Suddenly, a light bulb went off and I thought "I know. I will go and have a blood test to look for toxins in my system. I will tell them that I had been visiting with a relative that lived in the country and they had a well and that I got sick from the water. So, I wanted to make sure that the well was not contaminated. I could call Steve and ask him as he was an EMT and he could tell me how to do this.

And I guess it is time to fill Doc. in on all of this but if she tells me I am crazy, I am out of there. I picked the phone up and called Doc's number and when I heard the familiar Dr. Showalter", I almost hung up. It took me a few minutes to get the words out and Doc must have sensed it was me since she said "Charmaine, is that you?" I managed to squeak out a faint "yes."

I squeaked out that I needed to see her and she told me that I had a 2 o'clock appointment and she would see me then. She reminded me to bring my journal.. And I hung up. I wanted to run there right now but at least it was only a few hours away. Maybe I could get the blood work before I go.

Steve was awesome and I sat in my car after they drew the blood until I could remove the bandage. I did not want to go into Doc's office with that on. I am going to tell her about it but I wanted to tell her in my way, not her see the bandage. The results should be ready in a couple of days. At least that will tell me if someone is drugging my food. I just realized that I had not changed the locks. That is the next thing for me to get done.

I was going to write in my journal and realized that my second journal...the secret one was gone. OMG did I leave it at Doc's office? Surely I did not carry it there the day that I was there and did not know how I got there. Oh Crap. I am gonna call her. I HAVE to have that journal back.

Well, crap. She told me I had to wait for it. I am terrified she will read it because it has awful stuff in it. What will I do? It has all those entries someone else put in there. She told me I had to wait until tomorrow. I am so F'ing mad cause I want that journal. I think I will drink a beer. I feel like I am gonna explode.

What is happening to me? I feel like my world is falling apart and crazy things are happening and I can't stop them. I have asked a friend of mine that knows I have been through a lot with Jeremy and she is keeping the kids to give me a break. I am afraid I will totally lose my mind and Jeremy will get the kids.

If it wasn't so dam scary I would die laughing. Whoever thought I would have Dolly Parton Hair. Oh dear, now I am about to have a silly giggling fit. Oh yeah, I am crazy.

Doc does this relaxation thing and breathing stuff. Maybe if I do that I can go to sleep. I want to find some of that sage stuff like Doc has to burn too. There is just something about it that makes you feel relaxed after something has happened. One day we went outside and went around to the back and sat in the old wooden swing and talked.

I think Doc was worried about me driving home and I was too but after a bit I felt better. Why do I keep hearing fuck in my head? I don't say that word. Oh well...Sleep please come.

Chapter 8- The Revealing

I had scheduled time prior to our appointment to review my notes, to review all that I had gleaned from journal articles on cases that had been studied and researched on DID from noted and esteemed therapists in the field.

We seemed to have come a long way in our time together and I did sense her trust in me growing and it was evident by her body language and her ability to speak to me honestly. But, I was very upset that she had chosen to keep a secret journal. I knew it must be her fear of what was being written in there but I thought we had reached a better level of trust than that.

Speaking of honesty, I was glad I got her to sign our contract on the do no harm and the honesty the last session as we were delving into issues that will become increasingly difficult for her and I hope this will deter any more secrets like the second journal.

I believe that most people can cope with anything if they are treated with genuineness and positive regard and given the opportunity to know what is happening to them. It allows people a sense of control during a time when control feels hard to come by and loss of self is the primary concern and makes people feel like they are going or have gone crazy. I can only imagine the terror that they feel and how scared they are.

As I looked through my notes, I also found an initial statement from Charmaine in an early session about the grief of her father that kept returning to me; "I'm over that now, I am not grieving him, I moved to the other coast to get away from all of them." That had been and continued to be a red flag for me of abuse and perhaps this death had triggered some of the trauma experienced as a child for Charmaine, now heightened by whatever these episodes of dissociation were for her.

I felt that today may be a turning point in our trust and in our sessions, if she arrived at all. I believed that if only she would find the courage to walk through this door after her last visit, we might just make some great progress on this unfolding puzzle before us.

I had given Charmaine my word that together we would get to the bottom of this, had shaken her hand on the honesty factor and that it would involve work, but little did I know that it might involve so much along a journey of this magnitude.

I had studied, attended seminars, and read on DID and MPD as it is known to the point of making my head spin and my eyes bleary, yet I must admit I had not had a client before with multiple personalities. There may come a time that I would question whether I should refer Charmaine to another therapist if some of my suspicions were correct on this, or continue to work with her.

It was not my specialty, yet I felt strongly that once a trust was made with a client and a therapist was willing to put in the work to collaborate with others who were more knowledgeable as resources if they were needed, then we would be fine to continue working with her. That would be a decision that we, Charmaine and I, would decide at some point if we feel we are not making the progress necessary for healing.

I kept the idea of having to refer her out in the back of my mind should the time come that I felt unable to help her, while knowing that she would have to be in agreement and a part of all planning. Meanwhile I would continue to enhance my own therapeutic skills in this arena as well as build on my understandings where I may not be as sharp as I needed to be.

As these thoughts and the review of my notes continued, I heard the door open and soft footsteps coming down the hallway to the office. As I looked up, there stood Charmaine, and I felt a relief as I saw her standing there dressed in dark colors with dark hair and a watch with a beaded bracelet on.

She seemed apprehensive to come into the room and glanced at me with her *"hello Doc"* and I rose to greet her and we took our seats on the other side of that desk together. I also noticed that Charmaine's smell was distinctly hers as her hair was freshly washed and shining, yet with that smell that seemed to be fresh and belonging to her solely. The black ops one always had on manly cologne, Charie always smelled like baby powder and Charmaine had this distinct smell of clean outdoors. It is hard to explain.

She is a pleasant woman and I had come to enjoy her, the southern drawl and our shared times even with the complexity that seems to be rooted with unearthed trauma. I thought today would be very difficult, and I was right; I believe that during the last session when she realized that she was sitting in front of me in those clothes and when she realized she appeared as a child had really unsettled her and she seemed anxious.

I told her it was good to see her, and asked if she had been sleeping better as I tried to get her at ease at the beginning of the session. She seemed strained and our beginning was to a certain degree awkward for her and I could not help but notice that she was not making eye contact with me.

I offered her coffee yet she declined it, but I did have a bottle of water sitting near her chair and noticed that she immediately reached for and took the top off that and had a long drink, as we began what would become an intense session.

I realized that Charmaine was having great trouble feeling comfortable initially and I had to initiate our conversations; so I began with small talk with the idea that small talk leads to big talk, and so we began.

I asked Charmaine if her children were back at home, if she had new flowers in the yard, what she had been doing, and if she had brought her journal with her. She at first was hesitant to look at me, mostly looked down with her hands in her lap, and fingered her beaded bracelet and answered with "no, yes, uh I forgot it" as we moved on in the beginning.

I asked Charmaine was there something bothering her and she said yes, that the fact that I knew about the other journal and knew she had not told me was making her feel very bad and ashamed. She went on to explain that honesty was a big thing to her and she was not trying to lie to me but that she was scared I would send her away to some stranger and not help her anymore.

I told Charmaine that if we were ever to have a good relationship and I was going to be able to help her that we had to keep the honesty up front at all times and that is why I created the honesty contract.

With eyes overflowing with tears, Charmaine looked at me and nodded. I told her I did not ask her to sign the contract because I thought she was dishonest but because I felt it would make her be accountable when things scared her.

Charmaine looked me squarely in the eyes and leaned toward me for the first time, and said, "Doc, I have come to trust you and I am so sorry I hid the other journal from you. I have so much inside of me to talk to you about that I am about to burst open. The things in that other journal scared me and I was afraid you would commit me."

Charmaine wanted to know if I now had determined that she was in fact crazy after the last session and what had happened with her appearing in clothes that she had no idea where or how she came to be in them; no recollection of getting to my office or in that chair, nor what had happened prior to her looking at me in fright and trying to get out as quickly as she could.

She stated she could barely remember getting back home and the last thing she remembered was me standing on the porch and her in her car trying to get her senses together to drive home. Her speech was rapid and her breathing rate I watched as it increased with each sentence while her eyes never left mine, she continued to talk and tell me that she was scared to death.

Charmaine took a breath only to say that there are not a lot of people in her life that she trusts enough to share any of this with, and she had determined that she trusted me, and she only prayed that I would not send her off to somewhere or someone else or betray her trust, after all we had just signed that contract on honesty.

Charmaine also insisted that I too sign that contract that day and I still smile as I visualize her laying the pen and looking at me and then at the contract and then back at me. At the time, I had no idea of why, and asked her if she had a question, and she replied that no, she had no questions. She was just waiting for me to sign the paper as well. Touché Charmaine, I thought and could not help but smile as I picked up the pen, I do admire that in a person and sign I did.

As Charmaine spoke, I was writing notes and paying attention to her face, her body language and at times I found that I was listening with all my senses as this woman was like a volcano about to erupt. It was then I noticed her heart rate continually increasing and I stopped her and suggested that she just breathe for a few minutes and have a sip of water.

Only then I think did she realize that she had worked herself up as she was red in the face of someone who was usually pale, was animated and using her hands as she spoke to emphasize her points of trust and things that she felt were Important such as needing to bring me up to date on all that had happened.

She had been talking about blackouts, about the fear generated by the last session and not knowing what had happened to her; the devastation and gratitude that her boys were not at home while this was going on and as I stopped her, she had exclaimed, "I have one week to get this fixed Doc as that is when my kids will be home."

It was only after I stopped her that she took a deep breath and reoriented herself to everything around her that she seemed to notice that I had been writing notes as I had listened. She wanted to know what it was that I kept writing on that paper and what good did I think that was going to do.

I let her know I was making notes that were similar to puzzle pieces and that with those pieces we will eventually place them together, but for now they seemed to be hidden in hallways and rooms and it was going to be quite the challenge.

I asked Charmaine if she wanted me to tell her again about the last sessions and what had happened before she got so upset. She looked at me for what seemed to be a very long time before answering yes.

It seemed that she wanted to know but at the same time was fearful of knowing what had taken place in this place she now felt as safe.

I began by letting Charmaine know that she was safe here with me, that I had promised her to be honest and truthful at all times and to also remember that there is comedy in every tragedy and always hope in healing.

I then described the car that screeched into the driveway and the presence that walked into my office along with the Glock stories that occurred as I watched Charmaine look absolutely appalled yet captivated as if I was telling her a made up story or reading one of fiction. Her eyes were wide with complete and utter embarrassment and disbelief as I repeated the phrase "you have a fine ass Showalter" as said by the person in the ball cap" along with other anecdotes.

I then told her how just as quickly it seemed, she had been thrown into the outfit from somewhere inside of herself with no warning and was scared beyond words to find herself there in that outfit. I said "Charmaine, it was like someone shoved you out an invisible door into my office in this chair."

As I recounted the event to her, I watched the tears form in her eyes, her body stiffen and her breath all but stop as she listened intently yet worked hard to absorb what I was saying as truth. At the end of this synopsis, Charmaine hung her head and with a quiet voice whispered, "Well, I guess I am crazy as a loon then right Doc?"

Her tears flowed quietly on her face as she sat there and I watched her shoulders shake from her devastation on hearing this. I reached over and then gently placed a Kleenex in her small clenched fist and touched her arm telling her no, she was not crazy as a loon, but when she was ready, I wanted to tell her my thinking on this.

I encouraged her to take a few minutes to process this, to just be for a few minutes and concentrate on her breath in order to be present as I went to make us both a cup of coffee. Charmaine nodded her head and I left her there, with her head down as she wiped her tears to make the standard cream/sugar coffee as I pondered how I would now explain what I thought was happening to Charmaine.

This had been a tremendous amount of information to give her at one time and yet it was necessary in the work being done. As I returned to the room, I found Charmaine looking out the window, and rocking gently in the chair she sat in.

She had finished the bottle of water, and when she met my gaze and accepted her coffee, she looked terrified and desperate to speak but she wanted to know more. She asked me questions like rocket fire, what/how/why did this happen to her; can we fix it, will she ever be normal or better, will I not ever see her again now. It felt like being in a hail storm with her questions quite frankly and I barely got seated before the questions and pleading eyes found mine.

She wanted answers and she wanted them now. Yet, she had managed to let me know that she hated to tell me this, but she needed more time today. She said that she was willing to sit on the porch for as long as it took if I had other clients but there were things she had to say and she had to say them today while she had the courage. It seems we had hit an important place in the road and this was an opportunity that we had to take now.

I recognized instantly that Charmaine was at a point in therapy and emotional status that if we did not get all of this covered in this session even if it worked into two, she might regress on me. I began by letting Charmaine know that I was not going to stop our work together, once again reminding her of the very contract that together we had signed and its significance. I wanted to validate once again that she had courage in coming into my office on this day after such an experience just days before that had left her so frightened and confused and had listened intently as I gave her a review of what actually took place.

I realized that it prompted more questions than we had answers for and I also sensed that there was something pressing that she needed to talk about and could see by her face and body that it had to be something stressful and important and that she had to get it out now or emotionally she would shut down.

I assured her we would indeed get to it and wanted her to really work hard to hear what I wanted to talk with her about. It was then that I introduced the concept of DID to her and that I thought it possible that was what was happening with her blackouts and the times that she could not account for. Charmaine just sat there staring at me like I was talking with four heads and for a minute, I thought I lost her.

I asked her if she had ever heard of DID or MPD and her reaction was one of shock at first. The first association from her was "do you mean like Sybil and that movie *The Three Faces of Eve*? Doc, do you think I am making up this stuff and create myself personalities like those movies?" Interesting how movies and talk shows have given us images of things, people and disorders, cancers, mental illnesses, yet the realities are so vastly different from people's perceptions.

I assured Charmaine I did not think she was making anything up as I tried to clarify for her what DID was and what it meant. I explored and explained the disorder and likened it to compartments inside of the brain that take on different identities within a person. I said that they are usually born out of trauma or something horrible that has happened to a child; perhaps abuse suffered or witnessed as a child that was just too much to bear and so the person unconsciously created the many identities/ Alters/ personalities that they needed in order to protect themselves. I explained to her again that it was not a conscious action but subconscious.

Charmaine looked at me terrified as if I was talking about space aliens invading her body as I went on and spoke about "Alters" or those identities that come out as protection and often take over when a person is in crisis or being triggered or traumatized. As I spoke Charmaine's body was remarkably still, her breathing was shallow as she listened intently trying to absorb each word. She tried to attempt to understand as if to grasp this in order to see if it fit for her world and experiences.

I moved on to tell Charmaine that I now suspected that some grave abuse had occurred in her childhood and in her life, which perhaps she has blocked through the years. With that she leaned far back in her chair bewildered in her reaction to hearing that. I could tell by her reaction that Charmaine had no conscious idea of what I might be referring to, or maybe I was really off base on this.

I had put it out there as a possibility and my gut believed that this was the root of deeply planted seeds that may have created this creative coping mechanism we know as DID in Charmaine and this life saving mechanism that possibly saved a child's life; Charmaine's life. And now was a part of a grown woman who had yet to realize the many doorways in her mind and now feels she is losing her mind and living in hell much of the time.

As I paused and allowed Charmaine time to absorb that information I watched closely as her eyes moved and could swear I saw her mind moving to catch the thoughts as they went by her. I was also mindful of how I might be thinking if someone had just put all that information into my head and thinking, I do believe I would faint or say they were crazy and surely this could not be happening to me.

As I watched Charmaine, I knew she was looking anxious and processing all the information, and the first thing she said was, "I don't know of anything that could be traumatic that has ever happened Doc, so I can't possibly be those things or letters." I assured Charmaine that many people block out the terrible things that have happened in their lives and maybe within our work together and through her journaling, more memories would emerge and that together we can address and confront them as they do.

I noticed as I was talking, that Charmaine kept covering her ears and shaking her head on and off. I asked her was she ok and she said "It is that noise I get in my head like being in a bar Doc. You know like you hear the chatter of people but not really hear talking. I think I must have an inner ear thing as I hear it all the time but right now it is really loud."

Writing this down, I then asked Charmaine, "Can you think of anything that may have happened to you before our last session when you arrived in those clothes Charmaine, anything out of the ordinary?" With that Charmaine looked out the window again; looked at the door and for a second I thought she might try to bolt on me, and then the fountain bubbled so to speak.

Charmaine told me of an incident that had happened just the day before she was to come to the session where a man had grabbed her arm as she walked on the sidewalk and it was a man that she did not know. She went on to say that he called her by the name of "Laylee" indicating he knew her.

She was scared she said, and fought to get away from him as he blew her kisses and told her to meet him again that night, and was insistent that he knew her and had been with her. I sat watching her described these encounters as sexual intention from a stranger. She felt threatened and stated she felt "dirty" after that interaction and stated that she had no idea who this man was and had never seen him before. As I listened and watched Charmaine describe this, I knew that she was describing a very traumatic incident that may have triggered the new episode that led her into my office dressed in camouflage and combat boots just days before.

As I continued to listen, I found myself making puzzle pieces and wrote furiously as Charmaine was talking quickly. She said she was filled with what she described as shame regarding this incident where she had pulled from that paper bag clothing that she said she woke up wearing and described as clothing a hooker would wear and she would not be caught dead wearing that outfit.

When she had shown me those pieces of clothing, I could not imagine that Charmaine would ever purchase this for herself, nor be out and about with these clothes on Just as I could not imagine her purchasing camouflage pants nor wearing combat boots, or rolling cigarettes up in a shirt sleeve. As I listened more and more, I was sure that she was describing distinctly different personalities, or what is known as "Alters" within her brain used as defense mechanisms.

I asked her had she asked this man where he knew her from or where she was when she was with him.

She let me know that she could not think that quickly as her only immediate response was to make him let go of her and to get away from him as quickly as possible. She also indicated that she had wet her bed at home and in the bed at times like this and was filled with shame. And that she wore special pads in her underwear because she would have accidents if something stressed her.

Charmaine described finding herself dressed in this particular clothing and after the encounter with this man, she had rushed home and showered with such hot water that it was uncomfortable while scrubbing her body so hard that her skin would burn. She claimed she felt "dirty and ashamed" but she did not know why. She was terror filled as she recounted this to me. As I continued to write my notes, it occurred to me to ask if she had a history of urinary tract infections (UTI) to which she looked rather stunned by the question and answered yes as a matter of fact she did for a long time.

Charmaine continued to tell me candidly of the episodes that she had been told about and strange occurrences that she cannot make sense of which have her afraid to go outside her home and yet does not feel safe inside all the time as well. The more I wrote notes and watched my client the more I empathized with her wondering how long she had carried this burden alone and raised children as well with few resources.

Charmaine wanted me to know she is what I was looking at; a plain woman, who dressed the way I saw her right then and right now. She was not one to go out and party, and had never been that way she stated emphatically.

She let me know her idea of pajamas was sweating and a T-shirt, so when she woke up and stretched and was able to touch her navel she knew right away something was very wrong. And when she ran her hands over what she had on, sheer panic took over, more like terror and then she could not contain her bladder for some reason, and just like that her bed was wet.

She stated it was just horrible and she had no idea how it happened, but it was like waking up and finding your hair a completely different color and knowing what color it is supposed to be, yet she could wake one morning and it be blonde, or red, or who knows what else. Without taking a breath, Charmaine went on to tell me that on a particular morning of "these hooker clothes" that she woke up and felt like she had cotton in her mouth and her head was exploding. " I do not know what is happening to me." she would say over and again.

"Doc, it was just this morning I woke up in these clothes. Now you are telling me I might be like Eve? If something traumatic has to happen in your childhood to have this thing DID or whatever it is, then I don't think I have that because nothing ever happened like that to me. I feel like I was thrown into hell and don't know how to get out."

As I watched, listened and took in all that Charmaine had so freely let go of, I decided we really needed a separate notebook for her, one that she would use to record just these things. And I talked to her about events like the one experienced with people that she does not know should that happen again. We role played a bit of that scenario trying to empower her rather than frighten her with the wording that she is looking for in real time.

I asked Charmaine to work very hard on finding the words of "where do I know you from, where were we when we met, tell me again who are you" and similar things and then to write it in her journal with as much description as she could muster as we continue to work through the puzzle pieces.

I shared again with Charmaine that I thought trauma was at the center of this and perhaps by writing in the journal the memories would become clearer as we worked together. I then asked Charmaine how she felt after sharing all of this information that has been so safely guarded within her, and she looked at me for a bit before answering me.

For perhaps the first time since knowing and talking to Charmaine, I do believe I saw her relax for the first time and even grin as she stated that she actually felt good letting all of that out, and for perhaps the first time she felt like she could trust. She quickly added that she was not so sure about the DID though and would give it some thought, but still was not so sure on that one.

Charmaine did share with me about her children and an experience with the ex-husband as he took them away, as it seems that the same person who made a visit to "Showalter" must have come out and gave a few choice words to the ex-husband. One of the children told her about this as he hugged her and thanked her telling her that she was like Rambo with her ex-husband and her oldest loved hearing her tell his dad off.

Charmaine said that she had no idea what her son was referring to as she had no memory of that interaction or saying anything out of line to him in the driveway but whatever must have been said certainly made her son proud at the time.

Yes, I was more and more beginning to see pieces of this puzzle that appear to fall into the spectrum of DID here; yet we' have come a long way in the trust relationship in several months' time, and have only scraped the surface in my thinking.

Charmaine still strikes me as a woman who has seen much and is blocking even more from her conscious memory. I appreciated her openness today as she revealed so much but find it interesting she is in such denial of trauma in her history as it appears that what occurred last night with this stranger was traumatic and I have a feeling so are many interactions with the ex-husband.

By the end of the session, Charmaine had become emotionally drained. Yet, I do believe she would have gone on with revelations that she had come prepared to share. She had finally mustered up the courage to bring the outfit she discovered herself wearing upon her awakening,

As I looked at my watch I realized we had actually spent the equivalent of two sessions together yet I was not surprised by that. I had deliberately carved out the time when I had planned to discuss DID with her knowing it would take some time and I knew confronting her about the second journal would take time too.

I did not however know that she would have so much to tell me and that she had come so far in her trust of me to hold sacred her experiences and feelings. I knew we had entered territory that she had never shared with another and it had built up yet was frightening for her.

Can you imagine finding yourself at home in your bed wearing clothes you have never seen before? And you are with a memory of a strange and undesirable man grabbing you and indicating he knows you and wants to meet you that night as he makes sexual innuendos suggesting lewd behaviors that you should know about yet you have no recall and do not live your life in that manner or fashion. I know that I cannot. I would be horrified.

The sharing of the information about bed wetting by a grown woman had left Charmaine with feelings of great shame and disgust as she shared them. It also validated my feelings that she was abused as a child. It was sad to hear that she felt the need to self-punish through hot showers and scrubbing herself with a loofah sponge almost to the point of skin bleeding but I was not surprised at this revelation.

Yes, I believed after this session that grave abuse has occurred in this gentle woman's life, yet I had no idea of the extent of this abuse until much later when I was allowed to journey with Charmaine down the hall through hell with her. And we indeed walked a journey through hell with me only as a guide as she did the work to integrate those within the many doorways of her mind.

I saw such terror as she described the incident of not knowing where or who this man was, nor the experience that had occurred wearing combat boots, but that was just the beginning of walking this journey, and that was only the opening of terror as it is known from one who has lived through hell in ways that I still stand in amazement by.

Charmaine is a gentle spirit, one who has survived more than most people I have met both personally and professionally. Yes, this session opened the canvas for a puzzle like none I had ever seen up close and personal. As Charmaine was leaving that day, I suggested that she begin another journal, a separate one for those instances that she felt or experienced things she did not understand, or people or places she did not recognize but who seemed to know her.

Anything out of the ordinary was important and I told her; to pay attention to her surroundings, to take an inventory of her home, closets, shoes, her undergarments, clothing and bathroom personal care items. I asked that she do that daily and make lists including what was in her medicine cabinet and refrigerator.

We talked about the need to monitor things very closely in order to better understand what was happening day to day hour to hour in order for her to feel more in control of her life, her home, her goings and comings in the area. I stressed to Charmaine, under no circumstances do you attempt to tear out any pages of this journal; no matter how bad or how strong or offensive it may be when you later read it do not tear out anything.

I also explained to Charmaine that I had hoped the Alters might use the journal to share needs, feelings or experiences at times that she is not present; those times that she has no recall of. I validated that I knew this was all hard to grasp and we would spend more time talking about it next session, but asked that she just humor me for now and she smiled.

My hope had been that if the journal was explained to her, and it was available we may find that entries would be made from the one in the combat boots, or even by the one that had written previously that had upset Charmaine so much she had ripped it out of her journal. My hope was a reality for they were using the journal.

As I saw Charmaine's expression change, I had to ask her again, "Deal? To which she replied, "Yes Doc you have a deal. But I might not like it." I smiled and continued by telling her "In the other journal you write your thoughts, any questions or concerns, and feelings like always. Please bring both with you when you return. No more secret journals. Ok? Can we have truth here?

As Charmaine was leaving I took her hand in mine and looked her in the eye and asked her if there are any weapons in her home, any at all that she is aware of. Charmaine told me that her son had a rifle and a pistol at home, but it had been just a BB gun.

I asked her if she would mind bringing them to my office or giving them to the ex-husband for a while, and then we talked about the possibility of Charmaine hurting her. She readily agreed but said she would rather I keep them than her ex. She said he would do too much questioning and was trying to take her kids anyway. So, we agreed for her to bring them to the office later today.

Charmaine said that she would never do that to her children, but there have been times that if she did not have her children, she just did not know because at times it was so very hard. She said the closest she had ever come was just not caring if she lived or died not taking an action. I was greatly relieved to hear that.

I let Charmaine know that I valued her, that I was there for her and it was important that if she felt as though she was in harm's way she needed to call 911 or to call me. She agreed to that and thanked me for the concern and that she was glad we had signed the paperwork, and I in turn made a copy for her to take home with her.

It was a long session and I knew she was over flooded with information and her openness of all she had shared. I had asked if she needed to sit quietly for a bit before driving but she had assured me that she was fine to drive and actually felt lighter than she had in a long time. She said she had much to think about and yet no desire to watch those movies about Eve or Sybil again anytime soon and laughed.

As we walked out on the porch together, I felt the breeze on my face and I must tell you it felt good, and as I glanced at Charmaine, I saw her lift her face to the sky. She then turned to me and said, "Doc, may I give you a hug or is there a fee for that?" I saw the twinkle in her eye. With all this woman has lived through she was able to maintain some semblance of humor, and that is the mark of a grand warrior; as with every tragedy there is comedy and with all comedy there is tragedy.

I was tired but felt grateful that Charmaine has walked across the bridge of trust as we now enter into the hard work that is in front of us. I smiled at her, and opened my arms for a great hug knowing in that instant we had stepped across a bridge together; one that would lead us to the foot of a mountain. We had indeed established a much needed trust for what lay ahead.

As I bid so long to Charmaine until our next session, I watched from the porch as she sauntered to her car, and before getting in she lifted her head again to the sky as if a silent thank you was being given to the Creator that for once she was heard and it was her voice that did the talking.

I watched as Charmaine got in her car, listened as she turned the engine on and just as quickly turned it off and got out of that car. She came back to the porch with a fast step and told me there was just one more thing she needed to let me know. I leaned against the rail and looked closely at her and said "W hat in the world could that be?"

Charmaine wanted to let me know was that she had gone with a friend and had him run a blood test on her after getting rid of all the food in the house. She worried that someone might be trying to poison her. She said she had thought that maybe that was the reason she was waking up with odd colored hair and such strange happenings with no recall. She stressed that she did not want this to come out later and me to think she was keeping it from me.

I asked if the results had come in as of yet and she let me know she was waiting. She wanted me in on that loop though, as she thought perhaps the ex-husband may have something to do with all this. She said that he did not want to pay child support anymore and if he could, he would do anything to make that possible. She felt that he would even take the kids even though he did not want them and then they would suffer.

Then she also said, she was sorry for taking so much time but there was one other thing that was really bothering her, and it had to do with the locks on her doors. She thought she might need to get them replaced but money was really tight now.

As I listened to her describe what was happening I felt strongly that this may indeed be an Alter at work unlocking doors but we needed a plan, not new locks. I carefully described my thinking to Charmaine and told her perhaps we can enlist your children to help with this without yet telling them what we are thinking here. We can ask them to double check the locks to ensure your safety and normalize things at home at the same time.

So together on the porch, Charmaine and I came up with a plan that would involve her oldest son having some responsibility. I talked to her about how to make him understand that because of her sleeping habits and sleep walking, that she sometimes left the doors unlocked and it would be helpful if he could double check them.

Charmaine looked visibly relieved that we seemed to come up with a workable plan, as she thought through how she would present it and how she would implement it in her daily routines when the children returned. And she was thinking of ways she could check herself while they are away.

I reminded her to call about the blood work and if possible to bring her results and journals with her for our next session. As I stood up, she said, "Ok Doc, we have a plan then" and smiled; and it was then that I noticed a shift in Charmaine, a release of something powerful in her in that instant. I noticed the ability to joke in what had been an immensely stressful time not so long ago when she declined a cup of coffee and was not even making eye contact. I smiled at her calling her and said "Yes, we have a plan."

I watched until she was in her car and pulling out of the driveway. She waved as she pulled away in her car, and I returned inside to gather my papers to return outside and do my paperwork. I wanted to enjoy the breeze for a change as it did feel good.

I decided that I may want to give her a book to read on DID as it may help her in her understanding as she processes this as a real possibility for her life. The mind is an amazing thing and Charmaine is teaching me more about the mind than I have learned in a long time.

As I put notes together from this session, I was struck by how interesting it is that some can condense therapy notes into just a summary of a few lines. How does one lay a life like this down to three or four sentences I found myself thinking and yet maybe it is time to join the 21st century and join with those who check mark people into categories and call it a day. But, I knew that I could never do that.

I sat and reflected on the work done in this little eccentric office with all its color and brightness, knowing that the stones help to ground clients, the flowers assist in the energy flow, the sage will clear the room between clients and the art on the walls will calm the mind.

As I thought of all that has been shared between these four walls I am grateful for the safety that these walls have afforded the many that have found solace and courage here to tell their stories or find their way through the darkness and unearth their gifts beyond their pain.

Yes, that old saying is really true, if these walls could talk, what a story they would have; and now Charmaine has decided she wants her story told; she wants her life to stand for more and through the telling of this story she feels strongly that countless, many will find the courage to heal and to integrate the many rooms of their minds into one full life. If only I had known then what I know now but it is not only the client that learns, it is also the therapist.

Charmaine's Journal

The next day

I finally felt comfortable enough that I actually wanted to tell Doc what had been going on. She never gave any kind of reaction like she thought I was crazy when we talked and we had been talking for a couple of months now. If I am ever to get my life back again, I have to tell someone and she is the closest one I trust. The time has come for something concrete to happen.

As I walked into the office, Doc looked up and motioned to the chair. The session started off awkwardly and she had to do a lot of leading to get me to talk. I found once I actually started talking, it became easier.

I still do not get it about all these Alters thing and me changing appearances. What am I a quick change artist??? I can't even find all the stuff they wear. I feel so danged confused. Maybe those others are right and I am crazy. OHhh I want to run to my cubby so bad.

She asked me what had happened prior to my coming to the office. I had to sit for a few minutes trying to remember and it suddenly hit me. That was the day the man grabbed me and called me Jennie and was acting like he knew me very well and even blew a kiss at me.

I only wanted to run, run... RUN when that man grabbed me. I felt so filthy that I cannot even put it into words. Doc said "Did he mention where you met him?" I told her no, that was not the first time someone had done that and it was always a man and they would grab my arm and ask things like why I had not called them. Doc just nodded. And who the hell is Laylee??? I don't know a Laylee.

I watched as Doc was writing on her tablet. I asked her what she was doing and she told me she was trying to keep all the pieces of the puzzle so that we could put them together. She told me that from now on, anytime someone strange talked to me and acted like they knew me or anyone told me I was acting differently to be sure and write it down and if possible to ask them questions like where we had been when we saw each other.

I decided that it was a good time to tell her about the incident with my ex when he picked up the children. I told her I had not said anything to my ex but that my oldest son said I walked and talked like some Rambo and implied I told him off. Having accidents was a problem for me and I knew it was stress related but I felt it was time Doc knew that too. She nodded and said that it was something that did happen to people who had been traumatized in some manner. I don't get it......what trauma???

When I told her how ashamed I felt, she told me that we would get to the bottom of it. She told me not to feel ashamed, that what was causing it was not my fault. And all I could think was how the hell do you know? We don't know what is causing it."

I also started telling her about how my hair color changed constantly and my hair style and how I would suddenly find myself in clothes I had never seen before and with hairdos that I would never have. I told her that the last one was when I woke up and called her this morning.

This morning, I woke up and was laying there and my head felt like a bomb had exploded in it and my mouth felt like I had dirty cotton stuffed in it and I was dressed looking like what I called a hooker.

When I looked at myself in the mirror, I again felt that shame and deep fear and before I could stop it, I could feel my bladder releasing and the warmth on my legs. Fortunately, I was standing beside the bathroom door and made it into the interior of the bathroom. When I told her this Doc just kept writing and nodding. What the hell Doc are you a bobble head????

She looked up and asked me had I ever had problems with UTI's? She seems to be on target so much with what she asks that it is not funny. "Yes, I do have a history of urinary infections" I said. And she nodded and started writing again.

I pulled the paper bag out and pulled out items one by one and told "I had this on and I have no idea where I have been dressed like this." When she finished writing, I looked at her and said "I am crazy, right?" And she again told me no. She said she had something very serious she wanted to discuss with me and that she felt I was triggered by some trauma from the past and this was causing the problems.

She told me that first she needed to discuss the journals with me. I looked at her knowing when she said "journals" that she knew the truth. I had left the other one here. I told her right off the bat that I was sorry for not telling her and would never do it again. We even signed honesty contracts about it.

After that, Doc asked me if I had ever heard of Dissociative Identity Disorder and I looked at her and said no. She told me perhaps I had heard of it as Multiple Personality Disorder and I laughed a little and said "you mean like that three faces of Eve movie?" And Doc said "Yes in a sense. I think this is what is wrong with you."

All I could think was OH GREAT...she thinks I am making this all up. I might as well give up if she thinks that. Finally she got me to understand that she did not believe I was faking but thought it was an unconscious thing. I told her ok Fix it. She told me it would take hard work, often walking through extreme emotional memories and opening myself up to do it and that it was not done overnight.

I was the one nodding then. I told her "Ok, when do we start because I want my life back." Doc said "We start now. I want you to keep using the two journals...one for you and the "Alters" to write in and one for just you to put down everything every day that is odd or makes you feel funny. If we can open the secret places inside, then you will not need them anymore and maybe this will not happen anymore."

She and I talked about what having Dissociative Identity Disorder meant and what the cause usually was. When she said traumatic abuse, I told her that I must not have it then because I did not remember any abuse in my life other than the ass Jeremy that I was divorced from. She let me know that sometimes these traumas are hidden inside our heads and we do not realize it. She said this was where all the hard work came in and that we would have to start with accepting that this might be it.

She told me that the book for the Alters to write in too was an experiment she hoped worked. She hoped that they would put down information so that when I blacked out, perhaps I might know what was happening when I was "absent" from myself.

I asked her was that who wrote in my other journal and she said she suspected so. At least I had a game plan now. I was the kind of person as long as I knew what I was battling, and then I could make it. I just knew I could. Now, if I could just make it home without going AWOL, then I would be happy.

As I started to head to the car at the end of our session, I remembered that I was going to tell Doc about the blood work. I asked her if I could tell her one more thing before I left. While I was explaining my fear that Jeremy or someone was trying to mess with me by putting something in my food, she just watched my face. So, I said that I went and had a blood test just to prove to myself that everything was ok.

She nodded and said that it was a good plan for if nothing showed then I could remove that stress. After I told her about the doors being unlocked so much and what how I wanted new locks put on the doors, she told me that she did not think I needed to do that since she felt at least one of the Alters was doing it so they would do the same thing with the new locks. Tapping my fingers on the door jam, I nodded and said that made sense but my question was...what do I do then?

We developed a game plan to include all the kids without upsetting them. I decided to tell them that I needed their help because of my not feeling well, as they all knew I was run down because of the anemia and I have to take this horrible liquid vitamin tonic.

So, I am going to tell them, that sometimes I forgot to lock to garage door because I was so tired and so everyone had a new job. It was to check the locks every time they happened to be near the doors to help Mommy in case Mommy fell asleep and forgot to lock it. I knew my oldest would not really buy that so I will tell him that I really am afraid I am sleep walking and unlocking the doors. He will watch closer.

I like it. We have a game plan. I feel like I am gaining some control with a game plan. But I still feel like I have worms with all these people inside me. I wish I could go inside and talk to them. I wonder if they live in the rooms in my hallway?

How the failing hell do you have rooms in your head and a hallway? I was ok when it was one hallway and my cubby. But now I have a whole motel???? Oh crap now I am laughing. I can just see my regular doc looking in my ear and seeing rooms.

A drawing that appeared on the easel with a note labeled simply "Charie"

CHAPTER 9-Life in The Fast Lane

Charmaine arrived early for her session with me laden with her journals and had brought a thermos of coffee saying it was the least she could do. I found her sitting outside on the porch as I walked my client out after what had been a tearful session for them, and as we parted I sat down on the steps and heard a caring woman comment, "Oh gosh Doc, it seems they are hurting real bad huh?"

I smiled and didn't really respond, just allowing the question and the genuineness of her concern to wash over me and the moment, as we both enjoyed the quietness of the afternoon. I had scheduled a double session for Charmaine and then noticed her thermos and journals.

I asked if she was ready to go inside and she surprised me by saying she knew she was early, so if I had notes or something to do she would be fine waiting, but she had perked a thermos of real coffee for me if I wanted to enjoy some now. She also carried and handed me an envelope and told me I could look at it after she left when our time together ended for the day, it was just something she found for me.

Kindness is one of the reasons I do what I do, and this gesture touched me deeply. I let her know that I would just finish up my paperwork and would come and get her shortly if that would be alright with her. I then left her with her thoughts for a bit. She seemed to be enjoying the afternoon breeze and content to be early there sitting on the porch.

Paperwork is not something that anyone enjoys but is always best to be on top of it the moment when things are fresh in your mind and I knew that my focus would be on where Charmaine was today after she had time to process our last session. I wanted her to let me know how the last few days had gone with her new journal. I needed to keep my focus clear so that all matters of housework and paperwork would be completed.

I had noticed in that brief time that Charmaine had long dark hair, and was in simple dark clothes, so it seemed that she was herself for our session today. She was carrying both journals, so hopefully she will have some new insights for both of us.

As I wrapped up with the papers in hand, I heard the door open and the familiar now southern drawl of "Doc is it ok if I come on in now?" As I glanced at my watch, she was right on time and I said, "Of course come on in dear." I stood from behind the desk and offered to get us cups for that coffee and all the little things to color and sweeten hers for her before we began what would be an extraordinary session once again.

As I sat down beside Charmaine, she let me know that the results from the blood work came back negative and that everything was all good and nothing showed up. I told her I was glad to hear that and now she can relieve herself of that worry and stress and I hope that she had re-filled her fridge by now as well.

I did let her know that I felt she took great steps in making an empowering decision to follow through in doing the blood work, and it was one less worry she had to walk with. Charmaine looked at me and grinned with an eyebrow raised and stated; "now Doc, that sounds like that psychobabble stuff people say." I had to laugh out loud at that one, but I did tell her she could mark that off her stress list and I meant it.

With that she smiled and took a few sips of her coffee and said "Oh boy do I have a lot to tell you since I've become a DID detective." She was quite witty as we began the session and said her coffee was wonderful. I suspected that we were in for an intense session by the lightness of its beginnings. I was glad to see that Charmaine was allowing her sense of humor to emerge.

I too had been piecing more of my puzzle together and was feeling stronger in my belief that Charmaine has a diagnosis of DID and any doubts that were left, she took care of as she shared the journal and items that she found since our last time together. It seemed that Charmaine had decided to find out if things were hidden in her home and began a search, while trying to wrap her head around things we discussed in the last session together.

While still not sure she was buying the package of DID and other personalities, she also was not convinced that it was not true. She began to delve back in her memories for clues or for things in her home that might lead her to discoveries or a better understanding of what has been happening. She had no memory or recollection of many things.

In trying to think back to the traumas and childhood memories she was struck with the reality that there were long periods of time that she could not account for, memories and time frames that were just huge blanks or spaces of times.

She talked about finding the camouflage pants and black ops tee shirts hidden under her son's bed, along with cigarettes and then recognizing them since our last session while stating she did not know whether to laugh or cry.

She did not know whether to celebrate that her son is not smoking or to feel crazy as it was proof to what I had told her about in my office and as were the very clothes she found herself in when she came back into herself that day and fled from my office not knowing how she came to be dressed that way.

Charmaine was animated and seemed to be on a mission to find the answers to questions that have been alive in her for a long time, yet have only magnified in their intensity. She told me that she sat in her big chair in her bedroom after searching through papers and discovering writings and sketches much like the one that was on the easel, yet it appeared to have been drawn by a child; and while in the chair she had dozed off for a while only to wake singing "wubba ducky me wuv ou" in her mind.

When she awoke she could not for the life of her find the drawings and the writings she had before falling asleep but instead there was a child's sewing kit in her hand and in the other was a needle and yarn as if she were about to sew the cardboard kit.

She reported looking over at her dolls and noticing that they had been repositioned and were in different clothing than she remembered and could not remember doing it herself and at that point thought that perhaps she had sat in that chair and lost what little might have been left of her mind.

As she expressed these things I watched carefully her eyes, her body posturing and her comfort level in sharing this information. Once again I made notes, and once again I felt as though I was hearing the sounds of a person who was fighting with all their might to reach some understanding of their world and control of their mind and body and spirit.

Charmaine stated that it was so hard to imagine that she has lived all these years with things like this happening and not be able to account for major amounts of time as she thought about her life. As I listened to Charmaine I had to agree with her; I cannot fathom having such large chunks of time just be gone from the memory as she was telling me she could not remember an entire year when in 4th grade. Occasionally you get a client that truly works as if their life depended on it and Charmaine was one of those people.

I asked Charmaine to share with me times of her childhood if she felt comfortable, did she recall any times of great stress as a little one, or times similar to the one she had shared where she was daydreaming and was kicked by her father. My heart ached as I listened to Charmaine as she told me of times she slept and hid in a closet afraid of being beaten by her parents. Yet she felt she had not suffered trauma as a child.

This woman sat in front of me and with very little emotion was able to talk with me about hiding among dirty laundry from her parents. She spoke with clarity about sitting at a mirror with scissors in her hands after cutting her bangs as a child and being discovered by a punitive mother who then cut off all her hair as tears flowed from Charmaine's eyes.

The mother telling her to hush or she would give her more to cry about and a child who claimed to not have done it although she had scissors and fallen hair around her but no recollection. She had disassociated as a little child to save her from abuse by parents. The puzzle pieces were falling into place as if being put there so quickly my mind was about to explode trying to keep up while dealing with an aching heart for this woman who has probably suffered from dissociation since a very young age.

I was captured by her southern drawl and ability to maintain her composure as she spoke and told the stories in fragmented pieces of a child who wet the bed under such stress and fear of punishment that she often would sleep on hardwood floors with a child's brain figuring that if she should pee it would be easier to just wipe it from the floor or cover it up without being discovered.

She said these things with very little emotion, just facts to a therapist who was listening with amazement at a grown woman who seemed to be talking about the weather rather than expressing such anger and disbelief at such horrid treatment by parents. She recalled being called a "black sheep" in the family; of regular beatings with a belt, and bruises that covered her body in a way that it seemed to be a fairly regular occurrence. And being told to never tell anyone or else.

A remarkable discovery was made as she also related an incident where she was pretending to be asleep and was discovered by her Mother who then became very upset and told her Father. It seems the mother was angry and panicked over Charmaine sleeping at that time, and then asked the father what to do then and his reply was to "wake her ass up as the group will be coming and they would want her there."

Charmaine went on to tell me that she now recalled a group of adults who came to her home as a child on a regular basis, they were some kind of church group she thought yet she recalled a lot of hugging and kissing going on and drinking as well. My heart began to sink as I immediately thought of groups that used to meet under the auspices prayer groups, of adult gatherings yet children were sacrificed to sexual exploitation during those dress up parties , and I could not help but wonder if this was the origins of Charmaine's escape to the hallways of DID.

I listened intently and did not want to push on this as I was well aware we were entering into something that was fraught with abuse and landmines of a child now all grown up and blocked for years and years. Yet it was beginning to make the pieces of the puzzle fall into place in ways I had never imagined when I first met this woman and had no idea of such horrendous acts and courage to survive.

Could it be that within this woman lived a little child who had been the sacrificial lamb for adults having their evening cocktail parties of such sickness and lewd behaviors in a home with Persian rugs and grandeur while a child was given so freely by parents with no moral compass? I felt unnerved as she spoke with eagerness in her sharing of things that she had worked so diligently to discover and find, along with the few memories she had pieced together since our last session.

I was amazed at the detachment she was showing as she spoke to me on these things and the calmness while realizing that if I was correct in my assessment she had not actually witnessed the horrors that had occurred but instead she had been saved by the Alters who stepped in to protect her.

My mind was racing and I was fully present to bear witness to her at the same time, as much as even I know that is hard to imagine. As I listened to Charmaine I begin to wonder if perhaps she had many Alters we had yet to discover within her: Alters that were children along with the adults behind whoever was in charge of that long hallway in the brain. I was already seeing the image of the hallway in Charmaine's head.

I had done a lot of research and also remembered from those long put away text books, that those with DID have a "gatekeeper" of sorts, one who controls what and which Alter steps out and takes over when the stressor or trauma or trigger is pulled. These words conjure up the image of a body guard standing at the door to a person's brain.

I could not help but wonder who was the gatekeeper for Charmaine, and suspected it was a strong and trying Alter who guarded and maintained the doors of the entrance of that long hallway. All that I was hearing gave me ideas, and yet fears into the unknown world of this woman, and still admiration on the ability she had in finding clues to take control of her life.

I knew and appreciated her fear as she continued to talk in a manner that indicated her confusion and bewilderment at times with each question, discovery, and clue that was unearthed in her home. I only knew that our sessions seemed to end quicker than most I have held with clients in my recent memory, as I realized we were almost out of time.

I decided to ask Charmaine if she would mind trying something new in our session and utilize play therapy with her; as I stood up and showed her my corner where coloring books, a doll house, dolls and stuffed animals were tucked in a corner of the office. She looked at me rather oddly and said, "With all I have on my mind you now want me to color with you Doc?" I had to laugh at that one, as I am sure with all she had been telling me it did sound a bit odd, but as she had been talking with me about bits and pieces of the past, I was struck at her ability to disconnect of emotions as she shared information.

So I once again told her it was an experiment of sorts, as we talked she could just "doodle" if she did not mind, and we would continue our conversation at the same time, and Charmaine agreed. At first hesitantly and asking what in the world did I want her to doodle and how did I expect her to do that and talk to; before I knew it she was in fact doing both quite well.

What began as "squiggly lines to circles and squares", Charmaine continued to talk as I watched and listened to her speak, noting her gestures, facial expressions and her tone of voice. I asked Charmaine if she ever heard voices inside her head, and she stopped still at that point. The crayons, the paper, her voice all dead quiet. I watched as she cocked her head and leaned to the left and appeared to be straining a bit.

Puzzled I asked Charmaine what it was that she was doing and she replied "Well I am listening and I do not hear anything. What do you mean do I hear voices or sounds, you mean like a schitzo does, voices telling me to do things Doc?" I smiled at Charmaine and told her no, that was not what I was meaning actually and that schizophrenics actually heard voices "outside" their head talking to them. I was asking if she ever heard voices/sounds "inside" her head and that was the difference, but I did not want her to work so hard in trying to hear them.

We both chuckled at the same time as she looked relieved over my answer and I was amused at the way she paused and strained to listen to whatever it was she thought I had meant: she was quite serious there for a moment.

As she went back to coloring I noticed that the lines were different that she was now making; more childlike in their appearance and that her voice seemed to be much softer as well when she spoke. I was having to lean closer to hear her and realized that I was in the presence of an Alter who presented as a child now.

I watched quietly as she continued to draw on the paper, humming to herself and appeared to be oblivious of my presence. She was drawing little stick figures that seemed to be odd in ways and doors I think, yet the stick figures being drawn had shapes that I had to look twice at.

As I watched, I saw Charmaine's face change and the look of childlike innocence come across her face as she looked up at me with teary eyes and I heard a voice I had not ever heard say, "Pweeze no tell on me. Me get in twuble" and the humming stopped. Her eyes were big and she looked at me with such innocence that it amazed me and then she lowered her head as I sat quietly for what seemed a long time but was probably moments.

Then, I watched as Charmaine lifted her head up, and raked her fingers through her hair seemingly a bit unsettled, and she quickly asked me if she could go to my restroom there, and I guided her to its location, noting that she looked embarrassed, and seemed hurried.

While she was gone, I looked again at the paper where the doodles and stick figures had been drawn and noticed there was an intensity of the ink and pressure used by Charmaine. I was quickly writing my notes on the noted changes in her face and body language and that little voice saying, "Pweeze no tell on me", and trying to think of the tune she was softly humming and yet I could not bring it to mind. I had just been in the presence of a little one that lived inside of Charmaine, but who was I watching color and what was it I was not supposed to tell and who was I not supposed to tell it to?

We had gone into one of the doors in the hallway, I knew that we had. But how/why and why had we come out so quickly? The stick figures and doodles were quite telling as I glanced at them more and more noticing the details and I was lost in thought there and still trying to figure out that humming song as I began to hum softly in my office waiting for Charmaine to return so we could talk.

I was deep in thought and did not hear Charmaine reenter the room and sheepishly sit down. She had her hands in her lap and sat quietly for moments until I sensed her presence and it startled me. I apologized for being lost in thought, and she said, "No need to apologize, I think I have another one of those bladder infection things going on again." She looked quite uncomfortable and did not want to draw anymore, nor did she want to look again at what she had drawn.

She looked at me and said, "Uh Doc, were you just singing about a duck as I came in? Oh, that is so odd because after I had woken up with that sewing thing in my hands, I had some song in my head the other day but it sounded like "wubba" ducky" and I could not for the life of me remember the last time I've heard that. Is it on a commercial or something? I think my little girl may have come home singing it one day."

I thought I would just faint right there on the spot as once she said that it made perfect sense to me. Yes, that was the name of what was being hummed, wubba ducky me wub ou. Seriously??? She had awakened with the same tune playing in her head and yet she had it as "wubba ducky" as if indicating she had been hearing it sung by a child? As much as Charmaine had changed, as much as she seemed out of sorts now, she had just confirmed what I had just witnessed, a child Alter that came "in" to play or "out" shall I say, with no warning or invitation by Charmaine.

A little innocent child who did not want to get into trouble for drawing or doodling yet was trying to speak, and was humming until she felt threatened by something. Could it have been the stick figures she drew that looked like something projecting from the abdomen of each one like a pencil pointing outward?

Had we triggered the memory of this church group in Charmaine and the abuse that had gone on so very long ago that has been blocked by the gatekeeper of her mind to protect her? That was my first thought anyway, yet I was fascinated and most concerned by what we were now approaching at what seemed to be rapid speed ahead.

Interesting, something had changed in a flash in Charmaine and she was no longer as comfortable as she had been when she arrived. I asked her if she was feeling stressful since the drawing/playing with coloring crayons and she said she lost time doing it, and then to be truthful she felt she was losing control of her bladder and that something bad was happening to her, so yes she felt nervous now.

I assured her that she was safe, and ask her if she would like to do some deep breathing exercises in order to return to a calm place for a bit before we continued together. She said she did not know how to do that, and it sounded like "hogwash" but she would try it as she was feeling "jittery."

I tried to keep from grinning as I made a note to myself to add "jittery" as a technical term in my vocabulary as it was a wonderfully descriptive word. I described to Charmaine how we were going to do breathing exercises and led her into guided breath, and she was a great follower. It did not take long to notice her breathing change, her body become relaxed and for her to want to resume our session feeling more calm and less "jittery" from what had gone on in her mind as she drew those stick figures on paper.

Charmaine wanted to get back on track of sharing with me her journals and findings once she felt calmer, and I of course wanted to continue with these drawings as I knew I had tapped into an Alter who wanted to come out and be creative there in my office. I followed Charmaine's lead as it was really her journey we were on, and she was the one who was now wanting to lead; for that I was grateful and not about to try and sway her into territory she was not ready to traverse.

Charmaine told me of tearing her home upside down looking for clues, for things that would help her and guide me better in helping her since our last visit. She had found some papers and drawings that she said were hidden among papers and under things that she did not know about, and some seemed to be done by children and yet others by adults. It had her very confused.

I had asked her if any were made by her children and she adamantly replied that none were done by them as it was not like how any of them drew. Some were similar to the sketch on the easel though and others were quite different, she had brought everything for me to look at and for us to talk about.

This was a woman who could not account for blocks of time, for memories of her life as a child, often confused and committed to her life and wanting to do all that was needed in placing these puzzle pieces in order that would make sense for her. She was like a detective in her determination and I admired her bravery.

She had told me more than once that as long as she knew what she was fighting she was willing to fight like a warrior. She was indeed on a battle field within herself now, and there was no slowing her down in her quest to find out what in the world was happening to her, along with the fact that she wanted a fast resolve while her kids were with their father.

I had to let her know that there was not a "quick fix" for DID; it would be a long uphill battle I thought as we addressed each thing as it came and explored the how's, where's and why's of her life as she has come to know it. She did not like that answer and admitted that she still was not totally convinced of this whole DID thing anyway. I knew that part and felt for her in the vacillating between wanting a diagnosis and wanting it to all just magically go away.

I still had many questions but felt I was getting answers through her detective work, and most recently through her artwork. The puzzle pieces indeed were fitting to the diagnosis. I was not a magician and Charmaine was a complex client with many doors in a long hallway that I had just entered with her.

I had more questions than answers although the puzzle pieces indeed were fitting to the diagnosis I was not a magician and Charmaine was a complex client with many doors in a long hallway that I had just entered with her.

As we ended the session, Charmaine had returned to a more relaxed state and thought the breathing exercises were "pretty cool", and said that she had a question for me. I told her that I would try to answer it, and with that she said, "Doc, how is it that a parent or anyone else can beat you and then tell you that you better smile or they will give you something to cry about? I mean how in the hell can you smile after having a belt put to you, you know what I mean?"

I sat and just looked at this lovely woman with sad eyes who asked that question with such sincerity that I wanted to cry as I had no answer for her. There are times when no answer is the best answer, and I shook my head while trying to come up with something politically correct, professionally appropriate and still I came up empty.

I went with my gut and said "Charmaine, I am so sorry that this happened to you, so very sorry." That was the best I could do for an answer. Interestingly enough, it seemed to be the answer that she was seeking as she rose from her chair, and said "Me, too." Together we walked out onto the porch as the sun was setting and then I remembered that Charmaine had forgotten the journals and her thermos, so I asked her to wait for me to retrieve them for her.

She smiled and leaned against the rail, raising her face to the skies as if inhaling the welcomed air and freedom from her time of sharing such pain and intimacy in that safe place she has come to know. I realized we had not spent as much time on the journals as I had hoped to, yet had received so much information, much more than I thought we would cover in this session and I had met someone, though I did not yet know who.

When I returned I found Charmaine at the bottom of the steps in the flower bed. She was sitting in the dirt and picking the heads off the flowers. I came down those steps in a hot second and thought something was wrong as I said, "Charmaine, what are you doing there? " I can only imagine my own face as she looked up at me with a mean face, a scrunched up nose and put her hands on her hips stating "Who are you calling Charmaine Lady? My name BUCK. You got that lady, I BUCK." I looked at my client now Buck and said, "Well hello Buck, nice to meet you. How old are you? "

I guess that was not very impressive since the reply was, "I'm 6 shitin' years old, and I hate these darn flowers too. Everyone else likes 'em but I HATE 'EM. Why do you care lady, nobody listens to Buck, not no one. I hate everyone cos' they don't listen and don't do nothing about nothing, you know what I mean."

With that I watched as Charmaine, now introduced as the Alter Buck clumsily stands up and wipes hands all over the pants and proceeds to stomp all over my flower bed. I was ready to have one fine fit, as my brain exploded thinking what the hell is this happening here.

I said, "Buck, you need to stop that and who are you so mad at and why are you here?" As I watched, I realized that this Alter was really another child: a six year old little boy Buck who felt no one listens: a child whose movements were clumsy, the speech kid-like and the mannerisms awkward. Oh my, was Buck angry. I said it again, "Why are you stomping on my flowers, have they done something to you?" what came next shocked me yet cracked me up. Buck reared up and said, "Charmaine touches 'em, likes 'em, shit she even plants 'em at home. But I fix her, I sneak out and tear 'em up after she goes to bed at night... then you know what else I do? I leave the doors unlocked just to fuk with her that is what I do. Now, why do I care about your ole stink flowers, just try to make me stop stompin 'em lady." And he began to start chanting "My name is Buck. It rhymes with FUCK" and he stomped some more on my flowers.

Well I guess Buck the six year old with a mouth had just served notice and caught himself on the door openings at the same time. I would not be bullied by Buck I had decided as I listened and watched that fine fit being taken out on my flowers that I had given so much attention and care too.

Without a second thought I walked over to where the stomp anger fest was happening and put my hand on the arm of my client and yanked him out of my flower bed. With a firm voice and a serious eye, I lowered my voice and said, "Buck you are welcomed to come and visit me anytime you would like, and I will listen to you. BUT that is if you behave and you respect my property and me. For now, you have been disrespectful to me and I will not have that, as I have not deserved that from you. So for now, you need to go and send Charmaine back out to me. I am very sorry that you are so angry and we can talk about that another time, but you will have to stop locking and unlocking those doors and tearing things up to be welcomed here. Do YOU understand me?"

Buck looked like he was going to wet himself and pulled away from me and ran to a nearby tree and sat crying. I walked close to the tree and just stood there quietly to see what was next. Before too long I noticed that the body was moving and legs stretched, Charmaine sat up taller and looked around intensely and then up at me squinting her eyes and said, "Doc, what the hell are we doing over here?"

I smiled at her and extended a hand to help her up to her feet and then with my arm around her, we headed to the porch. I let her know that we would talk about it in a couple of days but the most important thing for her to know is that she is safe, and everything is alright.

She looked at me and shook her head like fleeing a fly on a hot day and then noticed the flower bed. "Oh my Doc, look at your flowers. What in the world happened to them today?" I smiled at her and said, "It looks like some kid had a hissy fit doesn't it?" and she agreed saying if one of her kids did that she would have a fit.

Suddenly she stopped dead in her tracks and told me that her flowers had also been destroyed more than once just like that and she never found out who did it, but sure would have liked to. She said she spent many hours on her flowers and that she was so proud of them and then would find them destroyed.

I suggested that sometime we should do a therapy session with restoring the flowers and getting our hands in the dirt as it would be a good session and quite healing. Charmaine thought that a grand idea but wanted to know what had happened. So we sat on the steps and I let her know in a nutshell that I had returned outside and found her in the flower bed and it seemed that there was a little kid version of her not real happy having that hissy fit I had just spoken of, but that she needed to know she was ok, and everything was fine.

We agreed to talk more about it in our next session. Remarkably Charmaine took this without her feeling the need to run, she only shook her head amazed. If only she could have seen what I saw as I walked out there or heard the words of little Buck. I picked up the things lying on the porch and handed them to her while letting her know that this had been an enlightening session and encouraging her to keep looking, seeking and discovering for us to continue next session.

Charmaine glanced at me while taking her thermos and journals saying she would continue her detective work and hoped she was not getting another UTI. I told her that I thought she had worked hard in session and between, and it may be a good idea to rest, drink a lot of fluids and to just relax between sessions. No homework was given to her to do for me, just to rest and to take best care of herself though part of me knew that she would not comply. She was driven to find out all the answers.

Sometimes more happens when we are open to just being, and she has now opened herself to the possibility that she has Alters living within, and has been validated consistently that she was not crazy. The relief on her was palpable in regards to that fear as she walks differently than she first did, was way more comfortable with me, and it was obvious that she was feeling safer in the way she shares her fears, her past, and her story.

As Charmaine left, I handed her the appointment card for our next time together, and she hugged me so long. We have come a long way in what is a relatively short time by therapy standards but months and months for her.

I watched as she walked to her car wondering what her evening would look like now that she had deposited a part of that past with me here today. I hoped that she would know peace rather than be haunted with the past that is being uncovered for the first time since a child which was what I feared for her. I watched her brushing off her sweatpants that were now filled with dirt from the flower bed, and it was not lost on me that she kept looking at the flowers that had taken a pounding during the meeting of Buck.

I returned to my desk, and found myself looking over my notes and at the coloring book once again. I heard and reheard that little voice in my head, the look, and the eyes. Yes, there was an Alter that had been hiding, abused within Charmaine wanting to come out and tell her story, wanting to play and know she was safe.

Then I was thinking of Buck, clearly male and a six year old who was filled with anger. I wonder where he learned to cuss like that, and now to find out through him that he is the one responsible for locking and unlocking doors while Charmaine is asleep.

I doubt he intended that information to come out while having his fit in my beautiful prized flowers and wanting to take sure I got it on his name. So now I have identified three distinct personalities that reside within the brain of Charmaine and have yet to have her convinced this is real; yet I have been in their presence, Buck is the one I had sense enough to ask, "what is your name."

This was going to be a long haul, and for now this therapist was exhausted and excited at the same time, yet honored as we seemed to have moved further into this journey of DID than I had imagined or thought even possible.

The brain is remarkable and as I thought of Charmaine in driving home, along with other clients and I found myself wondering had I had other clients who may have had traits, or come into my office with issues of grief or depression as their presenting problems but under that diagnosis could there have been layers of what could have been horrid abuse as children, and that grief perhaps have been that of a history of such things.

Some secrets are so deeply hidden that even we as therapists cannot uncover them and then there are some clients like Charmaine who so desperately want the answers that they are unearthing the clues for you.

It seemed I arrived home so quickly I think that I astounded even myself when I saw that I had lost track of time and the route I had usually taken my time to travel and admire the surroundings while driving on had sped by while I was deep in thought. Had I myself just "lost time" as Charmaine spoke so plainly about?

This journey was eye opening to me and at times I felt that I was exploring new territories although I had become well acquainted with the clinical presentations and manifestations of DID; to actually be "in it" was quite another thing as a person, as a healer, and practitioner I was finding.

It required truly allowing the client, the whole person to lead while trusting your senses and knowing when to step in and guide rather than to try and make changes or alter what was. And it was fascinating and painful to witness to be honest.

I stood in awe at times that anyone could have lived a life and raised children while fighting through such battles and loss of time, yet the children seemed to be well cared for and not in harm's way. This woman had managed to care deeply for others, yet talk of things that seemed horrific with little emotion and that was a key to understanding in the realities of DID; she was not present at the time but only recounting what she was just now coming to understand.

CHARMAINE'S JOURNAL
Two days later

The drug test came back clean. Maybe I sounded paranoid but after Doc saying she believes I have Dissociative Identity Disorder, I no longer think that someone is trying to drive me crazy. Now the idea of DID as it is called is a scary thought and kind of makes me think of having parasites. If I am really dressing up like different people, then where are the clothes and stuff? Why are they not in my closet? Where is all the hair coloring that seems to be put on my head? Doc even says I smell like man's cologne at times. Where is it???

As I was looking on my desk for something, I knocked a pile of papers off. All I could think was "crap, another mess" as I leaned over to start picking it all up. At first, I was not really paying attention but then something caught my eye on one of the papers. It was more pictures drawn like the one on my easel and also there were notes.

I sat down at my desk thinking as I glanced through all the papers looking for more and it hit me. Perhaps the clothes and other things are all hidden in plain sight so to speak. Doc said she thought I had Alters ranging from little children to adults inside me.

Sort of made me feel like I had worms or something and creepy crawly inside. Maybe that is the best place to start looking...in the little kid's rooms and in my room where my oils and children's books are.

Trust me to develop something that is not normal. I headed into my room and sat down on the big stuffed chair in the corner that held a lot of my dolls. As I looked around trying to figure out what exactly I was looking for, I began to flip through the books. I noticed coloring pictures and on them was written in really messy and rough writing "Charie." Hmmm, maybe this is something, so I pulled it out and put it aside. As I continued looking, I found many drawings and colored pictures but none like the one on the easel. These appeared to be more little children's artwork. I leaned back into the big stuffed chair that I loved so much and closed my eyes for a few minutes.

THE ALTERS

"Dat my picture" a small child's voice said as she took the picture and held it to her chest. Charie took the picture and hid it in another book and started playing with the big cardboard sewing cards that Charmaine had bought at a sale a while back. She sat there humming and singing to herself, playing happily. Her favorite song was "wubba ducky, me wub ou" and she sang it over and over.

CHARMAINE'S JOURNAL

I awoke to the sound of singing "wubba ducky, me wub ouuuu..ou so fun" ♪♪..... and I stopped mid sentence thinking "what the hell am I singing that for? And why do I sound so funny?" In my hand is one of the big sewing cards I bought at that yard sale. I loved stuff like this for it reminded me of my children when they were very small. In one hand I held the card and in the other I had the end of the string as if I were about to put it through the next hole. I felt as if it were burning my hands and dropped
it into my lap and looked around. "Oh, please do not let me ever do this in public" was all I could think.

Laying them back on the little shelf, I decided to go check out the other rooms and closets. Glancing at my dolls before I got up, I noticed that the clothes had been changed on them and they were not sitting in the same place I left them. This is downright creepy. I guess I better write this in my journal while I have it fresh in my mind and am aware and can show Doc next time. Now, where did I put those drawings?

It took me hours of searching through every nook and cranny in the house, but so far I had found combat boots, camouflage pants and black tee shirts under my son's bed AND cigarettes. I did not know whether to be glad I was about half nuts with this DID thing or thankful that I could now feel confident that my son was not smoking.

As I leaned against the bed staring at all the stuff I found, my mind started wandering in years past when so many strange things happened. Maybe my ex was right all those times that he told me I was crazy as a bed bug. I had to laugh at the thought of Jeremy meeting up with whatever Alter wore those camouflaged pants, baseball cap and combat boots. It was a strange feeling to be able to even laugh at any of this. I guess laughing is better than crying or being terrified. I have spent my whole life being afraid but did not want to spend the rest of it being terrified.

Oh great, now Doc wants me to listen for voices. So then I can be crazy and hear things. I was glad to hear she wanted to know of voices inside my head. Is that like a pretend friend???

She told me to write down history, so here goes as much as I can remember from my childhood. I remember all these people being at our house and supposed to be doing some prayer group thing. Only, vaguely I remember a lot of kissing and hugging going on but that is all.

When I was little, I was always getting the "belt" because I did not answer them when they called but I never remember hearing them call. I hated that belt and would hide in the dirty clothes basket in the bathroom praying they would not find me. And always after, I was told to get a smile on my face. How the hell are you supposed to smile after being beaten with a belt? But, it was expected and I learned how.

I know that I cannot remember a lot of when I was a kid. I do not know whether I blocked it out or if I had this Dissociative thing even back then. I was told often that I was the "bad seed" and for years I believed it and tried to live up to it even after I left home.

I remember that from three or four years old and older, I had a problem with peeing in my pants, even as recently as a couple weeks ago. It is a stress thing for the urologist had checked me and run tests and said there was no reason that it should be happening.

I wet the bed until I was about 13 and I was so ashamed and told how dirty I was. I can remember being so scared of wetting my bed and getting the belt that I would slip out of bed, take off my jammies and lay on the hard wooden floor and pull the throw rug over me to sleep. I think I had this idea that if I pee'd then, I could just wipe it up. I would wake up shivering and cold and wet.

My teachers would send notes home saying I daydreamed all the time and did not do my work and then I would get in trouble and carried bruises for days and days. Once, the teacher saw the bruises and asked me what happened and when she figured out that it was because of the daydream comment, she quit putting it on my report cards and no teacher after that ever mentioned it either.

I have many holes in my memory and I actually have a whole school year that I do not remember. It was fourth grade and I had no recollection of being in the class or what it was like. In other classes, I have missing segments and a few memories but for that year, I missed it all.

Another memory is of me sitting in front of the mirror and seeing that I had cut my bangs and really *wacked them up so that they looked horrible. I had no memory of doing it and kept telling my mother that I did not do it. I am sitting there holding the scissors and the hair is on the table so she did not believe me.*

I had really long pretty hair that I loved to wear in pigtails and she made me sit there and she cut it all off. She said it was to remind me to never put scissors to my hair again. When I looked in the mirror, I could feel the tears coming and she told me I better "knock it off" or I would get worse. I looked bald and got up and walked away and went to my favorite hiding place...the coat closet on the floor. This was where I would go to cry and I would hold my knees and rock back and forth and just sob and sob quietly.

I could hear them calling me and knew I better get out of the closet before they found me. I lay down on my stomach and looked under the door and did not see their feet, so I eased out of the closet and went to my room and stretched out on my bed and pretended to be asleep. The last thing I remembered was hearing her say "damn she is asleep. What do we do now?" And he would say "better wake her ass up cause the group is coming over and they will want her there." These episodes happened often and I would not know anything until the next day. I always thought I just went to sleep in my safe room inside.

This week Doc asked me to do "play therapy" and wanted me to doodle on paper while we talked. I thought she was a little nuts but I was willing to try. I will admit that I found it a nice diversion while we talked.

Chapter 10   Well, Hello Alters

Months have passed and Charmaine has been diligent about being present for all her sessions. I am seeing more signs of DID than ever before but still need to confirm for myself that this is what is going on with her. Today provided the proof I sought.

This was a day that will be forever etched in my mind, I do believe. It was the day before a session with Charmaine, and a day that was carved out for paperwork and relaxation for me. I had grand plans to arrive at the office early morning, get all that dreadful paperwork completed and spend a day just enjoying the beaches and sand. The plan was set and I was looking forward to each moment.

As I poured the second cup of coffee, music playing in the background, I had realized how much I was enjoying myself; jeans, T-shirt and the quietness of the day. I had taken only a couple of phone calls, and almost completed all the tasks as planned. I was feeling on top of the world, and then "the phone rang."

It would turn into a phone call that would stay with me for a long time; and that beach enjoyment would go out the window along with all my other plans for the day. I answered the phone with my usual greeting. I heard a pause, and then a voice on the other end, who I thought was Charmaine, but I was not 100 percent sure. Her voice sounded muffled. Perhaps odd was the right word. What came next brought me to attention. Before I knew it I had my pen in hand. I was leaning over my desk straining to hear her.

It seems Charmaine was calling to let me know that she was somewhere, but unsure where; as a matter of fact she had no idea where she was. She knew she was lost. I was the only person she could call. She was trying with all her reserves to get her words out. I heard a new level of desperation in her voice. She was so upset, I thought I heard her panting. I stopped her from talking. I actually had to say "STOP", before she could hear me.

I began to ask her questions. I asked simple questions, in a quiet but firm voice. "Charmaine, I need you to breathe now; and look around you. Do you see anything there that you recognize? Are there any signs on the street corners? Are there any signs on the buildings that you can read to me? Look around you. Tell me what you see; take your time, I'm right here on the phone."

I could sense her devastation on the other end of the phone as I listened intently for answers. I could hear Charmaine's rapid, shallow, breathing as she tried to answer my questions. She fought back tears as she spoke. She had no idea where she was. She was working hard to maintain some control in that moment.

I asked Charmaine where she was calling from at that precise moment. She was on a phone at a diner somewhere. I felt immediate relief, and suggested softly that she ask someone there to please tell her the address of the diner. "Charmaine, look at a menu, there might be the name and address on the front. Is there a sign with the name of the diner out front?"

I then said, "Charmaine, just breathe, you can do this ok?" There was a long pause on the phone as she said, "Oh Doc, what am I doing here?" I could hear her voice quiver. I repeated again, quietly, but firmly, for her to ask someone there for the address, and look around for the name of the diner.

This was not the time for me to try and address the why's or how's of her being wherever she was. In this moment I needed to gather information in order to find her. As I strained to listen, I could hear Charmaine asking questions to someone on the other end of the phone. She repeated the answers given to her.

I am writing everything I hear as she speaks, noting that her voice is sounding different with each word spoken; bit by bit, a little stronger. We have remarkable coping abilities under extreme stress. I think she is boosted in her efforts knowing she has made contact with someone familiar to her. It appears comforting to her to have some help on the other end of the phone. I keep listening and hoping that she will return to our conversation once she has determined where she is.

At some point, I interrupt the whole conversation and tell Charmaine to ask how far she is from her town or a town that is familiar to her. She says *"ok, hold on."* As I wait, I see my own plan for this day slipping further away. I find that I have tensed my neck so much it is stiff and hurting. Mindfully, I do a few neck stretches as I wait for answers, wondering how in the world Charmaine ended up in a diner she does not recognize. After all, this is not a huge city.

I hear Charmaine say "Thank you so much" to whoever she has been talking to, and "Yes I would love some coffee, with the pink stuff and cream too." She came back on the line. "Oh my gosh, Doc., I am at least 59 miles from home. How in the hell did I get here and what am I ever going to do now?" I took a deep breath. Upon hearing that; I told Charmaine to just calm down, and tell me the name and address of where she was. I was writing it down as she spoke. I found myself truly amazed. Indeed the question was, how did she get there?

I told Charmaine to stay right where she was, to not go anywhere, as I was on my way to get her. I wanted her to try to relax. Eat something if she was hungry. I was on my way and would be there as soon as I could. I told her she could call me if she felt nervous, or panicked, but to know I was on the road to her as soon as I locked the door. We would talk once I got there. I was glad she had called.

Charmaine said she would tell the waitress not to let her leave no matter what. As I was hanging up the phone, Charmaine said that she wanted me to know that she did not know how she could thank me for this. She really did not know what had happened to her. I did not say, "Well if you don't, you can believe I don't", but I bit my tongue. Sarcasm was not the right emotion to share.

I began the drive of 50+ miles on roads that were interesting, to say the least. As I moved further from my own familiar stomping grounds, I realized just how far she had gone. I had never even been near this town before. Once I arrived, it was as if I had entered a time warp. An old style diner from the 50's, a real old time silver streamline diner, quilted exterior and all. You know the kind of place; the coffee is strong and the burgers are good and greasy.

The counter stools were red, the booths were vinyl red/black and the space was not large but long, with a pie case at the cash register. Yes, I was lost in the 50's at this diner. I was looking for Charmaine; and was not expecting to find yet another Alter. I was ready for a cold coca cola and a long talk after an exhausting drive.

I looked around for Charmaine. I saw a woman wave from the back booth. I stopped in my tracks when I saw her. My client Charmaine, who dresses in simple dark clothing with no jewelry, had been replaced with a woman that looks completely unlike her. I had trouble with my own sense of focus for a moment. My eyes and my brain are in conflict.

I find my way to this woman and slide into the booth opposite her. I found in front of me a woman who was dressed like a hippie of the 60's. An eclectic presentation of the past, dressed in a long tie dyed dress, with a floppy hat, and later, what I saw to be old open-toe sandals.. Her face was covered in what looked like dirt with tear stains on her cheeks. I immediately noticed that this odd looking dress, which was so out of character for her, is torn.

She appeared traumatized. Her speech was uneven, her eyes had a dead appearance; like she was in shock. As I am making these observations, Charmaine began to cry. The waitress approached the table with a cheerful, "Well there you are. I am so glad you are the one she has been waiting for honey, can I get you some coffee or pie? I've been really worried about Laylee. I let her use my phone to call you to come out here. I was going to take her home with me after my shift if she had not gotten in touch with someone."

I was listening to this woman greet me, while watching Charmaine, when it occurred to me that she had just used a name I had never heard before, "Laylee?" Who was Laylee? Meanwhile, I was thinking, could this woman just bring me a coke?

As I watched Charmaine in front of me, I was wondering if I should take her to the emergency room, instead of trying to talk with her and figure out what exactly had happened. I decided to rely on the first rule of practice; one that has always guided me; even to the disagreement of colleagues at times through my career: "first rule of practice, Do No Harm."

Before I entered the diner, I looked around outside and noticed that it has a small parking lot. There was no sign of Charmaine's car anywhere. The road leading to the diner had little traffic. However she had gotten here, she must have not been alone, had fled from a car, or had been dropped off.

As I sat waiting on my coke, I reached across the table and took Charmaine's hands. I asked if she could help me to understand what brought her to this place. Charmaine was crying, trying to catch her breath. I suggested now that she knew she was safe, perhaps it would be a good idea if she went into the bathroom, washed her face, and cleaned herself up a bit.

I let her know that her face was covered with dirt. I told her that I suspected she might have been in a scuffle of some kind, as her dress was also torn. Since she had been crying, it might be refreshing to wash her face a bit before we continued. Charmaine looked puzzled as I spoke. She seemed to find comfort in my holding her hands, to ground her in reality for a moment, before rising to go into the nearby bathroom.

I watched her get up. I saw that she was wearing sandals. She seemed to have trouble navigating in them. The sandals got caught in the hem as she stumbled briefly. She seemed to be in pain as she moved. She was not gone long before returning to the table. She reached again for my hands as she began to speak. She clung to my hands like a scared child. The first thing she said to me was "How in the hell did that happen to my face? Where did these clothes come from anyway? I do not know how I ended up in here, or even what happened Doc. I just knew I had to call you. I had forgotten your number so I had that lady to look it up for me, or maybe she called the operator. I do not know exactly how she got your number. I don't know where in the world my car is, or where we are for that matter. I don't know anything."

She was talking so fast that she was losing her breath. I could almost smell the fear on her. At that moment, I looked into Charmaine's eyes and asked her to slow down, and start at the beginning. I asked her if she wanted to leave the diner and start our way home or stay there and tell me what she remembered. She opted to sit where we were. To be honest I was glad to be still for a few moments. I wanted to hear all the details she could recall, and I was enjoying the ice cold coke.

It is interesting how a person can tune everyone, and their surroundings out, when the need is there. To focus on what is important, and the person who needs to be heard. I think a parade could have walked through that little diner and I would have been oblivious to it as Charmaine went on to describe how she found herself outside this diner in an unfamiliar town.

Charmaine said she found herself sitting outside on the curb of the diner, looking around. Frantically trying to figure out where she was. She was so tired and thirsty; she started looking in her bag for change to buy a cup of coffee. She looked for a phone, a phone number, to call someone when she realized she had no earthly idea where she is. When the woman from inside the diner came out and spoke to her that helped her calm down a little.

She told me how kind the waitress's eyes were, and what a sweet way she had of talking to her. That allowed her the courage to tell her she was looking for change for a cup of coffee. She did not tell her at first that she was lost. Then the woman had helped her up and walked her inside to a booth in the back.

The waitress had poured her coffee and stroked her hair while offering kind words to Charmaine. That made her feel good for a moment or two, but panic set in after as she realized she had never been there before and it scared her even worse. She was alone with no resources. No idea how and why she was where she now found herself.

So we had the beginnings of the story now, and Charmaine looked at me and said, "Oh Doc, I am glad you came to get me... oops I have to run to the bath, I'll be back." With that Charmaine made a quick exit from the table. I sat quietly feeling gratitude to the waitress that allowed her a safe refuge.

It was as if the waitress was reading my mind. She approached the table the moment Charmaine got up, and said, "Hon, I don't mean to interrupt you here, but I was worried about her. I'm so glad you showed up. I thought maybe she had some kind of amnesia or something you know?"

At that moment, the waitress looked around as if to see if all her customers were well taken care of and glanced at the bathroom door. She leaned in close to me. She wanted to let me know what she had seen when Charmaine arrived at the diner. What she had to say was valuable. This kind woman said that she saw a man pull into the parking lot and force Charmaine out of the passenger door. It looked like he pushed her out of the car with force.

The waitress said she was pouring coffee for a customer at the time, but watching out the window. She felt so bad for her she could barely stay in the building to wait on her customer at the time. She said she thought Charmaine hit her head when she tumbled out of the car but could not be certain. She went on to say that Charmaine had gotten up and patted her dress off looking around like she was dazed; appearing to be lost. She just kept looking around then finally sat on the curb in front of the diner.

The waitress said that once all her customers were taken care of she went out to see if she was alright. Charmaine was looking in her pocketbook. She still had an odd look on her face. Her eyes did not look quite right, so she brought her in and got her some coffee and juice.

Neither of us heard Charmaine return to the table. She slid back into the booth. I do not know who was more startled, the waitress or I as Charmaine asked "What are you two whispering about? Me?" The waitress bolted to an upright position and said, "Laylee honey, you scared me to death."

I tapped my finger on my cup and said, "I did not hear you return, and yes, we were talking about you, are you hungry?" As the waitress left the table, I looked at Charmaine and asked her if she noticed that she had been called "Laylee." Charmaine replied, "Yes, I wondered why she is calling me that."

It was in that moment that I had an idea that I wanted to explore. Thinking outside the box is something that situations like this may be just what was needed. Yes, I had an idea, but I needed Charmaine to be willing to go with me on this, and I did not know how it would work, or even if it would work. We needed answers to what was happening now before we could leave this place.

I asked Charmaine if we could go outside and sit as the waitress had told me that there was a patio that was "out back" of the diner if we wanted to talk more privately. I thought that would be a great idea. Quite honestly our conversation up to this point had been playing "catch up." Although seated in the rear booth, it was a bit difficult to tune out others conversations and the clanging of dishes and orders being shouted over the counter. The patio would afford a more intimate, quiet area for what I had in mind. I believed that Charmaine would be open to my idea.

She agreed willingly. She said she had seen about all the people, and heard about, all the variations of burgers and eggs she cared to. She had sat there long enough. After getting refills of our drinks, I paid the bill. Together we walked outside to a lovely secluded patio area in the back side of the diner.

It was surrounded by old oaks and crape myrtle trees that were in full bloom. Both of us remarked how lovely and odd it was to have such a beautiful area attached to an old 50's style diner. I could tell

Charmaine was feeling more comfortable, and safer now that she knew she was not in harm's way any longer. As we sat down, I gently explained my thinking to Charmaine. I watched closely for her reaction.

I decided to try something new. We seemed to be on a train to nowhere at the moment. Maybe a new approach would work. I spoke slowly. I told her I had in mind a new plan. I told Charmaine that I wanted to see if I could call out this Alter Laylee. To see if she would present herself to me, with the hope that she would tell me what had happened. Perhaps she would tell us why she had taken over. I promised Charmaine I would share with her everything I learned in the process. I would keep her safe no matter what. I asked her if that was ok with her, and suggested we begin immediately.

Charmaine looked at me and said, "I'm game if you are Doc." With that I smiled at Charmaine and let go of her hands. Sitting across from Charmaine on that little quiet outside patio, I looked intently at Charmaine and said, "Ok, whoever brought you here, get your ass out here and show yourself. I want to know what happened, and I want to know right now."

I noticed a smile on Charmaine's lips. After a few minutes, I repeated my request. "I'm talking now, whoever it is that brought Charmaine here, I want you out here now... right here ...right now." I watched carefully as I leaned in toward Charmaine. I saw Charmaine's eyes close, flicker, and then her face changed slightly. I noticed her posture change as she began to shift in her seat. Her eyes opened.

I was making mental notes. I did not know quite what I expected. A part of me wondered if Charmaine would fall in the floor laughing at me; holding her ribs, thinking I had lost my ever loving mind.

Yet as I watched, I saw a transformation. She opened her eyes. She looked at me with an expression that I had never seen on Charmaine's face. I knew I was in the presence of someone I had not met before; an Alter who was about to introduce herself to me. Could it really be this easy? What might I learn from this "Laylee" that even Charmaine might not know.

As I watched, I noted a seductive woman size me up and down. She began to speak, with mannerisms, posturing, and a distinct clip in her speech that was unfamiliar to me. Her eyes even looked different if that was at all possible. Sitting before me is a woman who was pulling up her long hippy dress and crossing her legs. She stroked one leg as she flung her hair to the side. Her greeting; "Well ll lll, hell oooo sugg aah" with the most pronounced southern accent one could ever think of hearing. It was almost comical.

I responded "Well hello to you. And you are?" She smiled with an expression that was both seductive and filled with mischief; as she told me that she was "Laylee." She proceeded to call me "honey, dahlin, suga" and every combination to reference me, but my name. She dripped with a seductive, youthful, southern sweetness.

I could not help but notice that each movement, each word was exaggerated and stressed her sexuality. From hiking her dress up to her thighs, rubbing her legs as she spoke, and throwing her hair over her shoulder as if it were her mane. She was freedom personified.

She looked at me with a smug smile and said, "Well, hon, you pulled me out here, now what do you want suga?" She was laughing as she asked the question. I quite frankly, was gathering my senses. The Charmaine I had come to know, was truly nowhere to be found at that point.

I found myself sitting up straight in the chair. In my own mind thinking; "Damn, it worked, I did it. I called out one of the Alters and they came. Now what am I to do?" At the same time I was processing just how amazing the brain is; mine, hers, Charmaine's, all at once those millions of neurotransmitters were firing. She was looking directly at me, wondering why I had called her to this meeting.

Yes it was a momentous moment. Surrounded by great oaks, and crape myrtles, this therapist can say that this combination of "out of the box, and out of the office" can bring about a remarkable situation. This was unlike any teachings I had been taught, any video I had watched, any talk show, any textbook I had read. My client Charmaine has been replaced with this sexually free, wild and free southern spirit known as Laylee; asking me why I called her.

Quickly, I was back on task. I had questions, and wanted some answers. I noticed my body was taut.

I had called and the gatekeeper had heard me. If only Charmaine could see this, she would be amazed. Maybe more embarrassed than amazed, but I was astounded.

Laylee had gotten up from the chair and appeared to be doing a celebration dance of some type around the crape myrtle tree. I watched intently as she grabbed a flower and found a way to place it in her hair. She looked at me laughing. "Well suga, have you deci- I -ded, why u wanted me yet?"

I realized I must have been lost in thought for more than a few minutes. she was waiting for me to answer the question. I then asked her if she would rejoin me at the table, and she complied. I looked at Laylee and asked if she would please tell me why she had brought Charmaine here, to this place. I told her I needed to know what had happened.

Laylee said, "Oh lawd honey, I'll do my best but its chommmmplaaacated." With that, Laylee began telling me what had brought her to the diner. She had an acute recall of the events that Charmaine would only later have to be told about. It was painful to hear.

Oh how I longed for another coke, and a cigarette during her oration. More than that I needed my pen and notepad. Laylee, with each word elongated, took forever to share the details. The information she was sharing was complex, and in depth. I did not want to miss a single detail. I realized I would later be sharing this with a shocked Charmaine. I suspected she would have difficulty believing most of what I was hearing.

This would be a great time for a recorder, a video, something visual that I could share with Charmaine. I would later come to discover that Charmaine would have some difficulty imagining what had occurred based solely on my description of the exchange. Who am I kidding? There were parts of me that had great difficulty grasping this myself. I cannot fathom how Charmaine was going to handle my telling her what I was learning on the drive home. I knew I would find a way, but it would be a challenge. No wonder she had doubted her sanity. It seemed a little crazy to me at the moment.

As I listened, it appeared that the waitress's assessment of the man in the car had indeed shoved her out into the parking lot. According to Laylee, it seems that she had snuck out past the one who stands guard as the gatekeeper for Charmaine. There is someone called "Deseree" who usually tells the gatekeeper, whose name is "Bart," when to let the others out. Those others are known as "Alters."

Laylee was a wealth of information. I was most interested in how Charmaine had ended up so far from home and appeared in such disarray.

As she spoke with that long drawl, I was struggling to remember each of the names she was identifying. She readily provided a plethora of facts as she knew them.

I continued to watch her mannerisms, her posturing, while trying to capture every word, committing it to memory. Occasionally glancing around to be certain we are alone. Oh how I wished this could have been happening in the quiet of my office, behind the closed door. But it was what it was; when it was... and it was incredible, unfolding before my eyes.

Again, I had promised Charmaine to tell her everything once this was over. I am a woman who keeps the promise for good or bad. I just needed to trust my instincts for now.

One would have thought it was two old friends sitting in a private area out back of an old run down diner that day. If they only knew. Laylee crossed her long legs and threw that hair back, and said "Well it was not as great as I thought it would be, but at least I got away for awhile."

It seemed that Laylee had snuck out, past the gate-keeper that she referred to and grabbed the car, going to the 7-11 to get herself some smokes. She was pumping gas in the car when a man, in a "hot car," as she described, it pulled up and asked her if she wanted to go for a ride and have some fun.

As I later learned, Laylee was 16 and the wild Alter living inside Charmaine. She loved to ride, to feel free; so she jumped at the chance to take a spin with what she described as a "hunk" of a man. Thinking he just might take her away from all this boring stuff.

As it turns out, away they did go. Laylee ended up having more fun than she thought she would while being used sexually, and then being dumped in front of the diner. This man, who was much older than she, then sped away in his car, leaving her feeling wounded emotionally and physically. Yet, Laylee was ready to party on at the next available opportunity and I knew she would at the first opportunity.

Laylee indicated that she loved to have fun. She asked that I please not to let anyone in there know; she had her ways to sneak out when she could. She said she knew she would be in trouble with Deseree, and had left Charmaine standing in the road alone and scared. As I listened it was clear that she had been sexually abused during this outing, yet she seemed to have detached from that in the telling of her adventure.

I had wondered if another Alter had protected her from feeling the assault as well. I saw that she seemed to grow bored with recounting her story. She began to look idly around the patio. She was fidgeting with her hair and her dress. With a bored expression, she asked me if there was "anything else I just had to know."

I asked her if she felt ok and if she liked Charmaine. There was a pause and then she laughed. "Ohh hon you are so funny. Well, I feel kinda rode hard if you know what I mean. As for Charmaine? Well she's pretty boring and plain. She stays at home painting and stuff. SHE sure don't like to have much fun. Lawd she NEVER wants a man around. But overall, she's alright."

As I watched Laylee, it seemed that she faded in front of me; she just disappeared. In her place I observed a tired looking Charmaine. Resurfaced in the same dress, yet completely changed in appearance, posture, and speech. Her presence was completely different. It was not lost on me that this Laylee Alter had shown me a whole different side of Charmaine.

As I watched this transformation, I leaned in and quietly said, "It's ok Charmaine, you are safe... are you ready to go home?" Charmaine looked at me blankly. As if she noticed for the first time, the air on her legs, she looked down. Seeing that her dress was well above her knees, partly exposing her thighs, she quickly pulled it down. She asked, "Doc, did anything happen?" She looked tired, yet she was interested. She appeared completely unaware of what had just transpired.

Charmaine said she felt exhausted but wanted to know everything, if there was anything to know, and she sure seemed so very thirsty. I suggested we get a coke for the road. I would share with her the events on our way if she wanted, or we could just drive quietly so she could rest. I let her know we could also just sit where we were a bit longer. I could share with her what I had learned.

Charmaine decided that she was exhausted and would prefer hearing everything on the drive home where it would be private. If only she knew, I thought over and over. I had to wonder... was sharing this information while driving, my not able to visibly gauge her reactions the best thing to do?

I would drive slowly I decided. Take this one mile at a time. I went to get us beverages for the ride home, and hit the restroom on my way. She waited by the car: after all I had the keys. I asked her to not talk to any strangers while I was gone.

I wanted to thank the waitress once again, making sure to tip her generously. I could not remember if I had done so earlier. I was appreciative that she had kept Charmaine safe for quite a while, losing tips from "would be customers" as Charmaine tied up her table while I was in route there. My head was crowded with thoughts. My body ached from having held it rigidly at attention throughout the entire ordeal.

I found Charmaine in the car with her head back, eyes closed. She startled when she heard the sound of the door opening. I paused a second until she regained her senses seeing that it was me. I checked to be sure she was indeed Charmaine, (the real Charmaine) before getting in the car.

She tried to muster a laugh and let me know she thought she may have dozed off for a minute. She reached for the cold soda while thanking me again for rescuing her. She began to tell me once again that she did not know what else to do or who else to call. She asked where in the world she had gotten the dress she was wearing, as she gazed at it in wonder. She said she was fearful of what she may have done or said. She was curious about what happened behind the diner. She wanted me to tell her then and there. She did not want to wait until our next session.

I let Charmaine know that I had reservations about sharing it with her while I was driving. I could not see her reactions, nor tell what she was thinking. It might have been helpful if I could. She laughed a hearty laugh, while telling me that it might be good I did not see her reaction. She knew by my comment that something must have happened that was going to make her eyes bulge. That would not be a pretty sight to see. She did promise not to jump out of the car. As she furthered her case of my sharing right then she let me know she would tell me what she was thinking.

As we drove a while she commented that she had no idea what roads we were on. She was amazed by the GPS system. She then turned sideways in her seat, tucked her legs under her with the seat belt on staring at me. She then pleaded as she again asked me to tell her what had happened back there at that little diner. I guess this was literally where the rubber met the road. Once again we were out of the box in working this journey. I told Charmaine that I was going to be honest with her. I would give her the details, but I wanted to know what the last thing she remembered was as we sat on the patio. She said that she remembered me telling her I was going to try to figure out how she got there. I was going to attempt to bring out one of the Alters, and ask them about it. After that, she thought I asked if she were ready to go home. Talk about a memory lapse!

As I was about to speak, Charmaine said, "Oh Doc, I also remember you holding my hands I think, but then it was like you were gone, but I think I was too, if that makes any sense." Yes, it made perfect sense. She was gone as Laylee was there so of course to her I was gone as well. The conversation was between Laylee and I; Charmaine had nothing to do with any of that.

Yes, there are people that try to use DID as a means to gain fame or get attention. Once you have seen the real thing, those that are known as attention seeking people stand out in a way that lets you know that they are not really suffering from Dissociative Identity Disorder.

It made perfect sense now to me. It was as if she was gone, just like that. My hands had let go of hers as I called an Alter out to tell me why and how Charmaine had ended up at this place. Laylee had appeared. She was a 16 year old who had snuck out of one of those doors in the hallway of Charmaine's brain. She was out for a good time, she took over. It was not feigned. It was as real as I am. I knew as soon as I saw Laylee that it was not Charmaine pretending to be someone. Charmaine does not have the guile in her to be able to act in such a manner. The distress was too real too.

As I drove, I began to introduce Charmaine to an Alter that resides within her brain; that is able to come out and take control using her body. Laylee was the one that brought her to the diner before retreating leaving Charmaine there to fend for herself. She was stunned, and embarrassed. I took my time; I paused frequently; used short sentences allowing for it to sink it. I asked her if she needed some time, wanted me to stop the car and sit a while. Charmaine answered with "Are you making this shit up Doc; really, you have to be kidding me. Oh hell I am crazy as a bed bug huh?"

There were times when I glanced at her and saw tears streaking her face. Several times she reached over to touch my arm and said, "Wait." I became quiet, just nodded, knowing that she was hearing for the first time more than she could absorb. She wanted to know all the details. I had promised the truth.

She had yet to learn that I felt she had been sexually abused on this outing. I also knew she needed to be seen by a physician. I asked Charmaine to stop for a moment and just breathe. Breathe in deeply and blow it out through her mouth. I pulled the car over at a scenic overlook at one point. I found myself breathing the same way, hoping she would follow my breaths in order to relax, to calm her racing heart. I will admit, I worked to calm my senses as well. We sat in silence for a few minutes. Then I asked Charmaine if she minded if I stood outside to have a smoke. She laughed. She said "No, not if you don't mind me joining you!"

The two of us, just stood quietly looking at the scenery for a few minutes. Side by side our arms gently touching. She was safe. She was trying to absorb all that she had just learned about Laylee living within her. At one point while standing there, Charmaine looked at me from the corner of her eye. She asked if I would not see her anymore. Was I ready to hand her off to a shrink or send her packing to a psychiatric hospital or something?

She was fearful of being rejected, and so tired. I assured her that I had no intention of abandoning her, of sending her anywhere. That seemed to bring her comfort. She sighed deeply. She expressed shock and confusion. How could someone live like this and not know what they are doing? She said she felt she had been beaten. She was sore all over.

I knew then I had to share with her more of what Laylee had said to me. I asked if I should continue to tell her what I had learned here, at this beautiful spot, or while we were on the road. Charmaine opted to continue as we drove, where she could sit and be more comfortable. She said her body felt like it had been run over by a truck.

We returned to the car. Getting back on the road, thankful for the seatbelt she was wearing, I proceeded to tell Charmaine about Laylee and her love of partying with men. I delicately explained to her that Laylee was 16, as she presented herself and was rather a "wild child." She liked hot cars and slick men. Laylee did not have good filters on who she associated with it seemed.

I worked hard at trying to not be too blunt in my descriptions of Laylee. I knew that Charmaine was quiet, reserved and not a woman who ran the streets, or was sexually active, engaging with multiple partners. Charmaine had told me previously enough about her ex-husband to know theirs was not a marriage made in heaven. It seems there was abuse in that relationship. She had also told me that her ex was the only man she had ever been intimate with her whole life.

As I talked quietly, I could feel the moment that Charmaine had realized what I was telling her.

Suddenly she let out a loud, "Are you tellin me Doc that I have had SEX with someone and didn't know it? How the hell can that happen?" I was startled by the intensity of her voice, the loudness of the outburst, and the desperation in the tone of her voice. She startled me.

Try as I might to explain this delicately, Charmaine heard that she was a "slut, a loose woman" vs. Laylee; an Alter of 16, a promiscuous teen out to play, who had gotten in over her head and was sexually active/abused prior to getting to that diner.

Charmaine was crying, she was screaming, she was rubbing her arms and legs. Saying she "felt "filthy. Now I KNOW I'm crazy." If this had happened to her, and happened without her having any memory of it, what else had she done? She wanted to understand this, yet she was exhausted and upset. She could not be comforted. She had to let these emotions out, and here we were both strapped in a car, headed home from nowhere. She continued to babble. rubbing her arms, scrubbing her hands together, running her hands through her hair. She was devastated.

I was driving slowly; second guessing myself as to whether or not I should have told her this in this way. Yet, I had given her a promise, a commitment to honesty and integrity, and I will stand by that.

I found the next place to pull the car over. We sat quietly as she continued to process this news. She had finally wound down. Charmaine looked at me with the most sorrowful eyes I can ever remember seeing. I assured her that we would walk this journey, as we started out, one step at a time. We would find out all that resided within her, and we would find ways for her to heal and restore balance in her life.

I tried to instill hope, faith, and a belief that she would work through this. I offered compassion and even humor as we sat together. Reminding her of the promise we made to be honest. Sometimes the truth is hard to hear. I validated and honored her outrage, her humiliation, her horror in learning all that she had been told. Reminding her that this is her life, I am only walking beside her on the journey, but it is HER JOURNEY. We walk at her pace not mine. This is her story, not mine, in her time, not mine.

I admitted to Charmaine I did not, and do not have all the answers. Together we will get to them. The diner was a huge step, meeting JR was a huge step. I reminded her, and she was further now along the journey than ever before. Charmaine was nodding as I spoke. She leaned over, took my hand and squeezed it hard. She then wiped her tears and sighed deeply.

I told her that the most important thing was to get her home. She needed to rest, have something and eat and get her car back safely. With that I started the car, with the annoying voice of the GPS telling us she was re-routing us once again. We finally got close enough that I was able to cancel voice guidance. Oddly enough Charmaine and I both laughed at the same time as we agreed that GPS was indeed a Godsend, but she had an irritating voice. The laughter was a welcome relief.

We rode for a while in silence, both seeming to be comfortable with the silence. I'm sure Charmaine was processing all she had learned. I wondered if she was trying to determine if anything I had shared with her was less than truth, but I quickly dismissed that thought. I was certain that she had come to trust our working relationship completely. It was a welcomed respite to only hear the tires on the road.

I noticed that Charmaine had put her head back and closed her eyes for a bit as we neared her home. She opened them as I stopped at a light. I asked her how she was doing with all we had talked about. She replied she was still trying to wrap her thoughts around it. I nodded, I was too.

~~~~~~~~

"I used my two dogs as a therapeutic tool with Charmaine who loved holding them. She at times would love on them when talking of tremendous heartaches suffered during sessions." DRSES

"This was one of the journal entries that caused me great concern for Charmaine." DRSES

Chapter 11- Visit With Dr. Hope

As we were nearing her home, I asked Charmaine if she was willing to go to a Doctor friend of mine and be checked out. I let her know that I would be happy to take her. Charmaine asked me why, with a strange look on her face. I told her that since we both now knew that Laylee has been physically intimate with this man from the 7-11; and we did not know if the man had used protection, it seemed like a good idea.

I let Charmaine know that I was concerned about her well-being. I explored the possibility of STD's or an injury that may have been suffered during this event(s). I noticed that Charmaine hung her head. She slumped down in her seat as I spoke. Silently she nodded her head, reluctantly agreeing to the plan. She asked if I would really go in with her. She hated going to the doctors. I said that I definitely would. I thought she would probably like this physician. Dr. Hope was compassionate, gentle and kind.

I called my friend who was an OBY/GYN, and very connected to women's issues. She and I had a history. We had served together on behalf of women who had suffered sexual abuse and rape at the Rape Crises Center. She was a strong healer; one who gave freely of her time to those who had been victimized.

I called right then from the car and spoke to her briefly, with an update of what had happened. Luckily she said for me to bring Charmaine right to her office and that she would make the time as it sounded as though it was indeed something that either she or and ER should attend to immediately.

I felt blessed indeed. I definitely did not want Charmaine to be further traumatized by a visit to the Emergency Room after all she had been through. I told Charmaine we were going straight to the Doctor's office. Her reaction was as I thought it might be... "Now Doc, you mean I have to go there NOW, I thought you meant next week. YOU mean now, I have to go now Doc?"

I saw the fear, and heard the angst in her voice. We turned left and headed to the physicians' office. I quietly explained to Charmaine that yes, now was the time to go. It was critical that she be checked out for any signs of sexual assault, and tested for STDs. I continued to provide support as we made our way there.

Charmaine sat in silence for a long while as she tried to process this turn of events. It seemed the right thing to do given this new set of circumstances. I would from time to time glance at her, offer a pat on the arm and nod in her direction to show support. A soothing touch went a long way with Charmaine. Within a few minutes, we arrived at the office of a woman I will call Dr. Hope.

Charmaine was shaky as she got out of the car. She looked at me for reassurance. In the elevator she whispered, "Doc, I feel filthy. Look at me," as she looked down at herself. I felt badly for her, and understood what she was saying to me. Yet, it seemed important for this to have happened.

Charmaine really needed medical attention. I had no idea how badly she might have been hurt. Laylee might have been a willing participant, but Charmaine was an innocent recipient of Laylee's exploits.

We were the only ones there as we entered the office. Dr. Hope waited for us. The staff was gone, and she met us in the hallway, with a warm smile for Charmaine. Immediately Charmaine asked Dr. Hope if I could stay with her. Dr. Hope smiled as she let her know that I could stay if Charmaine felt more comfortable that way. Meanwhile I was praying that Charmaine remained intact, with no Alters presenting or taking over during the exam.

I knew that Charmaine was under duress and felt that if she could find comfort in this physician, perhaps she could find the strength to maintain for the exam. As we sat in the office, Charmaine looked to me for reassurance. I sat close at hand. I asked Charmaine to let the Doctor know what she felt comfortable with, no more, no less. Dr. Hope was gentle; she was accustomed to women in such fragile states, yet I had no idea if she was at all attuned to those with DID. I could not remember if we had ever talked about it before.

She asked Charmaine when was the last time she had a "PAP examination, or had seen and OBY/GYN." Charmaine looked at her intently, then glanced at me before she answered. "Well hell Doctor Hope, I guess when my little girl was born. I hate those exams and do not like anyone looking down there if you know what I mean. Since I do not have sex anymore I don't see any reason for it I guess."

Dr. Hope nodded and went on to ask her what she remembered about what had happened to her earlier in the day. Charmaine seemed to relax a bit as she sized up this Doctor, and went on to tell her she had a blackout, and felt maybe something had happened that she has no recall of.

She told Dr. Hope she would sign a release for me and the Doctor to talk if she wanted her to. She liked having me there with her, and she needed me there because she did not feel very sturdy at the time. Dr. Hope told her that was fine, that she was there to help, not to create stress for her.

I sat silently. I was there to only be supportive, not to offer opinions or to weigh in with information. I continued to pray that Charmaine would be Charmaine during this appointment and that no harm had come to her physically while Laylee was out. I had my doubts about that though. Actually, I had my doubts that this was the first time that a sexual encounter had occurred. From my studies I knew that those with DID often have a promiscuous Alter that is likely to be the one engaging in sexual activity.

At times Charmaine would reach over to hold my hand. When it was time for the exam, I could see her body tense. Her eyes moved from engagement to fear as she looked at me for reassurance. Dr. Hope told me they would be back in a bit, explaining to Charmaine they would be going into the examination room now. She also wanted to do a thorough blood work up too.

She stood beside Charmaine. I'm sure she noticed the look of fear in her face. She very gently placed her hand on her shoulder and said, "Charmaine, if at any point you need Dr. Sherry to come in the room, we will call for her, does that make you feel better?" I could see that made a difference in Charmaine, both the words and the touch as Charmaine looked at me and said with that southern drawl, "I'm ok Doc, she is a fine lady." She stood and walked out with Dr. Hope and down the hall to an examination room.

I stayed in the office and returned phone calls during the examination. I found some paper and jotted notes from my experience with Laylee and the rest of the day's events.

It was as I feared. Laylee had had sex with the unidentified man. The Doctor returned with Charmaine. I could see that Charmaine was crying, the Doctor looked deeply concerned about her. I asked if Charmaine was alright, and she said, "What am I going to do now?" The Doctor asked Charmaine did she want her to talk in front of me.

Charmaine responded with; "Well yes, she brought me here." She reached for a Kleenex on the table and tried to wipe her eyes and nose. Sadly, the pelvic examination was terribly painful for Charmaine they both shared with me. At times causing her to moan in pain as Dr. Hope examined her. What she found and discussed with us made me feel ill.

Dr. Hope appeared troubled. I knew her well and could see the concern in her eyes as she confirmed that Charmaine had been sexually active, or more likely abused in the last 24 hours. She spoke with a solemn voice as she described what she had seen upon examination. Charmaine quietly cried, sitting close beside me. I reached out and put my arm around her.

"There is tremendous inflammation and ripping of the vaginal tissue. I am prescribing broad spectrum antibiotics for her. I have samples here to apply topically as well. We are running blood work. I should have results back in 48 hours and will call you Charmaine with the results. We will need to schedule a second appointment for you, to talk about this and the blood work results in detail once you have rested. You will be better able to hear and participate in all of this, ok? I am so sorry the exam was so painful for you Charmaine. I cannot imagine having a black-out and then waking up to this realization. I have also prescribed topical Lidocaine to use for the vaginal pain. The instructions will be on the label. Do you have any questions for me?"

Charmaine had no questions. She kept her head down, quietly trying to stop crying. At that point, her exhaustion had kicked in and I could see that she was on over-load, ever so weary. I longed to get her home so that she could rest. Dr. Hope was not quite finished, so I leaned toward Charmaine; as I touched her said, "We are almost done, and can you hang with us just a bit longer here?"

She looked up at me and said she was trying her best. She was just listening hard, so she could remember everything at this point. This is one tough lady I was in the presence of, I kept thinking to myself, as Dr. Hope continued.

She went on to tell Charmaine, that since there is history of PID (pelvic inflammatory disease) followed by a radical hysterectomy, pregnancy is not a concern. However, she has run all tests for STD's including HIV. This compassionate Doctor of wise and vast experience went on to say that she suspected there is some history of past sexual abuse and that she is certain that this has been extremely traumatizing for Charmaine. She encouraged Charmaine to please feel free to call her at any time. Once again, emphasized the importance of the follow up visit. She would want us to all get together as soon as possible for that.

As I sat and watched Charmaine lean against the side of her chair to hear this, I remembered the first time I thought there was a history of abuse in Charmaine's past. I felt so terrible for her, my heart ached in her behalf. I had seen her bring herself into my office, walk through fear with courage, and now I could tell by the way Charmaine attempted to hold herself that this truly hurt her.

It was taking everything she had to sit up and look at the Doctor. On a day that she found herself in a diner after being with who knows who, doing God knows what; hearing about it second-hand, with absolutely no memory of it, only to be affirmed by a medical Doctor.

As I tucked my notes in my pocket, I stood up, prepared to leave with Charmaine. I let my dear doctor friend know that I would be sending her

Charmaine's insurance information the next day so she could process for payment. Somehow that must have startled Charmaine into gear. Charmaine stood straight up, looked at the Doctor and said, "Oh my gosh, I don't know how to pay you. I don't have any money or anything with me. Oh crap, I don't even know if I can afford you. What do I owe you Doctor Hope? I'm so sorry, did I even thank you for seeing me?"

With that the physician hugged Charmaine and told her not to worry, we would exchange her insurance information with each other and she would take care of it for her. Mostly she wanted Charmaine to take care of herself, to continue with her therapy and to know that she could always call if needed to discuss anything.

Yes it sounds like a story one does not hear every day, but there are still some physicians out there who care about the patients they took oaths to provide care for. Doctors who work collaboratively with therapists providing care, often without any desire for pay.

Charmaine looked stunned. She once again became acutely aware of what she was wearing, and apologized to the Doctor saying, "You can ask Doc, I never look like this" as she rubbed her shaking hands through her hair. I assured her that soon she would be safe at home. If she wanted to she could bury the dress and take that long awaited shower.

It had indeed been a long and arduous day for this dear woman, who now had to cope with the reality of something so wrong happening to her. She was so very offended by the thought that she brought this on herself. Yet here she was worrying about whether or not she had thanked the doctor.

We walked out, got in the car and started towards her house. She looked at me and said "Oh Doc, that hurt so much when she stuck that... what do you call it... inside me. I thought I would faint from the pain. I am just beside myself. This is just too much. What am I to do? Dr. Hope was so nice; she really did try not to hurt me. Oh, so much has happened. I hope she doesn't think bad of me. Can you even imagine that she is not even worried about getting paid and all? How in the hell am I suppose to go back there and see her anyway Doc? "

She had so many questions. She was in pain from the examination. She was just exhausted, yet her mind was still in overdrive it seemed. I just listened, and let her talk. I knew she needed to get it out, to process it in her own way. She was not really asking my opinion, not really asking for answers as much as she was ruminating. The incredulousness of it all as it was all coming into focus.

As we were driving toward her home, I told her she was doing all the right things. She would be home shortly where she could shower, rest and eat. I told her Dr. Hope and I had known each other a long time and that she had worked with many women who needed her. Charmaine could feel safe with her.

I validated her pain, her mind racing like a NASCAR driver on an endless track, and told her it was good that she was talking about it. I also reminded her she was exhausted. It seemed like a day that would never to end in some ways. She looked at me, puzzled and said, "But what about my car?" I had to smile. I told her not to worry. Tomorrow, I would swing by and pick her up. We could get it in the morning. Meanwhile, I would let the station manager know so that it was not towed. She was happy to have that resolved. Truthfully I think she was relieved to not have to get behind the wheel at that point. Charmaine was truly exhausted and each step was an effort.

As I pulled into her driveway I could sense the last bit of energy leaving, both of us. It had been one hell of a day. We both needed sleep. The kind of bone crushing sleep without I knew I would rest better knowing she wouldn't be out driving about. God only knows what Laylee might do if Charmaine had access to the car tonight. At least for tonight, she did not need any additional misadventures.

She sat still for a moment and said nothing. I just waited looking at the yard; a toy here, one there, a few beautiful flowers that had survived Buck's destructive efforts. Charmaine turned and faced me. "Doc, I do not know how I would have made it without you. I honest to God do not know what would have happened today, and I just want you to know, I trust you with my life. Whoever the hell is in here with me should be thankful too. I sure hope you know how awful this is; how awful I feel about what happened. I just had to tell you that." Straight forward and to the point, very much like the woman who first walked into my office, but more exhausted.

As she opened the door I said "I'll be here tomorrow to take you to your car Charmaine, but I will call first. Thank you for your trust, now hit the shower and go bed. I know I'm tired, and you surely must be exhausted. "She smiled as she closed the door, and told me she would see me the next day. She was "all Charmaine." I sat there in the driveway watching Charmaine walk into the house. She looked fragile, weary, and her shoulders sagged as if she were carrying the weight of the world. After all this time, I knew Charmaine well enough to know that after she processed today; after she rested and got her feet under herself again, she would be full of thoughts, and new questions.

We had a double session already scheduled for tomorrow. As I drove home, I thought about this Alter who called herself Laylee. She was totally the opposite of Charmaine and seems to be as provocative and wild as a bat. There is no telling how many times she has put Charmaine in harm's way. Who knows how many times she has had sex that Charmaine knew nothing about.

I asked Dr. Hope to check her first to see if there was evidence of recent sexual contact to determine if there was a need for a police report. She said there were signs of rough sex, but that it was not necessarily rape. She did a swab though in case they needed it for future prosecution as it is not easy to report a rape on a DID person who has no conscious memory of anything. From what Laylee told us she went willingly with the man and had sex with him. When one has something like Dissociative Identity Disorder, things can become very complicated. Dr. Hope would be unable to testify if it was rape or rough sex.

I did want documentation by a Doctor. Charmaine was adamant that she was NOT going to the police with this. I was fortunate in that in my line of work, I had met most of the law enforcement officials in the area and they knew that I did therapy. When I reported a potential problem they were kind enough to keep their eyes open for me. In this case, what could I report? Some man in some hot-rod car hung out at 7-11 and pick up a willing chick?

With any DID person, anything involving the legal system is very complex. Charmaine's experience is a perfect case of this. The individual may have no recall of the events, and no real way to report what has happened. It is unlikely Laylee would hang around and go with me to the police to report non-consensual sex. In fact, hearing her tell it, it was very much consensual. That changes the whole scenario. The courts don't easily recognize that a person can be a victim of their own Alters' behaviors.

Chapter 12   The Day After

It would be great to say that I went home without a thought in the world. That all my clients were files in a drawer, and that once I closed and locked the door to my office, it was over for the day. But not that night; it was not that easy for me to just let it all go. I drove to the 7-11 to speak with the manager about the car and let him know that I would be bringing the owner to pick it up tomorrow. He was curious about why I was there about someone else's car. He told me that usually that car was driven by a quiet woman that he sees from time to time, but yesterday it was driven by someone else. Some lady in a hippy dress got gas, parked it and left with a guy.

He had not called to get it towed because he recognized her car as belonging to a regular customer. He was concerned when the woman had gotten in a car with some guy known from a local beer joint. When she did not return, he thought it was strange and said "None of my business, but strange all the same." I asked had he ever seen the same woman driving it before and he said he did not remember ever seeing her. He thought the lady might have loaned her car to someone.

He asked if everything was alright and I of course assured him that it was. He said he would keep an eye on the car and suggested I recheck that the doors were locked before leaving. I gassed up while I was there, and checked the locks on Charmaine's car.

Nice guy. It is wonderful how some people take notice of random events. Just another tidbit of information in my detective work; might not help, but every detail so far has lead somewhere.

As I tried to pick through my memory to fill in the gaps in my notes, I found myself going back to the diner in my mind; had I forgotten any names, or other specifics that will be helpful I found myself asking over and again. I hoped that Charmaine was asleep and that she was at peace with all the information she now is aware of

I picked Charmaine up at her house the next morning. She had a fresh pot of coffee on. She greeted me at the door dressed in sweats and a shirt with her hair freshly washed and pulled back in a band; with her watch and beaded bracelet on her arm, and no hint of perfume, no flowers in her hair, nor fancy colors in her choice of clothing.

I asked if she was ready to go. She let me know that first we were going to just sit and have some coffee. As I took a seat for the first time since my initial home visit, I could not help but notice how clean and tidy everything was. What a remarkable difference from the day of the redhead who answered the door to a home of clutter.

As we sat, I asked how she had slept. She lowered her head and began to tell me about her shower. She had washed herself until her skin was red and raw. She had to scrub the filth from her body. She woke up this morning disgusted with the very idea that someone had touched her in that way. She said it was difficult to come to grips with this whole DID thing in its entirety, it made sense in many ways; but scared her to death.

She wondered if we could go pick up her car and have our session in her home. She knew in her heart that we were in scary territory and she just did not want to have to drive home afterwards from the office. That made perfect sense to me. I absolutely understood her wanting to be in her own sacred, safe space. She was probably still tired from yesterday. This way she could lay down if she needed to afterward.

I wanted her to know that while I had no idea what she was going through, I did applaud her courage. I admired her willingness to not run from it; nor deny it any longer, as a I part of her personal reality. I knew what courage that took for her, but I also knew what a courageous woman she was.

After our coffee, we left for the gas station. I asked her if she frequented that station often. Charmaine said that she had bought gas there from time to time, but seldom went in to shop. I let her know that the manager was aware of her and knew her car. Leaving it overnight had not been a problem. That seemed to surprise her.

As Charmaine stepped out of my car and walked toward, we were startled by a horn blow over and over again. Nearby an engine was being gunned by someone in a sharp looking car at the stop light. We both looked up to see a man, leaning across the driver's seat of his car waving furiously. He yelled loudly at her but I could not tell what he was saying over the sound of the engine. She looked perplexed and dropped her keys, bending over to retrieve them; I noticed her looking at me with panic in her face. As she rose back up, keys in hand, the horn blared again. The car raced off as the light changed.

I then followed her home wondering; could this be the man that had picked her up at the 7-11, blowing the horn and gunning the engine? How would we know? She did not seem to recognize him at all. She was clearly taken off guard at the incessant blowing of a horn, but then so was I. The timing was most interesting. There is a very real possibility that this could have been the man that found and took advantage of Laylee while humiliating Charmaine.

I had rearranged my schedule to accommodate up to three slots if necessary with her. I felt she might need it after yesterday. When doing intense work, one does not know where the road will lead at times. Usually a 50 minute session is 50 minutes, but this was not that kind of client.

The day began with me thinking that Charmaine would follow me to my office, but since that cup of coffee and her request that made such good sense to me; we were now heading back to her home where she felt safe.

There have been many times in therapy when I wished I had a separate room for clients to lie down prior to having to return to their cars and homes after working through trauma or intense sessions. This is one great benefit of seeing someone in their home, I will always believe. Yet it has to be done with great care and caution for all Practitioners in working therapeutically with their clients.

For Charmaine, it worked out very well. She suggested we use the session to do a "hunt and find." She thought we could continue the search for more of the stuff she had found in her home. Perhaps there were more journals, or sketches that had been hidden by the Alters.

As I pulled in behind Charmaine, I noticed she was at my window before I had time to get out of the car. "Did you see that man Doc did you know him? Why do you think he was hammerin that horn at us, and did you hear him on that engine, I thought he was gonna blow that thing up."

Whoever he was, he had stirred Charmaine up and had created suspicion in my mind, as I cannot imagine that a stranger would just begin laying on a horn and gunning an engine for no reason. I had hopes that perhaps I could call Laylee out again or maybe the child. But mostly, I just wanted to get Charmaine on a better level from the trauma of yesterday.

I motioned for Charmaine to back up. I opened the door and got out, noting her anxiety as I told her I did not know who was in the car. I could not understand anything he was saying. She seemed nervous and agitated by the experience. I asked if she understood anything that was being said. She responded that she had tried but was so unsettled by the horn and the engine sounds it was hard.

We got inside and Charmaine made fresh coffee for us both and had a seat at the kitchen table. I had brought a book on those with Dissociative Identity Disorder for Charmaine to read; a book that I had hoped would give her a better understanding in the way of the brain, of how it was that a person had no awareness of the Alters who seemed to take over in times of duress and distress.

It was not lost on me that she made a face when she accepted it, and then pushed it aside on the table. She thanked me saying she would try and look at it later. It would be a book that perhaps she would later pick up when she was ready, when she was more at peace, or when curiosity got the better of her I thought.

I looked at her and realized that her face looked bruised. It was the first I had noticed it. I asked if she had noticed her cheek bruising. She said no, but her whole body was aching. That is where we picked up from the diner events. I then said, "Do you think it was possible that was the man who attacked you?" Charmaine flinched and said, "Oh, God I hope not, I pray he does not live in the same town I do Doc."

Charmaine then spent time telling me her thoughts after learning of Laylee; hearing about the new sexual event and her thoughts about DID. She was grateful for the waitress, and my arriving. She felt ashamed once she learned what had happened.

She also talked about her marriage and other memories that she had held onto before she allowed me to see the updates in her journal. As Charmaine handed me her journal, she seemed nervous. As I read she got up and busied herself in the kitchen. I could feel her looking at me, looking I think for reactions or comments.

I read sorrow and horror at the same time in her words, the slant of letters and her new found understanding of what was and had been happening to her on those occasions that she had at first spoken of "black outs" and fears of brain tumors and her being "plumb crazy."

As I sat there, I realized that Laylee had provided so many pieces to the ongoing puzzle that we had begun piecing together. There are so many parts now coming together. The pieces all led to a hallway that indeed had many doors; all within this weary woman who I sat with at a kitchen table. I knew she was waiting for me to say something... to say anything; now that I had new facts to support my previous thoughts and assessments.

As I flipped through the pages, I realized she had rejoined me at the table, so I scanned the journal as quick as I could, grabbing only the words that jumped out at me. Her words validated what we already knew. Charmaine was trying to fight with all her might.

She wrote in her journal about the fear of not knowing who she was, who she would wake up as, or what she would look like in the mirror. I could not help but try to imagine the horror of that as an individual, a mother, a woman living and trying to provide a home and a life.

I laid the journal down and looked at Charmaine, knowing she was waiting for a reaction; something from me. She looked into my eyes with so many questions, so much fear. The best I had was this; "I cannot imagine what it must be like for you." I watched her smile as her body relaxed. She seemed at peace in some way, that I did not diminish her writing, her life, her feelings, yet acknowledged that I had no idea what it would be like to walk in her shoes. Nor look from within at her face in a mirror, after waking from what she called a "black out," not knowing why her hair was red, nor why she was dressed a certain way. The horrors of that alone: much less the abuse she had suffered, made the Charmaine's story: one that would remain etched on my heart for years to come.

We sat and talked about the journal. We explored how Charmaine was feeling about the new discoveries she was making with the help of Laylee, with her own work in her journal and conversations in therapy. She had come so far along this path in understanding herself. She was coming to accept that this was a result of deep and long standing trauma. She recognized the brilliant coping strategies of her brain; working hard to protect and save her.

While she was still struggling with these concepts, she was moving toward a deeper understanding. She was willing and she was a fighter. She was honest, was a warrior of spirit, and a woman of great faith. I had come to realize that it just may be that it had been that faith that had allowed her to survive all these years. Charmaine was to be a teacher of how hope the size of a tiny flicker, can help a person survive the most horrendous of acts. She had hoped that the next day would be better.

I had decided that this was not the day to risk trying to get Laylee to make another appearance. Charmaine had been through too much, was weary, and needed to know peace while catching up and absorbing the events of the last 24 hours. She wanted to hear more details, to talk about it and to talk about her journal in more detail.

I listened closely, and repeated much of what I had shared with her on the ride home from the diner. Speaking slowly, allowing time to pass while I watched as she tried to let it settle; then ask questions as they came to her.

She asked many times if I had worked with anyone who was like her before. Had I read about things like this, or had known of anyone who could just go away and another "personality/Alter/identity" or whatever the hell you want to call it just come and take over? An Alter that would create a mess, and leave you standing in the middle of the street not knowing what has happened?

I was frank with her; I let her know I had limited experience in working with someone who was exactly like her, and yet I had done much research, had attended many seminars, and had consulted with others in the field about DID. I let her know that each person with a diagnosis of DID was unique in their presentations. Many described a similar detachment when describing traumas. Many talked about the ability to compartmentalize things in their minds in ways that most people cannot. Nearly all described "blackouts" and a type of amnesia in ways that she had.

We talked more about DID that day than any day before. We talked about the triggers of stress, anxiety, revisiting trauma, unresolved grief. The numerous traumas that are recorded in one's brain that may be responsible for individuals to be diagnosed with DID. Charmaine was like a sponge. She listened intently; even took notes at one point in her journal, writing down things as I spoke. She nodded her head in agreement when I spoke about sexual abuse being one of the main traumas suffered by those with DID; along with the trauma of death, or witnessing horrible events and being subjected to terrible, unbelievable things.

She seemed to want to know as much information as she could hold. As we talked, she would write in the corners of her journal "Ask about this" and then make a note for later. At the end of our session, I asked Charmaine if she would use the time between now and our next session to make a list of anything that she may be able to remember from her childhood: things: anything that may have occurred in her young adulthood that she thought might have triggered any significant upset. I wanted her to see if there were any trauma, or horror for her, now that she knew more about DID and its roots. She wrote my instructions down as well; agreeing to think about it.

She seemed more alive, more alert, more wanting to be involved in figuring out the whys of all this, in hopes of controlling the gatekeeper and definitely hopes of keeping Laylee behind a closed door from now on.

I had asked Charmaine if she thought she would be safe alone in the house. She let me know that she thought we may soon have to let her oldest son know something about all of this. She was starting to wonder if she was safe anywhere now. I had been thinking the same thing, yet was not yet ready to broach that with her. Charmaine had her "get it done" stance on and was ready to figure out how to regain control of her life.

It may be that we will soon have to meet with her oldest son and fill him in. Charmaine will have to decide how to involve the family with DID, and enlist their support, while ensuring everyone's safety. We made an appointment for the next week. Charmaine knew to call if she had a crisis between now and the time we had scheduled. She knew what to do in the way of homework, and she was ready to take that on.

We had also worked on de-stress exercises for her to practice: ways for her to practice controlled breathing for times when she felt anxiety rising. As she delved into past memories, she would need to remind herself she was in her home, she was safe.

Together we worked on a plan of action. We wrote a list together, and mapped out some future efforts. I asked that she bring all of her material to her next session at the office.

The week went by with no calls from Charmaine. I figured she was doing alright, but something kept niggling in the back of my mind. Perhaps there was something that had happened, but I could not put my finger on it. On the day before our scheduled session I had been calling clients to remind them of appointments for the upcoming week. I was also making some follow-up calls that I had arranged earlier. I decided that I would call Charmaine to remind her of our scheduled session for the next day.

The phone rang several times. Just before I was going to hang up, I heard her voice on the other end. It sounded as though I had awakened her. After what sounded like a groggy "hello?" I said who I was and heard, "I was just talking to you." I sat a bit straighter in my chair with that and said, "Excuse me? What did you just say Charmaine?" There was a pause... Charmaine then said, "Oh hell I must have been having a dream. Hello Doc, I think I was dreaming about you. In my dream we were sitting at the table talking."

I immediately felt reassured that it was Charmaine on the other end of the phone and that she was alert, aware and cognizant of the here and now. I told her I was calling to remind her of our session the next day. She quickly let me know she would be there with bells on. She had much to share, including a few new Alters that seemed to let themselves be known since I had seen her; but she was alright for the moment.

My interest was piqued, yet I hoped against hope that she had not been out and about without her own knowledge. It was a brief conversation. She assured me we would have a lot to discuss at our session together. I wrote a note to myself that simply said, "ALTERS" on her chart with the date of my call to her.

The rest of the afternoon was difficult. I was with clients, who had the night before been with their son, only to wake in the morning to discover his body; lying dead in his bed. Their profound grief and shock had consumed the better part of the rest of the day.

Prior to leaving my office that evening I had lit some sage, opened one door and mindfully burned sage through the building; praying that they might find peace. It was days and nights like this that made coming home to my sanctuary even more blessed; warming my soul, allowing me to see that life still has beauty.

I was working on the last of my paperwork for the day when I heard tires hit the parking lot. Somehow I knew it would be Charmaine. She was the last appointment for the day, which probably ended up being a great thing after all.

I continued getting the last of my papers put away rather than go out to greet her. She knew now how to come on in, find the office and make her way to her chair. She was comfortable enough after all these months to stop at the restroom if she needed to. She had become very used to the routine by now.

I hurried to wrap things up. I could hear the door creak shut; yet I did not hear the usual sound of her footsteps that I had grown accustomed to. I thought perhaps she was wearing different shoes. I looked up and thought I heard someone singing; but it sounded like a child's voice at the door in the lobby. How odd. I could not imagine Charmaine would be bringing a child with her to a session. Could I be so tired I am hearing a child singing in my mind? Surely not.

As I put the last of the papers in a cabinet I sensed someone at the door. I glanced up to see a head peek around the corner at me. It was Charmaine, but wait... was it Charmaine? I had never seen Charmaine wear pigtails before. As I said "Hello, come on in and let's get started," I motioned for her to come into the office. I did not see anyone else with her. I saw her "hop" and go directly to the corner where my toys, dolls and books are kept. She just sat right down in the floor singing "hippy hop here me tom." She began to play. She looked up at me and smiled as big a smile as one has ever seen.

She looked at me and said, "pway, me wanna pway wif u tois otay?" What/who is this? She spoke, in the voice of a little child, with a lisp. I realized I was in the presence of someone I had yet to know. Where was Charmaine? How had this little one gotten past the gatekeeper after Charmaine drove and parked that car?

I was rather taken aback by this new appearance, as there was no evidence of a little one other than the one day when I thought Charmaine had regressed from fear and acted in a very childlike manner. I had not seen any evidence since then of a child. This child did not have a care in the world; and oh my, was she precocious.

I smiled at her. Immediately moved from behind the desk and got down on the floor beside her as I tried to regain my senses. I tried to think; three or four, play therapy; a fast switch up for me with a completely changed Charmaine, now a little one who called herself Charie.

She was a wealth of information. The lisp took a bit of getting used to I must tell you. Particularly my name; I had to figure that out and ask for a repeat from her more than once. She was having the best of times as she sized me up. As I sat beside her she looked up at me and smiled.

She called me "S" but with a lisp, it was hard to understand: "S-*th cos* da*t ur name." A*s she talked she would pick up little dolls that were in a bucket there on the floor beside her, and hand me the boy dolls; keeping all the girls for herself. I found it fascinating that these little dolls were being separated in such a manner. I was intrigued by her, her body movements were that of a little one, her facial grimaces intense, her manner of speech and words were so young.

When I asked who she was, she said "Me Charie". I found that watching her was as fascinating as learning her name; she became more precocious as the minutes passed. She was shy, yet wanting to share, her hands twirling a pigtail, her eyes were rolling around making faces as she said, "Me Charie" with a lisp, and the hint of a smile. When I asked her age she held up fingers and replied "me free" to indicate three as she put her thumb and two fingers at me in the air towards my face.

I was mesmerized by her movements and her innocence. As she reached into the bucket where the dolls were kept, she pulled them out one by one. She would immediately scowl and hand me any that appeared to be male. When I asked why she did not like them, she scrunched her face and replied, "Dis one bad. Ou teep it."

I was perplexed as my hands became full with the ones she thought bad. I asked her to tell me why were they bad; thinking that perhaps they had been broken or damaged in some way as I looked at them... This child of three responded, "Dey dot sticks in der pants and dey hut ou." As I looked at them, and looked at this child with a face that was contorted, in disgust, it occurred to me what she was saying.

They have sticks under their pants and hurt you. Had Charmaine been hurt at the age of three years old by men who abused her under her parents watch? Have I just discovered the beginning of a life of such trauma through the Alter named Charie and some little dolls in a bucket?

As I sat with Charie and joined in her play, I held all the "bad men/boy dolls" with those things in their pants that were bad. I watched, and asked in small sentences what she was doing. I asked Charie how she came to my office to see me. Causally she told me Bart lets her come because he loved her so much and knew she wanted to play with the toys in my office.

From the mouth of a babe, I am now having validation of the gatekeeper in Charmaine's brain. I reach for my pad and pen to jot some notes, allowing

Charie to color or draw if she wants to; and then it hits me to ask her if there are others that she might know.

Children are marvelous in their openness and innocence if asked the right questions. They have no reason to be guarded, or to lie if not forced to. If treated with positive regard and warmth they usually respond with candor. They can also be brutally honest as she had just been about those dolls in the Bucket.

I asked her if she wanted some water or something to drink. Her reply was "no but did ou know dat thomeone pooped on ou porch s'th." I almost bit the inside of my lip in half when she said that. Then she made me bite even harder as she followed it up with "but it not me, coth me poopeded at home, me pwomise me did."

She looked at me when telling me this, with eyes that were big as saucers. Fully animated; a proud three year old, making the most important announcement of the day, with a sincerity that one could not help but believe. I had to bite hard on the inside of my mouth to keep from laughing. I still laugh as I recall that moment.

Here I was sitting with a grown woman on the floor of my office, who now appeared as a little three year old. She was so convincing that I found myself seeing an honest to God three year old who was just over grown. Telling me there was poop on my porch and not to be mad about it. Can you even imagine? I do not mean someone play talking as a child. I mean a child.

If only I had thought to hit record on the phone's video for this session to replay later for Charmaine. I am certain she will not believe me when I try to tell her about this. I had tears in my eyes as I reassured Charie that it was all alright. I explained that there is a stray cat that comes around; the cat probably pooped on the porch. I would take care of it later. I was proud of her for pooping at home.

I jumped right in; quickly asking Charie if there were others where she lived with Bart. Oh my, did she enlighten me; much more so than Laylee. Spoken through the eyes of the child; it seems that Bart is the Gatekeeper in the hallway. He has a soft spot for little Charie. He loves her, and takes very good care of her as a little one. I wish Charie were able to draw a picture of this Bart.

She cuddled a teddy bear. I felt as though she was telling me a fairytale. In her best voice, Charie told me about the inner workings of Charmaine's brain. She described a long hallway; with many doors, behind each lived a unique resident. According to Charie, she had come out of her door, gotten to the end of the hallway, wanting desperately to "tom out and pway." She said that Bart loved her. She held her arms up, to him, squeezing her hands open and closed saying *"up pweeze"* for him to pick her up. He scooped her up in his big arms hugging her tight. He told her it was not time for her to play yet.

Charie then she told him how much she wanted to "pway in s-th office wif de toys. Me see dem when tharmaine dere." Charie's eyes twinkled as she spoke about big Bart taking care of her, and her love for everyone behind the doors in their hall. She also gave me some delicious new insights. When Charmaine is "out front" the others, see what she sees and what she is doing; but Charmaine does not seem to see what they do when they are out.

Charie continued talking for quite a while. She would look away and play a bit, drawing in the little sand tray with her finger, or the small rake that was laying there. She had the dolls now lined up in a row, neatly along the bookcase.

I would wait patiently, or join her in drawing in the sand before returning back to the subject at hand. I had a million questions but did not want her to lose interest. I surely did not want to lose her at that time.

I asked Charie if Bart talked to her. What did he say when he held her in his arms? She thought a minute, smiled and said to me, "him sthay, not now baby, ou stay wif Bart. Ou know Tharmaine haf to go theee Dawkter S-th." Chattering away; she told me that she hugged Bart as soon as Charmaine parked the car, and he let her out. She had hopped out of the car singing.

She told me about the pretty flowers out front, and that she was singing all the way to the door from the car. She just could not wait to get inside to the toys. I knew I had heard a child singing. Now was the time... "Charie, can you tell me the names of the others there? Just take your time honey." Taking her little fingers, she tapped each finger, one at a time. As she spoke, Charie started rattling off names: JR, Tina, Laylee, Jennie, Anna, Zoe, Boo Boo, Deseree, Buck and baby. I was writing quickly. Then I thought of the drawing on the easel, and it hit me that she could tell me who was who.

I had to stop her for a moment. Quickly I jumped up and flew to my file cabinet to retrieve the drawing. I returned so quickly to sit again on the floor that I was almost dizzy as I asked Charie, "Do you know who any of these people are honey? Can you tell me their names? These people in the picture, are they the ones you are telling me about?"

Charie giggled and clapped her hands with sheer delight. "Oh doodie S-th ou already took dey picthures"... see em? Der is..." With pure delight, little Charie pointed to each caricature in the drawing as she told me their names. I frantically wrote them down. She had just identified the Alters that lived within Charmaine, with utter clarity, including herself. It was remarkable. She had the joy that only a child gets from looking at pictures and identifying them. She was proud of herself. I was delighted too, although for different reasons. "See s-th, dis is and der is ME, dat is JR, him sumtime say bussthard and cusses a bunch, and him smoke too, did ou no dat?" Charie was very animated in her descriptions. She candidly revealed their habits and behaviors as only a child would. Charie told me that Boo Boo could not talk, and that Zoe hurt Charmaine all the time.

I asked if she knew who drew those pictures of everyone. She looked at me with a puzzled expression. She shook her head, put her hands out, palms up, and said, "But Sth, ou took dat picthure. Me not know. Me only know dey names s-th." I was taken by her honesty, her joy, as she clapped her hands and then changed the subject all together. She went right back to the toys, as if I had not interrupted her play at all.

I let her play as I finished writing down all she had given me. This little Charie had shared a wealth of information. After a few moments, I re-joined her in play in the toy corner, with the sand, and the little dolls. I had thrown the male dolls back in the Bucket and moved it further away, thinking that she would not notice.

Charie was singing. She was happy. At times she would sit up straight and look at me, clap her hands and say, "me wuv you s-th." I found her to be enchanting. Such a sweet child, living inside Charmaine, who had suffered such trauma all these years. I asked Charie if there was anything else she wanted me to know? Anything she wanted to talk about while she was here playing today? It was then that Charie said "Me do s-th. Do ou know where beeths poop?" With a look of utter innocence, eyes wide open, she had asked her question in a very serious voice. I looked at her, biting the inside of my cheek, and said "No Charie, I sure do not." I was so hoping that she would talk more about the Alters. Charie was surely thinking as a child. We chatted for a few more minutes when Charie proceeded to return on her own to the subject of the Alters.

She started with BART who was the gatekeeper; he was always there and she "wuved him so bery much.

He took care of things." She said Bart was mad at Laylee and "her tannot go out no mo Bart say, tos her get us in twouble all time and acts uggy."

She let me know that JR was tough, and he took care of things too. He looked out for everyone. He was a cusser, and a smoker. She seemed to delight in telling on him. Just as a little one would it seems, "you thee s-th, him say busstard a wot an that weally a bad word ou know." As she told this there was a grin on her face and a twinkle in her eye.

She let me know that Deseree watched over everyone as well. She also had a say in who got to come out. She was the one who had locked Laylee up in her room for her bad behavior, but she also had the ability to talk Bart into allowing her out. Deseree had taken special care of little Charie it seemed: apparently Deseree made the others "toe the line" from what I was gathering from this little one.

I knew the adult size of Charmaine, but somehow, Charie appeared much smaller. It was as if she folded her body up into a compact her. It is hard to explain, but Charie appeared to be a "miniature" Charmaine, and I was not sure how. At times I felt like my eyes were playing tricks as I watched her. I finally decided that it must be the way she sat curled up that made her look so small. Her mannerisms and facial expressions kept me enthralled as I watched her.

Charie used her hands to gesture as she spoke to me. She would often turn, use her finger to run through the sand, then pick up a doll for a moment, and then return to what she was saying to me, or reach over and rub my arm, and smile at me. At one point near the end of our conversation, she noticed the dolls that I had put back in the bucket. She looked at me with a scowl on her little face. "S-STH...ME tole ou dem bad..dey back in dat bwuket get dem OUT!"

She was clearly not happy with my having put the bad dolls back in that Bucket. I quickly pulled them out and laid them on the floor. Asking her what she thought we should do with them. She said, "out of here, dem need go way, away from here otay?" She looked at me with big crocodile tears in her eyes.

Before I could answer her, I see Charie lean forward like she was listening to something, or for something. I watched her closely as she tipped her head slightly. Then I heard her say sadly, "otay otay Bart me toming, me sthay bye bye to her, otay? Me just say bye bye to s-th and put way me toys. Me toming, otay Bart?"

Having said that, Charie turned and placed everything back in the now empty bucket, tidied everything in the corner and moved to get up as she said "Me haf to go now, s-th. Bart sthay it time for tharmaine to tum out and me to go now and me pways long time today."

As she stood up and moved toward the door, I stood by the desk and watched. She turned to me looking so very serious. "Sth tan me tum back sthomtime and pway wif you agin sthomtime tan me?" I looked at her serious little face, smiled and told her absolutely she could. Anytime Bart said it was safe she could do just that.

She continued to stand there, looking at me. Finally she extended her arms, with hands opening and closing, opening and closing, she said, "Me want to hab hug sth for me go cos me wuv you."

I walked over and hugged Charie tight. I realized I was hugging a 3 year old who was occupying a grown woman's body for the moment; a child who had opened many doors for me as we had sat in the floor. This had been a time which was filled with innocence, and honesty, beyond measure. Filled with love that only a child can give so openly, I was grateful for her visit.

I told her "I love you too Charie, now go to Bart honey, and thank you for visiting me today." As I stepped away, and moved back to my desk, I fully expected Charie to skip or sing and go down the hall and out the door to Bart. What happened next, once again surprised me.

Charie turned to leave but just stood there motionless for a bit. After a few long seconds, she turned around. I hear Charmaine's voice say: "Hi Doc, I'm here, were you getting ready to walk out to meet me? What's wrong Doc, you look like you've just seen a ghost, did I scare you?"

I am not sure I can describe what my expression must have looked like. Stunned might be the right word. I don't even know what my feelings were at the time, what I was thinking, I only know that I was expecting that Charmaine who was Charie at the time was on her way out of my office. I guess I did not think she would turn and not be Charie. Nor did I think she would turn and be Charmaine saying *"I'm here,"* as though she had just arrived.

Truth be told, at the time, I believe I was so absorbed with all that I had learned and was so touched by Charie's sweet good-bye, as I was watched her leave; I was wondering if she would someday be allowed to come out again. Now that Deseree and Bart would know that she had spilled all the beans, would they keep her too under wraps.

I had no idea that she may just turn around, and be a clueless Charmaine, who thought she was just at this moment arriving for her appointment, oblivious to the fact that she had been here all this time.

I bet I did look as though I had seen a ghost. I tried to quickly get my wits about me and welcome her. She walked past me, laughing at how I appeared "frazzled" while making her way to her chair for our appointment. Yes, it was Charmaine, her posture, her voice, that slow drawl, her mannerisms and charm sitting in the chair. I felt as if I had entered a time warp for a few moments.

She was here for her appointment. In her mind, she was on time, having no idea that she pulled into my parking lot more than two hours ago. She had no idea that an Alter had jumped out of the car, skipping up to the porch singing "hippy hop here I tome." Charie had paused only to pick a flower, looking at life through the lens of a three year old, with such joy and honesty. Charie, playing on the floor, one by one was revealing the many doors and their occupants, in the hallway in her brain.

How would I begin to share all this information with Charmaine was the question at hand. I realized she had just noticed the sketch lying on the desk with names written under each face. She looked at me quizzically as she spoke; "Doc, why in the world have you got the names under each of those faces? Here we go. Charmaine wanted to know how I knew the names to put on the pictures.

Before I could answer, Charmaine had picked up the picture and was studying it intently. Looking at the names I had written below each face. She looked back and forth, between the drawing and me. I could tell the lightness of her mood was changing. I was still trying to regain my balance. Shall we move directly into the introduction of Charie? I asked Charmaine if we could go for a brief walk before we started our session. I asked that she humor me for a few minutes, I just needed some fresh air before we got started.

As we strolled around the yard, we stopped for a few minutes and sat in the old swing. We talked about the clouds and how the sun came shining through, in the midst of storm clouds building. I was able to try to connect the dots for Charmaine. How the good times shine through after the storms of life.

She wanted to know if I was alright. I assured her I was fine, just needed a few minutes of sunshine and a little break before we began our session. Sometimes fresh air, just leaning against a tree can give one a fresh perspective. It can allow strength to find its way to you, can provide energy when one feels a bit depleted of their own, or when you just need to clear

your head. My time with Charie, now so quickly shifting and changing to Charmaine, made me realize I needed a moment to realign my own self in order to be my best self for Charmaine as I got my thoughts together. She was kind enough to indulge me. She too enjoyed the outside.

So we walked a bit, quietly and peacefully, around a block. Pausing to admire the flowers, comment on the trees, find shapes in the clouds. She talked with vast knowledge about the plants, flowers and herbs, as we strolled. I learned more about Charmaine the person: I and realized that she had always grown plants. That she learned to take cuttings and make different varieties of flowers and plants.

She was comfortable sharing the intermittent silences as I observed her gait, her posture, and mostly just enjoyed the quiet. As we headed back to the office, and to our session, I thought; this was just the respite I needed, a break between sessions. One of which I had been totally unprepared for. Two distinct personas; a child/adult, an Alter and her host; how now to bridge the two? I was hoping the connection would be made once I filled Charmaine in on Charie's existence and her visit.

We got back into the office and sat down; only for Charmaine to ask again about the paper with the faces. She said that she did not remember any names being on the picture when she had given it to me in her home many days before. I told her that I had a lot of information to give her and asked if she was ready to hear it? She might want to buckle her seat belt.

Charmaine said, "Well, dang Doc, it can't be any worse than what happened at that diner can it? I mean if I have to go home and scrub myself raw again, I just might go on and put a bullet to myself. So, I'm thinking, it just can't get any worse than that that CAN IT? Now calm down Doc, I don't have no bullets, and do not plan on getting any, but what can be worse than that right?"

I had to smile. Here I was, telling her to buckle her seat belt, after what we had been through together with the emergence of Laylee. She was absolutely right. She could hear this. She would cope with this. I have grown very fond of this woman. She is a warrior who wants to understand how to live her best life. But, I also fear that we will reactivate traumas that she has been protected from, her by her Alters. Once again, I decide to tread lightly.

I asked if she recognized any of the faces in the sketch now that she was holding the paper again in front of her. She was looking at them very intently. I leaned in often gently touching her forearm for reassurance. She was safe here. Knowing that this was going to be difficult; no matter how strong she was.

Charmaine squinted her eyes. She told me that driving here she was having a good day, looking forward to seeing me. She had a good feeling because when she looked in the mirror, she was grateful it was really her that she saw.

She went on to say, "When I got here Doc, you looked like you saw a ghost when you saw me. You wanted to go get some air, which you rarely do. I see this picture with every face labeled with a name; and now you are telling me to buckle my seat belt. Gosh, I don't know what to think about my day now. Let's get to it... what do you know, that I need to? Have I gone and done something else that you heard about since the last time I saw you?"

One thing about Charmaine; she was plain spoken, honest and to the point. That set her apart from the Alters that I had met to date. She wanted to know everything; she wanted to be in control of her life, to be totally responsible for her comings and goings, and to make her own decisions.

I found that she was consistently missing the emotions that would have followed from the traumas that she had obviously been through in her life. The connections were not there for her. The Alters stepped in, leaving huge blanks in her memory. Somehow we needed to fill in all those blanks.

Charmaine said it was time for me to let her know what had really happened. So, I began. I shared with her, in great detail, Charie's visit. I watched as this client, that I have come to know so well, once again held her breath. Her eyes grew bigger and bigger: she was shocked at the news that a three year old Alter named Charie visited for two hours in her place.

I then pointed to the sketch. I introduced her to Charie; to each of the others that Charie described, starting with JR. I reminded her of the clothing she had found under her son's bed, and my description of this masculine person that appeared in my office dressed in black ops.

I then asked her; given the detailed description I had given her, the description of how he spoke to me, the clothes she found, can you look again at the drawing and tell me, "Do you think that one would look like JR?" Charmaine's mouth dropped open and tears fell from her eyes as she nodded. Charie had opened the door. Charmaine now had a visual of what Charie and JR looked like.

We then did the same thing by the description of Laylee provided by Charie. I let her know what Charie had said about her now being locked up as a result of getting everyone in trouble. When I shared that, Charmaine laughed through her tears and said, "Well thank God for that anyway, the bitch should be locked up!"

I asked Charmaine if she would like some coffee at this point, knowing we were in deep here, realizing that sometimes it is good to pause, to sit with information rather than bombard the system, the heart, the soul all at once. It is better to just sit quietly as it is absorbed, rather than be too quickly overwhelmed.

Charmaine seemed grateful. "Oh yes, please." I left to make a pot of fresh coffee. I left her to her own thoughts for a few moments of space. I also left a pad of paper laying on my desk with my notes from Charie that I had not had time to move, and frankly had forgotten they were there, during the quick shift from Charie, to Charmaine.

When I returned with our coffee, I saw Charmaine sitting with Kleenex lying beside her. She was reading those notes intently. So intently that she did not hear I come into the office, set the coffee down, and resume my seat.

When she saw me she was startled. Immediately she said, "I'm sorry Doc, I saw this pad and was going to make myself some notes on all this, but then I saw where you had some stuff here about all this and I started to read it, I hope you do not mind, after all it is about me right?"

I smiled at her. I assured her I did not mind, telling her I did not realize that I left it out on my desk, even though it was face down. That yes, those were notes I was trying to take as Charie spoke in her fast baby talk. I also told Charmaine that Charie spoke with a lisp. At times I had trouble understanding her and had to write it as I heard it. We picked up where we left off.

There were times when Charmaine would stop in mid-sentence; mine or hers, it did not matter. At one point she exclaimed, "How in the heck can I be me one minute, and three years old the next? What if this happens when I am with the kids, or in the store, and I do something like this? I know someone will lock my ass up doc. This is crazy stuff."

I told Charmaine that I wished I had made a video of this for her to see. I told her about Charie's cute comments about the "poop on the porch." I must tell you at first; it was met with an incredulous look and I "got it," I probably had the same expression on my face when Charie first told me about it.

Sketch after Charie identified each person while visiting the office. DRSES

Charmaine laughed until she held her ribs. She insisted I must be making that part up. Then in her southern drawl, as loud as she had ever spoken, she said, "ARE YOU KIDDING ME DOC?" Me a grown woman, sitting in the floor playing with toys, talking with a lisp, and I said I did not poop on your porch, I pooped at home? OHHH===My ===gosh."

With that we both laughed heartily. A much needed laugh I have to tell you. Once again, we dug deeper into Charmaine's mind and its brilliance. I imagine this was a lot to grasp. Unlocking unknown and potentially frightening doors for a person who must now fully accept that she is living with DID. She was discovering so much new information, all at once. While absorbing the unbelievable, she was still able to find humor and light amid the shadows of darkness.

As we continued, it seemed that Charmaine stayed totally present. She was, and remained, an investigator. One who wanted to dig deep into what's and whys of how she had become this way. Mostly she was driven to understand so that she might gain control of her own life.

She looked once again closely at the sketch, as though she was trying to see if she could remember any of the people or their names. Then she looked at me and said, "Doc did I tell you about the man who grabbed me and insisted my name was Laylee that time? Do you think? Do you think he really recognized me?"

She bowed her head. Just as quickly, her head snapped back up, before I could answer. "Oh gawd

Doc, I've found little notes, written like a child wrote them, hidden under things. Think about all my dolls, and coloring books, all the things I have. Do you think I have those because of this Charie? Do you think, oh gosh I don't know what to think about all this. I think I just need to go home and lay down Doc. This is a lot to try to think about. It has me spinning now."

I watched as Charmaine was trying to process all this information. She had worked hard, had absorbed much; maybe too much for one day. We brought our time together to an end with a guided imagery for relaxation. It was difficult to get her focused as her mind was filled with thoughts, feelings, emotions and questions. Finally, she was able to get to a place of relaxation in imagery, before leaving the office intact, as Charmaine. We walked out of the office, and said our good-byes.

I asked if she was alright to drive or needed to sit a while? She assured me she would be okay; her plan was to go home, take a shower, eat and rest. Her kids would be going from the ex-husband's to their Aunt's home for a week, but were coming home for the weekend between the two. She was thrilled to be seeing them, and was looking forward to time with them. She indicated that she was somewhat nervous, and hoped that all this would not interfere with her time with them. She did not know what she would do, if an Alter came out, and especially one who poops in floors, or talks about pooping, with her kids around.

Oh how I hoped that it would go well for her. Standing on the porch, Charmaine said that she sure could use a hug before she left. I gladly hugged her, telling her I wished her a great weekend with the kids. I watched her walk down the steps, then turn back to wave. I waved, and pointed to the right. I realized Charmaine did not seem to remember she had parked near the back of the building beside my car.

She had forgotten I think, with all that we talked about. Or maybe because of how quickly Charie had jumped out, as soon as that car was turned off. It is ironic. I can visualize the car stopping, Charie hopping out and skipping up the porch steps. That is how real these Alters are; just like JR, with all his swag. I remember smelling his masculine cologne. It's uncanny how changed each of them are. I really forget that I am dealing with Charmaine when these Alters present. This is hard work.

CHAPTER 13   IN BETWEEN SESSIONSE

I received a phone call from my old friend Dr. Hope. She wanted to remind me that we had a meeting at the Rape Crisis Center coming up. She suggested we meet for dinner prior to the meeting, and asked if we could talk about Charmaine. She had some other things to discuss with me as well. I was eager to see my dear friend. It would be wonderful to sit and enjoy her. I had forgotten all about the Board meeting during my busy weeks and Charmaine's many sessions.

Dr. Hope was a remarkable woman; she had an active practice and yet made time for service to women in the community on so many levels. She had served on boards throughout the year, in grassroots organizations. She was one to donate time, money and her talents where they best served women in need.

We had known each other for years, she was a great friend. One I had turned to professionally, for and with clients as the need had been there many times before. We had referred patients to each other as well through the years and had worked collaboratively for the best interest of our patients and clients.

A rare and special friendship, personally and professionally is hard to find, I found myself thinking as I drove to this great little steak house with private booths that I just loved. Dr. Hope was an elegant but down home type of woman. She arrived right on time, with her phone in her hand, a folder under her arm, and that beautiful gray hair flowing around her shoulders. She looked great as she slid into the booth and smiled a smile that lit up the room.

We immediately engaged in conversation. The talk moved from football to the latest trends linking spirituality to wellness in grief, sexual abuse and psychological stress, in the workplace. The conversation flowed, with ice tea and salads. Dr. Hope wanted me to know that she was honored that we had such a great working relationship. She was proud of the many years of our joint work on women's issues. We talked about some of the women we had learned from, had ministered to on so many occasions.

Then we came to Charmaine, and her findings in the examination. That helped us both settle into the real reason for our getting together for dinner before going to the annual Rape Crisis Board Meeting. She told me that she knew that Charmaine had a long history, perhaps stemming from childhood abuse based on her examination. We both concluded that Charmaine needed to see her again in her office as soon as we could schedule the appointment.

As she talked to me, I realized that some of my thoughts from our early sessions were being confirmed about Charmaine, that perhaps as a child she had detached as a result of severe abuse. That detachment or disassociation had in fact saved her little life back then from the horror and the pain she must have endured.

Dr. Hope explained that the extent of her injuries, seen upon examination, were old injuries indicating trauma done to the vagina and anus. She felt that Charmaine was in need of surgical repair as a result of her recent encounter. The procedure could be performed in her office. Dr. Hope would donate her time to do this, but could also utilize a fund that had been established for women who have been sexually abused to help cover any costs incurred.

I could tell as I listened to her speak, that this was a situation that she was all too familiar with through the years. As she educated me more these physical tears, I found myself wondering how some women survive, not only physically, but emotionally and spiritually, without the Dr. Hopes of the world.

In addition to the physical pain, the scarring, we have to consider the emotional pain, the shame, blame, and feelings of punishment that women often talk about. I wondered about the women who have no one to talk to; no one to turn to. My thoughts drifted back to Charmaine, as Dr. Hope asked me my thoughts on her psychological status. Did I think she was ready to even approach such a procedure? Dr. Hope had seen many women's lives greatly improved after treatment, but did not want to suggest it to Charmaine if I felt she was not ready to consider it.

I found myself fascinated that the procedure could be done in an office suite rather than a hospital. It was also rather remarkable to me, now that we were talking to hear that women felt more whole, more psychologically sound, to have vaginas that were "intact" once again after sexual abuse.

It seemed there is a procedure that could be done that allows a woman's vagina to be tightened, with a relatively simple procedure; that restored the tissue its natural state. No stretching, no tears; remarkable. I frankly, had never heard of this before, but was not surprised that Dr. Hope had not only done the research, but was skilled at it. She was up to the minute with gynecological issues, as it was her passion, her profession. She was all about taking care of women.

I glanced at my watch and realized we had talked so long that we were certain to be late for our meeting. We quickly called for a check, and ran like the wind to the car to get to the next task. We could return later in my car.

In the car we were able to continue our conversation. I thought she should give Charmaine a call to set the appointment, to let her know that we had talked, and that I would follow up with her at the next session as well.

We were the last two to arrive for the meeting. Interesting that the agenda being covered as we arrived was the fund we had discussed. An anonymous donor had just contributed 15,000.00 to that fund for women in need of GYN services. The Creator seems to know where the need is, was my first thought as I took my seat. During the meeting that evening we heard the most recent statistics on the number of rapes that were occurring in the area.

The Center had made plans to increase the public awareness through a new campaign.

Informing the community and reaching out to women was always at the core of the work the Rape Crises Center did. We wanted to tie the rape statistics to the issue of STDs; not only for rape victims, but to heighten awareness in general. We talked about how to best approach our new campaign. A guest speaker was being sought to talk to the local high schools about STD's in the coming months. Of course all eyes were on Dr. Hope. I was almost certain that she would volunteer, but oddly, her hand never went up. Little did I realize what that would come to mean to me and so many others.

As I listened to the discussion, my thoughts kept returning to Charmaine; to her life as I imagined it. From the little one that had shown up to "pway" in my office; to "JR" who thought I had a "nice ass" and was in special OPS clothing and a ball cap, to Laylee who was 16, promiscuous, a carefree love child of the 70's... all Alters of this woman who once was an innocent baby girl. A child that I know must have seen and experienced hell at the hands of grownups, adults who should have been there to love and protect her.

This little girl, now a grown woman, that I know must have been abused, manipulated, beaten and feel certain now, that she was used, as a child, for adults to sexually exploit. After my enlightenment at the hands of Dr. Hope, I accepted that much of the old scaring could indeed have happened many years ago.

She was able to finally see what she felt, was very old trauma, deep scarring and fresh ripping.

My God I found myself thinking; once again I am seeing someone who has been damaged at the hands of others when they were but a child. In a way I'm glad that Charmaine was protected by Alters, but now, to unravel it all. Perhaps, the next steps would become clear as we worked together to meet Charmaine's physical needs in the moment.

I was brought back to the topic at hand, as I listened to the frequency of transmission of STD's from sexual contact, whether consensual sexual contact or that which is forced. The consequences were staggering.

We would come to find out through blood work that Charmaine was one of the ones who had indeed contracted a particular virus through forced contact that was unwanted. For Charmaine, she did not even know or remember any of this. From Dr. Hope's perspective, this virus could have been lying dormant for years. In the car Dr. Hope had told me that the blood work revealed that Charmaine had HPV; genital human papillomavirus, HPV. It is the most common sexually transmitted infection (STI).

As I let my ears now really hear what was being talked about in our meeting, since I believe I was not fully paying attention, my mind was focused on Charmaine; it hit me that HPV was the subject at hand. I began taking notes as I knew this would come up in our session in the near future. I would need to be very well informed. Knowing Charmaine, she would have a thousand questions.

Part of me was really hoping that Dr. Hope would be the main player in this conversation, while I was the wing woman on this one. Yet I needed to be prepared. Charmaine looked to me for the truth. She wanted me to have the guts to walk this journey no matter what. We were going to be in some sensitive areas in more ways than I could count.

As I listened, I wrote as fast as I could. How relieved was I when the speaker passed around detailed handouts. As we broke for coffee, the room got louder, with everyone catching up on each other's families; the latest statistics in the neighborhoods and the Nation. There was enormous energy in the group. These women, working for others; churning with ideas, sharing their passion, I was glad to be a part of it. Yes, it is in the service of, and for others, that we receive so much in our lives; standing for difficult issues; women, their rights and choices. Not always easy, but necessary.

As Dr. Hope and I drove back to the restaurant at the end of that meeting, we laughed as we talked about our tardiness. Great timing; we entered at such a perfect moment, since it was she who was the one the center sent rape victims to for treatment. Given that there was a new influx of funds for treatment, she would be able to do even more in her work for these victims. Charmaine would be a perfect candidate for assistance in helping defray Dr. Hope's cost of care.

Society often judges women by the tough choices they have to make. People often judge others by what they see on the outside, yet seldom stop to think. They have no idea what may have happened on the inside, literally and figuratively.

Dr. Hope and I had a plan at the end of the evening. I had learned much; we had enjoyed each other's company, in spite of the sad news we would have to share with Charmaine in the days ahead. It was late by the time she dropped me off at the restaurant where I had abandoned my car. This had been another long day.

As planned, Dr. Hope called Charmaine to let her know that she needed to come in for an appointment. The appointment was scheduled. The reason I knew exactly when that happened is that I received a call from Charmaine. She was not a bit happy. I answered the call with my usual, "Dr Showalter, may I help you? Before I could finish the "you", I heard Charmaine's voice on the other end. She had just hung up from Dr. Hope. She was upset and afraid that something bad was wrong. She had called to see if I knew anything that she did not yet know.

It was hard to get a word in edgewise, hard to reassure her; or to speak for that matter. She was on a roll that was difficult to stop, for several minutes, with her thoughts free flowing on the other end of the phone. When she paused to catch her breath; I asked her if it was my turn to speak. She laughed just enough to let me know that she could hear me.

I told her I had a cancellation. If she could come now, we would talk. I had an open hour; she grabbed it, saying, "Ok Doc, I'm on my way, bye." I looked at the phone, realizing that was shortest phone conversation I had with Charmaine since I met her. I readied myself for her arrival by taking out my notes from my conversation with Dr. Hope. I put on a pot of coffee.

I had just finished making phone calls when I heard the car roll into the parking lot. I went to meet her on the porch, like so many other times. Mostly I wanted to see firsthand who stepped up onto the porch. I was not in the mood to be surprised that particular day.

Another drawing that appeared one day on the easel in Charmaine's bedroom. Charmaine is portrayed at the top of the drawing with the others around her. DRSES

CHAPTER 14 YOU CAN DO THIS

Charmaine stepped from her car in black sweats and a dark shirt. She had something in her hand as I watched her walk toward the porch. She looked up to see me watching her. I saw her grin as she approached the steps with her hand behind her back. She reached out without a word and wrapped her arms around me with a hug saying, "Dang it's good to see you standing here Doc, and I'm sure glad you had someone cancel today, but I hope they are ok."

With that we walked inside. I motioned her into the office as I walked on and got our coffee. I returned to see that she was sitting in her chair. On my desk, she had placed a little vase with one bloom in it, a flower from her garden. She said that she picked on her way out the door in a hurry.

The vase was a little jar of some kind, I had never seen one quite like it but it was just perfect. Charmaine looked at me, looked at the flower and told me she thought that with all that we talk about, maybe something beautiful will come of it. Maybe, just maybe, it will take some of the ugliness away.

She was blooming; growing in ways that were astounding. Even as traumas, both old and new were being unearthed, she was finding ways to heal, to transform through the beauty that was still hers to embrace.

I felt she had come further than she even realized. Yet part of me had to wonder if somehow, Charie, Laylee and JR; her acceptance of them played a part in her growth. In the face of her call from Dr. Hope, she was seemingly resilient. I can remember a time when such a call would have inspired a complete meltdown. She was developing new skills, new coping mechanisms.

Charmaine thanked me for the coffee and started right away telling me about Dr. Hope's call. She told me she had scheduled an appointment. She was concerned, in fact a bit afraid. She spoke in detail about the painful examination, and her hatred of those kinds of appointments. Probing "down there" was embarrassing.

I let her talk until she was finished. She finally asked me if I was ever going to say something. I smiled and told her I could not have said anything if I had wanted to, unless I had taped her mouth shut with duct tape. She was talking a mile a minute. I wanted her to be able to get it all out without interruption. She laughed, and then took a long sip of her coffee. Good to see that she could laugh even though she was worried about the pain and personal intrusion of the impending doctors' visit. I saw that as excellent coping in the moment.

I let Charmaine know that I had spoken with Dr. Hope; and that yes, we had talked about the need for her to come in for a follow-up appointment. I was sorry that it was so very painful for her to be examined. Many women had expressed that; particularly women who had been sexually abused, or had conditions that caused sensitivity in the pelvis. She told me that she didn't have any "conditions." She had not had cancer, had not had any surgeries down there, and to her best knowledge, she had not been abused. She followed her comments with, "Well unless you count that useless and sex crazed x of mine."

We talked about her fears regarding this next appointment with Dr. Hope. She was insistent that I check my calendar right then to see if it was possible for me to go with her. She knew she just could not, go alone.

As I was checking my calendar, I asked her how she had been doing. Had she discovered any new clothes or other items at home? How she was feeling? Charmaine did not want to talk about any of that; she was focused on the Doctor visit, and my availability. She would not speak until I had confirmed that yes, I would be available to meet her there.

Once that was established, she said that she would go. That she felt better now that she had all that off her chest so to speak. She was still afraid of what the Doctor was going to say to her. We talked for a bit about what Dr. Hope had said to her on the phone. I wanted a better idea of what she already knew. Charmaine told me that Dr. Hope had indicated that she wanted to fully discuss the results of her blood work with her. She said something about tearing she had seen when she examined her. Dr. Hope said she wanted to assess the damage she had suffered from this last incident.

Charmaine said, she sensed that the Doctor was not telling her everything. "She was cagey doc. She was not telling me everything, know what I mean?" I told Charmaine that I felt that some conversations needed to take place held face to face. That way she could ask questions, and get a better understanding of what Dr. Hope had to say. It sounded like Dr. Hope certainly had told Charmaine enough to prepare her for the appointment, and to alleviate her stress until then.

I answered a few questions that Charmaine had, from the phone conversation. I did not want to go further, as I knew that Dr. Hope wanted to talk to her in person, and that it was her area of expertise. That satisfied Charmaine. She seemed more relaxed.

I wanted to ask her about her parents, about any memories that may have come to her, particularly from her early childhood, to push a bit more on Charie and the little dolls.

It was as if Charmaine was reading my mind. Just then she asked me, "Do you think it is possible that those little dolls Charie talked about could be why it's so painful even now to have an examination down there?" She went on to describe her experiences with childbirth. With each child, she thought she would die from pain or months and months after their births. She had experienced excessive bleeding and often felt as if she were being stabbed "down there."

She talked a lot during our times together about her marriage with her x-husband. She openly recalled his sexual frequent sexual demands. She hated that he forced sex on her. Her one consistent statement was her disdain of sex, and the constant pain that accompanied it.

Charmaine stated that she always thought it was fear that caused her to "dry up down there," making intercourse painful. She felt it was always like he enjoyed raping her each time he forced himself on her. She recalled that he swore at her, called her frigid; and flaunted his cheating with other women throughout most of their marriage. She admitted that he was also physically, and verbally abusive. The subject was embarrassing to talk about, but she never showed any emotion.

Charmaine then told me at one time she realized that just the thought those experiences could bring up the smell of semen; and that would still make her vomit. It disgusted her. It made her feel physically ill. If she ever had to be with a man again she just did not know what she would do. She emphasized that was how much she hated sex.

It was beginning to come together in my mind. Between the childhood sexual abuse, and this destructive marital relationship; riddled with pain and rape, I was getting a better understanding of the physical observations Dr. Hope had talked about.

I heard the door open, indicating another client had arrived. We had not even begun to discuss the possibility of STDs, the HPV, or even what she could expect at her next appointment. I took Charmaine's hands into mine and looked her into the eyes. "Charmaine, I am truly honored that you allowed me to walk this journey with you. I just know Dr. Hope will be an important part of your healing. Try to trust her. I promise it will all be ok."

I asked her to write in her journal any thoughts she may have about those little dolls, about all that Charie had to say, any dates she might remember, or the specifics of that group of grown ups that had gathered in her parents' home. To think about her parents, the way they spoke, how they acted. We would continue our conversation at our next session.

As she left, I reminded her that I would meet her at the Doctor's office at the date and time she had been given. My phone was available if she needed to call. In all the time working with Charmaine, she had only called my number a couple of times. In each instance, she was in need; not once had she overstepped boundaries with phone calls. Nor had she called when she could find some way to get through to the next session.

As we walked out together, my client, who had been sitting in the waiting room, looked up at Charmaine. They exchanged hellos. I continued to walk Charmaine out to the porch. My clients are used to that; they are considerate of each other and my time with each person. They know that periodically we run over a few minutes. Everyone is generally polite and respectful, knowing that should the need arise; they too will be given the time they need.

Charmaine hugged me tightly. I knew she was feeling vulnerable with all that was going on. She thanked me for our time together. I thanked her for the flower, promising to save the little vase for her. So much was represented by that little flower, and the way Charmaine's life was unfolding.

CHAPTER 15 JR AND DR HOPE

I had called Dr. Hope to let her know I would be meeting Charmaine at her office. We chatted a few minutes between clients. She asked if I minded arriving a bit earlier than Charmaine, letting me know she had something to discuss with me. I checked my schedule and let her know that would be fine.

I arrived and found her office with one patient, so sat in the lobby reading as I waited. I saw her come out for her last patient. She glanced at me and motioned me into her office to wait for her.   I appreciated that as I needed to make use of my time, so I used her phone to make calls. There was always something to do. It was great to have a quiet place, while she was finishing, to catch up. After a while she joined me. She sat on the other side of her desk and we began to talk about Charmaine and her visit. I shared that Charmaine had called me panicked after their phone call.   Dr. Hope was not surprised. Her conversation with Charmaine had been purposefully brief. She had wanted to see me first, to talk about how she planned to discuss her findings with Charmaine. She suspected that it would be difficult for her. I knew it would be hard, yet I know somehow she would handle it. I braced myself for what was to come next; although a part of me felt as though I already knew. Dr. Hope let me know that as a physician, as a woman, as one who had seen many women who had suffered sexual abuse; she was convinced that Charmaine had a long history of such abuse based on her initial examination. The damage was extensive, although during the initial exam Charmaine had been under great stress.

She was impressed at the fact that Charmaine was established in therapy. She felt that was important in her healing. Dr. Hope planned to ask Charmaine to share her diagnosis with her when she met with her today. She wondered what Charmaine might say.

It was then that I asked Dr. Hope if she was asking me to share with her Charmaine's diagnosis. She said no, she wanted to ask Charmaine directly when talking to us. I knew then, at that moment, that Dr. Hope was thinking deep and hard about something. She had a lot to talk to Charmaine about.

We sat and waited for Charmaine to arrive. Dr. Hope told me about some of the work she had been doing to repair the damage to those who had been harmed by rape or abuse. Something told me that Charmaine was in her mind as she spoke. It seemed that many survivors of sexual abuse suffered from tears to the vagina and rectum, some minor; many were much more than that and often required surgical interventions to correct, to comfort, to heal the frequent or periodic pain that was experienced by women.

Some, Dr. Hope reported, always complained of burning upon urination, bleeding for no apparent reason, pain upon intercourse or even when using tampons. Others reported psychosocial damage so severe that many of her patients entered therapy, secondary to sexual abuse that had occurred many years earlier. After seeing Dr. Hope, receiving a diagnosis of internal damage, many women welcomed surgery; but had no idea how to cope with the painful emotions and shame they felt. She was glad that Charmaine's problems came out as a result of therapy, rather than the usual way.

As we were talking, she heard the buzzer on the lobby door indicating that Charmaine, or someone, had entered the waiting room. She went out, returning a few minutes later with Charmaine; who let out a sigh when she saw me. She had a lump in her throat when she walked into an empty office.

I smiled and greeted her. Letting her know that I had been there a while using Dr. Hope's office as my own for a bit, as she was seeing patients. I moved from behind the desk to allow Dr. Hope her chair, but she motioned for me to keep my seat. She had pulled up a chair to sit beside Charmaine. That seemed to surprise Charmaine, and quite frankly, it delighted me to sit in the big chair and be the observer for a change.

Dr. Hope began by saying she would like to start by re-examining Charmaine. That since Charmaine was dreading that part, they could get it out of the way first and be done with it. She asked Charmaine if that was alright with her. I was a bit surprised to hear Charmaine reply that she was in total agreement by saying, "Might as well get the hell over with first is my way of thinking."

They both excused themselves and walked out of the office with Charmaine looking over her shoulder, saying, "Thanks for being here Doc, it means a lot to me." I nodded and smiled giving her thumbs up. I prayed she would not have horrible pain on the exam table and that maybe, just maybe, Dr. Hope would find she healed. Maybe the outcome would be better than she thought the first time.

It seemed to take a long time before I heard footsteps in the hallway. They both came back in the office, Dr. Hope carried a file folder with her, Charmaine, a Kleenex. Charmaine had tears in her eyes. I kept silent. Stilling my inner voice, wanting to ask if everything went ok in there, somehow feeling that would sound shallow or disingenuous.

Dr. Hope sat near Charmaine and asked her if she would like me to stay in the room as she discussed her findings and thoughts. She was kind, yet serious, her face held no trace of the words she was about to say. Charmaine was herself, she was adamant. She wanted me in the room at all times, whenever possible. That meant today, and every time she might have to come back.

She looked at the Doctor, looked at me, and asked, "I'm not about to die or anything am I? I already think I'm crazy most of the time, so don't go telling me I'm dying ok?" With that, Dr. Hope and I both had to laugh. It was only then that Charmaine laughed as well. I guess she figured if we were both laughing the odds were pretty good that no matter how bad things might be, she was not dying, at least not right that minute.

Dr. Hope reached over and took her hand. She told her that she was a very strong woman. And no, she was not dying, although it looked like someone had tried to kill her in the past based on what she saw. She then told Charmaine she had a lot to talk to her about. She promised her that she was safe, and that she would be honest with her. She asked if Charmaine was ready to hear everything.

Dr. Hope told Charmaine that some of what she was going to tell her was complex; was hard to comprehend, especially if things occurred when she was under stress or had black outs or had amnesia. She wanted to begin with a question. Charmaine was listening intently as Dr. Hope asked the first question. "Charmaine, what is the diagnosis, or the problem that you and Dr. Sherry are working on together? Can you tell me in your own words?"

There was silence in the room as Charmaine looked at the doctor, then looked at me; she looked as if she was asking me what to say, what to do now. I looked back, said nothing and waited... This was a moment that I will always remember. It was the first time Charmaine had to move from wondering about DID, to owning DID to another person. I was not sure that she had completely embraced it, nor truly believed it.

After a long pregnant pause, Charmaine told Dr. Hope that she thought she was crazy so she had come to see me. She had these black outs and now it seems that maybe she was DID. She had these Alters in her who did things she could not remember. She was not yet 100% sure but it beat thinking she was crazy as a loon.

Charmaine went on to tell Dr. Hope that it was like someone else lived inside of her it. They lived their own lives, but she never knew what they did. "Whether you know anything about DID, I don't know, but it is hell."

I watched closely, both her and Dr. Hope, for any reactions in body language or facial expressions; fascinating to watch from the outside, as these two women interacted. I was not used to being privy first hand, to such intimate sharing between a patient and their physician. I felt my body sigh; not me, but my whole body sigh, as Charmaine spoke plain and simple truths to this doctor. Recognizing she had just said what Dr. Hope was really looking for: "I trust your doctor."

It was hard to know how much, if any experience Dr. Hope might have had in caring for a patient with DID. I know she and I had discussed Charmaine's case, but she never indicated that she had actually had a patient change into a second personality in her presence. As I thought about it, we had never explored that situation in depth.

I did know that Dr. Hope never changed her expression as Charmaine spoke to her. Charmaine was plain in her wording and clear in her message. Now the work could begin on a true bio-psycho-social-spiritual level with holistic care. Once again, I was in awe of my client, and was flooded with respect for my friend; the physician and healer who sat before me.

Dr. Hope told Charmaine that there were many things she needed to talk with her about. That she had consulted with me on some things, but not all of them, prior to today's appointment. She went on to discuss the results of her examination. It was not all good news. Charmaine's examination revealed that she had old scarring, vaginally and rectally, as a result of sexual abuse. There was tearing in her tissues which had damaged her severely.

That was probably why she felt so much pain during the examinations. Dr. Hope asked if she experienced pain during intercourse. She looked embarrassed and lowered her head. Barely audible, she responded that she "Never had sex no more. It was unbearable, and dirty. It makes me sick to even think about it." I was surprised that she was so candid.

As Charmaine listened, she became more and more upset. Dr. Hope continued gently. The chart was open in her lap. She paused from time to time and handed Charmaine a Kleenex and offered a hand, or a gentle touch acknowledging that this information was difficult to hear, and she understood that.

Dr. Hope explained the varying degrees of vaginal tears in women and their severity. The recent encounter Charmaine had experienced had resulted in a severe third degree laceration that needed attention. It had opened old wounds in the vagina. There were multiple fistulas that had been there a long time.

Charmaine also had HPV as Dr. Hope went on to talk about her findings. She explained that this virus could have lain dormant for many years as well. I was acutely aware that Charmaine's stress level was being ratcheted up with each additional bit of information. The explanations were complex, even though Dr. Hope broke it down in layman's terms. I watched Charmaine closely.

Dr. Hope asked Charmaine if she was following her; if she had any questions. The room became very quiet. We waited to see if Charmaine had anything to say. She sat silently, her body stiff; nothing; no words no questions. Dr. Hope continued.

"Charmaine, I would like to help you. I suggest that we repair as much of the damage that you have suffered as possible, here in my office. You would not have to go to the hospital. I think we should consider doing this as soon as you would like. I have worked with many women who have had similar damage. I know that you have suffered. I think that we can reduce the pain and correct the problem you have with dryness. Your issues with burning and pain on urination can be easily resolved with medication.

There is a surgical procedure that we can do with conscious sedation to repair the tears and address the fistulas. You can have Dr. Sherry bring you into the office and stay here with you while I do the procedure. Afterwards, you will need to spend a few days recovering at home. Because of the type of sedation we use, you will be completely comfortable during the whole surgery, and most likely will not be able to remember any of it. For a couple of days, we do not want you to do any heavy lifting or very strenuous activity. You will have antibiotics and pain medicine to take while you recover."

Dr. Hope continued; "You do not have to worry about any costs. We have access to a special fund that will cover everything, even the medications. We will repair the fistu..." Before Dr. Hope could finish the sentence Charmaine burst into sobs, she began to cry so hard her body shook, as though someone she loved desperately had just died in front of her. Dr. Hope glanced at me wide eyed. I quickly moved from my chair to Charmaine's side. She was crying, shaking terribly. Her reaction came on so quickly that we were both taken aback by it. It seemed to come from such a deep and mournful place.

She had been sitting so still, so stoic, throughout the presentation. She seemed to have heard all this as if she were a second party. I did not see this sudden meltdown coming. I suppose, given my past experience with Charmaine, I should have anticipated this response.

I placed my arms around Charmaine as she sobbed. Dr. Hope sat near with her hand on Charmaine's arm attempting to provide comfort. Finally, Charmaine quieted a bit, and ultimately sighed. Suddenly, with no warning, she reared back in her chair, tossing me off balance.

My arms were swept from her in one violent movement. She quickly brushed us both away from her. She stood up, re-adjusted herself; wiped her nose with her sleeve. In a loud baritone voice, she tossed her head to the side, one hip thrust forward and pointed a finger at me.

"Fuck THIS Showalter! Now just look what you and your damn doctor have gone and done to her. You damn well know she ain't strong enough to take that, what the hell are you thinkin' here you bunch of bastards. Hell. One more thing I'm goin to have to go and do for her so she don't get hurt again. You know those girls can't handle this kinda stuff. Hell, it won't hurt me, cos' I ain't got a vagina. Bring it on doctor, I can take it. Let's get this shit done right now. Then I'm goin to the range and shoot the hell out a something. Y'all got me hot today! You know better than to piss me off. You Showalter know better than this. I mean damnnnn."

With that he sat down hard in the chair; threw his leg up on the desk. Crossed his foot over it and leaned back, glaring. JR, the Alter. Oh my God, Charmaine has gotten so stressed that JR has stormed out in front of Dr. Hope. She looks absolutely mortified. I realize I am standing with my back to the wall as this tirade is going on. Of course he would be the one to emerge. He protected Charmaine. He would be the one to come out when she a perceived a serious threat. I knew she had heard enough to feel threatened by the conversation. I had seen her breakdown before, but never quite like she did today. Even when she learned about Laylee and the stranger, she had been upset, but was able to maintain some control. JR leaned down and rummaged through Charmaine's bag. He came up with a cigarette and lit it. On his face a look that said, "Just say something to me about it. I dare you!"

Dr. Hope looked at me amazed as I said, "Well hello JR, you do realize you are smoking in a physician's office?" The reply was simply, "Fuck you Showalter, you do realize you have just scared her to death DON'T YOU?"

"Touché JR, you made your point, put the cigarette out." I asked Dr. Hope to please get a cup of water for him to extinguish the cigarette in. She literally dashed from the room to find a cup. I told JR that yes, I realized that Charmaine was afraid, and yes I realized that he was there to protect her, but his service was not needed.

JR seemed to be hearing something. I noticed he had his head tilted to the side and looked angry, but resigned. He muttered out loud, "Yea Desire I hear you." I had to ask. "What is Deseree telling you? What it that you hear other than you are out of line here today?" I was that blunt with my question.

Dr. Hope returned with a specimen cup of water. She tentatively held it out in JR's direction. He laughed at her. "What do ya want me to do with that sweetie? Pee in it or drink it?" I looked sternly at him. With that he dropped the butt into the cup, and made a face.

JR let me know that he would be the one getting fixed because Charmaine was not strong enough. For him it would be a piece of cake. He had no idea what a "fist you lah" was, but how bad could it be. He said "Deseree told him to tone it down, or zip it up. I'll do it, but not because you two deserve it. What the hell is wrong with you all?"

Dr. Hope sat down in her own chair behind the desk. I glanced at her, noticing that she continued to watch JR/Charmaine intently. She was glancing between him and I as if watching a fast paced tennis match. Dear Dr. Hope had a little of that deer in the headlights look in her eyes, but I knew she was taking it all in with rapid speed.

I was standing closer to JR, looming over him. Letting him know that I was not flustered, nor would I be disrespected. I was quite calm when I spoke. I let JR know that we would take good care of Charmaine. I knew he wanted what was best for her. He grinned and said, "Hell Showalter you haven't been around long enough to know what is best for her. I have been the one that had to be there, and I will be there for this. Got it?"

I told him I got it; I understood what he was saying. I would like him to go and have a seat in the waiting room so that Dr. Hope and I could talk about scheduling the date. I would come and get him when we were done.

JR grinned and looked at both Dr. Hope and I and said, "Yup I'll go but let me say this to you first right here and now; I don't really get why ya'll have to have vaginas anyways, but if something is wrong and needs fixing you can just fix it on me not Charmaine cos' she just ain't strong enough for stuff like that."

That was how it was. He said that would be alright with him to wait outside, but if I did not mind since he could not smoke in here he was going to go outside and have a smoke. Just show him the way. I agreed only if he would be sure that Charmaine got back in the office safely. He assured me that he and Deseree would see to that.

I excused myself from Dr. Hope, who I am sure was grateful for the moment alone to gather her thoughts. I walked JR outside to the smoking area, and secured a firm promise that he would return. It helped that I also had the car keys, I was thinking in the back of my head. As I returned upstairs to Dr. Hope, I found her sitting behind her desk with her head in her hands. She looked up at me incredulous and said, "Was that for real? My God I've read about it, heard about it, but I have never seen it, I've never been 100% sure about it until now that is. I have to tell you, it has blown my mind here. How did you know who it was, how to react to this, and how did you stay so calm?"

As I sat down, I began to reassure my dear friend that yes, this was real; she interrupted me with a laugh that startled me. I said to her, "what the hell are you laughing about my friend?" She said "I've never had anyone light a cigarette in my office. And I have never had a patient with such attitude before, NEVER! That was a first; somehow it just made me laugh to think about it."

Here we sat; two professional women as I was about to tell her, yes this was a very real episode of DID. Before I could do it with any real authority, my dear friend gets tickled over the antics of JR the Alter, of Charmaine lighting a cigarette in her office, with a foot on her desk to boot. We must find humor where we can, and I have to tell you, now that I recall it, that was very funny.

Yet, in that split second, where a woman sobbing beyond comfort became the JR who was there to protect, ready to fight while taking one for the team. Ready and to stand in front of anyone and let them know what he thought, could be intimidating to be sure.

JR had said he had no vagina, could not be harmed by the actions of others to that area; JR would stand in, if any repairs were done to protect Charmaine. Dr. Hope was fascinated and a bit shaken by all of this. I was worried about how Charmaine would react knowing an Alter had presented in front of her physician at this critical time.

We were still talking when the buzzer sounded to let us know that JR had returned. We quickly finished our conversation. We had already talked a bit about Dr. Hope and how she would speak to JR as if he were JR when he returned to the room.

I left to go out to the waiting room after getting a cup of water in the hallway. As I approached the lobby, I found a bewildered Charmaine standing there looking around like she was lost. She said, "Doc why in the hell am I out here?" Before I could answer, she asked me if I smelled smoke; not knowing that she was smelling the cigarette smoke on herself from JR. He had probably been chain smoking outside the office prior to Deseree calling him back. Charmaine was confused, trying to figure out how she came to be in the lobby again. I smiled at her, and placed my arm around her shoulder as we headed back to the office. Saying, "JR has been here my dear, I think he thought you needed a hero to rescue you while Dr. Hope was talking." I led her to her chair.

She looked stunned and asked that I sit beside her, which was easy since Dr. Hope had not yet moved from behind her desk where I had left her. There was a silence now, where before it seemed comfort had been established, it now was replaced by an awkward silence. I felt I should be the one to break it and to re-establish where we had left off.

It had all happened so quickly, and at such an important time. I leaned into Charmaine and placed my hand on her wrist. I started by saying that it was great timing in many ways that JR had chosen to come out today after Charmaine had let Dr. Hope know about her diagnosis of DID.

It seemed that JR wanted to be sure that Dr. Hope understood that this is very real. He made a very real appearance at a time when stress was felt to be a threat to Charmaine. I looked at Charmaine and smiled at her with all sincerity, trying to normalize what had happened.

I asked Charmaine what was the last thing she remembered. She looked at Dr. Hope, and then at me. She said, she remembered going into the examination room but that was about all she remembered. Then she thought some more and corrected herself and said she did remember telling the Doctor about what she thought was the reason she came to see me and what we had figured out about Alters and DID, but that was all. She had no memory of anything Dr. Hope had told her about her findings from the examination. No recall of any discussion of surgery.

Dr Hope, I noticed seemed amazed. To Charmaine, she seemed caring, kind, compassionate and totally accepting of what was happening in the moment. I tried to help Charmaine understand that she was in need of surgery, outpatient surgery there in the office. It had been scheduled and that was all we needed to focus on right at that time. I asked her if she thought she could hear more at that time or if it would be better to discuss it later in the week, as she had just gone through this with JR and was obviously feeling rather bewildered by it all.

Charmaine said she felt embarrassed at the moment, but she wanted to know why she had to have anything done. Why she needed to be fixed or anything, since she really didn't understand what we were talking about. She asked if we could try to explain it to her if we had the time. She asked again why she was in the hallway. I tried to explain that part of it again, as I watched her concentrate on her breathing. I spoke, this time she appeared to have absorbed it.

Charmaine did very well and heard what I was saying, staying present. Once she interrupted me to apologize to Dr. Hope for what had obviously just happened with an Alter showing up. She asked Dr. Hope to please not think her crazy and stop allowing her to be a patient of hers now that she has seen this.

She seemed worried about what the doctor would think of her now.

It was then that Dr. Hope let her know that in fact, Charmaine had given her a great gift in those minutes. A first in her career, she had been allowed to meet face to face with DID. She let Charmaine see a side of her professionally that few see; a time where a professional admits that they do not know, what they do not know; yet they are eager to learn. They still want to be all that they are to help their patients. In her way of talking to Charmaine, she was able to calm her fears; to enhance her relationship with her patient, at the same time reaffirming the trust that they had established. This made their relationship stronger in many ways.

We then tried to go over the things that Charmaine had no recall of as I held her hand. I would apply pressure during the parts that seemed scary to her, in order to keep here present, in control and with us. We would pause often for her to do some controlled breathing in order to lower her anxiety while hearing about the 3rd degree lacerations and tears, the fistulas that needed to be repaired. No Alter appeared. Charmaine wept silently, but remained Charmaine.

It was an abbreviated version of what was wrong I noted as Dr. Hope spoke carefully, calmly and looked to me as if to ask was she giving enough information. She was being mindful not to overwhelm Charmaine with too many details. I felt that Charmaine was doing well. The support offered seemed to be working, for that I was grateful. The surgery in the office was scheduled. We did not revisit the costs or lack thereof. That it was already taken care of through generous donors and the fund set up for women who have survived sexual abuse. There seemed to be no need and Charmaine never asked about that part.

The important thing was that she was able this time to hear it; we gave her a fact sheet about it. Something tangible she could look at once she was at home. We made it through the information, including broadening Charmaine's vocabulary to include her word for the day; "vaginismus" which she repeated several times, shaking her head, saying, "Now I have heard it all. I guess this is another diagnosis I have to have."

Dr. Hope did tell me as we left that she would never again think that she has seen it all in her life. She thanked Charmaine for the privilege of providing care. Charmaine, good naturedly, with her quick wit said, "Oh hell, Doctor Hope, hang with me honey, I doubt you've seen anything yet! "

As we walked out together to the parking lot, at one point Charmaine leaned into my shoulder and said, "oh goodness doc, I cannot believe all of this is happening … can you?" I leaned back toward her. We We kept walking until we arrived at her car, two people leaning against each other. No answer was needed, no words could be found anyway.

Why do things like this happen always crosses my mind. Why are good people suffering bad things? Why are little children exposed to horror by adults who exploit and harm them; leaving them to grow up damaged, or never get to grow up at all... questions that boggle the mind and turn stomachs if we dwell on them.

At the car Charmaine told me she was sure I needed to go but she just had to know what JR did and how bad it must have been up there in the office with such a kind doctor. She let me know she was just mortified at the thoughts of it. What the doctor told her was bad enough but to think that she had that happen while she was there, made her want to disappear into the chair.

So we took a few minutes; I gave her a re-cap of what was being talked about before JR's appearance, and that I thought it was because she just could not handle hearing about the damage that was done to her, so JR appeared.

I did tell her that if she were in a good mood and could have seen it she would have probably laughed when JR lit a cigarette in the good doctor's office and propped a foot on her desk though, and Charmaine's eyes popped open and she replied, "Ohhh dear really?" and then she giggled.

After giving her enough to let her know what had happened without making her feel guilty or awful as she had in the past, we parted company. She knew that she was going to see me for our next session soon. She seemed to have had a good working under-standing of what the surgery would do and why it had to be done, and I knew we would be talking more about it when I saw her. Charmaine made it through the appointment. JR let his voice be heard. I had a feeling that we had not heard the end of what he might have to say.

For a brief moment on the drive home that day I wondered if he would have a few choice words for Dr. Hope under conscious sedation or that very effective drug Versed. I quickly dismissed it from my mind as I listened to Patti Labelle sing on a CD. I cleared my head of all the traumas and hurts of the world.

I stay amazed at peoples buoyancy under circumstances like this. This woman never ceased to amaze me. I had to believe that we were making progress along this journey. It seemed that so many things were happening at once, or so quickly that it was difficult at times to keep up. It was a challenge. This experience was filled with opportunities beyond belief both personally and professionally that would walk with me all of my life. I had learned more about a woman's physical anatomy than I had ever known before. I thought I had a great understanding given I was a woman, had served on boards representing women, and had worked with women for years, yet I was still learning.

Charmaine may have been the most time consuming client I ever had, but all the time and the energy was worth it. I spent many hours on weekends and after hours, studying other cases and how they were handled. The one thing I knew was that this was not a normal, textbook case and could not be treated as such. I would be using many out of the box tools that I found to be quite helpful when dealing with clients with abusive histories.

I have always used Alternative methods in my work; even when working with those dealing with chronic pain. I have found that far too often trying to fit the wonders of the mind into a box only limited what we are capable of accomplishing. This was the beauty of dealing with Charmaine. She had been through enough to know that she needed something beyond "standard" treatment. She was willing to work outside the box for her own healing. We are but the guides, sometimes leading, but usually following our clients as they travel their journey and learn what it takes for their own healing.

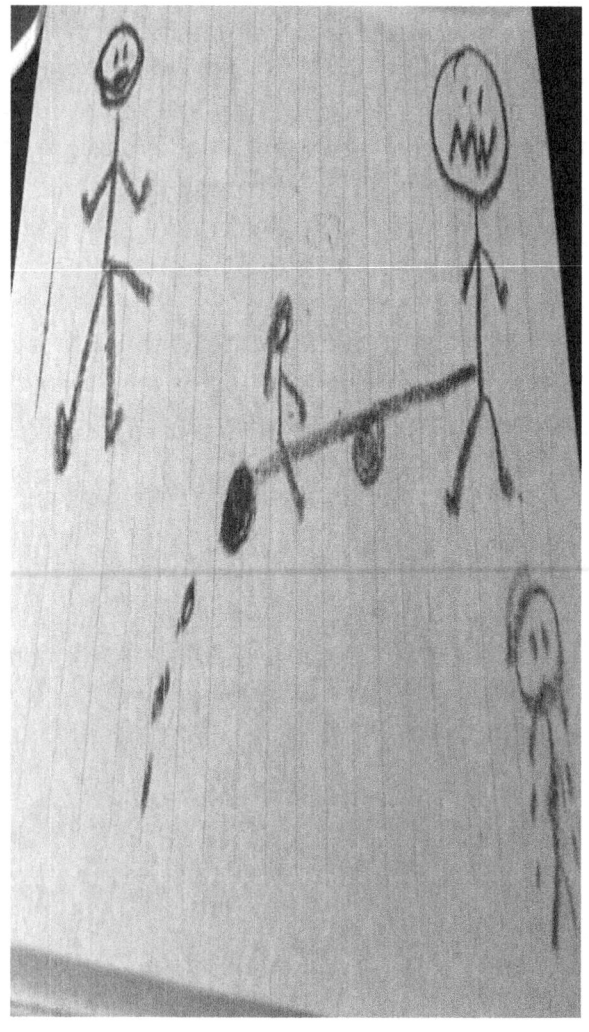

CHAPTER 16 BEFORE THE SURGERY

Charmaine arrived for her session a little early; she seemed to be nervous and had her journal in her hand. I found her sitting on the porch as I was running late from my previous client who left through the back door and only knew Charmaine was there as I noticed her car in the lot when the previous client and I walked out together.

I walked up the ramp on the side of the building and found Charmaine pacing on the front porch and mumbling to herself shaking her head back and forth. I wondered if I had walked in on a private conversation, or just rambling rose like thoughts as she would have expected me to walk out with a client, or perhaps she was just anxious that she was early and I was late.

I had no way of knowing until I spoke to her and at risk of startling her, I stayed my distance and cleared my throat to let her know I was there. She quickly glanced up to see who was around and then laughed nervously and asked me why I was sneaking up on her from the back of the building? I let her know that my last client had left from the back door, so I saw her to her car.

It seemed that she was herself, and had just been pacing, as she told me she was getting worried as she looked at her watch and had not seen anyone come out. Charmaine went on to tell me she had been trying to figure out if she should come in and make a lot of noise in case something was going on and if

she could help in any way as it was making her
wonder if I was safe.

I assured her that all was well, that I just ran
overtime and it sometimes happened that way. She
seemed to be relieved but I could tell that she was
working on a plan to possibly storm the building and
wondered if she might have been calling on JR to call
out the troops on my behalf as I found myself
chuckling with that thought.

I walked in with Charmaine and thanked her for her
concern again. Again I noticed her watch and beaded
bracelet, her hair freshly washed and smelling like
sunshine it seemed. She was in her traditional dark
and simple outfit; today it was dark jeans and a
sweatshirt with no colors, just plain and simple, and
tennis shoes.

As we walked in the office she told me she liked
the corner I had arranged and I looked to try and
figure out what she was talking about. I did not
remember changing anything in that corner since she
was last there. As I looked I saw immediately what she
was talking about. The corner that held the books and
toys and little things on the floor had been moved
around and I guessed it had been done by a client's
child or the cleaning people.

I had not noticed it though and found it interesting
it was Charmaine's first glance and what a keen eye
she had for details. I was going to have to up my
game as Charmaine was extremely observant and I
believe that this was probably due to her childhood of
abuse for abused children must learn to read the signs

and expressions of those around them and read them quickly.

The more I looked at the corner, the more I was also amazed I had not noticed it sooner, and yet she walked in the door and it jumped out at her, making me wonder what Charie might be thinking of the new set up as well.

Charmaine took to her chair and I noticed she seemed to be uncomfortable as she sat down. I asked her if she was ok today as she whimpered as though she were in pain. She sheepishly let me know she had been having some pain and discharge since her visit at the Doctor's office and not feeling really well. She attributed it to the exam and stress of being there, and said it was worse when she sat a lot she thought, but she was alright.

Charmaine had brought her journal, and in it were writings she said she did not quite understand and wanted to talk about them. We got right to work, as she told me about her thoughts, her writings and her discoveries of entries that she said she did not make.

In our conversations, as I held the journal I listened to Charmaine's reactions to the appointment with Dr. Hope, her fears and thoughts of the upcoming surgery. She said she was unable to sleep the night she got home after the appointment and when she would almost get to sleep she kept having nightmares and would wake up in a cold sweat scared to death, and it involved gruesome scenes that were blurry to her, and her heart was racing so hard it felt as though it would come out of her chest.

She said at some point she must have passed out from exhaustion because when she woke the next morning it was almost noon, and the journal was laying on the bed, the covers looked like someone had a wrestling match in the bed and she felt like she had done battle with a cage of monkeys and the monkeys won. I told her it sounded dreadful, and she assured me that it was, as she continued by telling me she had made coffee and taken a shower and then had a seat at the kitchen table to write in her journal.

That was when she discovered some of the writings. The first one looked as though it was written by a child in bold print saying,

"me no go pweeze no me go."

The writing on most of the page was sideways with frown faces and rough little stick bodies drawn that were all out of proportion. The next page said:

"why do you have to have a damn vagina I'll take care of it don't worry"

And it was written fast and furiously and hard to read. It made me think of a mechanic diagnosing a bad engine and all that was lacking were the charges. I was sure this was JR. One page had doodles, lines, angles, drawings that Charmaine said she did not do; no patterns just random "doodles" that one might do when trying to get their minds distracted.

Yet another had the following words:

, *"I hate you, I hate you, Just go somewhere and do not let them find you, you are going to be punished"*

I felt like this was the writing of a young adult, and one who was angry, very angry and blaming. Yet Charmaine again said she had no idea and no recall of writing it. I had seen Charmaine's writing in the past, cursive and printing and none of it looked like any of these pages.

We decided that when she felt that she just passed out from exhaustion and slept, the Alter(s) must have decided to leave some messages while tossing around in the bed, particularly if she had no memory of any of it. I asked Charmaine if she woke in her own clothes, her own hair coloring, had checked to see if her car was where she had parked it and the marker was in place.

We had come up with a plan since the event with Laylee of putting a piece of a 4x4 under the rear tire each evening as a marker of where exactly she parked her car. This would serve as a reminder hopefully to let her know that if it were moved in the mornings an Alter had taken the car and returned it but not necessarily have remembered to place that piece of wood exactly how she had placed it the night before.

Charmaine said that all was good in those departments as she had gotten up in basically the same shape she had gone to bed, with the exception of the pain she was experiencing since Dr. Hope examined her and the condition of her bed. She said that the covers are usually not in such disarray upon first awakening.

The journal was the clue that Alters were at work in the night, and it seemed as though JR, perhaps Charie, and one other who was quite angry had made themselves known. I told her I was sure that it was a result of her visit to the Doctor and the stress that had been triggered regarding the sexual abuse that had been suffered and blocked by Charmaine.

Every once in a while I would notice Charmaine glance over at the things on the floor, as if committing to memory where and what was there; the books, the dolls in the bucket, the stuffed animals and sand tray. I brought her back to task and ask her if she had any questions or thoughts she wanted to share about the upcoming surgery at Dr. Hope's office the next week. She looked at me intently and spoke:

"Doc, I have been thinking about that and wonder, do you think it will make me feel better about myself with this getting done? I mean hearing all that, I feel like this is just more proof that I'm being punished all over again, punished when I was little, punished when I was grown for even having these parts, and now punished cos I let it all happen and am having to go through all this to get everything fixed. Just punished."

And then she cried softly, steady, and enough to bend a heart the way she wept. She was feeling punished by the Creator, by the Alters who she said that she still had trouble accepting as living within her, punished by herself, and by those no longer alive or near to harm her.

She wept and said she felt shame, felt unworthy of the help she was now receiving and the compassion that was being shown to her; the care from two professionals when others had looked and treated her like she was just trash and crazy trash at that.

She had been processing all of this; the sorrow, the horror, the realities of pain; physical emotional spiritual pain that was inflicted upon her by others, yet she was thinking it was her fault. As many do, she somehow twisted abuse into something that says, I am not worthy and it must be my fault thinking.

I had yet to hear her sound angry at the person(s) who had done this to her, yet today she sat in front of me, wept softly at times while saying that she now felt as though this was once again a punishment like the days when her dad would beat her until welps and blood was visible from a belt for daydreaming, or when she was sleeping in front of the television on the floor when he wanted something from her as a child and she did not hear him. In my mind I had to think what kind of sick bastard was her father to treat a precious child in such a way, although I would not say that to her; you can bet I was thinking it.

I then asked Charmaine to stay with me as we worked on something incredibly important along this journey of healing; the realization that none of this was her fault; that she was not being punished now, that she chose to heal and be healed. She was listening hard and taking each word to her heart, in her mind, and I suspect the others were listening behind the doors in the hallway as well. I told Charmaine that I had long suspected she was an adult, who had survived child sexual abuse, that I had also felt she had been abused horrifically beyond the natural scope of child abuse.

I wanted her to know some important things if she would and could listen to them and to know she was safe within the walls and with me. I let her know that most adults who realize that they were abused are also known to have been made to feel like they were to blame for the actions of adults. I also let her know that these same children carried that into their adult lives somehow, filled with shame and fear, afraid to tell anyone for fear they would never be believed or that they would be thought of as bad or judged.

I helped her to see that many are taught to believe that something horrible will happen to those they depend on if they tell, or others will be hurt if they tell. They are brought up in a world of lies and secrets and deprivation of so many things. Seeing her face of relief when she learned that many children when abused disassociate as they cannot bear what is being done to them happens often was rewarding to see and was and even more so when she learned that the dissociation was when they just detach from the pain, the reality, and the emotions and shut down. Many survivors go through this process where the mind distances itself from the experience because it is too much for the psyche to process at the time. It is a protection mechanism that the human mind seems to have to help in cases of extreme trauma and helps them survive what has been done to them.

There is where she made the connection, I could feel it, see it in her eyes, her body, as she listened and leaned in closer to me and I continued. I told her that there are times when this loss of connection with thoughts, memories, feelings, actions or sense of identity, is a coping mechanism. I slowly explained that this may affect aspects of a survivor's functioning and may have been when she developed Alters to keep her alive and also explained that when she had what she thought were blackouts so very long ago or times of daydreaming, it was when Alters were out.

This is brought about by trauma, and can be triggered by flashbacks, by re-visiting old wounds, and when memories begin to surface or in this case the visit to Dr. Hope and hearing what she found upon examination and what needs to be done. I let Charmaine know that when Dr. Hope was talking to her, when she began to discuss what needed to be done, that Charmaine began to sob, to weep with such depth of sorrow like I had not seen, and it was when I came to comfort her that JR appeared in a hot second.

The combination of stress and what appeared to be absolute mourning of the realization that she had been so deeply wounded and perhaps even wounded by those that were held in trust and loved had some how triggered a warning. I told her that in those very words was something that made her feel the need to hid, that caused her to detach and JR needed to step forward as he was her protector.

Then I paused and there was silence between us, and I watched as Charmaine as she just looked at me, looked at her hands, the office, over her shoulder at the sand and the stuffed toys, for a moment I thought I had lost her. I waited... I hoped she would speak, finally she leaned across and took my hand.

"Doc, I think I understand what you said. I have never had anyone explain it like that before. The pain was too much physically and emotionally, so I hid because it was too much for me to handle what they did. Somehow I created parts of me to be the warriors or to stand for me when I was hurting too much, only I didn't know it. I have felt so ashamed. I understand that I did not do the abuse to me and I should not feel ashamed. I will have to keep telling myself that because I was made to feel so long like it was my entire fault. These are MY HANDS, this is me, I am me right now right? I mean me Charmaine, I am me right? Did I stay me while we were talking here or go anywhere Doc?"

I smiled at her and squeezed her hand. Yes she was herself, she had been right there, but she sure had been looking at the toy corner a lot while I was talking. She said she had not been aware of that, but she felt she had heard all I had been saying.

She was still scared to death about the surgery and hoped that Dr. Hope would give her something for her nerves before she got there to calm her down. She wondered if she should apologize before going in, case something should happen that she wouldn't know about. She expressed concern about being alone after the procedure and asked if I thought it alright if she call Dr. Hope and ask her about that. I told her that it might be a good idea to call Dr. Hope. I would pick her up for her appointment as scheduled.

Prior to our ending that session, I asked Charmaine if she minded if we took her on a guided imagery before ending for the day. She said that she was hoping for that as it always relaxed her. This had been a hard session. Once she had said that she likened guided imagery to anti-acids for the soul.

"Ok Charmaine, I want you to hold this tablet on your lap, (11x14 art pad). In your hand is a magical wand (large purple marker with a tassel on the end). Please close your eyes now. You have just walked on the beach with the warm sun on your face... you hear the ocean rushing to greet you. You want to put your feet in the wet sand and feel the water as it gently rushes up to caress your feet as you feel the refreshing sand and water, use your magic wand to draw this on the paper on your lap now....your pad has just turned into a sandy beach. As you hear the water, use your wand to draw the motion, feel your breath, the air, the sand. Take a deep breath and slowly blow it out when you exhale... exhale now as the water is touching your feet..."

I watched as Charmaine took a deep breath with her eyes closed, her shoulders relaxed in front of me. I noticed her feet move as if having just felt water on them. Her hand began to move. Swirls were being drawn that looked like waves. She slowly drew as she breathed in and exhaled, slowly blowing it out. The pen moved around the page creating circles, and soft flowing marks, as though she were there with the water and the breeze in her mind's eye. I spoke softly and guided her to a peaceful place as her hand guided her magical wand.

As our imagery ended, Charmaine became still, her breathing slow and steady. Without opening her eyes she whispered, "That was so wonderful. I could even taste the salt of the ocean." I gently took the pad she laid on her lap but left the magic wand in her hand and sat quietly until she was ready to rejoin me. It only took a minute or two before she opened her eyes.

She looked at the pen and smiled, saying what a beautiful "wand" this is. I told her it was hers to keep. She might want to journal with it, or use it to recall the feeling of relaxation it evoked. We stood to walk out into the sunshine. Our session had been long, arduous and productive. It was good that we ended it in such a peaceful way.

As we got to the door Charmaine paused, with a tired smile, she said, "Doc, do you think sometime when I'm here I can play in that sand thing there, or you can tell me what you do with it with other people? I think it's fascinating."

I assured her that I would. As we walked outside I told her that Charie had really enjoyed the sand tray when she was here. That made Charmaine laugh, saying she wished she had been there to enjoy that too. I watched as she walked casually to her car. She had worked hard, had absorbed much and was moving full steam ahead along her journey.

I had paperwork to do. I made a note to bring the sand tray to the desk for our next session. Many a great story has been shared with the use of the sand tray. Whatever works. It was time to wrap it up for the day. I found myself looking at the toy corner again before finishing my case notes and packing them away, making a mental note to double check my calendar. It was amazing to me that I had not noticed the changes that seemed to jump out at Charmaine as soon as she walked in for her session; even with all she had on her mind.

Note to self; be more aware of what is in your office.

I wrote that note on a sticky pad. I laughed at myself. I had written the date of surgery on my calendar, had put it in my phone, with a reminder the day before as well. There was no way I was going to overlook that appointment.

Charmaine's chart had gotten rather heavy. I might soon need a wheelbarrow to move it from the file cabinet to my desk. I was submitting claims to her insurance company as I had promised, but it was not lost on me the number of visits that I would be writing Off as pro Bono on next year's taxes. Some work you have to do, regardless of payment. I had one other client who at the same time who had suffered a tremendous loss, secondary to prescription drugs which had claimed the life of her son. She too needed help that would otherwise not be available.

As I reflected back on the number of lives I had walked journeys with, I found myself humbled all over again, and counting my blessings. I thought about the fragility of this complex, beautiful thing we call life, in all its fragile moments.

I had to get this paperwork completed. It was one of those days that had turned to night as I sat alone in my office, lost in thought. I realized I had been there longer than I anticipated, pen still in hand, yet had written little. Some days seemed to just end up that way.

Charmaine's Journal

I feel as if the wind is knocked out of me. I am still processing what Dr. Hope told me. Now, not only do I feel like I have worms inside me, I feel like I have the plague. What is that HPV stuff anyway? It comes from sex so it must be horrible.

I still hear the bar sounds in my head. I wish it would go away. It seems worse right now. Why are they writing they hate me? If they are supposed to be part of me why do they hate me? I have not done anything to them. I just cannot tell Doc about the cuts on my arms and legs. I know I am not doing that. I just know it. I KNOW IT. Maybe if I scream they will hear me.

Hello? Anyone there? Dam I sound like a lunatic. Can I come sit at the table with you? I understand better what Doc said to me. I saw a commercial for one of the satellite companies and it had a person's head and on the front was their smiling face and the back was cut away and inside was like a living room with a TV in the head. Wonder if that is how I look inside?

I like Dr. Hope. She is kind like Doc. I do not think I could handle anyone being cruel to me or telling me I am not trying when I am working myself to death trying to get answers.

I was so relieved to hear that this was not genetic. I worried that my kids would get it or their kids. And now I know they won't. Doc would laugh at me if she knew I had literally tied my hand to the bed to make sure I did not leave. I am so afraid I will end up in bars again or at parties in that old house down the dirt road. I tried to show someone where that house was but could not recognize it in the day time. And I did not think they believed me at all. The parties there were horrible. I have found myself there more than once but not since Laylee has been locked down. I have tried to find that house so many times to prove I was not crazy or lying but in the day time, it never looks the same.

Doc would laugh if she knew I actually had my oldest son look in my ear to see if he saw anything. He thought he was looking for infection. I was looking for Alters. And now I have to figure out if I have already eaten before as when the boys are gone, I find dirty dishes and the only one here is me. And of course the Alters.

So, now I look for dirty dishes before I fix food. I never was a big eater but if this keeps up, I could weigh 200 pounds. Luckily, none of my clothes feel tighter. I could save a lot of money if my hair quit changing colors and styles. I like my dark hair. I am just thankful that none of them cuts my hair. They just shove it in hats or roll it up in buns or put it in pigtails.

I feel like I want to cry tonight. I cannot explain it. I want my cubby and to just lay in the quiet. The kids are gone on a camping trip with the church group. Maybe I can lay around in my jammies and do nothing. Only I am afraid to sleep for fear what one of THEM will do.

It is strange. I hear a soft voice at times telling me "it is ok honey. It is ok" maybe it is an Alter and I just am starting to hear them .I still get the willies...sorry guys if you hear me...but it feels like I got parasites or something.

CHAPTER 17 FLY IN THE BUTTER

Two days before I was to see Charmaine for her appointment with Dr. Hope I received a phone call at six o'clock in the morning. It was Dr. Hope calling on her way to an airport for a family emergency. I could tell by her breath that she was walking and talking at the same time. She told me she was trying to get to me before boarding the plane. She wanted to call me personally, rather than have the office call. I could tell the news would not be good. For my phone to ring at that early hour, never indicated pleasant news; when I heard the word "airport," that confirmed it. A sense of dread immediately overcame me.

It was the beginning of a new week, Dr. Hope kept a busy schedule. I could not recall her mentioning any out of town conference she was to attend prior to Charmaine's appointment. I immediately became concerned for my friend. I detected stress in her usually calm voice as she continued to speak. She told me that Charmaine's procedure would have to be delayed. She was not sure at this point when she would be returning. She had a family emergency. Once she got back she would have to catch up before being able to attend to this procedure with Charmaine.

She expected it could be as much as three weeks on an outside guess. She wanted to let me know. She felt it best that I be the one to tell Charmaine. I agreed. We decided it best that I have Charmaine come into the office to give her the news rather than have her receive a call from a stranger on Dr. Hope's behalf. That would probably not be well received. Dr. Hope stressed that she would reschedule Charmaine just as soon as possible. The delay was unexpected. She asked that I let Charmaine know how sorry she was to postpone her procedure.

As she was approaching security, she told me she had to get off the line, but that she might need to talk with me during her trip, on a personal level, she'd be in touch. I wanted to express my concern for her, but time did not allow for that. We ended the call with my telling her to take care, reminding her I was always available should I be needed.

As I hung up the phone I realized that I was dreading talking to Charmaine. I hated to tell her about this delay. A deep sense of foreboding came over me. I could not pinpoint why. Charmaine would be both happy and disappointed in the change of plans. She wanted to get it over with, but was dreading it at the same time. It may have been that we had worked so hard to prepare her. I shook it off. I'd just have to explain the situation. I was worried too about Dr. Hope.

Charmaine had finally agreed to treatment with the understanding that it was probably going to be painful. It required that she trust Dr. Hope to care for her physically, and to be there for her. Trust was not easy for Charmaine. I knew that many had lied, had used and abused her trust for many years. I worried that she would take this news badly. She had gone through so much to accept its necessity in healing her physically and emotionally.

The next step involved me calling her to arrange for her to come in; or should I ask to go to her? I had to think this through. I decided that I would have her come to the office and see me; it would normalize the news I was going to share with her rather than make it a momentous occasion that she would interpret as so significant that I had made a special home visit spontaneously.

I called her mid-morning. She was in the middle of cleaning her house. I asked if she had some free time to come in and see me late afternoon for a session. She became wary and asked if there was something wrong, if I had discovered something in our puzzle. I laughed, telling her she was always the detective. The answer was yes and no, yes I had some things to talk with her about, and no, there was nothing wrong.

I think she halfway believed me. She laughed saying she was "fixing to call you today Doc cos' I found some stuff under my table this morning and I did not put it there, so I was going to see if I could see you maybe tomorrow. Today is ok with me though. I can come around 4:30 if that will work for you." I told her that would work just fine, and to bring her findings with her. We would figure it out when she got to me.

Interesting, I was thinking as I hung up, wondering what she had "found." Who had emerged in the night as we neared the day if her procedure. I made a note for myself, dated it, and started my day not giving any more thought to it at that time. Life is like that; one often has to multi-task, do what is needed, when it is needed.

The day flew by. Before I realized it, the afternoon was staring me in the face. I had seen more clients than usual and felt my energy waning. I had gone for a walk, spent some time admiring the flowers out front before returning to my office. Somehow it was past our appointed time.

It was not like Charmaine to be late. I was about to call her when I heard the car pull in. Perhaps she had gotten caught in traffic was my thought. I made sure I had the sketch out, and all my other paperwork put away.

I shook my head in amazement once again as I realized it was not going to be Charmaine who popped in the door this time. I was hearing that cute little voice of a happy Charie coming down the hall singing, ♫ ♫ "oh me off to sthee S=th to pway with S-th me goo" ♫ ♫. As I looked up, Charie/Charmaine sprang through the door as happy as could be. She flopped down in the corner clapping her hands in excitement. She looked up at me with a smile and said, "me isth here agin S'thh, to pway wif ou, isnth that wunnerful for usth s-th?"

Coming around the desk, I said, "Well, hello to you Charie." She lifted her arms indicating she wanted a hug. "Me wan hugs S=th me misseded ou, wets pway otay?" I sat in the floor, leaned over and found myself hugging Charie who was out and playing on a day that I had planned to discuss the postponement of surgery.

Charie leaned back smiling. Bart had let her out of the car again to play, because she had been very good. She had been telling him about the new "stuff" in the corner of the office.

She let me know that she was a "very good girl." Waiting until the car stopped and the door was open, she was so excited she was afraid she would "pee her pants." I watched as she suddenly cocked her head a bit and then said, "otay Bart, me det it and gib to her, otay."

As I watched, Charie reached into her pocket and brought out a piece of folded paper telling me that Bart said to give it to me. She turned her back to me and began pulling the dolls out of the Bucket again as I looked at the piece of paper.

Just as I unfolded the paper to look at it; Charie turned and threw a handful of dolls at me, hitting the paper, knocking it out of my hands. "S-th, me tole ou dey bad bad BAD!!!... Ou now frow dem way. Dey is bad. Take outta butket now me mean it tooo." Oh my, little Charie was pissed. There was no mistaking the temper tantrum. She scrunched her face for battle. "Dey hurt ou with sticks in dey pants. Me tole ou dat. Ou no bweave me s=th? Me ole u dey baddd. No like, no like, no like. Make em go way NOWW..." With a beet red face, she looked at me and said "Why ou no bweave me sth?" Big ole crocodile tears rolled down her face. My heart hurt.

I told Charie I was sorry that I had not made them go away before. I stood up right then and there. I put them all in a pile on the floor and with all my might; I crushed them with my feet. I stomped and stomped on them, one at a time as she watched with big eyes. Then I got the trash can and one by one put them in there saying "They will not hurt you or anyone else Charie, never ever again honey, See, I am destroying them right now." Charie watched intently as I put them all in the trash. I took them outside the door of the office and returned to sit beside her. "They cannot hurt you anymore honey, they are gone from the bucket and gone from here now." Charie looked wide-eyed at me. She leaned into me, crying softly; saying "S-th ouu killeded dem and now dey is gone. No hurt me no more wight? No more eber not no eber hurt.. me wuv ouu s-th..me wuv ouu."

She then looked at the remaining dolls and said, "Ou isth safe now S-th and me make ou safe now." She returned the girl dolls to the bucket. I watched as Charie played now in the sand with her fingers and a little matchbox car she found. I could not remember seeing the car before and had to wonder where and how it gotten there. Maybe a gift from spirit, one that would let her drive away to a better childlike place, now that the bad men were gone and no longer a threat. I told her a story. About angels that surrounded her. They sent a little car for her to drive. They wanted her to feel safe, and have fun. She smiled, enjoying the idea of a gift from her angels.

All of a sudden, Charie sat straight up and looked at me; saying nothing for a moment, then began to pat her chest. I wondered what in the world was going on now. I said nothing, but only watched as she looked more and more perplexed. She pulled her top away from her neck and began to peer down toward her chest. She looked down her top, and then up at me; down at her chest and then back up at me. I could not figure out if she had discovered a bug on her, if she had an itch, or what in the hell she was doing, but I sat silently and just watched her.

This went on and on. Imagine, you have a grown woman who is now three sitting with her little cute ways; obsessed with her shirt and what lay beneath it, an expression of wonder on her face. I just could not imagine. On probably the fourth time, I thought that I heard the elastic neck band snap as it went back against her neck as she exclaimed, "S-TH... tharmaine weft her boobies in me thirt. Do ou wanna thee em? Ohhhh no s-th!!! her weft her boobies in me thirt wook!" I felt my jaw drop. I said in a choked voice, "what did you say baby?"

Acting like she was talking to someone hard of hearing, Charie said very slowly in a loud voice "ME THAID HER WEFT HER BOOBIES IN ME THIRT. S-TH ISNT OUUU WISTENING TO ME? WOOK HER WEFT EM IN ME THIRT." She was preparing to pull the neckline away from her chest once again to show me what Charmaine had done. She was aghast in this new discovery. She was none too pleased that Charmaine would leave her breasts in little Charie's shirt. How she happened to make that discovery, in that moment, is still beyond me.

I reached over and took her hand. I told her it was all ok, not to worry about it. I said Charmaine had trusted her to keep her boobies safe for her a while. I tried to let her know that she was being handed something like a treasure; her shirt was the treasure box, and only she had the key. Talk about some fast thinking.

I went on to tell her that the person with the key had to guard it very carefully and never ever let anyone else in the box, never let anyone else have the key. Meanwhile inside I am laughing to myself; wondering about the magical mind of Charie and her discoveries; yet another first for me. Flying by the seat of my pants on this one, figuring at least she did not poop on the porch. We would get through this.

As I spoke of the treasure box and the key, she was absorbed in the little story I was creating. She still held the little car in her hand. I could hear her little mind thinking *"otay me keep da tweasure box, now wet me drive me car."*

Without skipping a beat she again told me she loved me. She leaned against me as I heard her say "I know me haf to go. Tan me hug her firth? Otay Des." Then she looked at me and said, "Des say me haft go now and no can take dat car efer. Me wuv ou. Me tell u sethret firth tho." Charie leaned into my ear and quickly, in a childlike way said, "me wuv u S=th and me keep tharmaine boobies thafe in me thirt eve if me change thirt me hide dis one otay? Our sethret"

I hugged Charie tight and told her yes it would be our secret; oh how I loved this little one. I believe Charie is the child Charmaine never got to be. It brings a tear to my eye that Charmaine endured so much; she never got to be Charie, but somehow I felt like Charie was going to make up for it now. I stood up and watched Charie go to the door. As she turned back, she waved, humming as she walked out.

It was then that I laughed. I looked out the window to see if I could see Charmaine's car. I thought, now what am I to do? Our time was spent on the floor with Charie and Charmaine still did not know about her appointment being postponed. It occurred to me I had not heard the door open or close; I had not heard a car start. Oh God, I felt my pulse quicken.

I had been sure to get the trash can out of sight before Charie left, I had said good-bye, had seen her leave. Where was she? I could not see the car from the office window. Ok, maybe I just didn't hear her leave... doubtful, after all I was not laughing that hard.

I quietly walked out of my office. There, sitting in the lobby, was Charmaine, magazine in hand, as if she were any client on any given day, waiting. She looked up when she saw me and said, "Good afternoon Dr. Showalter, are you ready for me?" Her voice was so quiet that I could barely hear her. Her posture perfect, she sat erect in her chair. There was a slight tilt to her head that I had not seen before. When she stood, I realized I had no idea who I was looking at, but I knew I was not seeing Charmaine.

I asked her to please join me in my office. I took a couple of steps back and allowed her to walk in first; my head was spinning. She sat in the chair that I usually sit in when meeting with Charmaine. I sat in the one next to it, beside her.

She said quietly, "Excuse me." She stood and moved the chair so that we were facing each other directly, knee to knee, face to face.

I was in for another first, meeting a new Alter. She began by apologizing for her appearance, saying she would never be seen out in public dressed like she was now, so please pardon her appearance, but she felt it important that she meet with me.

I suppose she saw from my expression that I had no idea who I was talking to. Before I could even ask, she offered, saying, ever so quietly "Dr Showalter, I am Deseree; I know you have heard of me. I want you to rest assured I have done everything to quarantine Laylee, hopefully we will not suffer that kind of embarrassment anymore. I apologize for the trouble she put you through. Little Charie just wanted to play today. I fear that she does not know yet how to talk when she is out and about. I can assure you she meant no harm today, she is but a child you know. Charmaine is another story. We have to protect her at all costs you understand."

I was sitting in front of Deseree, AKA Charmaine, who had felt such an urgency to bring me up to date that she had come out. I had to strain to hear her soft voice. She seemed to be the perfect matriarch. I sat in awe listening to her talk, trying hard to not miss a single word that she was saying. I was trying to memorize the inflection in her voice, her mannerisms.

She was patient and kind beyond words, yet she was firm. She did not seem to grow tired of me asking her to repeat what she had just said. She was nothing like Charmaine. She spoke with wisdom, frequently gesturing with her hands.

She continued, "Dr. Showalter, I also want to tell you that JR is hard to control. His mouth and his antics I can usually manage, but he does have his moments. When you were in the Doctor's office, I could not get him to calm down. He is just that loyal to Charmaine, and feels tremendous guilt that he has not always been able to protect her.

He would die for her. He is always ready to fight like a soldier if anyone tries to harm her; that is if he can get out of his room in time. There are times now dear, that he just explodes out; and as you saw. It can happen so harshly that there is no containing him at all. I am glad you were not hurt when he blew out of Charmaine. I know you were thrown against the wall. You were not harmed were you?"

Deseree was so prim, so proper, so very genuine. She was waiting for my reply. I assured her I was not harmed by JR. No one was trying to do harm to Charmaine, but rather we were trying to help her heal from the physical traumas she had seemingly suffered through the years. Deseree nodded her head from time to time as I spoke.

I asked Deseree if I might be able to show her something while she was there with me. She indicated she knew what I wanted to show her; it was the sketch. Why would I think she had not seen it before? Surely I knew that she had been watching over Charie, Charmaine and even JR as I thought about it later. As she looked at it, she made a face that I interpreted as not approving the likeness when it came to the sketch of her. She shook her head, saying it looked quite different now that she was holding it in her own hands. She carefully laid it back on the corner of the desk and refolded her hands in her lap. She told me that yes, she did recognize everyone there. Charie had correctly identified who each person was for the most part on that sketch.

Deseree looked deeply into my eyes and said that she wanted to try to explain a few things before she left. She told me Tina did the drawing. The sketches were meant to reassure and educate me as well. She meant no disrespect regarding my abilities, nor to my profession. She felt it was important for me to realize that she knew each one, longer and better than I: these people that I called Alters.

Deseree let me know that Bart, the gatekeeper always tries to stand sentry in the hallway. He has his back to the rooms, watching Charmaine. He is a guard of sorts (if I could understand that) she emphasized. She again reassured me that Laylee had been "locked down" due to her bad behaviors, but often she played to his soft side and enlisted Bart to help her sneak out. Deseree felt reasonably certain that she had finally put the "kibosh" on that.

She went on to tell me that at times an "Alter" would just "burst" out, particularly under stress. At those times no one could do a thing about it; it just happened in the wink of an eye. That is what she hoped to help me to understand, although she knew that I had already seen it first hand with that foul mouth JR. She said that he was a work in process. Although he meant well, he just loved to get a rise out of people. She then praised me for my ability to not let my "feathers get ruffled by his rough ways and brusque manners."

Deseree finally got to the meat of her message with a warning that she felt I needed. I listened, watching intently. She reached for the sketch once again. She pointed to one of the faces and said these haunting words: "Dr. Showalter, you need to beware of this one. That is Zoe. As I have told you, I am working very diligently to rein everyone in now, especially with all that Charmaine has learned. I realize that there is much more that she will eventually come to know, but sometimes they just burst out. It can be very disconcerting."

She continued after a brief pause, "Zoe hates Charmaine, and has been known to cut her in the past. She has cut her badly. I am not sure if she has shown you the scars, or if you have seen them as she mostly wears long sleeves, but you must be aware of Zoe now that Charmaine is suffering so much stress.

I was working and Bart was on guard, with high alert now to keep everyone in their rooms as much as we possibly can. It was difficult for me to bake, to keep the house up, to comfort Charmaine with all that I have to do. Now I find myself concerned for your safety as well. Do you understand me Dr. Showalter?"

Oh mercy, I was sitting in the presence of the matriarch of the Alters and she has just told me one of them can harm Charmaine under duress. I was quick to let Deseree know that yes, I understood her. I valued her time and appreciated her visit. I also asked her that if I wanted to talk with her, would it be possible to call her out, asking Charmaine's permission in future visits, now that we had met.

She seemed amused by the question. I swear I saw her eyes twinkle as she indicated that she was always there. She was always watching over Charmaine. I took that as a yes, and felt hopeful, yet a bit unsettled on hearing that there were episodes of prior cutting.

I tried to go back in my mind, to look for visible scars on Charmaine. As we talked, I thought I found that particular file in my mind's eye. I put it aside to revisit after my talk with Deseree. It was as though she read my mind. She then said to me, "Dr. Showalter, I know you have seen scars; I well can remember you wanting to ask about them. I am certain you are taking good care of Charmaine; as most of us have tried to over the years. She has never known as much about her life as she has learned since she started talking to you, so now it is all going to come out. The truth always does you know..."

With that, Deseree stood up and extended her hand, saying she had taken up too much of my time. She recognized that I was a busy woman. There was a formality, yet a special kindness from this woman who seemed to be a very motherly protector of her nest of characters.

I shook her hand and escorted her to the door. I held it open as she walked outside. I followed her onto the porch and again expressed my appreciation for her visit. I did not wait to watch her go to her car, but rather I walked back to my office and dropped into my chair. I just sat there.

I heard an engine turn over, the car leaving as I sat. I had just been educated on DID by an authority. She had shown me great respect, and provided me with many new insights as she spoke lovingly to a large degree about the many Alters of Charmaine. She was there to educate me, to reassure me, and to warn me about Zoe, the Alter known to cut and who hated Charmaine.

I had been with two Alters on one afternoon while I was supposed to be talking to Charmaine about the postponement of her appointment with Dr. Hope. My phone call must have triggered some stressors for her. I had almost forgotten about the note Charie had given me. Oh damn, where did I put it? I looked all around the desk. I could not find it anywhere. I looked in her file, under the sketch, and even in the trash can with the dolls that I had all but destroyed. I even searched the bathroom. I caught a glimpse of myself in the mirror and was startled to see myself. God, had I aged that much today? My hair looked like I had stuck my finger in an electric socket. My face was drawn and tired. I looked gray.

It had been one helluva day in the life of the ole' therapist and play pal of Charie I muttered to myself; still wondering where in the hell I had put the note she had handed to me. I was ready to go home. As I walked toward the car, I reached in my pocket for my car keys. Low and behold, I discovered the note. I must have jammed it in my pocket while killing the bad boy dolls for Charie and just forgotten.

I came back to the porch and sat down on the steps. I looked at the note; on it I saw the same stick figures again with what looked like sticks shooting out from between their legs. I again interpreted it as a Charie drawing of the bad dolls, with the sticks in their pants. Then I saw the words written in anger across the top of the page in bold pencil, traced over again and again: "*I HATE YOU I HATE YOU I HATE YOU DIE DIE DIE.*" Now that was some kind of anger.

I sat staring at the writing. Over and over, written boldly, with scratches where the stick figures had been on the paper drawn by a child. The writing was more like that of an older child, or a young adult; an angry one at that. I stood up, and then glanced at the back of the paper. I saw where I had missed two things on the back. In different writing, on two lines, were what appeared to be "Get over it ok" and "Ok folks you are getting out of hand." It looked like they were penned by separate hands; one statement written beneath the other. The "I Hate You" writing concerns me the most for Charmaine's sake. I now fear she might very well be in danger at the hands of Zoe. I need to talk to Charmaine about this at some point, but first to Deseree.

Note to self-ask Deseree who is writing these. None of them looked like they had been written by Charmaine. As I was walking up the steps, back to my office, I heard the phone ringing. Even the line "why are you writing in my book" does not match Charmaine. Charmaine has distinctive handwriting. It is the reason we do not display copies of her actual handwriting in the journal like we do the Alters' writing.

JR in his baseball cap and that finger up like he does when he is very animated. DRSES

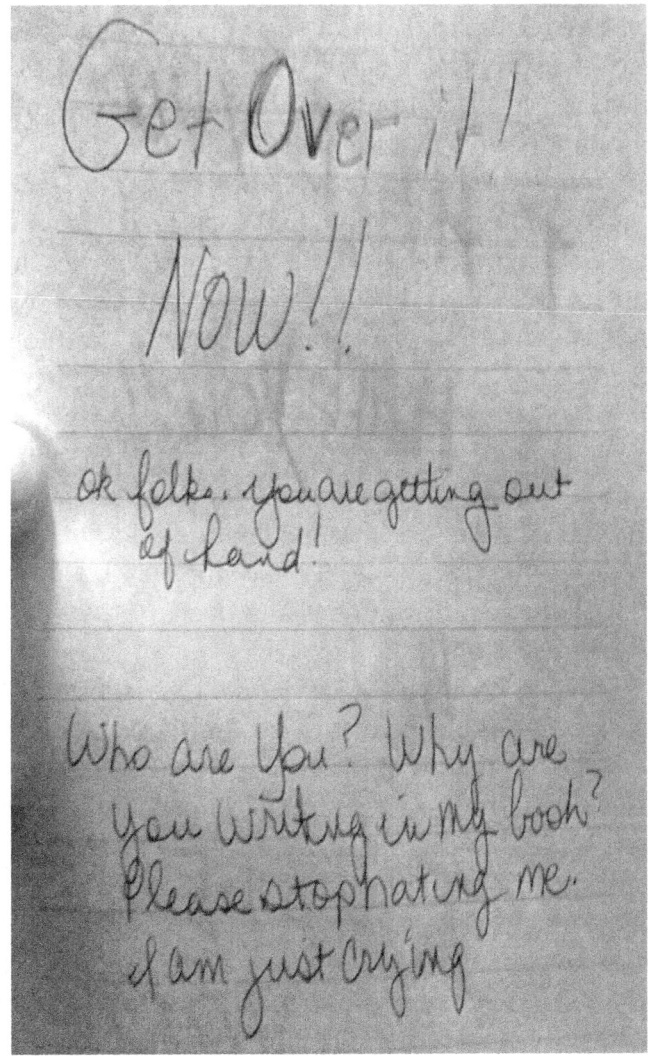

I picked up the phone; it went dead. I was a ring or two late getting to it. I looked to see who had called; Charmaine's number came up on the caller ID. I hit redial and heard a tearful voice on the other end of the phone, "Oh Doc I am so sorry I missed my damn appointment with you today. I am so sorry. I guess I must have laid down for a nap. I just woke up and feel like I've been running a 10K marathon. I'm so tired, can I come tomorrow? Please forgive me, you know it is not like me to miss an appointment, so I wanted to see you."

I tried to get a sentence in but she continued babbling apologies. She was very upset. She sounded winded. I glanced at my watch, thinking she had only been back home less than 45 minutes by now. She had no earthly idea that she had not only been here, but that she had driven here and back. Her Alters had taken her session.

I finally told her we would re-schedule for tomorrow. I asked her to place the wood under the tire as we had done in the past; to be aware she was under stress now. I wanted to remind her that the Alters tended to come out when she was under stress. We did not need another episode with Laylee.

Charmaine was listening, but I could tell she was not in the mood to talk about Alters. She was filled with remorse over missing an appointment and wasting my time. Little did she know. I was brief and let her know we would talk about it in tomorrow's session, but I was running late and had to go. I was unable to continue the conversation at that time. As much as I wanted to tell her the reality that she had been in my office, sat on the floor; we had destroyed the dolls, and lastly, the Matriarch Deseree had warned me about Zoe. That was just too much to talk about after such a long day, and way too much to discuss by phone.

She seemed a bit surprised that I was ending our conversation so quickly. I could tell that she was perhaps a bit hurt by my telling her I had to cut it short. It had been a long day. It was one of those times when working with people that one has to remember the importance of "self-care and boundaries" in order to continue to do good work for the long haul. I was spent.

It could all wait until the next time we were together. I needed to restore myself from a day that was too long and complicated to continue at full throttle any longer. We set our appointment for 3:30 the next afternoon, with me suggesting that Charmaine work on breath exercises one hour before she come to see me; thinking it would ground her, that she would come as herself and that we could get through the entire session with no interruptions.

Yes, there was a fly in the butter from the beginning to the end of that day so long ago... and it would ruin the popcorn if we did not properly attend to it. The story continued to unfold. The puzzle of what life is like with DID grew daily.

Chapter 18 THE NEXT DAY

I heard the door open, and found myself holding my breath. I sensed someone coming down the hall. I waited near my desk, and saw what looked like Deseree; coming through the door, a bottled up expression on her face. She looked like she wanted to tell me something right away.   I looked at her with anticipation. I hear "Hi Doc, how are ya?"

I tried not to look surprised. Her casual greeting did not match her facial expression. I recognized the voice (I thought) to be Charmaine, but not the clothes. She moved to our chairs. Then looked at me a bit odd and asked why the chairs were positioned as they were. She went about moving them into their regular places. It was then that I knew for sure that I was in the presence of Charmaine, yet she seemed unaware of how she was dressed. I quietly put my phone on record. I told her I was happy to see her and had some news to share with her. She sat down. She seemed happy to be here, but a bit anxious as well.

I asked how she was doing and was not surprised to hear that she had been having difficulty sleeping. She reported feelings of being "out of sorts" the last couple of days, but could not "put her finger on why." I decided there was no time like the present to explain to her that the surgery had been delayed. I wanted her to know that I needed her to work hard today to stay with me. I understood that the postponement would be stressful, but we needed to talk.

Her immediate reaction was fear that I was going to stop seeing her for some reason. She was concerned that I was ill or leaving to go somewhere. I assured her that neither was the case. I asked her to please focus solely on our discussion.

I began by telling her that this was not the first time I have attempted to share this news with her. It seemed that the stress or worry had caused several Alters to come to the office rather than her yesterday. We had some interesting pieces to add to the puzzle. She seemed astounded by that revelation and became tenser.

I immediately regretted sharing that bit of news. I feared I had put the cart before the horse even as the words came out of my mouth. Knowing I had just created more tension; I thought I should have saved it until the end of the session.

So I asked her to hold that thought in the back of her mind for now. We went into a breathing exercise in order to relax her. I wanted to change the rhythm of the neurotransmitters, while desire calmed the others down, preventing them from bursting out past Bart. That was my hope. It seemed to work for the moment. For that I felt extremely grateful. I needed to talk to Charmaine and not an Alter right now.

Note to self; do not do that again.

Charmaine asked if what I had to say was a "bad thing." I responded, not at all, it was just a change in plans. I then went on to tell her that Dr. Hope had to go out of town for personal business and she had to postpone the upcoming surgery. I went on to say that both Dr. Hope and I recognized that she had worked hard to accept the surgery. The date was upon us, and we knew that she would be disappointed by this change in plans. It simply could not be avoided. Dr. Hope had an emergency.

Charmaine looked at me, and then laughed; saying, "Well hell Doc, you had me scared to death, and is that all? I mean, with all we are dealing with, a change in the date of that operation is the least of my troubles, don't ya think?" With that she laughed and shook her head. I saw relief on her face. The energy in the room shifted. She did not tense up, or feel upset by this change in plans. She was almost "giddy" knowing that it was only a change of dates. She was not being abandoned, nor diagnosed with yet another thing wrong with her.

We both laughed. I realized I was infected by her relief and her laughter. I watched look down to see her watch; and then it happened; she noticed the pearls. The laughter stopped as quickly as it started. She looked at me and said, "Whose are these, and where in the world did they come from Doc?"

Oh my, Charmaine just now sees something that she has had on since our hello. More to come, I thought. She took a quick survey of her attire. She was suddenly aware of the smock/dress and shoes she wore. She looked at both, then looked at me with a very pained expression. "What in the world?" she exclaimed. I reached over and took her hand. I said that Deseree must have been out. Charmaine wanted to return home and change clothes, but I really needed her to stay here. We had work to do. This was no time to make a fashion statement.

Charmaine began to cry. "Oh no Doc, not again, not again... look at me." She then excused herself to go to the bathroom. I sat and watched as she got up, stumbling awkwardly in the shoes. She said she could barely walk. She left to go to the bathroom down the hall. Oh, please let Charmaine return and not an Alter was all I could think. We still have things to do in this session. I turned the record button off on my phone after saving it. Knowing there would come a time to show all of this to Charmaine. To allow her to see firsthand who walks through her mind. Who lives behind the doors in her hallway.

As I waited for her to return, I went and made two cups of coffee, took a phone call, and returned to my desk. I started to worry as it seemed that it took forever for her to return. Just when I was starting to get very nervous she returned, carrying the shoes in her hand. I looked at her and said, "Charmaine, is that you?" She smiled at me and said, "As far as I know it is Doc." She sat in her usual chair and sighed.

I moved from behind my desk and motioned to her here her coffee was sitting. She thanked me as she reached for the cup. It was a blue cup and written in gold were the words "Kick some brass." Charmaine looked at me after reading it and laughed out loud as she said, "Yup, I think this fits this day Doc." She laid her head back still laughing.

It was funny. I had not really noticed the writing on the cup. She did not miss a beat. I asked her if she was alright. She told me she had just been staring at her hair, the colors on that ugly dress and thinking "Oh God, why?" She finally took her long hair down, and decided she might as well get back out here and find out what was going on.

I asked Charmaine what she was thinking. What was the most important issue for us to talk about? Surprisingly, she responded by saying "Is Dr. Hope alright Doc?" Of all that she had just learned, the restraint she was employing to stay in control; she expressed genuine concern for her physician and her emergency.

This woman continually amazes me in so many ways. I let her know that, yes, Dr. Hope was alright. She had been called out of town which was why her procedure had to be postponed. She had wanted me to assure Charmaine that it will be rescheduled as soon as possible. She was thinking maybe three weeks. She wanted me to apologize for her, as she knew this might create stress and anxiety for Charmaine. I also thanked her for her concern for Dr. Hope, in light of all she was dealing with. Her ability to care deeply for another in times of stress is a mark of great understanding and compassion.

I then repeated my previous statement asking her what we should focus on. The first thing she had to tell me is that "Deseree sure does dress matronly. I hate these puny pastel colors. No way will I even try to walk in these dumb shoes. Who, exactly who, wears pearls anymore?"

She then wanted to know everything about the new Alters; how can this be happening to her. We explored the stress of my wanting to talk to her, her perception of it being not good news, which may have triggered the appearance of Deseree in an effort to protect her. I wanted Charmaine to understand how stress triggered the appearance of these Alters so that she might work toward controlling her anxiety in the future.

I tried to explain. With her history of abuse, the detachment she experienced from events in her own life, the Alters were her coping mechanisms. They may have saved her life. It is the brain's way of providing emotional protection from things she was not prepared to take on. Charmaine was leaning into me as I spoke. She was intent on trying to take every word in, absorbing each word, concentrating on each breath.

She finally spoke. "Doc, I just cannot....cannot hear another word today. I'm about as full as I can be with it all. I feel like I'm about to bust. To be really honest, I think a lot of it is these clothes. These damn pearls are choking me to death, but I hear you, and I have to think about all this.

I'm O.K. about the surgery being put off. I'm just trying to breathe here about all this other stuff. I trust you with my life, you know that. Now you tell me there is someone who hates me, someone who wears boys clothes, someone who watches after me, someone who has loose morals running around having sex, and someone who sits in this floor and colors. They just come on out here and I don't know any of em right? Now if you were me... wouldn't you think me and you are both crazy as hell here?"

I had to smile. I felt a tear on my face at the same time... how to answer that one? Professionally and personally, how to answer that one; the truth has always worked best for me, so I said: "Charmaine, it may seem crazy. If we were to read about it, or hear someone across a table in a restaurant have this conversation, we may in fact look at each other and say, are you kidding me? But the fact is this; we are not crazy as hell, and YOU have all those folks within that brilliant and creative brain of yours. They are Alters. They all came out of a little girl who was brutally traumatized and harmed. Each one has played an important part in your life.

You were a baby girl who was severely damaged. You grew into a woman who now is just meeting all the ones who loved and protected her all these years. Ok, so one of them hates you. Maybe she just hates in general, and thinks it is you she hates. Somehow you and I connected by the Universal Oneness of the Creator: created to work together to unite you with them. So that you might co-exist, living as one beautiful woman, who not only has survived, but is thriving.

So as to answer your question; I'll use the words of one of my favorite singers. A country singer once wrote a song about going crazy that I think fits this situation. Sometimes that is the only answer that fits. Yes, I fully appreciate that you are now on overload from hearing all of this... is that a helpful answer?"

Charmaine had quiet tears streaking her face. By the end of my dissertation she was once again smiling. She said she thought he wrote a song about that, and laughed out loud at the reference. She even sang a bit of it out loud. Charmaine nodded her head in understanding and appreciation of my description. We had come so far together. I had to agree with her on Deseree's out of date smocks and weak pastels. Charmaine did not look her best in that outfit. I was much more used to seeing her hair down, her black jeans, sweats and dark shirts. She wore them well.

As we ended the session, Charmaine asked if I would smudge her with sage. I agreed it would make for a good ending to our session. It would be healing and cleansing for us both. We walked out together. she carried the shoes in her hand. After giving me a big hug, and thanks, I watched as she walked to her car. She was swinging the shoes by her side singing, " ♫"I've all wayyyys been crazy" ♫ ♫. She turned and waved goodbye to me, promising to continue writing in her journal. She would bring it with her to our next session.

It had been a great session, an empowering session; one that I had remembered once again to get bits and pieces of on tape. Later we would look at them together. I had to complete my notes and transfer the video to my laptop before leaving. That night, I was attending a session on DID and hoped to glean additional information that I would be able to share with Charmaine. I was constantly enhancing my own knowledge in the work we were doing together.

It was not lost on me that I was learning more from this client than I had from any textbook, any research or seminar that I had attended in my professional work over the years. Yes, she had been a blessing professionally, personally and spiritually. She posed a challenge daily. There were measurable joys and much heartache in this experience; along the moments of utter exhaustion.

It continues to stay with me, the saying that "people don't know what they don't know." To walk through fear is like walking through a glass door. Many will go as far as to hear the crack, and jump clear of the danger. Others have no time to anticipate the agony of the falling glass. They just crash through the door, suffer the shards slashing through flesh, and only then realize their fear as the adrenaline rushes in.

It is with guidance, with fierce determination that one goes through that pain, to the other side of it, continuing through rather than to step forward, back, forward, back while ripping and tearing one's self. It is a battle that happens to so many, physically, mentally, spiritually, daily, hourly, in the light and in the darkness.

I understood and admired Charmaine saying she had heard all she could hear during our session. She knew she was at her limit. Like a sponge we can only take on so much at one time. She had done better than many could under those circumstances. Wed had talked through the delay of her procedure; the one where JR had burst through and said he would take it on as Charmaine could not go through something like that.

I would forever remember that moment in Dr. Hope's office, as I stood behind her as she sobbed in such deep pain. My arms around her to comfort her, as Dr. Hope leaned in with her hand on her. In the blink of an eye, JR had burst through her, jumping from the chair, knocking me back against the wall and toppling the chair in the process. Frightening Dr. Hope to death as he took over, trying to protect Charmaine from a perceived threat.

I half way expected him to appear during this session, while I spoke to her of the Alters, and the postponement of the surgery. I guess that Deseree had kept him at bay, with the help of Bart's steady eye on the hallway. It was complicated, the more I learned about the Alters, the more questions I had. I did know that they had saved her as a child. Now, they had very distinct roles in her life. I could not imagine trying to live the life she had, managed the fear, thinking myself crazy, experiencing time warps, whole chunks of my life, lost to me. Now, she was coming face to face with those who lived behind the doors, along that hallway in her brain. She was taking it in, accepting it, working with it.

She has come a long way on this journey, yet we still have puzzle pieces lying here and there. There is still much work to do in the process of integration of these Alters to facilitate Charmaine's healing. She is the one who will drive the course. She is the one who must set the pace. It is after all her journey. I am but the guardian of her story. She has allowed me to walk with her, beside her, not to lead her down any path she is not ready to walk... it is she who is leading me. I am honored.

Long after she was gone from sight, I had smudged the office with sage. Moving outside, I had smudged myself, ending this day with gratitude. My notes were completed, I had watched the video of the visits by her Alters, and was off to attend my seminar on DID that evening. With an open mind, I was hoping to learn about interventions being used by others, along with the latest research being done.

It was later with a colleague, after we had sat through the seminar; that we talked. We both came to the same conclusion ... we were disappointed by the seminar. The seminar was held by a clinician that was speaking around the country on DID. We had signed up a few months prior and found about 45 people in the room when we arrived.

We received handouts at the door. She worked from a PowerPoint slide show. As we looked around the room, felt the diminishing energy, it seemed that we both felt it was going to be a long two hours. Over dinner we both agreed that it was disappointing that the speaker basically read from the slides with a completely monotone voice. She had no life to her. Perhaps that is why the energy seemed so flat. The information was less than hopeful, and less than impressive than I had hoped.

Perhaps the saddest commentary from my colleague was that during the seminar she noticed no one taking notes. During the break she had engaged with other clinicians only to hear, "I think this speaker has never even encountered a client with DID." We both agreed that in work with clients who have not only DID, but in any kind of therapeutic milieu, boxes are best used to hold files, not to constrain the working relationship.

Needless to say, dinner was the best part of that particular evening. We both have become more careful in determining which speakers we sign up to hear. I like folks who "fire me up, fill me with enthusiasm, inspire me, restore and intrigue me, and educate me all at the same time." It is a large bill to fill, but I know those folks exist. I have been in conferences and seminars where I have had the pleasure of hearing them. When that happens, the energy is high, the folks walk away with something tangible that is then transferred to others. Those are good times, money well spent.

Charmaine would have been a good speaker for that seminar I thought. I still think she would have given folks something to gnaw on, and improve best practice. I told that to my colleague without mentioning her name. We both laughed knowing that, yes, every once in a while there comes a great diamond from a polished piece of black coal.

On this night, I had the very life sucked out of me just trying to get through the seminar. I was so glad we picked a great restaurant for our late dinner. Good food, great conversation.

~~~~~~~~~~~~~~~~~~~~~~~~~~~

Charmaine's Journal

I am sitting here not knowing whether to shit or go blind. I know I know Doc when you read this you will not get it. It is old country expression. So, we now know there is a person called Laylee who got me in a hell of a mess. I am still feeling banged up and bruised.

Doc took me to a Doctor that she knew works with some of her patients and asked the Doctor to give me a complete exam. I was not completely happy about this but understood why she was doing it. The Doctor said that I had sex and the minute she said that with Doc and me, I immediately threw up. I could not help It. I felt like a demon is inside me and now she is going out and having sex and I do not know it.

I am sitting here with tears streaming down my face and feeling so sick that I just do not know what to do. How does this happen? Why does this happen? And who the hell is Laylee? I would slap the bitch except I would just be slapping myself. And I will admit, at that statement I actually laughed for the visual was just too much, almost like a cartoon.

I keep having this visual of a long hallway that I run down when scared and rooms on each side with doors that slam shut as I run past them. But at the end is my safe haven...my cubby. And I flee in there and curl up on my soft white bed and hold my pillow and just lay there feeling safe.

I do not think I can absorb anymore right this minute. I am going to go lay down. Doc said that she wished she had her camera when Laylee appeared for she said that she did not think that anyone could put on an act like that.

And the waitress who was there and saw me thrown out of the car by that guy backed up a lot of what was being said. I admit when she described what this Laylee was wearing, I busted out laughing for it was not me at all. I mean seriously Tye Dyed? Be back later.

I think I have showered at least ten times since I was told what Laylee did. I still have a hard time understanding how Laylee is in me. Am I possessed? Maybe it is time I look at the books that Doc wants me to read. I scrubbed so much, feeling so dirty that my skin looks scraped. I douched over and over and I do not think I can feel clean enough. Some strange man having sex with me???. I want to cry every time I think about it.

How can part of me be so promiscuous when I am the opposite? As a matter of fact I hate sex and have since I was little. Jeremy used to mock me and call me frigid and use all sorts of creams because the first hint of him wanting sex and I would dry up down there. Why do I hate sex so? My friends tell me it is wonderful and lovely.

Where was the one that calls Doc "Showalter" and wears an OPS shirt and cammie pants and baseball cap with boots on? Why didn't he stop it? Well, I guess that sounds dumb. If that one was out, the man would not have wanted to have sex. If this were not so dang scary and crazy it would be funny. I swear I feel like I was dropped into some Alfred Hitchcock show and everything is strange and there seems to be no answers.

I woke up this morning and first thing looked in the mirror and said "who are you?" because I was afraid one of "them" was present. And I was happy to see me, to see my eyes, my hair and my expressions looking at me. I even made faces to make sure I was in control of my body.

Doc was coming to get me to go get my car and then we were having a long session to go over yesterday. She is going to ask me the last thing I remember and that would be the day before, going to bed. I have no memory of waking up or any of the earlier day until the waitress found me. I had no ID on me, no money, and looked like something from the the 60/s. And I was over fifty miles away from home. Now talk about scary. I have to get control. I have to get control. You all hear me inside...I won't have this anymore. I have to get control. Why do you keep doing this? Why?????

Charmaine's Journal
Days later

The more I think about this the more I think that I do not NOT NOT have this stupid Dissociative Identity Disorder stuff. It cannot be true. I think I must just be exhausted, stressed from Jeremy and physically not feeling well. I have decided to tell Doc that I think she is wrong. Ohhhh boy, she will not like that but I think she is wrong. I mean how can a person have all these people inside them? What am I doing running a half way house for crazies ??

It has been two weeks and I do not know of any lapses and there is no writing in the journal but mine. I swear I think the kids are doing this to make me think I am crazy. They say they do not want to live with their Dad so I can't figure out why they would want me crazy

I think I will keep on seeing Doc though because I think the stress of the divorce and my being sick and all the Doctor stuff coming up that she will help keep me balanced.

Crap I hope she does not ask me to read those DID books again. I think somebody made those up. I remember that movie The Three Faces of Eve and how crazy that woman acted. She reminds me of a woman from church who goes around telling everyone she is DID. Now, that is one thing you will NOT hear or see me doing. I will never tell anyone I am DID. NEVER EVER.

I do not want anyone to know about the things I have done. And if I look like that woman acting like she does and it is so fake looking that anyone around her knows she is pretending...then someone just shoot me. I do not pretend to do things. I might be reacting to meds or something and acting a little wonky but I am not DID. I am not. I am NOT!!!!!

THE ALTERS

Oh crap. I knew this was coming. She is denying us. I HATE HER I HATE HER. First she lets them hurt us and does not stop it and now she denies we came to help.

Dat ugy.

OK DUDES let's not panic. CHILL.

Zoe, Tina, Charie, JR and all of you. It is ok. I will take care of it. Let me get my dress on and I will go talk to the kind Doctor so she understands what is happening. And the rest of you, stop being upset.

She might want to deny us right now but we are here. Now, Laylee is locked up. I am going out and the rest of you behave. I come back to arguing and fussing or planning ugly things and we will have a serious talk. Do you all hear me? And with that

Deseree turned and walked out the door to the murmurs of yes mam...yes mam. JR held his finger up and said for them to behave or else. He was in charge while Deseree was gone.

Taking one last look in the mirror, Deseree patted her bun and headed out the door to drive to Doc's office. When she got there, she quickly powdered her nose, opened the door and started walking up the sidewalk. Her high heels were making a tapping sound on the steps of the porch and down the hallway to the Doc's office.

As Deseree reached the door, she looked to see if the session door was open or closed. It was open so, she decided to stick her head in and speak to Doc. She noticed that Doc was working on folders on her desk.

Tapping lightly on the door frame, Deseree said "Dr. Showalter, may I have a moment of your time. I hate to bother you when it is not session time but I figure this is important enough that it needs to be said now."

Doc looked up and blinked her eyes a minute and looked like she was trying to take it all in when suddenly Deseree noticed a flicker of recognition.

"Oh, Deseree, please come in. Yes, I have a little time between clients." Deseree entered the office and moved the chairs facing each other and sat down in her very erect form of posture with hands together and the Doc came over and sat in front of her.

Deseree started off "If is very important that I talk to you for we have a crisis in the hallway. I need you to know….."

CHAPTER 19 Complete Denial

Oh, how I hoped that it would be Charmaine who walked through my door today and not one of the Alters. I wanted to hear from her; to look at her journal as we had planned last week. I had been busy with a new influx of clients and had just finished up with one when I heard a car come into the parking lot, but had not heard a door open, nor the engine turn off.

I went back to my work thinking perhaps someone was just turning around in the lot as it sometimes happens. Folks missing turns or getting turned around I supposed. I was lost in thought again; thinking about that seminar. Some people are so rigid in their thinking. They live in boxes with their set of rules and ways of doing things. A must lead to B and then C must follow. How can that be helpful if a client or loved one wants to begin at Z and then hit P out of nowhere? What about the training that teaches us to begin where the client is?

I looked up in time to hear a voice. "Excuse me Dr. Showalter; I have to speak with you." It had been a few days since our last session; Charmaine was due in an hour and I looked forward to seeing her, to hear how she had done with all the information she had received. To see what she had worked on in the past few days. Oh crap, I thought... there stood Deseree. She had come in so quietly, but more importantly she had come in when I was hoping to see Charmaine. I shifted my focus, changed my state, and greeted her warmly as I stood with an extended hand, "How lovely to see you Deseree, please come in."

I let her know that while it was lovely to see her, I was expecting to see Charmaine for our session to follow up from last week. As I spoke, Deseree went about arranging the chairs face to face and then sat in what was usually my seat. She smoothed her dress and patted the well-coiffed bun she had coiled her hair into, waiting for me take a seat.

Deseree is well spoken and very calm. She let me know there was trouble within. Charmaine is now having one fine fit with all the information that she is finding herself confronted with. That is the reason for this visit. As she spoke I noticed that she reflected a different degree of matronly pressure and angst. While still well-coiffed, and composed, she seemed desperate to share this most recent news about Charmaine. She said she was on limited time. She would need to get back home and change clothing in order for Charmaine to not be upset when she returned for her appointment.

I asked her to please just start at the beginning. Take her time. I could see that she was quite upset. Deseree had something on her mind. I assured her that if Charmaine was late today it would be fine. I did not have anyone scheduled after her session, so that was of no concern.

Deseree, as the matriarch, as you may recall. She was the one who kept the Alters at bay, kept things to order if you will. It appeared from the look in her eyes that all hell was about to break loose. She did not like it when things seemed out of order. She produced Charmaine's journal. Deseree said that she had watched as Charmaine wrote in it, listened as Charmaine looked in the mirror ranting on about not having DID. Charmaine had said that her dear "Doc was just wrong about this."

Deseree would pause briefly; as if she were hearing the others, would make a face and then look at me once again. She told me that the others were upset, each weighing in with their opinion. She said each had a desire to come out and speak their minds as she struggled to keep everyone in line now. She absently smoothed her dress, although there were no wrinkles there. I listened intently, holding the journal. I rubbed my hand across the pages, not yet reading, but listening and looking at Deseree as she spoke.

She went on to tell me that Charmaine was determined this time that she did not have the others inside of her. That had created havoc. The Alters denied; were ready to explode. I asked her if she knew what had prompted all of this. We both knew that Charmaine had been unaware of the Alters for many years. She was only now coming to believe in their existence. Deseree's upset stemmed from Charmaine's firm decision now that the others did not exist. She had decided that this whole thing was just crazy sounding. Charmaine preferred to think that she was just having dreams, nightmares, and now has denied all thought of childhood abuse.

Since seeing me, Deseree said that Charmaine had seemed to have a complete reversal in her belief in

DID and was totally denying that the Alters were real. Charmaine had begun to change, to grow in her understanding of what was happening to her. Yes, there had been other times when she had trouble believing that she was DID. Now it was an outright denial of everything. Charmaine was convinced that her "dear doc" was totally wrong; yet she still wants to come and see you. "She plans on telling you all this today when she comes. The others are mad. They may just burst out with their thoughts on the subject if I cannot keep them calm as well. I had to come and warn you about this, I think we might be in for a hard time with her" Deseree said quickly.

With that, I looked at the journal. In her newest entries I could sense the denial, its strength and stronghold. I suspected it came from our last session. After she had processed it, perhaps she had become too overwhelmed with the reality, and was struggling to come to terms with it. Hearing about Laylee, JR, Charie, Rene and Deseree; "It was a lot to wrap your thoughts around." She had told me and she had been working very hard, yet it is quite possible that she is replaying the denial tape. Acceptance is a process.

Deseree then said she needed to "scoot" so that Charmaine could come for her session. She stood quickly. That is when I had an idea that we needed to act upon. I decided to risk going outside the box once again to validate that which we shared just last week by asking Deseree to please stay. I explained to her that by staying and allowing Charmaine to reemerge, I could; when the moment was right, show Charmaine herself in the mirror. That should confirm for her that she was indeed DID beyond a shadow of a doubt. I then told Deseree that I had some video of JR and Charie; that I intended to play it for Charmaine to help her to overcome her denial. Perhaps this would help her to calm the others.

It was imperative for the others to trust that I too was caring for Charmaine. We all wanted her to be safe. I told her that I would rely on her to ask the others to please trust me. Perhaps even allow me to call them out for a brief visit. As I spoke, I could see that Deseree must have been trying very hard to maintain the Alters. She looked very stern, her face distressed. She listened, and nodded at me, but this was a side of Deseree I had not seen in our few brief encounters.

She told me that she would agree to what I suggested. She had her doubts about Charmaine, but the others wanted their turn to come out too. She said she would do her best to control as much of this as she could. Deseree suggested that she go home and allow each alter to select just one outfit they liked best. She would return with them in a bag. Since they were so anxious to come out, I could video them in person. Charmaine was frightened of finding herself "dressed" in unfamiliar clothes. She hated the hair dye, she felt confused by it all. Maybe if she could be herself, and see each of the Alters the way they really were; while she was not confused, it would help.

Deseree said she would far rather have Charmaine "come to" in her own clothes so that is why she came back again. I told her that this was a very good idea considering how hard this was for Charmaine. She used Deseree as the mother she never had. I was beginning to think Deseree was going to talk a bit more when suddenly Charmaine looked at me and said "Hi Doc. Sorry I'm late. I think I was day dreaming or something as I was driving here. But here I am." She suddenly noticed the chairs were moved again and said "What's wrong with these chairs? Whoever comes here before I do must have to sit almost in your lap. Do they always move your furniture Doc?"

Then she went about moving the chairs back to their original places and sat down. I knew then it was Charmaine. I wondered how long it would take her to notice her feet in those high heels, or the dress she had on. Perhaps she was just focused on what she had come to tell me. I'm surprised Deseree had not donned Charmaine's normal attire before she left. After all, the costume parade was her idea. She was the one that felt Charmaine found it too stressful when she discovered herself in strange clothing. I probably should have suggested it to Deseree. Too late now, at least it won't be the first time she has to deal with the issue.

I welcomed her again, and took a seat beside her, having put her journal out of sight for the time being. I turned the video on, as I knew it would probably come in handy for her later on in our session. Many may wonder if recording her was ethical, and I did struggle with that early on; I would remind myself often that we had talked about the use of the camera before.

She had signed a release for me. I knew I would be recording at times during our sessions. I purposely did not tell her for several reasons on each occasion that I did record.

The primary reason was I did not want her to feel intimidated by the camera. I also did not want to sound the alarm for her Alters who may have observed videos as an opportunity to come out to be "on stage." I knew that there would come a time when "seeing is believing" for Charmaine.

I also had promised her long ago that I would never do anything that would harm her. The videos would never be seen by anyone other than her and me. I also promised her that when our work was done, the tapes would be destroyed in her presence. It was a promise I would never break. As a result, I felt no ethical or moral conflict in turning the video recorder on from time to time; although many times the device was rolling, and no one came out. The best result so far was Charmaine laughing about how she sounded on tape.

However, when one has absolutely no memory, tapes can be instrumental in helping them believe and accept a reality that is beyond belief. In Charmaine's life we needed more than words. In this case she needed to accept her own diagnosis of DID. Seeing first-hand the actions of the Alters would be concrete evidence.

She was truly not present during those times. The only complete way to help her accept that reality turned out to be the trust in our relationship and the proof the tapes provided. There are times when creativity is vital. The only limitations are our own potential to use whatever tools we have. That particular technology would become increasingly important as we continued our work together.

As she sat in the chair, Charmaine let me know that she had been very busy thinking about all the times we had spent together, the work we had done; her complete trust in me. Charmaine stressed that she wanted me to know that she appreciated me. She had never known anyone quite like me before. That she had so much respect for me. As she spoke I kept thinking of Deseree. At one point I smiled to myself, thinking "Oh boy, this is quite some build up to let me know that she is not DID and I don't know what I am talking about."

Charmaine said that she had gone through a really hard year. That she had come to the conclusion that her increased stress, her health problems, along with her ex-husband's antics, had about driven her to the hospital on more than one occasion. She now had come to the conclusion... then she stopped talking. She looked at me for a moment, then looked on the floor beside her bag and blurted out "Oh crap Doc, I forgot my journal."

I watched in surprise. She had stopped mid-sentence, realizing she was looking for her journal and thought perhaps she had left it in her car. She started to stand up, saying perhaps she needed to go and look in her car. I stopped her. I went to my desk, pulled it out of the drawer and handed it to her.

Charmaine looked at me, let out a sigh, saying "Oh God, Doc, you scared me. I guess I dropped it on my way in huh?" Before I could reply she had opened it and began to use it to regain her wording for what was to come next. I could tell that she was getting nervous, having a little trouble finding her words. She was so tense that she had yet to realize that she was in Deseree's clothing. I sat quietly. This was her time to speak. I watched as she flipped through the pages to get to where she felt she needed to be, and then continued.

She was able to tell me that she had read "those damn books" and never wanted to read another one of them. While she appreciated them, she really did not think she was like "those people." She had watched the "Three Faces of Eve", and she knew for sure she was not like that! After all that was a movie about someone "crazy as a loon. You're the one who said I'm not crazy, remember?"

She had written notes to explain and defend the memory loss. She was in complete denial of many of the issues, and her own history of abuse, that we had covered. She went as far as to explain that perhaps the damage done to her vagina may have been a birth defect aggravated by her husband's sexual appetite and roughness.

As I listened to her, I noticed her breathing change; her body became even tenser. Her eye contact lessened. She desperately wanted me to agree with her, to be able to say she was right; that I had made a terrible mistake in my assessment. That we had put the puzzle together all wrong.

I felt terrible for her. I had seen over the years this utter strength of denial in so many that I had worked with professionally. I had witnessed it in loved ones as well. Denial is a strong coping mechanism, one that is often fueled by fear.

Charmaine had taken on so much through her work in this office; the revelations that the Alters, who walked daily with her, or burst forth unbeknownst to her had given me a lot of information that she did not yet have. With her history of abuse, and their longing to take over or protect her from harm, she was still trying to deny it all because of fear.

She said she wanted to continue coming to sessions, but only to work on other things; to work on her depression, to learn to deal with stress better. She no longer wanted to entertain this DID thing as a possibility in her life. She just "did not believe such things really existed, and if it is real, it is not really about me."

Charmaine was talking quickly. At one point, telling stories of a woman she knew from church. How this woman used "fakeness" to garner attention from others, in her assessment this woman was just not "being real." She was very animated as she described detailed examples of the "crazy woman wanting attention" in her church. This of course confirmed her new found revelation that she did not have Alters or DID. Perhaps she had her own ways of seeking attention. She had now attributed her personal issues to health conditions, stress, raising kids and her crazy ex-husband who she now could safely say she only had to see when he picked up and returned her kids.

She had this all figured out, she proudly told me. At times I was lost in her voice, her face, and her body language. I said little as I listened to her. At one point she had even asked me if I was listening to her? "Why are you smiling so much." My reply had been that only one of us could talk at once. It took fewer muscles to smile than to frown. I asked her to continue. She did after a brief chuckle, telling me she thought I was funny.

I listened long enough to know it was time for us to now allow her to see herself on the video. It was time to get to the hard nuts and bolts of reality. While affirming that I would like nothing more than to be wrong about this, it was time for a reality check; probably past time. I had noticed several times changes in Charmaine's face that concerned me. As she talked, there had been distinct pauses in her speech, her face changed a bit several times, and more than once her head would tilt.

It was those times that I thought an Alter was trying to come out; perhaps saved only by Deseree and Bart, buying time for Charmaine to continue. Hoping that I would soon take control before things got out of hand in my office. Yes, it was time to introduce Charmaine once again to the reality of her life.

When Charmaine paused for a moment and glanced at her journal, I leaned in toward her and placed my hand on hers; over the journal page. I looked at her, and told her I needed her to stop for a minute and listen to me. I had listened, I had heard her; but now it was time for her to see something important, to realize that it would help her beyond words.

She looked at me quizzically and said, "Well Doc, what in the world could that be, and don't you think I am right after all I've told you? You can see I've been very busy, and I can account for all of my time." I took the journal gently from Charmaine's hands and carefully laid it on my desk, asking her to stand up. I took her by the hand and led her to a big gold framed mirror in my office. I wanted her to look closely at herself. As I stood her in front of the mirror, I moved behind her and placed my hands on her shoulders. In a soft voice, I quietly said, "Charmaine, who are you seeing looking back at you right now?"

The room fell still, the only sound, was Charmaine's' breath as she gasped. I felt her shoulders tense. I watched her look at herself. Her eyes widened. She was incredulous as she reached up and traced her hair in the tidy bun that Deseree painstakingly had in place on her head. Her eyes then fell to her neckline where the pearls lay. She glanced at the neckline of the pastel dress. She put her hand to her neck, touching the pearls, rubbing the fabric. She looked at her face and hair again, and at me through her reflection in the glass. An expression of utter shock and dismay was on her face, as tears streaked down her cheeks. A sob came from deep within her echoing off the walls.

Charmaine was standing stock still, yet her body felt as though it would melt into the floor under the weight of this reality. This immediately on the heels of her elation, fueled by denial of DID. She stood and faced herself dressed as her Alter, the matriarch Deseree. I witnessed that reality sinking like the Titanic into her very being. We continued to stand there as she stared, sobbing. There were no words to express her thoughts in that changing moment. Her eyes were taking it all in on a cellular level.

My hands never left her shoulders as she kept staring at herself in the mirror. I waited; it was not necessary to speak. At the moment, my job was to let whatever was happening to happen. The best I could offer was a gentle supportive touch to ground her. "Oh Dear God why is this happening to me, it is real isn't it Doc; everything I've tried to think, everything

I've tried to hope, everything I've tried to explain to you. You knew when I was saying it, I looked like this. You knew I looked this way and you did not say a word. You just let me go on and on, just so you could let me get it all out. Now you've shown me with my own eyes, and oh my God look at me. I need to sit down Doc. I think I might be sick." Charmaine turned around and faced me. She looked utterly pale. She was a mess, but now looked resigned to the reality that she indeed was a person who had to accept reality; the reality of DID.

We moved back to our chairs. As quickly as we were seated Charmaine excused herself to the restroom. She said she "had to pee", and made a hasty exit. She got as far as the door and realized she had on high heels. Catching herself as she tripped, landing against the wall, she let a litany of cuss words that was definitely out of character for her. She yanked the shoes off her feet, and ran down the hall to the bathroom. Part of me feared that an Alter had managed to escape.

I sat and looked through her journal, again struck by how denial protects in times of distress, loss, grief, and devastation. Yet when denial is overcome, and someone is faced fully with reality, they can step beyond fear and become open to hope. I was still looking through the journal when Charmaine returned. I had not heard her as she was barefoot. It startled me as she touched my back re-entering, the office. Then I heard her.

"Well hellfire Showalter, you sure do know how to do it don't ya..." As I watched; I saw that it was JR who had returned from the bathroom Taking a seat, spreading his knees, tucked the dress between both legs like it was nothing to him to be there; he was oblivious to how he looked. I assumed he broke loose in the bathroom or in the hallway on the way back.

"Hi JR, how's it going, good to see you too." He gave me that wicked grin that I had seen before, and leaned back in the chair. He said he had to jump out here before he got caught. "Charmaine freaked out in there. She got scared, they all are real now, but she would have to "just deal with."

I asked him how that would affect him now, knowing that Charmaine would know about all of them in the days and weeks ahead; how would he be with all that? "Well hell Showalter, it's like this. I ain't goin nowhere so don't be getting any ideas to try to get rid of me or anyone else, you understand? We've been around a hell of a lot longer than you and we'll be around long after you and your cute ass are gone. Yea, yea, I hear you Deseree; I'm comin, just give me a minute. Now, Showalter, now where was I sweetcheeks?"

I grinned at JR, he loved to get in your face and to let you know he was the "baddest of the bad." He knew I was not shaken by his presence or his words. I also knew he was a great protector of Charmaine. He had jumped out to let me know that she was upset over this reality. I took that as a good thing; a good sign.

I let JR know that I appreciated his visit, but he really needed to go for now, and in the future to not sneak up on me as he might just get shot. I gave a tongue in cheek grin. He looked surprised at that comment and then he laughed. "Showalter, you are one helluva woman, I might just have to take you out for a ride and a cold one." I asked him to please trust that I would take care of Charmaine. Right now I needed to spend time with Charmaine to assure her that he and the rest of the Alters are real. I needed her to feel safe with me now, but may need him to help me later.

He seemed to like that idea and rose to leave saying, "Catch ya later Showalter, shake it easy babe." He walked out the door with his cocky walk, which was hilarious in that dress. What JR did not know, and I had forgotten at the time, the tape here was still running. At least it was focused on the chair so I would have that information to also share with Charmaine, but I did not realize that until long after the day's session. I had forgotten about the tape running at all.

Once again at the end of that day, I would be glad for the technology. In the meantime I sat. Once again I felt the presence of someone walking in; only this time that someone would be Charmaine taking her seat. I knew it to be her as she began to speak before she sat down.

That familiar drawl, and what she had to say made me laugh, although it was not really funny at the time. She told me she thought she was going to wet her pants all of a sudden. When she jumped up to go to bathroom she had almost fallen in the high heels. However now that she had returned, as Charmaine, she let me know she had seen herself in the mirror, she had now seen her clothing, she was once again beyond words for her feelings. I explained to her once again that it was important that she be able to say all that was in her heart and mind. I only hoped she understood that.

Charmaine took it in, she was leaning toward me in her chair and listening intently as I spoke words that I knew had seldom ever been said to her: words of apology to her, said in earnest. We talked about the words mental illness and their impact on people; about the fact that DID actually saves lives in reality.

Although DID is diagnosed as a mental illness, it is actually the "brain's brilliance" in saving someone from trauma. It is born of creativity, from the Creator/ God/ Goddess; a creativeness that enabled her to endure such horrid acts at the hands of others, witnessing things that she just could not bear.

Charmaine then wanted to talk about her journal, the entries made by what seemed to be the "others", and her lack of any real memories. She also wanted to see the sketch again. She admitted that she was getting tired. She assured me she could not go backward now. "I guess today seals my fate. This really is my life. DID explains why everything has been so messed up. What now?"

I told her, as I retrieved the sketch that there was something I wanted to show her as well. As she looked at the sketch I handed her, she marveled at the resemblance of the one face in the picture to herself, although she thought she had not looked like the sketch of herself in many years. She reflected on the toll her health and ex-husband had on her physical looks now. I was not sure if she was talking as much to me, as to herself. I had gotten up and was hooking my camera into the computer, re-adjusting it to be seen from our chairs before rejoining her.

I asked her if she would bear with me. I wanted to share something with her. It was important for her to see it, now that she has come face to face with her own DID. Her immediate reaction was to ask me if we were going to sit through the movie, "The Three Faces of Eve." She laughed, telling me she just wasn't up to that. I laughed so hard I thought I had broken a rib over her remarkable sense of humor. I assured her we did not have to watch Sybil or Eve. I had something that was far more powerful and more real for her; I had "HER" in a light that she would now know was real. It was necessary for her to witness it, as she had no memory of the experience.

I spoke slowly and concisely, introducing the tape of the Alters to her. I wanted her to hold on to the sketch while it played, but needed her to pay close attention to the video. She would for the first time meet some of her Alters. Charmaine looked at me incredulous and said, "Oh Lord Doc, you have ME in THERE and we're going to watch it together NOW?" I told her yes, there was no time like the present. I told her that Deseree knew that we were doing this and was working hard to keep all the Alters in check, but they may be watching with us.

They might just want to come out. I was asking for all of them to stay put. "There is no need to be afraid. You are safe here. This will really help you Charmaine" She agreed with me and I moved closer to her as I pushed play. I found myself watching Charmaine more than watching the tapes. It was only then that I realized the true importance of what we were doing by watching this today; the remarkable significance of recording this in bits and pieces.

The tape began with Charmaine speaking to me. She laughed when she saw and heard herself for the first time on tape telling me she "hated her voice on that thing," but grew silent as she watched. Her eyes got larger as she reached over and grabbed my hand squeezing it with all her might. That woman has one hell of a grip I might add. I hoped JR would not come out and add his strength to the pressure I was feeling. I could not help but think of him, the protector, as I watched her observe Charie playing on the floor.

There were moments of laugher mixed with "Oh shit that cannot be me" followed by "oh my God that is ME", then, more emphatically, "Doc, how in the hell could you stand my acting such a way?" There were clips of desire, the inflection of her words, her mannerisms, completely different from Charmaine. With each movement Charmaine was leaning closer to the screen, captivated by every second, finally asking me to "shut it off, stop it, stop it, just stop it, please Doc."

I thought my hand was either bruised or broken as she had not loosened her grip. I placed the tape on pause, looking at her for a clue as to what she was thinking; some sign of how she was coping, yet she sat still; looking at the paused image, staring at the screen.

Charmaine looked at me. As she did, I looked at her hand in mind, my hand in hers, wondering if she had any idea how hard her grip was; and yet, I did not attempt to move my hand as she began to speak. Charmaine told me she just needed to catch her breath. This was so much to see. She knew that it was her, but she still could barely believe it. "Doc, it's like watching a movie where you are staring at someone's picture or something, but just can't remember being the star, do you understand that?"

I assured her that I did understand the principle behind what she was saying. She had said it very well, but no, I could not imagine being in her shoes. I asked her about Charie, and if she thought I had given her a good description of her. All she could tell me was that it embarrassed her, "Being a grown woman, coming into her therapist's office and plopping down on the floor. Speaking with a lisp and talking about someone pooping on the porch."

She thought I should get rid of that corner. She could not imagine I saw that many kids to make it a good use of space. I could tell that she was hoping that Charie never made another visit, any time soon. She spoke from the mind of an adult, trying to reason and be rational, about the child Alter who wanted to play. The child had spoken so openly and innocently about those bad men.

She was struck by the similarities of the sketches as she looked once again at them. She talked about the way Deseree and Charie looked and acted on the tape. I noticed her breathing change back to a calmer state as we talked through what she had seen. As she relaxed, her grip lessened on my now numb hand that she had released for a moment.

She then said she thought she had calmed herself enough to see more, but asked that if she needed to take a break, would that be all right. I assured her it would be. Charmaine looked at me before I pushed play and said, "Doc, I think I'm going to start carrying an extra set of sweats, a T-shirt and pair of sneakers when I come to see you cos' this dress is damn uncomfortable, what do you think?" I smiled, and had to laugh to myself, telling her that just might be a good idea, but our hope for her was to ultimately integrate everyone into one healing presence. Then it will be Charmaine who gets to make all the decisions. When I pushed play, Charmaine was sitting on the edge of her chair with her hands tucked under her chin, watching as awestruck as a child discovering birds in a nest, as Deseree made another visit to the office. As Charmaine watched, Deseree walked in and shook hands with me, arranged the chairs and then sat down. Charmaine said, "How in hell does she walk in those shoes Doc and don't you think she would keep a headache with that hair so tight up in that bun?" I laughed out loud. We both watched as Deseree left and Charmaine returned in her stead.

I watched Charmaine for reactions as each Alter came through. The tape continued, including the part when Charmaine left for the bathroom and returned as JR to startle me. That is when I became aware that JR was completely unaware that he was wearing "Deseree's lady clothes" during our conversation. Charmaine's eyes once again popped open. She covered her mouth with both hands. "OH Doc!"

I watched her, as she watched JR. He called me Showalter and said his piece about what was happening. He declared his desire to protect Charmaine, while spreading his legs to make his point; not knowing he had just thrown a dress between his legs to do so. Charmaine looked at the screen. Clearly she was trying to figure out what was happening. Deseree's dress, JR's voice... All at once she looked me in the eye and asked, "Is this the one who smokes and wears the boots?"

I assured her that yes, it was. I had another tape of JR that we would look at the next session. She wanted to know if my feelings were hurt when JR spoke to me that way. "Did it make you mad?" She said she felt mad on my behalf. He was rude, and offensive. How dare he speak to me that way.

I smiled and told her I actually liked JR. He spoke what was on his mind. He was a fierce protector of her; he wanted to be sure that no one harmed her or took advantage of her. Charmaine's response to that was "Well I think he might be all smoke and mirrors, cos' he sure didn't help me when I was lost and had sex with that man at the diner did he?"

As I turned the recorder off, I had to think about how to best answer that. I told Charmaine that I believed that in that incident JR may have not known at the time what was happening. Laylee was out voluntarily, and she had voluntarily had sex with the man. JR would not have felt a signal of distress from Charmaine.

It was an unfortunate circumstance, a terrible thing that happened, yet I did not think we could fault JR. Even though I knew that was hard for her to hear. It seemed the Alters could be unaware of each other's behavior at times too. In some instances, some of the Alters knew more than others. I knew this was still confusing to her. I was only just beginning to get it, and I had far more exposure to them than she had at this point. I asked Charmaine if she believed now that DID was the correct diagnosis of her condition.

She mulled the question over for a few moments. She looked first at me, then the computer, and finally at the mirror. "Well I'll just tell ya Doc, mirrors don't lie, and just seeing this movie thing here, that is me. I would be a fool to tell you I don't believe it now wouldn't I? It doesn't mean I like it, not one bit. I probably will never say I like it … but I sure can't deny it, can I?"

As our session neared the end, I asked Charmaine if I could take a picture of her, one for her file; a marker of this day when she moved from denial to understanding that; 1. DID is real, 2. SHE has Alters who are residing within her, and 3. She saw firsthand those who had come out on the tapes.

Charmaine laughed and said, "Oh what the hell, but you have to promise you'll never let anyone see it. At least let me take this god awful bun down first." Charmaine got up and went back to the bathroom fix her hair. I had planned to keep a copy of the photo for her file and to print one to give her at our next session. To mark the date that Charmaine came face to face with DID. She returned with her hair down, barefooted.

As I went to focus the camera I told her to smile for DID, as I was about to snap the shutter, though I was not prepared for it, she hollered; "No, No, No, No, no picthures pweeze, no picthures. Me no want. No, no, no." She quickly turned toward the wall, crouching down, crying like a child. The key word I heard was "pweese" and I all thought was "oh no, this is little Charie." I felt my heart sink.

As I ran to her, she stood and turned around. It was not Charmaine's voice I heard, but the voice of Deseree who said "Dr. Showalter it's alright dear. I wanted you to see little Charie, when she saw that camera she panicked. She was so pitiful I just had to let her see you. Charie was so afraid. The camera makes her remember what those perverted adults did back at that house when they exposed her little body; when they committed those acts on her and took photographs with their Polaroid's. Those harsh light bulbs would almost blind that child and scare her.

When she heard you say picture and saw the camera in your hands... well dear, I just wanted you to see it."

I was shaking, my heart heavy as I tried to hold back tears, looking at Deseree, remembering that child's cry. Remembering Charie when she was here and playing. Now having heard of the horror, the very, very real trauma that happened to Charmaine and the Alters, knowing now that Charie remembered so much of what had happened that she had been frightened by my camera; I was upset that I had caused her fresh pain. There was simply no predicting what small event would trigger a huge reaction from any of them.

I took Deseree's hand in mine and told her I was saddened that she had felt it necessary to teach me such a painful lesson. I was humbled once again. I needed Deseree to go to Charie and to the others; to hold them and assure them I would never ever harm them with photographs. I asked that she please let them know that the photographs were meant for Charmaine...meant for her to meet them; to accept them and involve them in her life for goodness, for right way relations, in a healing and loving way.

I asked Deseree as the matriarch of this tribe within, to reassure Charie that what those mean people did to her so long ago was now over and no one would harm her again. She was safe, I wanted her to come again soon to play here and visit with me. I thanked Deseree for her kind vigilance, her warmth and her guidance. She had managed to remain strong through all this.

For the first time since meeting her, Deseree reached out and hugged me. I heard her sigh as she said, "God Bless you Dr. Showalter, you are so precious to us." As I was holding her in my arms I could feel the energy shift. I felt her arms move, gently pulling away. I was looking at Charmaine, and she at me. She scrunched her face at me and said "Doc, have you been crying just now? Oh, don't tell me one of THEM came again, didn't they, I was standing here at the mirror and now you are hugging me... did you take the picture?"

I told her I was just about to take the picture, and asked her if she was ready, I could not tell her at that point what had happened. I was not ready for the emotional impact that it would have on Charmaine. Not able to "go there" just yet. I needed my own regrouping time and it was late. I just wanted to take the picture, let her go home and process all that had come out in our session.

I stood back and said to Charmaine and the tribe within: "Charmaine, I am going to take a picture of you, just you. It is a picture for YOU and I. You are safe. This is to mark the day that you acknowledged all the ones that are on that sketch as living in that beautiful brain of yours, ok?"

Charmaine smiled and told me that was the longest "cheese" to a picture she had ever heard. As I focused the camera, I saw her eyes sparkle. She smiled. With the "Click" of the shutter, we had captured the picture. Surprisingly enough, I even remembered to get the mirror in the frame. For Charmaine it was the mirror she would come to call the "mirror to her brain."

Charmaine's Journal

Damn things did not go like I wanted. I have no memory of going to the office. I looked up and there I was in the office with Doc. I figured maybe I was day dreaming all the way over. I could wait to tell her that I am sure I do not have DID. But, I did want to keep her as a therapist. Doc smiled and told me to sit down and I am so excited to tell her my new found discovery that I started talking before I sat and I realized that I have lost my journal. I started to get up and Doc hands it to me. As I am telling her that I do not believe in DID and that I do not have it and that I think that she has made a wrong diagnosis, she just sat there looking at me. I repeat myself wondering if she has even heard me.

Finally, Doc got up and reached down and took my arm and asked me to come with her. I jumped up wondering what it is she wants me to see and she stood me in front of the big gold framed mirror in her office. And she says "Charmaine... what do you see?" As I look in the mirror, I felt my knees buckling. I do not recognize the person in the mirror. I looked like an older woman like from the fifties, with my hair in a bun and a shirtwaist dress on. OMG...no no no my mind was screaming and my knees were buckling again. It seemed like time moved in slow motion and there were no words to express what I was feeling. Damn!!!

I think stunned beyond comprehension was the best description. I Felt like I was Alice in Wonderland as she looked through the looking glass. I really am crazy. I really am. Doc catches me under both my arms from the back and gently sits me in the closest chair. She tells me that she wanted me to see myself like this because I DO have Dissociative Identity Disorder and I have got to come to grips with that. She also tells me that denying it is part of having it and happens with many patients.

I feel sick to my stomach as once again I think "oh my gosh, I am stark raving crazy. Either that or I am caught in a time loop and can't get out." I ask Doc to let me run to the bathroom as I did not want to have an accident and as I took off half way running down the hallway, I almost fell down. I looked down and saw I was wearing these high heels. I thought I was going to break my ankle. I pulled them off and rushed into the bathroom and started running to the bathroom and then suddenly I was running down the hallway to my cubby.

THE ALTERS

Deseree takes off running down the hallway after Charmaine, yelling to JR to get out there quick so that she can comfort Charmaine and get her where she can go back out. She told him that this was too

important and they have to get her where she can see the video.

Grumbling, JR exits the hallway door thinking to himself that Showalter sure knows how to screw things up as he marches back to the office looking rather ridiculous in a shirtwaist dress, carrying high heels, swearing every step of the way. At least he managed to pull that stupid bun down before he got there.

"That Doc think she is getting rid of us she has another thing coming" JR mutters to himself.

Striding into the office, JR tells Doc that she sure has screwed things up and had to smile inside when she greeted him with Hi JR. *"Oh how I wanted to just rattle her one time"* he thought. They talked a few minutes with him trying to sit in that dress and finally pushing it between his legs so he could prop his leg on the other one. She better not ever tell anyone he was in a dress.

Doc tells him to let Charmaine back out because she needs to talk to her and that she will need him later. JR smiles glad she seems to appreciate him.

Charmaine's Journal

(A day **after** the mirror session. DRSES)

I can't believe the last session. I ran to the bathroom when Doc showed me the videos and then myself in the mirror. I got back from the bathroom and Doc told me that she also had something else she wanted me to see and went and plugged her phone into her laptop and once she was set, she came over with the laptop and sat down beside me. She took my hand and said "Charmaine this is going to be very hard for you to watch but maybe it will help you to get further along in your therapy. You cannot move forward if you are denying all the time." She turned on the video player on her laptop.

I sat there in stunned silence as I watched this video of me but it was not me. There was the woman with the bun who talks very motherly and sits very prim and proper and wears a dress and high heels. Then there was the one in camouflage pants, black T shirt with a black ops hat on and boots and talks like some rough neck and swears and calls the good Doc with simple "Showalter" and this one smokes?? OMG

I found myself trembling as I watched. I was mortified when I heard the word fuck come out of my mouth. I think I am going to throw up. Doc just patted my hand as we sat there and watched and told me it was going to be alright. I asked her to stop for a minute because I felt so sick. It was like being caught in a cyclone and everything was whirling around and all was confusion.

One of the ones on there was me in my jeans and shirt only it was not me. It was the voice of a small child that talked with a lisp and played with the toys and was the very essence of a small child. She even had pigtails. Doc asked me what I saw and I said that it was me but I sounded like a little kid. Suddenly it hit me...this was why I have all the toys and dolls and story books.

And then there was the sexy actin one; dressed like a slut and was flirty with Doc...only not on there for very long. Everyone I saw, their faces and motions and their mannerisms changed and while they looked like me; their clothes, expressions and even voices made them not look like me.

After the video was done, Doc told me that the provocative one was called Laylee and is the one that had me lost in that little town at the café and that Deseree allowed her out long enough for me to see her and she was "locked" back up. Doc named each one for me from JR with the combat boots to little Charie the child and even one called Boo Boo whom she said was a young girl that could not talk, not because she was too young to talk, but because of the trauma. Doc said she thought Boo Boo had taken most of the worst trauma and that is why she was voiceless.

She said Deseree told her that Boo Boo joined them when I was beaten so badly for making noise when those people hurt me and Boo Boo could take it and not make any sounds. I feel like I am in the cast of some horror movie soap opera. I look up at Doc and could not even speak. I found myself throwing my hands up and then just dropping them in my lap. Doc reached over and told me that it is ok, that we would get through this and that it was important for me to realize that they are a real part of me. Once we figure out why they came, we would know how to have them integrate into me. But, I am not sure I even heard her words at first. I hear them now but not then.

She told me that Deseree is the mother I never had and that she came to tell Doc that I was denying them and had everyone upset. So Doc worked out a plan for me to see it all face to face so to speak and over the two hours between Deseree's visit to Doc and my session time, Deseree went back and told the Alters to each pick their favorite outfit and they were going to the Doc to be filmed. Deseree said she wanted to come back dressed to be there when Charmaine was let back out so that she would see Deseree's clothes first and maybe feel the comfort of her mother figure.

I asked Doc if I could watch it again. There were times it was almost comical until the realization that this was inside of me. This was me. Doc said "I think all those doors you see in your head down that hallway to your cubby, are their rooms. You have separated all these parts of you into separate compartments. Our job is to learn about what brought them and to help open all the doors and release them so they are all inside you and not separated. Before leaving, Doc had asked could she take a picture for the files and I said yes.

CHAPTER 20   The Good, Bad and Ugly

I arrived at the office exhausted, still with a splitting headache from the events of the night before. It had been more than I would have ever imagined. I had heightened my visual imagery skills since beginning my work with Charmaine in more ways than I thought possible.

After the last week, with a hectic schedule I had made some relaxing plans with friends; having looked forward to a night of music and good food. To just enjoy my friends in a wonderful place I seem to not visit near enough. I waited briefly at the bar, people watching. Cocktail in hand, I made my way to the table when I saw my friends had been seated. The music was wonderful, the place packed with people enjoying themselves. It was lively, just what I needed after such an intense week.

I glanced around the room and thought I felt my heart stop. I walked past a table with a couple sitting close together, looked twice; only to realize that it was Charmaine cuddled up to a man in the booth that I was passing. I walked by, and then turned around to take a second look; realizing that yes, that was her, or rather, one of her Alters.

I feared Laylee had escaped, but was relieved to see that it was the Alter Tina. Tina, in all her glory; ready to make yet another mistake that could have a horrible effect on Charmaine, when she realized that once again; she was out with a man unknown to her. I stood there a moment, just observing Tina who was wearing a fancy dress, big earrings and high heels. She seemed quite enamored with her gentleman friend. Tina was younger than Laylee; she looked like a child playing dress up.

I knew that my plans for the evening would have to be postponed for the moment. I made my way to my friends table. I let them know that I would be back, but something had just popped up. I needed to attend to it. I found my way back to Charmaine, who was now engaged in a bit of "making out" with her male companion, while holding a drink in her hand.

As much as I hoped to not cause a scene, I interrupted the moment, saying, "Excuse me, Charmaine?" Her head spun around at the sound of my voice. Her voice replied, "NO", yet I saw dread in her eyes. I then looked at her sternly and asked her again, "May I speak with you in private?" Her reply was crisper as she responded, "Dr. S, Charmaine will see you in your office tomorrow I think, please leave us alone." I glanced at her companion who began to look a bit uncomfortable; looking perplexed, between the two of us. I did not back down. I asked her if I might speak to her in the ladies room. She reluctantly got up from the table assuring her friend that she would be right back. I ignored him; walking away from the table with her.

I led her to the restroom, scrambling in my mind to figure out my next steps. Knowing I had to get her away from this potential mess. When we walked in the restroom, she turned quickly toward me. She announced that she was NOT Charmaine but was Tina

I was trying to mess up her evening with her friend. She boldly crossed her arms, rolled her eyes and asked what I wanted. I was relieved to see we were alone, and firmly said, "Deseree I NEED YOU OUT HERE NOW." Tina puts her hand to my mouth. "Dr. S, sssh, I'm not supposed to be here, please don't..." I looked at her sternly and again called for Deseree. Tina's eyes flashed anger as her body language changed before me. Deseree's voice replaced Tina's.

"Oh my goodness Dr.Showalter, I was so busy with the others that I allowed Tina to go out and take care of things at the house. I thought she was at home, I had no idea she would do something like this. I guess with all that has been going on, I just was not paying close enough attention. I am so very grateful you happened to be here. I just do not know what to say.

I did not believe that Tina would have placed Charmaine in harm's way intentionally; however with so many things happening right now we cannot be too cautious can we? Is it possible for you to call me a taxi? I will go home and get out of these ridiculous clothes before Charmaine sees them. I am tremendously appreciative, and so very sorry to have taken your free time tonight. You can rest assured that I will hold counsel with Tina and the others."

This whole situation was amazing. How could I possibly have been in this place, at this time? At the moment, I decided not to ignore what I saw happening. I was also thankful that I knew how to bring forward the matronly Alter, Deseree, who could intervene and provide some safety for Charmaine. As I stood there, she reached over to hug me. Three women walked into the restroom and just looked at us as if we had two heads.

Deseree stood straight up, looking aghast at her own public display of affection. She reached to straighten her bun only to realize her hair was down. She caught a real glimpse of herself in the mirror and shuddered. We quickly left the restroom. I had all but forgotten my friends; who by now were probably wondering if I would ever rejoin them.

As we made our way to the front door, I wondered about the man who was waiting for the return of Tina. Who was he? How she had met him? Did he know where she lived? I filed the litany of questions somewhere in my mind as I called a cab, and waited until Deseree was safely in the back seat. I gave the driver the address; with money to get her home, and strict instructions to stop nowhere, make no detours; to wait until she was safely in the house before leaving. Deseree quietly thanked me and they drove away.

I returned inside and walked past the table where Tina had been with this man. He was gone. The table was clean as if no one had been there. I was left with all the questions I intended to ask him. This event had to be addressed when Charmaine came in for the next session which was intended to get her ready for the surgery.

We were also supposed to go through some of the journal entries. Many that had been written by the Alters, some that seemed to be threatening, others were fearful, pleading messages. We never seemed to have enough time with all the ongoing issues that found their way through the life of DID.

Luckily my friends had amused themselves with appetizers, clever exchanges of days gone by, and several drinks. As I approached the table, they applauded. They thought I had been kidnapped by space aliens. The joke of the night was why I did not wear a foil hat to prevent potential encounters with extraterrestrials' in the future. Little did they know. Our visit was light, playful, and very much needed.

I sat at my desk the next morning turning this all over in my head. I realized that I had almost forgotten Zoe's threats until Deseree and I talked. I thought about Buck's anger, Charie's joy and her desire to play, but her fear too. Added to all of this, there was the ongoing day to day life of a really lovely woman named Charmaine, who wanted nothing more than to live her life in fullness and wonder as she enjoyed her kids.

She was open now, receptive to therapy, and guided imagery. I believe the Alters had also been receptive to meeting this therapist, now that I felt comfortable with their appearances and their disappearances. It was a good that Charmaine had come so far, but it was challenging to execute my therapeutic plan from moment to moment. One thing I had learned through all of this was that treating the Alters with respect and talking to them helped in the healing of Charmaine. When the Alters felt threatened or Charmaine felt threatened, all hell broke loose.

We could never spend as much time as I hoped or set out to, on the journal. There was never enough time spent in reflection with Charmaine as I planned for. There was always something pressing, an issue from the session that needed follow-up, a new discovery that she had found in her on-going detective mode, or the appearance of an Alter instead of Charmaine.

I had long ago decided to go with the flow of my client. I had learned to listen keenly to the sound of the tires coming to a halt in the lot, the footsteps on the porch when she arrived. Sometimes I held my breath as I looked at her, noting what she was wearing, the inflection in her tone of voice, to see who it was that I would be spending time within each session.

The stress had taken a toll on her. It seemed that now, that the Alters had been acknowledged and accepted, they were having more difficulty staying in the hallway. It was good, bad, ugly and downright comical at times. I felt as if we were in one of those revolving doors. You never knew who would come out the other side.

The plans had moved along for Charmaine to in fact have the outpatient surgery in Dr. Hope's office the same week as this session would be. She had probably forgotten the upcoming surgery between her sessions; trying to convince me (as well as herself) that she was only under stress rather than a woman with DID, and all the many times of disassociation where the Alters had burst out and wanted to bring me up to speed on their fears, thoughts and their perspectives.

It was a challenging time, keeping up with so many issues and personalities. Information was constantly changing. Charmaine was changing. As her understanding of what was going on in her life deepened, she grew. I had no idea what might happen in the office during this session. This was our first since the infamous picture, and the parade of Alters.

As my thoughts wandered I realized I was taken back to the visit where Charmaine had told me she heard sounds inside her head; sounds that were muffled and far away. Distinct sounds; I had to wonder now if she was hearing the voices of her Alters as they gathered in the vast hallway in her head. This woman was working hard to understand things that even the most brilliant researchers struggle with at times.

I had a visual of all the Alters being mothered and monitored by Deseree; trying to maintain order, under her guidance and watchful eye. I would not want that responsibility for love nor money. Although I understood Bart to be the gatekeeper, it seemed that the Deseree had a lot to do with gate keeping also.

I knew that the video had opened Charmaine's eyes and mind to the reality of her life. She had watched it very intensely. After seeing herself in that mirror, coming to the decision that her attempts at denying this diagnosis could no longer work in any way, shape or fashion for her.

Once she had settled in, discovered the pearls, and questioned the outfit and heels she found herself trapped in for that time and place, she was lost in seeing herself as Deseree, then JR, as Charie, and all the others. Those times when she needed to pause, to absorb it. Wanting more, needing to sear it in her brain as further proof, or evidence of her truth was paramount in acceptance.

Allowing her to witness this in her time, in her way was the most important thing. Watching her as she viewed her other personalities was painful at times. It was also affirmed as it spoke louder than I would ever be able to. She had expressed a wish that she could know why she was hated so by Zoe. She would like to sit face to face with her and have that discussion. Then smiled at me saying "Did you just hear what I said, Doc? Now that is a hoot..." She was able to find humor in the good, the bad, and the ugly as it were, and that was perhaps her greatest point of healing resiliency.

As I looked back in my thoughts of the Alter JR, his toughness, his roughness; I could not help but smile thinking of him coming into the office from the bathroom in Deseree's dress and plopping down, tucking that dress between his legs.

I am certain that had he been able to see himself, there would have been a holy terror in the office that day. But I was more surprised to realize that it was caught on tape for Charmaine to see. I felt certain that by now he was giving Deseree an earful about that in the hallway of Charmaine's brain; cussing like a sailor, as Charie was asking to come back to the office to play and tell me more secrets.

Little Buck probably grabbed hold of every word being said in hopes that he could repeat it like a parrot, and use those words for the attention he longed so desperately for as well. While everyone else would be silent as JR ranted on until Deseree brought him to silence by letting him know it was time for him to calm down, and he would, at her insistence.

Yes, the more that I thought about our sessions together, how far Charmaine had come in her work with me, the more I was astounded at the workings of DID, the triggers that seemed to activate the different personalities, with the call to come out and take over.

The best thing I knew was that while I was thinking about this, my client would be investigating, would be planning on how she would fight through this. She had long ago told me that she would fight hard if she only knew what it was she was fighting. The more I thought about that, it seemed that statement might have been born from a combination of her and her most helpful Alters working together in unison.

As I was thinking about Charmaine, and her next appointment with Dr. Hope later in the week, I heard the door open. I got up from where I had been sitting and heard footsteps; realizing I was holding my breath. I had by now learned to listen with all my senses. I was desperately hoping it was Charmaine. I did not hear singing or heavy footsteps or heels clicking, so I felt good. Then I heard "Hello Doc" as Charmaine came into the room. I felt even better as she hugged me on her way in. We took our seats. I noticed that she had on dark colors, and reached for her water on the desk as she smiled at me. She did seem to enjoy that I had water nearby or offered coffee for sessions; that was never lost on me.

I let Charmaine know that I had much to talk with her about and together I had hopes that we would accomplish a great deal today. She let me know right off the bat that she did not like the sound of that. I sounded much too formal for her, making her wonder if something was wrong.

I assured her that nothing was wrong, but that some things, as usual, had come up and that we had a lot to do. That her surgery was approaching and she might also want to spend some time on that issue. I wanted her to focus. I thought that by letting her know we had work to do, it might just help. I was wrong.

Charmaine let me know she did not like the beginning of that pronouncement. She liked it best when we were "laid back," when things just flowed. "Now you have made me nervous Doc" which was followed by laughter, talk of her flowers, the weather, and that she liked what I was wearing. Charmaine was getting tense. She then began to tell me she had no recall of leaving the house. She had planned to tell me about watching a movie last night, then waking this morning not knowing if she ate dinner or why she was on the couch rather than in her bed.

It was time to let her know about my evening. That is when I showed her the title of my notes for the session, "The good, the bad the ugly." She looked at me with a haunting stare. I went on to explain to her the events of the night before. She became silent, with the exception of gasps from time to time, and "oh no Doc" at others.

At one point she pulled out her journal and showed me the writing that she had found as she drank coffee before leaving for her appointment. She could not understand it. As she listened to me, the journal entry became crystal clear to her. She was reading Tina's account of the evening's events. To me it was enlightening, in fact quite remarkable; for Charmaine it was frightening, yet reaffirming of her diagnosis.

Often I would reach over to her and touch her hand, hoping to ground her in the now, the present, offering support. She needed to know that she was safe. That last night had happened, but no harm had come to her.

There were times we sat in silence. She asked why I had written those words on top of my notes. I told her that I felt our time today would be all those things and more. She agreed. She wanted to know if I had video of the man from the restaurant; sadly I did not. I am fortunate that she knows I would not lie to her. She seemed to believe it was true.

She said she believed me, but that it was still hard to grasp. I let her know I could understand that feeling. I was there when it happened, yet I had walked past the table and stopped to make sure I was really seeing her or an Alter. I had done a double-take, deciding whether or not to intervene. It was a hard decision to make, but one that needed to be made. I saw her appreciation and felt her fear of what could have been.

Charmaine thought some more, then wondered where her protector JR had been. Why had he not appeared and kicked that man's ass for her. One more time she felt vulnerable with no one to help her. I tried to explain once again that Alters like JR come out when a threat is perceived; because Tina was having a good time, no threat was felt. That is why he did not jump out and do anything.

We were trying to make sense out of something that was beyond making sense of it, yet on some level, it did make sense. As we talked, and as Charmaine pondered the situation, she asked for a cup of coffee. She said that she felt so tense that it was as if worms were crawling inside of her body. Perhaps a cup of coffee would help.

I left to get us both a cup, knowing that Charmaine's description indicated to me that there was unrest and agitation; wondering if the Alters were perhaps being talked to by Deseree or if her nerves were just raw. When I returned I found her in the chair looking uncomfortable. She was deep in thought, her shoulders tense, pulled up almost up to her neck. We definitely needed to do some visualization and relaxation therapy before she left today.

Placing the coffee cup on the table, I sat down. Charmaine launched herself from the chair with such force she knocked me into my chair. I yelled at her

"CHARMAINE WHAT..." Her eyes were wild with hatred. A child's voice screamed "I HATE HER I HATE HER, AND I HATE YOU TOO FOR ACTING LIKE SHE IS SO WONDERFUL, SHE LET US BE DESTROYED AND DID NOTHING TO STOP IT."

All of a sudden, I found her arm had come up and the letter opener from my desk was in her hand as if she was ready to stab me. I instinctively grabbed her arm; trying to get my balance and get her away from me. I knew that this was not Charmaine, but Zoe who had come out now and was pissed.

Her rage was unyielding. She was wild as she flailed about, trying to speak at the same time. Spittle was coming from her mouth, profanities spewing from her lips; her body intently aggressive in her attempt to use that letter opener. I was struggling with all my might to move her away from me and to keep her from harming herself or me. Things were flying across the desk. My chair and hers were knocked over.

I screamed "Charmaine, stop" to no avail, and then I realized it was Zoe. I realized Zoe was not going to stop, could not stop, as she raged on, trying to free her arms from my grasp to hit me, kicking me in the frenzy.

I then screamed for Deseree, then for JR to get his ass out here NOW, to hurry. "JR I NEED YOU TO GET OUT HERE," I remember screaming as Zoe broke loose. She took a swipe at her own arm with the letter opener and I saw blood. I reached once again for her arm, wrestling her against the wall.

I was fighting like a street fighter when all of a sudden I heard a voice stronger and stronger saying, "Calm down Showalter, damn it stop fighting me, it's JR, relax. I got you woman." I was out of breath, sweating like a dog, and could taste blood on my lip. Still rigid, I heard again, "SHOWALTER IT'S JR, IT'S ALRIGHT I'M HERE, I GOT YOU BABE... Damn you are one tough ass woman, it's me JR. It's alright, I'm here now."

I felt my body relax. I let myself breathe saying, "Hell JR, what took you so damn long friend?" He laughed, "Damn Showalter, you are one tough ass woman, but your lip looks like it's bleeding; you ok? I think we need a smoke don't you?"

JR let go of me and went to pick up the chair that was now overturned, across the office against the wall. I stood against the opposite wall watching as he picked up the papers that were now all over the floor, and stacked them neatly on the desk without saying a word or looking in my direction.

I just stood there, unable to move for a moment, or several, as I tried to get myself together. I noticed the coffee cups on the floor, the coffee spilled both on the desk and on the carpet. I worked to catch my breath, then moved to get a tissue to wipe my mouth and look in the mirror to be sure I had gotten all the blood off. Then I walked to the desk, cleaned up the spill, before looking at JR who stood quietly before asking if I was ready for that smoke with him, on the porch.

Oh yes, I was more than ready, I could once again feel my own heartbeat; I could hear my breathing, feel my feet under me. I smiled at JR and let him know I was ready. We walked out to the porch in silence. I could see the swag in his walk. Once again I was reminded how grateful I was that he came out when called. I wondered how the hell this had all happened so quickly, and how I had forgotten about that letter opener.

As if he had read my mind he said, "I got here as quick as I could Showalter, I really did, but damn, Zoe is a mean one. I'll take care of her little ass when I get back, don't you worry about that. I'll take care of her. You know how to hold your own Showalter, impressive I have to tell you... you were on her ass like white on rice. Are you sure you're alright now? I mean damn, I know you're alright, but did you check to see if you are bleeding anywhere else is what I mean..."

I had to laugh at JR. He was so tough, yet tender at the same time, in his own way. As we talked I realized that it would have been hell had he not come when he did. The reality struck me that someone could have gotten seriously hurt. The letter opener had been lying out on my desk for months. I had not paid a bit of attention to it, in fact had used it just that morning to open some boxes that arrived, leaving it there without a second thought.

I was waiting for JR to say something about that but he did not. It seemed he was a bit winded himself, and more worried if I was going to be alright when he left. He expressed his concern about how "She was going to handle this shit" when she finds out. He kicked the porch with his toe of his boot.

I told JR that I had to let Charmaine know what had happened, and why I thought it had happened. I felt strongly that she would feel badly, but she had to know the truth. As I watched JR, I knew that we had to get back inside and that he would have to send Charmaine back to me.

I also felt confident that Deseree was dealing with Zoe and that she would not come back to express her rage now. I was feeling calmer. I knew that I was ready to continue. I thanked JR, and asked that he also thank Deseree for me, while hugging the little ones.

JR winked and gave me his devilish grin saying, "You know Showalter, if I ever get in a jam, I would want you with me, you are one helluva woman in a fight... I know that now first hand. Glad to be here for ya. Take it easy with her; she is going through a lot of stuff now with that appointment coming up. I'm goin to have to do that for her too you know."

Together we walked back into the office. I assured him I would take best care of Charmaine. I walked down the hall to get more coffee as he took a chair in the office. I stopped in the bathroom to make a quick assessment of my hair, my lip, and my face. To do a quick once over, making sure I did not look like I had been in a barroom brawl.

A few scratches and a bit of bruising, but all in all, I was good. I poured coffee and then heard a voice from the hall saying, "Doc are you alright down there?" It was the voice of Charmaine, I was sure she was wondering what was taking me so long. I let her know I was on my way as I poured two cups of coffee and smiled to myself, walking back to the office.

Charmaine took one look at me and said, "Lordy I thought I would have to come and find you it took you so long." I smiled, handing her the cup as I sat beside her in my chair. In my head was the question; how to proceed? With what had just happened, we had just entered a new realm and it was ugly.

Before I could speak Charmaine leaned into me and touched my face exclaiming, "Doc what in the world happened to your FACE and lip... oh my God." As I went to take her hand, I noticed the blood on her wrist. All I could think was "oh crap, Zoe cut herself with that damn opener and Charmaine has yet to see it."

I took Charmaine's hand in mine. With my calmest voice, I said, "Charmaine, I need you to listen to me very carefully, to work harder than you ever have to stay with me in the moment ok?" She did not move. I reached for a Kleenex and placed it on her wrist holding it tightly there and continued. Her eyes remained on me.

"Charmaine, this is not the first time I brought coffee to us. When I returned from making it the first time, I sat it on the desk. When I started to sit down, Zoe flew out and it was not good. She was in a rage and went ballistic on me. She directed all that anger at me, and she tried to harm you too. I tried to protect you, but it looks like, when she got away from me, she was able to graze you with the letter opener. I think you are ok, but just noticed you are bleeding.

I continued talking calmly to Charmaine. I told her that the scratches on my face and lip were from ZOE. Calmly I said, "I am alright. I need to look at your arm now ok... stay with me now." Charmaine's breathing was shallow but she stayed present, just sitting, staring at me incredulously as I blotted her wrist; noting that the cut was not deep enough to require stitches. It had almost stopped bleeding as I looked closely.

I had her walk with me to the bathroom where we cleaned it up and put a bandage on it. Together we returned to the office. I kept my hand on Charmaine's arm. I had hoped that by talking in a low tone remaining calm and in control, she would not feel the need to flee; or that another Alter would not want or need to burst forward. I was not real sure what I might say or do if another Alter jumped out at me in that moment. Oh yes, my nerves were a bit raw!

I could only hope that Deseree and JR kept Zoe in her room. Please Creator, lock that one up with all the help of the others that could be mustered I found myself saying over and again. I realized the adrenaline rush from Zoe's attack had left me weak in the knees and on high alert.

Charmaine wanted to know more. Her concern for me seemed to keep her in the here and now, or now and then as it is. Her concern for me had trumped her upset for herself. She was right there in the moment, listening hard, as quiet tears of concern streaked her face. She just kept staring at me with the look of "holy shit, did I do that" on her face.

I continued, describing what had happened when Zoe appeared. I shared that I had called on Deseree, screamed for JR to help. Zoe had required every bit of strength I had while defending myself against Zoe. Her rage was scary. That Zoe also was working through her past trauma. As I talked, I found I was able to relax a bit. It was Charmaine I was talking to, only Charmaine.

I found myself laughing as I recalled JR's words telling me to calm down. I recalled for Charmaine the words JR used to assure me that it was him, there in that moment, struggling to get me to hold still.

That was the first time I saw the expression on Charmaine change from absolute fright and concern to a smile. We both laughed with relief when I quoted JR saying, "Dammit Showalter it's me, JR" as he shook loose from my grip.

I had to admit to Charmaine that it was intense; it was in fact frightening while it was happening. It all happened so quickly that I felt like I was in a street fight. She let me know that she was so very sorry. She kept repeating that she could not imagine it. She then, for the first time, looked at her wrist and arms.

We looked at each other as she held her arms up for me to see. They were both red with marks. Aside from the gash, it was obvious that I'd had a strong grip on her. Knowing it was Zoe, not Charmaine that I had fought. It was self-defense at that point. I needed to be sure I kept that clear in my head, as well as hers as we talked about it.

Charmaine wanted to talk more about the whole thing, how I felt about "her" now that it had all happened. I needed to reassure her that this was not her, it was an Alter. The most important thing was to realize that we had to work together in order to figure out why it had happened. We had to dig deeper in understanding the rage, the messages in the journal, and to be alert for those triggers if possible. She was concerned that this altercation would change our working relationship; that I would feel differently about her as a person. While I listened to her concerns, I assured her again, it was not her Charmaine, it was her Alter working out the rage within.

I was convinced that I had been lucky in those moments. That part of the lashing out was a result of Charmaine becoming more aware of the Alters. As Charmaine was becoming more in control of her life, the Alters were becoming more threatened or at least I believed that to be true. That had to be extremely threatening to Zoe as we had moved closer to understanding the traumas that caused her behavior.

Zoe wanted to harm her, to harm anything that was associated with her. It seemed that the warning from Deseree had come to fruition at a time when I had not been paying full attention. The opportunity presented itself in that session, Zoe grabbed it.

Once again JR had appeared just in time to take over to protect Charmaine from harm. This time he also protected me. I was indeed grateful for his help as I sat there, realizing my body was feeling the effects of the rumble. It could have gone very badly as I think back.

Charmaine wanted to know if we could spend more time together once she noticed that we were running over our allotted time. I had actually forgotten all about the time. Interesting how that happened. I quickly jumped up to check what was on my appointment book. I realized I had a client coming in later that evening, but only for resources, not a session, so I was good to continue.

We decided to take a walk for a change of scenery. I needed the opportunity to get out of the office, Charmaine was grateful for the opportunity as well to get air. I gathered resources for the next client leaving them in the waiting area with a note in order to not be interrupted later.

The break seemed to do us both good. I knew for me it was a necessary thing at the time. I needed to clear my head with some fresh air. We walked quietly together around the block admiring the flowers. Charmaine seemed deep in thought. I was just glad to be outside stretching my body. The silence was restoring to my senses as well.

We returned to the office and sat down, both of us looking more relaxed than we had just a short time before. Charmaine wanted to talk more about what had happened. She wanted to understand why Zoe hated her so much. She wished that she could sit down with Zoe to attempt to explain that she had no memory of what had happened to her years ago. Charmaine said she only wished she could convince Zoe that she never meant her any harm.

As I listened, I could not help but want to move on to talk about the impending surgery with Dr. Hope, yet I was drawn to ask Charmaine the last thing she remembered before Zoe burst forward. I asked her what was she thinking as I went for coffee the first time. As I asked the question, I noticed Charmaine shift in her chair. I knew she was trying to remember what we had been talking about.

I saw her tension building. I reached over taking her hand, reminding her that she was safe. She smiled. Charmaine told me that she remembered sitting in the office when all of a sudden she felt like she had worms crawling inside of her, saying it was the strangest sensation she had ever felt in her life.

I then remembered her telling me that when she had first asked for coffee. She had told me about this, saying that perhaps a cup of coffee would calm her. I recalled that she appeared to stiffen and grimace about the same time. I wondered as she spoke, as that happened to her if those feelings were Zoe trying to get out of the hallway in Charmaine's brain. Had the anger building within Zoe created that physical feeling of turmoil in Charmaine? I wanted to know had she ever experienced a similar sensation before. I sensed discomfort in her body language, and feared another Alter or Alters were fighting Bart even as we sat together.

I quickly switched gears wanting to engage Charmaine in breathing exercises. Guided imagery focusing on breathing had worked beautifully with

Charmaine in her high stress times. My hope was to try to restore balance to her while stabilizing her fears and anxiety, thinking it would allow Deseree, Bart and JR to manage things, while giving Charmaine a sense of renewed control.

As I led her in a guided imagery, I saw her relax. I continued on as I watched she became more comfortable. Her breathing slowed down as her body let the stress move through and out of her. She was able to just let it all wash away. She sat there in a totally safe relaxed state. For that I was grateful. She had her eyes closed, her breathing was easy.

I asked her to allow herself to return to the room, to me when she was ready. I encouraged her to take her time enjoying the visual we had created. I saw her smile; watched her as she slowly returned to the moment. She looked more refreshed, ready to continue. She opened her eyes, adjusting to the light, the room and her surroundings. She said once again she enjoyed visualization and imageries in therapy.

The techniques and interventions she stated "Always seem to calm me Doc, to soothe me and to ready me for whatever is next." She seemed to always use them as a solid coping tool for what lay both within, and in front of her. I was grateful that she had started using the breathing exercises at home when she felt increased stress. I let her know this was going to be a part of her daily homework now since we had gotten the Alters moving within her more. My hope was that more interaction would occur within her.

Charmaine was ultimately one of the most committed clients to her own well-being I had had the honor of working with. She struggled to accept so much of what she had been confronted with, remaining dedicated to the process of peeling the onion of trauma. Grief? Yes, she had grief issues stemming from abuse, from the way things should have been for a child, to an adult, a marriage that was abusive, a life that was confused by others that left her feeling crazy as one woman struggling with huge lapses in memory, no one to talk to or a way to figure it all out alone.

Once she had re-centered in the guided imagery, I changed tracks. It was time to talk about the impending surgery while she was in the office. I asked her if she was ready for her appointment with Dr. Hope. We discussed the details, her fears and concerns. I made arrangements to pick her up at her home for the surgery.

Once again we talked about her not having anything by mouth after midnight, the standard preparations to make. Then I stressed the need to monitor, maintain her stress levels during the evening. I suggested she journal her thoughts feelings to maintain control for the evening, get a good night's sleep.

We both knew that it was possible that an Alter could come out and take over at any point. Neither of us knew what might occur after she left the office, but hoped for the best while trying to make plans for the "what ifs."

We discussed the idea of "self-talk" while enlisting Deseree in the process to keep the others in check while Charmaine used all of her own coping skills. I hoped she would be reassured, knowing that I would arrive and be with her during the procedure.

Once again I went over again the trust that she had established with Dr. Hope. Charmaine hoped that the surgery would put an end to the physical pain she had lived with for decades. She felt that Dr. Hope was an angel for offering to help her for free. I asked if she had any questions about the surgery. She felt sure that Dr. Hope's explanation of the surgery was still fresh in her mind.

As we wrapped up our session, I reminded Charmaine that she could call me if she felt nervous or anxious. I felt strongly that she was in control. Charmaine had grown in many ways since our work together began. For that I felt she should applaud herself.

She looked at me with such intensity when she spoke, "Doc, please do not patronize me, we both know that I haven't done that good or you would not be sittin' here with scratches on your face, looking like you've been in a barroom brawl and a busted lip... I would not be sittin here with a bandage on my arm either. I HATE this, and still don't know enough to prevent any of it from happening again. As far as tomorrow goes, I am scared to death about it, but I've got to pull up my panties and get through it. So I'm going to do the best I can and trust that you are not goin' to leave me. We are goin 'to get through this, all right?"

I met Charmaine's eyes with my own. I realized once again that here I was, with a woman who was a genuine steel magnolia in many ways, one who was constantly teaching me. I was not patronizing her, yet that is what she heard. She put her best voice out there. I heard her loud and clear. I realized that much of what I had said in my effort to soothe and comfort her, she already knew. She would have called if she needed to. She knew that without my saying it. She only needed my presence not my words.

Lesson learned I was grateful for it. It was another one of those reminders a practitioners' best teachers are our patients and clients; Charmaine was one of my greatest teachers. She and her Alters taught me well along the journey and into the hallway and out.

I remember walking Charmaine out to the porch, noticing that the materials I had left for the client wanting resources were gone. Interesting, I had not heard the door open, nor heard a car come or go. We both said our goodbyes for the evening with plans made for when I would arrive to pick her up for her surgery.

Charmaine would call to touch base between now and the appointed day. She seemed to be fine with the plan. As she walked to her car, she turned back and held her journal up in the air, "Well, Doc, I guess I will just keep writing. One day we'll get to look at this together." I waved thinking to myself then, it seemed we were living that journal faster than she could write in it. I did look forward to reading it with her someday.

Charmaine called me a couple of days later. She said that she would have me a cup of coffee ready for me when I arrived to pick her up. She wanted to know how my face was, had the swelling subsided, if the scratches would leave a scar… "Doc, are *you* alright is what I am trying to say?" I could hear both concern and nervousness in her voice.

I laughed, while letting her know I was doing fine. I also let her know I would be bringing my own coffee as I did not want her to have to smell the pot brewing, knowing she could not have any. I could tell something was on her mind, so I made small talk for a few minutes. I inquired how her day had been.

She said she had found some interesting entries in her journal, wondering if I had a few minutes to talk. I had just finished with a client. The beginning of paperwork could hold for the moment. I asked what was on her mind. It did not take long to ascertain that Charmaine had found an entry by an Alter wanting me to know about it. I knew something more than concern for my face was on her mind.

Charmaine went on to tell me that when she sat down at the table to write in her journal regarding her fear of the surgery, she saw in bold print, not her handwriting "I COULD HAVE HURT YOU BAD BITCH, I HATE YOU" glaring at her. It was the most recent entry as she opened the new page to write. She went on to tell me that she almost spit her coffee across the room as she stared at the page, remembering what had happened in the office. I was listening intently as she continued with her discovery.

Praying that she would not lose her train of thought, I asked her to read more of it to me. She continued to read aloud, mostly about entries from JR. I wanted to know her thoughts about what she had read. When I tried to ask she dug in, insisting that I tell her what I thought. It was then that I detected her voice change. "Enough of this crap. Now Showalter, what time are you coming to get me in the mornin darlin'?"

That was followed by a deep laugh. I realized that JR was on the phone. Charmaine had vanished, "poof gone." Just telling me what she had read in the journal had once again been too much for Charmaine. "Well hello JR, good to hear your voice", I heard myself say on my end of the phone. In my head I was saying, (oh crap here we go; now I have to talk to JR, while wondering about what else she found).

JR let me know that he was on his way to the office, so I had better clear my schedule, he said. This was not going to wait. With that, the phone went dead. End of conversation. I sat there staring at the phone wondering what in the hell had just happened. JR was on his way? No appointment, no request to be seen? The Alter JR wanted, no demanded to see me! Well how about that now I stood in a bit of pissed disbelief to be honest.

I quickly took a look at my appointment book, tidied up the toy area, glanced at my desk to see what was lying in the open. I tried to put my paperwork in order, neatly in my drawer. Noting the letter opener lying out, I found a safe home for it in a hot second. Then I piled up any and all sharp objects dumping them in the drawer as well.

This certainly was not on tap for the day. I could not imagine what issue had prompted JR's objective to rush over to the office. I had no appointments scheduled for Charmaine or anyone else for that matter. I had intended to catch up on paperwork. The well laid plans of mice and women I found myself thinking, oh crap now I have to deal with JR and who knows who as a result of a simple conversation with Charmaine.

\\\\\\\\\\\\\\\\\\\\\

Alters

JR told Deseree that he needed to go out for some air before the surgery tomorrow and would be back later. Deseree nodded assuming that he was taking a walk. He liked to take long walks, she thought.

JR eased into the garage and uncovered the motorcycle and rolled it out, closed the garage door and eased down the driveway before starting it.

He took off down the road, loving the feel of the air on his face. Boy was the doc in for a surprise this time.

JR sat at a light with his motorcycle idling. He loved when the women walked by and flirted with him.

CHAPTER 21   THE WIND IN MY FACE

I had planned on paperwork for the afternoon, maybe some sand in my shoes walk on the beach as well. JR jumping in on my phone call with Charmaine put a wrinkle in that idea. I sat there sipping my coffee that I had brought with me while nibbling on a donut. As soon as I finished, I realized that JR still had not shown up. It usually did not take him this long I thought as I glanced at my watch. I was about to lose my patience. If he had messed up my afternoon, I swear. I got up, stretched extending my arms to the sky then walked out to the front porch.

I was rather amazed when outside. There sat a motorcycle parked with someone leaning against it, smoking a cigarette. Legs crossed, gazing up. Then I heard a familiar voice. "Well hell...good lookin' whatcha got cookin on this fine ass afternoon? And why in the world are you here at your office Showalter?" As I walked closer, I see JR grinning, his forefinger tipping his ball cap, leaning against a motorcycle, one leg crossed over the other as he greeted me. Oh crap flashed in my mind as I see that wicked grin hearing the greeting play again in my mind.

My first thoughts were what is JR's game?: followed immediately with amusement at such a funny greeting from the old Hank William's song if memory serves me right. As I got close enough to say hello, JR straightened up from leaning on the bike. He stubbed out the cigarette with his boot. Then he bent over to pick up the butt putting it in is his pocket. I liked the idea that he was so courteous. The grin had never left his face as he raised back up winking at me.

"OK, JR, what brings you to my office so urgently? And what was so important that I had to clear my schedule?" I attempted to sound firm, but found I had lost my "ready to kill him" feeling. I admired the bike as I waited for the reply. I was not about to let him know that I had nothing but paperwork on the schedule.

He continued to grin as he told me that he figured he better get a ride in before the surgery as the "girls" might not feel like riding for a few days. "Showalter, you look like you could use a break. We're burning daylight just looking at them clouds you know... how about that ride you been promising me." With that JR patted the seat of the motorcycle and grinned wide. "Hell you're not afraid of ole' JR, are ya Showalter... c'mon let's go for a ride together!"

I smiled at JR, all the while knowing that this was another test. JR, wanting to see if I was capable of trusting him, me stepping way outside of the box; in our work together on behalf of Charmaine. The Alter who rushes out to protect his host Charmaine, now wanting me to trust him it seemed, or to see just how much he could really trust me perhaps.

As thoughts flooded my mind, I recalled Charmaine telling me she had no idea how to ride a bike. She denied ever having a bike, ever driving a bike or ever being on a bike as a passenger! I must be out of my ever-loving mind I heard myself say, "Well alrighty then JR, just give me a minute to close the office and lock up. I'll be right with you, but we can't be gone too long, I have things to get done today." With that I winked and said, "I'll be right back, do you need to come in or are you ok here?"

As I started to walk off I noticed shock flash across his face. His grin got even wider as he replied, "Damn Showalter, really? You really gonna take a ride with me? Hot damn, I'll be right here waitin.' I have an extra helmet, even though you don't have to have one in this state, but I have one if you want it."

I pretended to not notice the excitement in his voice. I just walked inside the office to grab my phone, sending a quick text to a friend of mine noting I'd be taking a spin on a motorcycle with a client, just in case. Note to self. Never leave home without letting someone know, and always take your phone.

This should be most interesting; I do love the feel of wind in my face. As I walked back out to JR, I found myself saying a small prayer that JR stays JR while driving. I found JR in front of the stairs, the motor being revived as I walked down the steps. JR sat tall on the front with a wicked happy grin. He patted the back of the seat indicating for me to mount the bike. I had to laugh at his raw enthusiasm. He gunned it to impress me.

We hit the road slowly making the turn. Off we went to parts unknown as JR found the throttle shifting through the gears, picking up speed. I noticed that he glanced often in the rear view mirror at me sitting back there. I wondered if it was to see my reaction, or to make sure that this ride was real.

Oh it was very real. The wind hit stronger as the road went by faster. We approached a wide stretch of country style road. There was nothing but open space, black pavement for miles with a few curves that allowed me a different view. On that open road, JR was having the time of his life. I on the back of that bike, now holding on for dear life, leaning up to notice the speedometer had hit 88.

As we approached a curve I let out a loud, "Slow it down JR" only to hear his loud laugh. As we rounded another curve I noted that we were closer to the pavement that I would ever want to be again. That was when JR got to feel the real strength in my hands. As the bike straightened up we hit 95+ MPH. The trees rushed by and the wind began to sting.

I punched him in the side so hard I swear I bent his rib as I leaned close yelling, "Slow this damn thing down JR, and I mean NOW!" I had a hold of his side not easing up until I could feel the decrease in speed. Only then did I release my grip, realizing that Charmaine would at some point see a fine bruise that I would probably have to explain to her. At that point I just did not care; I had to get JR's attention. It seemed that was the only way at the time!

I looked in that same mirror and caught sight of JR absorbed on driving that fine-tuned bike, still grinning. I once again felt more comfortable on the back of that bike, once again enjoying the wind and the scenery. The smells of grass, dirt, wind whirling were really mixing with my thoughts; all went by like the two black tires that surrounded those chrome wheels.

We had been riding for almost an hour. I noticed a billboard sign for a burger joint coming up. JR was in his glory, relaxed. He was quite capable of handling the bike I might say. I motioned to the sign and said, "Stop when we get there ok." JR nodded as he took one hand off the bar, placing it against his ball cap, gesturing with his pointer finger as if saluting me.

It was indeed a glorious day for a bike ride. The sky was remarkable I found myself thinking once again, as I felt the bike slowed down. I noticed the place ahead of us, on the right with a few cars and a lot of motorcycles parked. JR beautifully maneuvered off the road pulling right into the lot before coming to a stop. One last "revv" (rumble ~ rumble ~ rumble) of the engine before it was cut off as he flipped the kickstand down leaning that bike to its side like a pro.

I dismounted from the back stretching my body realizing it had been a while since I had ridden on a motorcycle. My muscles were wondering what I had just put them through as I glanced at a laughing JR. "You wanna smoke Showalter; you ride fine, just fine. But damn, why did you go and pinch me back there? My ribs are killin me. I thought I would wreck this baby! This place looks like a damn good juke joint don't it?"

I laughed and let JR know that if he had a bruise later to remember that's what happens when you take curves too tight or hit that speedometer to high. I grinned as I watched JR dramatically rub his rib cage as if he had been punched several times over. I lit a smoke as together we stood admiring the other bikes. Seems we both were a bit stiff from riding now that I think back.

After we smoked, we went inside this little place that looked like it was lost in time. A fair number of bikers were seated in booths, others sat at a long worn bar. A juke box was playing country music in the background. The booths had vinyl seats with dark wood tables. The tables were old, stained with the circles where many bottles had marked them.. Yes, I thought, this place had been here for a long time.

We found a booth as far away from the crowd as possible. I was ready for a cold beer and a cheeseburger. JR sat down across from me, stating he sure would like to know how I enjoyed the ride, the sights, and the speed as he laughed loud. He wanted to "order us a couple of cold ones, being that we were in such a fine establishment." That made me laugh so hard I thought I would split a gut. He was "Joe Cool" but like a little kid with questions, statements as he took it all in looking around.

The waitress appeared to glance first at JR, then at me. She was friendly, wanting to know what she could bring us. JR sat quietly looking at me as I asked what kind of beer they had. JR was watching me, watching the waitress, grinning the entire time. I ordered a Michelob Ultra in a bottle. JR jumped in quickly saying, "Make that two and make em' cold darlin!" as he winked at her.

The waitress giggled as she walked away. Quickly returning with two beers, along with menus that appeared to be as old as the building we were sitting in. As we sat there, I was amazed by JR, the ease of him, his persona; remembering that it was Charmaine's body that had been taken over. Charmaine now nowhere to be found, JR had taken over so well in fact, that I had easily transitioned to time with JR. I was with her Alter JR, and he was so very different than Charmaine. For starters he was all male!

In no time, the waitress appeared again, ready to take our order. We were not complicated; cheeseburgers' and fries for both of us. Once again JR waited until I ordered then followed with a comment for emphasis yet the order was the same. I waited until the waitress was gone, beer in front of us, order placed. Now I wanted to hear what he had to say.

I wanted to know more. More about JR, the others, about Charmaine; about his role in her life, now was the opportunity. JR was open in his conversation with me, his great love for Charmaine's kids and his role as her protector. He talked at length about his strong dislike of her ex-husband, referring to him as a "Pig", a "sorry excuse of a man." He got a bit too loud in his descriptions at times, leading me to place my hand on his arm and remind him to lower his voice.

JR also talked about the regrets. He felt remorse at times that he could not get out to make things better; to be more, to do more for Charmaine over the years. At one point JR met eyes with mine stating, "Hell

Showalter I was just a kid too. I didn't know what was happening I guess. That sure did tear me up though, all the shit she has been through, I should have been able to protect her. You know what I'm saying?"

As I sat looking intently at JR, I felt such emotion, such sadness for all he had endured through the years, trying to be the one to protect Charmaine, to be the hero. I watched him take a long drink of beer as he shifted in his seat. Then he sat up straight, rubbed his hands briskly together and stated, "Well hell, that was then, this is now. What else we goin' to talk about Showalter? Surely there is something good we can talk about ain't there?"

In JR fashion, and as is usual in a restaurant, just as I was about to say something, the food arrived. The waitress had a huge smile on her face for JR. JR decided to flirt. I thought I would just crawl in a hole when that happened and pull it in after me. Instead I kicked him swiftly under the table. That got his attention. Quickly he leaned toward the table as he grabbed his shin, "Damn Showalter"!

"What the hell did ya go and do that for? I will be black and blue before this day is over Showalter!" I laughed, letting him know that he would survive. We both commented on the great burgers. Oldies but goodies continued to blare from the juke box as we ate.

JR seemed to thoroughly enjoy our time together. As we finished our meal and our beer, I asked JR how things were going in the hallway. I was curious how the others were doing. Charmaine and I had come so far together, the Alters seemed more ready to speak, ready to revolt, perhaps ready to accept this thing called DID.

He shrugged his shoulders letting me know that as long as I understood that he had no plans to ever leave Charmaine, we would be all good. Deseree was the chief bottle washer attending to everyone. He only helped when he had to, but he sure did love getting out on a good day riding that bike. JR gave me bits along with pieces as we sat there. He wanted the time to be enjoyable, to be almost celebratory that he had managed to get me on the bike with him. He switched subjects; he often became quiet as he enjoyed the music, the people watching and the beer. I enjoyed watching him.

I could tell by looking at JR he was getting tired. Although he would never admit to it; his sparkling eyes seemed to work harder to sparkle. His laugh was not as easy as when we first sat down. Maybe it was a combination of talking, the beer and the burger.

I asked JR if he wanted dessert, but he declined saying another beer would be great though. I had to let him know then that I wasn't comfortable with that since he was driving; especially since he was driving with my butt on the back of the bike. He seemed alright with that and the twinkle returned to his eye once again as we got up to leave.

I grabbed the check as we headed toward the front door to pay. JR walked right past me. Letting me know he would be outside waiting. I wondered then if when the Alters are out if they ever think about money, the means to pay, the need to provide as JR seemed not at all concerned about the bill or paying it. That's not something I could ask Charmaine about since she is not aware of them coming, going, and doing on any level.

As I walked outside I could see we had been there much longer than I thought. Dusk was falling. I had completely lost track of time. I had enjoyed JR, our time spent. Being unplugged from a dedicated session or his usual walls of defense was a welcomed respite.

It was remarkable actually, the depth of character, of caring, of compassion beneath that tough guy exterior. In that little juke joint, he had let down his James Dean bravado, becoming just a guy who wants it all to work out. Doing what he can backstage, yet willing to come to the center of the stage if he has to.

He did love to shake you up, to try and rattle you, or get a reaction. That was the trickster inside of him. I found it endearing. The playful kid that was lost somewhere in the 50's, a rebel on a Harley, out to have some fun. As I got closer to the bike, JR was again leaning against it with a smoke in his hand. He said, "Well Showalter, I guess we've really been burning daylight, better get back I think. Deseree is goin' to have my head. I have to get home and hide this bike before dark. You ready to ride?"

I smiled at him but before I got on the bike. I looked him right in the eyes. "JR, I want to thank you for this day. I never thought my afternoon would have involved a bike ride, a juke joint, needless to say time with YOU... you are a fine person and I am glad that you trust me." With that statement I leaned in and gave him a hug, mounted the bike and then said, "So what are you waiting for JR, we're burning daylight here!"

JR looked stunned for a moment, actually blushed. He then let out a loud laugh. He kicked the bike into action, revving the engine for the entire world to hear it seemed. He pulled out onto the open road slowly; with me reminding him that I did not want to make a matched bruise on his other side should he think about opening up the engine again.

I could feel the smile in his body language as he revved the engine a couple of times shifting gears as we set off for the office. I enjoyed the curves, the straight road. I truly enjoyed the final destination when the kickstand when down. As we pulled into the parking lot, I was amazed that the sun was setting, the day over. The gifts were plentiful. With me knowing more about Charmaine and Alters than I had to date.

JR pulled right up to the steps and stopped the bike, kickstand down, dismounting. We had a quick smoke together. He let me know he had heard Deseree telling him that he needed to "be quick about getting home" on our way back. "Showalter, this has been one of the best days I can remember in a long time, hell in a really long time. Thanks for listening, and for trusting me enough to get your ass on this bike with me. I gotta get out of here and hide this thing so no one finds it. Oh yea, before I go... that stuff we talked about over that beer? That stays between us babe and I'm holding you to it Showalter. Luv ya."

I stood there absorbing what he had said. I saw JR's shadow with that signature forefinger salute from the tip of his hat. I smiled, tipping my imaginary hat to him as he drove off. I walked up the stairs to my office. I did not get one thing done that I had set out to do on that fine Saturday, but oh boy did a lot of puzzle pieces fall into my lap, along with more blessings than I could count.

Charmaine's Journal

The days have seemed to run in a blur lately. Doc says it is cause of all that is happening. All I know is the hate mail in my journal is getting higher and higher. I thought things would calm down. I do not know what everyone is doing but now that I know about Zoe, I am really scared. I don't know how much to tell Doc about Zoe. I wake up with cuts and bruises and nasty posts in the journal.

My gosh if she fights Doc like she did, she would kill me if she could. Does she not get it that if I die, so does she. I think. I need to ask Doc about this. What if she kills me off and takes my body and lives the rest of her life as Zoe. Is that even possible?

At least my hair stayed the same color for a while. I got where I was investing a lot of money in hair dye to turn it back and where were they getting the hair color from? Where do the clothes come from?

CRAP, CRAP, CRAP...my money is almost all gone. There is a twenty left in there. This was from selling my art, I used it for emergencies. Now, what will I do?

CHAPTER 22 DR HOPE'S CLINIC

I pulled up in the driveway to pick up Charmaine. There standing in the driveway was Charmaine, holding this big doll by one arm. What the hell???? Using my phone, I snapped a picture quickly because I wanted this one for her folder. I pulled into the driveway, got out saying "Good morning Charmaine, are you ready to go?"

She said nothing... she just stood there looking at me, the door to the house was closed. As I got closer I again said, "Charmaine?" I looked again at Charmaine, doing a double take at the doll. It was when she spoke that my brain exploded first thing with "Oh crap am I really in deep" as I heard, "Anna." I stood still watching Charmaine, I mean Anna bow her head and scuff her feet in the dirt driveway clutching an oversized doll in her hand. "Now what Therapist?" I found myself asking myself as we stood there in front of the car.

Quickly I spit out, "Well hello Anna, we are going for a ride, we have an appointment this morning. Let's go get in the car"! The words I had just heard and the name "Anna" resonating in my head. Of all the days, of all the times, here I was standing outside the car with a sad and very quiet Alter, now heading to Dr. Hope's office. Oh my goodness, seriously? Now I have to meet an Alter named Anna?

I start to walk to the car, glance to see if she is with me. Oh no, she is standing where she was before waiting for me I guess. I walk back, she extends her hand to me, and we then walk to the car. I open the door, but oh no, she does NOT get in. Crap crap crap, now what? I look at her, she points to the back door. She wanted to ride in the back seat of the damn car. Where is JR flashes through my mind? I guess he is in the hallway laughing hysterically perhaps. That does me no good right now as my brain continues to send transmissions of "seriously" throughout my nervous system.

Just my luck, was all that crossed my mind. I smiled at her. I opened the door showing her how to get in the back seat, finding myself pulling the seat belt around her until I heard the click of the safety buckle latch. I was sprinting to get into the driver's seat only to find Anna wanted a seatbelt on the doll. Oh crap, it was going to be one of those days.

I leaned between the front seats to belt the big ass doll into the seat beside Anna. She watched it all but did not say a word; no smile...no nothing. She just sat there quietly watching me. I took a picture because There was no way would anyone believe this. Here I am driving a grown woman; now a child carrying a big ole' ass doll. Yep, it was not starting out the way it had been so carefully planned.

I turned around in the driver's seat, backed out of the driveway as I glanced at my passenger with her doll both carefully buckled in. With the car in drive off we went to Dr. Hope. I kept glancing in the rear view mirror. I tried making a couple of attempts at small talk, getting no response. Several times I caught her eye, watching me, watching her. Occasionally I would hear her whisper to her doll, her head turned to the side.

My mind was spinning as I wondered why this Alter had popped out at this particular time. Maybe she just wanted to go for a ride. Surely Anna had not come to take Charmaine's place for the procedure. I had no idea, but it was stressful for me to grasp at the moment. It seemed to take longer than it should to get there, but I finally found a parking space. I had to grin when I thought of taking her hand, walking into Dr. Hope's office. This will be another first.

I jumped out to unbuckle "Anna." She cautiously got out of the car inching away from the door. I turned around only to see her standing stock still. She had stopped. I motioned for her to join me but oh no, she stood there motionless. Now what?

I went back to the car. I asked her if something was wrong, and she pointed at her doll. "CRAP", I thought and then told her I was sorry. She just stood there, said nothing. I scooted around the car keeping one eye on Anna, opened the back door unbuckled the doll and grabbed the doll and ran back around the car, Anna meanwhile had yet to move. I handed her the doll and started to walk sure that she was right beside me. I turned again, and wouldn't you just know it, she was just standing by the car, holding the doll looking at me. She had not moved one step! I walked back to her and said, "What is wrong Anna, let's go ok?" She just stood there. Finally she whispered, "You have to hold our hand." As soon as she spoke she again lowered her head.

I looked at her again. My brain was exploding; I realized I had broken a sweat! I reached to take her hand in mine, starting once again toward the office. Oh come on. At this rate, it would take all day to make it to the lobby. Again she stopped in her tracks. I looked at her and said "Now what Anna?" She said "You have to hold both our hands." Really... oh my goodness was all I could think as fireworks like the 4th of July were exploding within me. I did not think my day could get any worse, but it had. Here I am walking a grown woman with a big ole ass doll between us; her holding one hand of the doll and me the other. This was definitely one for the books. At least I did not have to be in the middle holding her hand along with the dolls hand... or did I? It seems so long ago that I do not remember, but it was a distinct possibility now that I think back.

Not another word was spoken after that. We drew a few stares from other people coming and going that day. At that my goal was to get in and up the elevator to Dr. Hope's office before she sent a posse out looking for us.

As the elevator door closed, I felt the doll's hand tug in mine. In a wink, the doll flew across the elevator hitting the wall. As I looked at her, I saw the strangest expression on her face. She backed up against the wall. Before I could speak or act, I hear, "Showalter what the hell are you doing here, and what the fuck is this?"

It was JR. He was not a bit happy. He looked at me, looked at the doll that he had thrown across the elevator. He was cussing a blue streak at the top of his lungs as the elevator door opened to the 7th floor. I was still standing there, mouth agape as he flew out of the opening door saying, "What kinda shit are you pulling on me Showalter with that pansy ass doll you put in my hand.. Bad enough I have to do this for Charmaine, but I ain't carrying no damn doll in there. You've lost your fuckin mind Showalter, what are you pullin' on me here?" Oh my goodness JR was pissed to be certain. The truth of the matter, I was not the happiest camper on the trail.

I picked up the doll from the floor while trying to gather my wits, the doll and calm JR down. "Listen JR, I DID NOT give you this damn doll to carry. You need to calm down NOW." I told him that he had just showed up in the elevator, it was Anna who had been with me. Anna was the one who was carrying the doll. I told him that I needed him to get himself together and quickly if we were going to get this done. JR was still upset, Anna was gone, the big ass doll in my hand dragging it on the ground as we entered the office finally. Oh yes, this was a great morning.

JR was rattled as he took inventory of himself, what he was wearing, how he looked. He glanced in a mirror in the hall as we passed by it. He insisted on going outside for a smoke before anything else and searched his pockets to see if he had any cigarettes. He let out a huge sigh of relief when he found a pack in the pockets of the sweat pants he was wearing. My mind was reeling as I thought "YOU' are rattled?

JR was mumbling, grumbling, cussing under his breath, as I kept telling him we needed to get inside. He was rattled? Try standing in my morning for God's sakes. I had half expected JR to be waiting in Charmaine's place that morning when I arrived at her house. When it was Anna there, well, I just went with it. For JR to explode onto the scene in the small space of the elevator; flinging the doll away, quite frankly shocked the bejesus out of me. We had 7 floors to ride, and he jumps out within seconds of the door opening… and when I say "jumps out" that is truly how it happened!

I made him walk into the office with me so that I could let Dr. Hope know we were there. I needed to take a few minutes before we would be ready; Dr. Hope needed to get on board the current train. I wanted her to know what was happening. As I ducked into her back office, I left him standing in the waiting room. JR leaned against the wall, one foot propped against the wall, hands shoved in his pockets, a cigarette dangling in his mouth unlit and a scowl on his face. Quite the sight for an OB/GYN office if ever there was I thought as I glanced over my shoulder.

The sight of me, a bit disheveled, dragging a life size doll made Dr. Hope chuckle as she said "My friend, who have you brought with you today? A new client?" I looked at her and said "Oh sure, you laugh my friend, you have no idea. I need about 10 minutes before we are ready. Oh, you might also want to know... you are operating on JR, so take some time to get your head wrapped around that thought. I'll be right back. On second thought, I think I am not sure who it will be when we get back, so don't hold me to it. Oh yes, and this doll is your new assistant. Just call it the big ass doll that greeted me this morning." I placed the oversized doll in her chair suggesting she may want to consult with it while I stepped out.

Dr. Hope got wide eyed, stopped laughing as she wrapped her head around my whirlwind announcement. She immediately let me know that I would be gowning up for whomever we might be working on. She was not the expert in that area. She grinned, wondering if the doll was going to sit in on the surgery. I left the doll with her and returned to a not very happy JR, in the waiting room tapping his feet and checking out his surroundings. Looking like a trapped coyote searching for an escape route.

JR started talking to me as soon as he spotted me walk out. He was giving me hell from the time we walked out the door. Back down the elevator 7 floors nonstop he talked, out the main door, to the smoking area. He talked, he ranted, he paced, and he cussed like a sailor in a row boat. Finally I put my hand up. Enough! I placed my hands on both his shoulders shaking him saying, "I need you to get your shit together and to do it in fast order here. I am not used to seeing you rattled. It does not look good on you Clint Eastwood. I need you to make my day. Pull your act together, ok?" I had had enough of the rant, the cussing, the non-stop talking. I wanted a cup of coffee, some normalcy.

With that said I lit a smoke. JR looked me in the eye, and I hear him start laughing like a mad person saying, "Showalter you are a piece of work, do you know that? Damn woman, to be holding a damn doll, in one hand and yours in the other? C'mon now; even you have to know that is some crazy shit. Only thing worse would have been a pacifier thing in my mouth and a dress on right? Just you wait til' Deseree and I have words about this. I tole her and I tole you, I would do this for Charmaine. But damn, she didn't have to go and embarrass the shit outta me and let little Anna out did she? I mean, I know Anna has never been in a car ride and Deseree told her she could come out and meet you sometime, but damn she didn't need to do it today did she?"

Ah, it was making sense now. I had to agree with JR, it did not need to happen today. My thought exactly. Poor JR, he was on total overload. I had to admit it did not do me a bit of good either. I had to ask JR if he knew whether or not Charmaine had stayed in the house last night; whether or not she had had anything to eat or drink after midnight, had every-thing had been calm. As I asked the questions, I realized I was asking too much from him. He just seemed so out of sorts. My plan was to try and get him back in control as the protector. I addressed him as the one with information that could be helpful. If he had been willing to take this on, he needed to feel in control. That seemed to help him to calm down. The cigarette didn't hurt either. He was chain smoking.

JR let me know that Deseree had been cleaning house the night before and he had taken care of things in the hallway. He had almost gotten his hands on Zoe. Deseree had her on lock down now too. But he had been able to give her a good piece of advice first. Deseree had not stopped him from coming down hard on her. He felt proud of that.

He also said he would be damn glad when all of this was over. He could not understand why women had to have all these things attended to. Women had such complicated parts. He didn't really feel pain, so he couldn't relate to any of it.

"Showalter you do know I'm not goin anywhere don't you? I mean, I'm here for the long haul. As long as Charmaine is alive, then I'm going to be alive, you get that, right? I just want to be sure you get it. Now let's get this shit over with. Don't you ever let me have no damn doll in my hand unless I am playing with one of the little kids. Got it?? You hear me, or I will kick your ass from here to the state line and back and you can bet on that; even though you have a cute ass at that. I mean what I say and I say what I mean. You can take that shit to the bank! Now, I'm ready to do this. Let's go see that Hope Dr. of yours."

I met JR's eyes with mine. I was laughing so hard I felt tears on my face. I promised to never have a doll in his hands, extended my hand and told him, "You have got a deal, no more dolls if I can help it, no more dresses unless it just happens that way. Now JR you have to behave when we get up there, no bullshit with the Dr. you got that part right?" He laughed giving me that wicked grin. We then made the trip back into the building, up those 3 floors on the elevator and into the office together.

JR's walk was distinct. I realized I could spot that walk in a crowd; it was uniquely JR with attitude and I liked it. I definitely knew I would want him around if I found myself in trouble. I had to remind myself that this was JR, but Charmaine too.

That was that day that had been dreaded for so long. As we got off the elevator for the second time, I watched JR pull himself up to his full height. Shoulders back, I watched as he took a deep breath. I held the door open. "Ladies first... Showalter, and a fine one you are. After all, here goes nothing. Hell, I've had worse scratches in my eye than what this is goin to be honey." I walked in ahead of JR halfway wondering if he would turn quickly running for the open door of the elevator.

JR was throwing all the bravado he could muster out there. Heaven help Dr. Hope was all I could think. I heard the door close behind us. The receptionist looked up as the door closed. She was saved from any dialogue as Dr. Hope appeared in the foyer, walking us straight into her office.

JR belted out a greeting to the good Dr. Hope. "How the hell are ya doctor? Are you all ready for some JR love?" She glanced over at me for a bit of reassurance as she extended her hand tentatively toward JR. I laughed saying, "Dr. Hope you remember JR, I'm sure. Are we all set to start?"

Dr. Hope glanced down as she felt the tight grip of JR's hand. She looked at him with a smile while letting JR know it was good to see him again. She stated she was ready if we were. Dr. Hope then directed him to go empty his bladder (which tickled me). When done, she then directed him to a small room to undress, and to put a gown on.

JR looked at me with a funny expression saying, "Well good God, am I gonna be completely naked in there, my ass showin' Showalter? I do not like this Showalter; don't like showin my ass to you women here. Where exactly am I supposed to empty this bladder of mine and what if I don't need to pee?"

I assured JR that his ass would not be shown. If he put one gown on covering his front the other covering his back he would be all good. He seemed to be more comfortable with that. I also wanted him to leave the cigarettes in the pocket of sweat pants. He chuckled at that, and then wanted to know where the "head" was. Dr. Hope showed him both the restroom along with the changing area as I sat down in the office staring at that big ass doll across from me. When she returned I saw her facial expression, I had to stifle my laughter. I quietly told Dr. Hope that everything was going to be alright.

Once JR was situated in his gown, he appeared at the doorway of Dr. Hope's office. He thrust his hip out asking if I thought it looked manly on him! I laughed telling him he could start a new trend in clothing, then asked if he would like to have the doll in the exam room. Oh the look I received was one of "go to hell" if ever there was. Dr. Hope let him know it was time, to follow her. Like little ducklings we walked behind her to the exam room.

Once there Dr. Hope invited him to get on the exam table as she busied herself with things on a counter. I was on the other side of the room trying not to pay attention as he jumped up on that table making chatter and off color remarks. I had no idea what would come out of JR's mouth next, so I had decided to just sit back for the ride. He was on the table; he was off the table, looking over Dr. Hope's shoulder at instruments, at the cabinets looking at me. He was as antsy as a cat on a hot tin roof while talking trash a mile a minute, pacing from one side of the room to the next. He was a mess.

Dr. Hope had her assistants stay out in the hall until her patient was sedated to lessen the stress; which I had thought was an excellent idea; less people less anxiety. I was truly happy given that JR was moving from side to side, unable to be still, unwilling to get on the table until the last moment it seemed. I had put on surgical scrubs and shoe covers; flattering attire indeed. "Well, I'll be damn Showalter, are you goin to operate on me yourself? You look kinda sexy in that outfit but I didn't know we were going to get so personal... you know, me and you. Uh, what do you want me to do now, stand here or throw my happy ass up on that table?"

He just stood there clad in hospital gown; barefoot, pressed up against the wall near the door. He still managed to be funny. I assured him that I was only there to hold a hand or to kick his ass if needed. The banter made him laugh. Trying to look cool, he leapt onto the table once again. This time he almost fell off the other side. I'm sure that Dr. Hope joined me in gasping at that visual before us.

Dr. Hope moved close to him and telling him that he needed to lie down on his back. She then proceeded to tell him that she would be placing an IV in his arm to administer the sedation. She directed him to put one foot in each stirrup at the foot of the bed, to scoot down a bit further on the table.

JR looked aghast. "YOU are going to do WHAT with that needle? You want me to do what with my feet? YOU'VE got to be shitting me... scoot down so my ass hangs off the edge." Showalter you did not say nothing about any of this stuff." JR's voice got louder as he pointed at the stirrups glaring now as he spoke, "She wants me to do that with my feet and spread my legs like wide open for what? Oh hell no. I don't think so honey, I don't do shit like that. And put a needle in my arm? What the fuck would you want to do that for anyway? Why?"

Dr. Hope looked sideways at me, a touch of anxiety in her eyes. My mind began to spin, looking for answers. Of course JR did not know what stirrups were on an exam table. Of course he did not know why or how a person was put to sleep or anything about IV sedation. We had never discussed what to expect with JR. Those conversations had taken place with Charmaine. He had never gone through anything like this. What had I been thinking? I saw panic in his face, he was in high gear. I stepped in close to him. I needed to get his attention quickly with the answers he could handle and understand.

Glancing at Dr. Hope, I winked knowing she would let me take the time to talk to him. Focusing on JR, I explained IV sedation. I had to rely on the bond we had established. Our bond was much closer with trust than that of him and Dr. Hope. He trusted me for the most part to keep it real with him. I told him that the sedation would make him more comfortable during the procedure. He would not feel a thing. He would only experience a pinch, and not as a painful one as I had given him while on the motorcycle ride. I let him know that he would sleep through the whole thing, so that he would not have pain. I reassured him that I would be right there during it all. That seemed to help him in understanding the why's of it.

I let him know he had to trust me; that was why I was in the room with him. He was doing this for Charmaine, her lady parts needed to be fixed. There was no other way. It was the only way just as he had said when he talked about doing this for Charmaine. I reminded him that only the Doctor would be looking and doing the surgery. I would be right beside his head the whole time. I promised I would make sure he stayed safe while assuring him that he could be ornery as ever. I told him he did not have to put his feet in the stirrups, only to lay there for right then. I wanted him to relax. JR's mission was to relax while Dr. Hope pinched him with that needle. I played to his macho bravado. I used his own words as I reminded him that he had "worse scratches in his eye" than what she would be doing. For him this would be a walk in the park.

That seemed to calm him. I nodded to Dr. Hope to continue as I stroked his hair telling him not to get used to my being so good to him. I watched him smile. He started to talk JR trash to me. I saw him glance at Dr. Hope as she put the needle in, back to me as he sang country songs until his voice became fuzzy. It wasn't long before he was out like a light. I had to wonder if that day would ever end at 10am. Dr. Hope and I grinned at each other as she moved to the door.

The assistants were called in. They put his feet in the stirrups. JR was none the wiser, out for the count. I stayed right there by Charmaine's head just as I promised while Dr. Hope repaired a terribly damaged woman. I was in the presence of a gifted physician and her team. It was noteworthy to watch them work in such timing, speed, focus.

It felt like hours, but I knew it had not been. When the surgery was completed, Dr. Hope informed me it had been successful. More so than she had initially thought possible given the extensive damage Charmaine had suffered. With that announcement, she left the room returning with two cups of hot coffee. I love that woman!

We waited for Charmaine to come out of the sedation. I watched as her eyes fluttered, opened and closed, I stroked her hair thinking about her life. Anger rose inside of me once again. I felt that those, now long dead, were rotting in hell for the sordid things they must have done to her. I felt anger on the behalf of all women, men, children who have suffered at the hands of abusers. Those who find the innocents and take such horrid care of their bodies souls while damaging them in ways that are too horrific to wrap your head around in real ways and times are an insult to humanity.

I am continually amazed at the resiliency of the human spirit. My hope was that Charmaine would recover from this surgery quickly. That she would notice the improvement in her physical wellbeing soon. Dr. Hope was so generous, so kind and caring to have provided this care pro Bono. I stood quietly basking in gratitude.

I heard a soft voice, "Doc, what is happening? Am I alright? Was I hurt or something?" I looked down and saw bewilderment, concern along with confusion in our patient's eyes. Who was asking? Who was laying there so vulnerable on the table before us? The questions were asked in a soft southern drawl. "Doc what happened, where are we? Was I in a wreck or something? What's wrong?" It was Charmaine. JR had gotten her there, through the surgery. Somehow JR knew that she was now strong enough to do it.

The workings of her mind once again rendered me speechless. Charmaine started to curl up on her side, moaning a bit. Before I realized it, I had bent down kissing her forehead like one would kiss a small child that needed comforting. I smiled at her. I patted her shoulder, telling she was going to be fine. The surgery we had talked about was over. Dr. Hope had taken care of everything, and it was a positive outcome. Charmaine was fast asleep so I had no idea how much of the great report she heard from me.

As I watched her, something in me suspected a baby was trying to come out. I had seen no baby Alters to date though. Sometimes we have to follow our instincts. This was what a very confused Charmaine. Once she was reassured and began to drift off, I turned my back when I heard JR speak again. "HELL, I would have stayed had I known you were gonna kiss me Showalter." My head snapped so quick I almost did a pivot in the room as I looked preparing to see JR sitting on the side of the bed. It was Charmaine laying on her side as she began mumbling again in her southern accent. I pulled up a chair sat there by her side as she rested. Half asleep, half awake, in and out of consciousness.

JR had done what he said he would do. I had met a shy very quiet Anna who got to have her first car ride. What a day. Charmaine had returned after surgery repaired, calm and intact. I was looking forward to taking her home for the healing to begin.

As I sat beside Charmaine, I watched the monitor over her bed, the constant pulsing of her heart beat, the oxygen saturation levels remained stable. She slept. I heard the door open, with my friend Dr. Hope entering. A fresh cup of hot coffee for me, oh boy was I glad to see that. I smiled a quiet hello let her know that Charmaine had briefly awoken not knowing where she was and wondering if she had been in an accident. She seemed reassured when I let her know that she was fine, safe, and that the procedure was over. Dr. Hope said that was expected as the sedation wore off, but she was intrigued that JR had left. As we talked more I let her know that before Charmaine drifted back to sleep I had heard JR almost killing myself flipping around to see along with his comment. Laughing, I told her about JR's comment to me in his drug induced state.

We both smiled a knowing smile. We were both glad to know it was Charmaine coming out of the sedation not a gruff ass kicking, cigarette wanting JR. As we whispered, Dr. Hope made her way to her patient. She did a pad check for bleeding. It was then Charmaine moaned pulling her legs up tight, curling into what seemed a fetal position. She began to quietly whimper, moan and put her hand up to her face as if she were going to start sucking her thumb. We looked at each other, eyebrows raised.

As we watched she took her hand with the IV, still in dripping saline solution into her vein. As we watched, she put her thumb in her mouth. She began to rock gently as a baby does, now sucking her thumb. We both went to her; me gently stroking her hair, Dr.

Hope placed her hand on her shoulder, speaking quietly to her.

Charmaine did not open her eyes. She did not speak. She kept rocking gently, sucking her thumb in silence. Was this the baby Alter I had silently anticipated? Could it be Boo Boo? Maybe Charie, curled up, moaning, tears leaking from her eyes?

I whispered to Dr. Hope, wondering how long she would be asleep. Perhaps the longer she was in a sleep state, the better. Dr. Hope let me know she would need to stay in the office another couple of hours before it was safe to leave. She suspected that Charmaine or whoever was coming out would sleep off and on secondary to the sedation for a while.

She was concerned at what we were seeing. She asked if I too saw the infantile posture and mannerisms. I did, but that did not disturb me as much as if it were JR having a fit coming in and out of consciousness. This was just a baby needing comfort it seemed, not Charmaine feeling vulnerable and frightened, not Zoe wanting to do harm, not Buck feeling like he was not being heard. She was just a babe needing comfort, an eye and assurance which we could handle fine.

We continued to stand over her. Dr. Hope leaned in close softly singing to her with faith that it would be comforting. Finally, Charmaine had rocked herself to sleep. I looked on with admiration for Dr. Hope, stroking her patients' hair as I sat, sipping on my coffee.

Dr. Hope assured me that physically everything looked great. We would let Charmaine sleep, would continue the saline solution until time for discharge. Then she would roll her to the car in a wheelchair. Charmaine may still be a bit woozy from the sedation. Given the possibility of others coming out it would be better to be safe, rather than surprised. I agreed with her completely as we had already been surprised enough for one day.

Together we sat and talked. It seemed that Charmaine was once again sleeping peacefully, yet we both commented that her thumb was still solidly planted in her mouth. Her position had not changed. We both hoped she would not be stiff from being in such a tight ball when she did wake up. I'm not sure I could have put myself in that tight a ball, but who knows? If I were a baby, who seemed to be out of the hallway, I might not respect the limited agility of an adult body either.

I was undecided on whether to tell Charmaine about the baby Alter as I knew she would be mortified to learn she sucked her thumb in front of us. All I could think was "please do not let her relieve herself in her clothes or on that table." She would be so humiliated. Thankfully, that did not occur.

When we put our heads together quietly, Dr. Hope voiced her concern about Charmaine going home alone. The possibility of the Alters coming out in the next 24 hours alone and unsupervised could pose a problem she stated. I agreed with her on that. Dr. Hope went on to say she felt fearful of trying to get someone to volunteer as a sitter with her given that Charmaine was DID. I once again had to agree with her. I was surprised at myself. I had not thought this through before now.

I admitted to Dr. Hope that I had really thought she would be fine to be alone until just this moment seeing what appeared to be an infant moaning sucking her thumb. I too was now wondering if she would be safe. We both agreed that it would be best if we once again, thought outside the box that had long been discarded in this case.

We decided to take turns spending the night, as Dr. Hope and I were both looking at a rare weekend with no patients or clients. She decided I would take Charmaine home. She would arrive around midnight and stay the night. I could get some sleep and then relieve her the next morning. I could then spend the day with Charmaine. By then we both hoped that Charmaine would be back to what her normal self with no remnants of sedation. Her pain after 24 hours would be more than manageable. At least we could provide a watchful eye in the short term.

So we had a plan. As soon as I would leave the office with Charmaine, Dr. Hope planned to go home. She would then be rested, arrive at Charmaine's for the midnight shift. At the same time, we both said we would get caught up on paperwork while we sat, bringing our laptops with us.

It sounded like a great plan to me; I felt like I was getting the easy end of the bargain. I only had to hope that Charmaine would be comfortable with it. If not, she would just have to hear it was Dr. Orders. As both of us felt it was best for her given the recent appearances of the Alters.

I felt sure she would go along with the plan. I was perplexed by seeing her so vulnerable, so baby like. I had not discovered infants in the sketch. I would have to remember (as if I could forget) to ask Deseree or JR about this. I felt it important to know about this piece of the bigger puzzle that we were still fitting together.

Dr. Hope left the room to refill my coffee. She also wanted to personally thank her staff letting them know she really appreciated their help. While she was closing down here office, returning some phone calls, I took my chair closer to Charmaine to watch her sleep. There were a few times I saw her wince as if in pain.

Slowly I watched her legs stretch out. That was the moment of the loud moan. She slowly moved her head, taking her thumb from her mouth. She was frowning. She wiped the spittle from her mouth, drying her hand on the sheet that covered her. She batted her eyes open and closed several times. She looked at me lazily. "Doc is everything alright... I had the strangest dream, are you sure everything is alright here?"

Pulling my chair closer, I patted her arm, letting her know the surgery had been done, she was doing great. I let her know we were just waiting for her to wake up enough for me to take her home. She asked if she could have some water, saying her mouth felt like cotton. She said her mouth felt like someone had shoved their fist in her mouth. I smiled at her while thinking, "oh... if only you knew how close you are on that one." Instead of saying more I went to check with Dr. Hope about water for her. I found Dr. Hope in her office on the phone so I slid a note to her saying Charmaine was awake, in pain and wanted water. She looked up, nodded yes wrote quickly on my piece of paper; only sips and ice chips. She would be there shortly to give something for pain.

I returned with a cup of ice chips finding Charmaine lying there with tears streaming her face. She was crying softly murmuring to herself. As I got closer to the bed I saw her shake her head back and forth quickly as she wiped her tears. I gave her the cup of ice chips, pulled my chair closer to her. I placed one hand on her arm the other with the cup of ice so that she could reach it easily. "Charmaine, can you tell me what's going on?" She asked for a Kleenex. Then let me know that the ice was the best she ever had put in her mouth! I knew she had to be parched as she had not had anything by mouth since the night before, or at least I did not think she had.

"Doc, it was like I was hearing a bunch of voices inside of me, whispers like I've told you before and I feel all crazy inside of myself. I was laying here saying hush, just hush, not now. I can't stand this. I am starting to feel pain DOWN THERE, you know what I mean? I mean, I think I know what I mean, but everything feels like it's spinning from the inside out."

I understood what she was saying. Coming out of sedation causes a bit of fuzziness. It may be that the Alters were confused too as well causing an internal stir. She may also have been hearing their voices. Maybe Deseree was having a round table with them. Now that she was aware of the Alters, she may be more conscious of their stirrings. I knew it was important to soothe Charmaine the best way I could do, as well as normalize the pain she was feeling "down there." "Charmaine, I want you to really listen for a moment. You have just had major surgery, and it was complex. You don't remember walking into the office because JR is the one who walked in. You've had a lot of sedation that makes you feel off centered now that you are coming out of it. It's ok to feel woozy and confused, in fact, it's to be expected. The sedation takes some time to clear."

She did not like the sensations, the feeling, the discomfort, but she did seem to like the fact that she was not alone. She did seem to feel better in understanding that these were normal feelings. "Doc please do whatever it takes to keep me in the here and now alright? I mean I want to stay in control of things since I was not here when I got here... dang that sounds crazy. I know... Did I act alright when I got here, Doc? Tell me the truth now... oh goodness I'm having a hard time keeping my eyes open I think. Did you say JR came in the off..." With that her eyes closed again.

I assured her she was fine. Maybe she just needed to relax again, close her eyes and rest a bit. We would talk more when she woke up again. She tried to fight it but soon was fast asleep. When the door opened, her eyes popped open. She apologized to Dr. Hope saying that she was sorry if she was not herself when she first arrived. Dr. Hope assured her she did fine; everything went better than she had hoped. She would be better than ever before once healed. She asked Charmaine if she needed something for pain. Charmaine said, "If you wouldn't mind, I think it would help."

Dr. Hope smiled at her saying she thought it would be a good idea as well. With that she explained to Charmaine that she just needed to check her for bleeding once again. Charmaine let her know how much she "hated" that part. She did not complain as Dr. Hope lifted her sheet. Charmaine stared at the ceiling. It took but a minute. Dr. Hope was happy to report that everything was just as it should be. Charmaine could anticipate leaving the office in an hour.

Dr. Hope decided to explain to Charmaine why she was waiting to remove the IV. Charmaine seemed to only then notice that it was in her arm at all. We both laughed at that, as we knew what a fit JR had pitched at the idea of it happening at all. With that Dr. Hope asked Charmaine if she had any questions. We noticed that she did not have a clue if she should have questions. She still seemed dazed by the whole process.

That was when Dr. Hope told Charmaine about the revised after care plan. Charmaine immediately became more alert. The moment she heard that we planned to be her caregivers for 24 hours she reacted. For a moment I thought we were going to see JR bellow, "Oh hells to the NO you are not." Thankfully it did not happen that way.

Initially she resisted. Her main reason was that it would be an imposition on us. "Oh no, that would be just too much to ask of either of you, I cannot pay you for your time. No one has ever been that kind to me to do such a thing... I will be ok I promise I will."

We made an effort to convince her by sharing all the reasons that it would be a good idea. The reality to face was that Charmaine was worn out physically. She had been through a lot of stress. The potential of an Alter(s) coming out, were at play. Most importantly, there was the very real danger of her being too active, at which point she might harm herself unknowingly. We would also monitor her pain levels; administer medication if it was needed. It was not unlike Charmaine to change a tire, or do some other very physical task, unknowingly. In fact, at this point, I knew the Alters did a lot of things when Charmaine lost time.

We tried to be light as we talked about this real need. We needed to help her understand that we did not mind. We wanted what was best for her. Given the lack of support she had intact and our desire to make things as easy for her as possible. She finally agreed, but only after I tried to bribe her with her with her favorite pizza, delivered for dinner and a movie of her choice.

She determined that the two of us were as crazy as she was to do such a thing. She said she hoped her house was clean when we got there, and if not, maybe an Alter would come clean it while we ate pizza. Then she laughed as she said, "Oh darn, it doesn't work that way does it Doc?" With that declaration all three of us laughed. She announced that she wanted more ice. We could tell the pain medicine had kicked in. Charmaine with her wit had returned. The relief of knowing this dreaded surgery was now behind her had provoked her humor.

I continued to struggle mentally with the infant child that I witnessed while she was in and out of consciousness. Seeing, hearing her moan as she pulled herself into fetal position while thumb sucking was hard to observe. I kept thinking that I remembered there being no babies in the sketch we had been referring to in therapy. Who was that? Where had he or she come from or gone? I decided to wait until she was over the surgery to tell her of this new observation.

In the meantime, I watched her stable heart rate beating, as she became more alert. She was itching to get home, wanting to get inside her house before me. She wanted to see if the place was clean enough for her two favorite people to spend the next 24 hours with her. I found this comical because however it was going to be is how it would be. We talked about how great the ice was as she gulped it wanted more.

Again she let me know how much she appreciated that I had not abandoned her. The voices that earlier seemed so close to her head bothered her. She said that at one point she thought her eyes were going to pop out of her skull from all the whispering going on. I wondered if Charmaine recognized any of the voices. She had heard the videos. She had watched them; maybe she could place some of the voices from that session. I watched her as she thought about my question.

I knew she was still groggy, but she seemed more open to the question than she would have been if she was firing on all cylinders and her defenses intact. I was just wondering. I watched as her feet moved back and forth. As if she were on cue, her eyes got wild. She looked at me with excitement saying, "Well, I be. You know what? I swear I heard a voice that sounded like the one with the bun on the video telling someone it's ok. Then I heard JR sounding gruff like, that's IT, that's IT... I DID recognize some of the voices from the video DOC. I DID!."

I felt my heart racing. I could see in Charmaine's eyes that she had made a breakthrough. In her half drugged state, she had for the first time recognized the voices in her head that she had suffered through so many years. Perhaps it was the sedation that let her not be so afraid. Could this be the key that opened the door to the hallway in her mind?

She closed her eyes, but had a smile on her face. I could see her eyes moving beneath her lids. I spoke her name just to be sure she was still with me. "Charmaine, don't leave me now, it is time for you to try to wake up so we can get ready to get you home."

She opened her eyes to assure me that she was only resting. She was thinking about what we had been talking about. Now it made so much sense to her. I asked her if she was hearing anything right now. She quipped that my voice was all she was hearing. She closed her eyes again.

I could tell by her breathing that she had drifted back to sleep so I finished my coffee sat patiently waiting. It had been one hell of a day in that little room. I was ready for air, music, or something other than being there.

I heard the door open. Good, quite frankly I was becoming bored as hell sitting in that room with a sleeping patient. Dr. Hope checked Charmaine without disturbing her and shook her head. Looking at me she whispered, "You are going to be hamburger meat tonight if JR jumps out and wants to ride that bike you told me about. You do know that don't you?"

I laughed quietly and rolled my eyes letting her know to not be too quick about wishing that on me. After all, she had the midnight shift. She got a bit wide eyed once she processed that thought. She let me know in a quick hurry that she had my number on speed dial. Dr. Hope assured me she would not hesitate to use it if she needed it. She had no idea what to do if an Alter or anyone other than Charmaine was in her charge for the night.

We both smiled. I let out a chuckle. It was time to start waking Charmaine up. She was good to go. I was happy to hear that, not realizing how much I longed to walk outside; to be finished with this part of the whole medical procedure.

I reached over gently rubbed Charmaine's arm while I was quietly speaking her name to try to get her attention. "Charmaine, Charmaine..." I said, again and again until I saw her begin to stir. Finally she began to open her eyes. Dr. Hope was on the other side of the bed standing close to her. We each looked at each other hoping and praying that JR would not jump out of the bed asking us if we wanted to go and throw back a cold one.

Charmaine opened her eyes, looked to Dr. Hope and then to me. "Well dang, I must of gone back to sleep huh?" She stretched her legs out moved a bit as we told her it was time for her to sit up. Dr. Hope was ready to take out the IV. She immediately pulled her arm back, wanting to know if it was going to hurt. Dr. Hope laughed and told her the worst part was over. She would not feel more than the tape being taken off. With that, she went ZIP, and it was done.

Charmaine did not have time to react it happened so quickly. We both asked her how she was feeling, whether she still felt a bit goofy, or was dizzy. We wanted to know if she thought she could sit up. Charmaine got tickled at the word "goofy" asking me if that was a technical term that she should get familiar with or if I had borrowed it from Dr. Hope. We all laughed.

I swore it was a result of her being sedated that she was so funny. She pulled herself up seemed to be doing alright until it was time to put her clothes on. As she stepped down from the table, with minimal assistance, she took her first steps toward the bench where her clothes lay. She leaned against the wall, and then lost her balance a bit.

Once again she managed to amuse herself. She thought it funny that she was so wonky on her feet. She could not stop laughing at herself. She wanted privacy to get dressed. We had to let her know that she had just failed the "sobriety test for privacy." One of us needed to be in the room to be sure she was safe. Guess who she picked?

Soon after Charmaine was dressed, Dr. Hope had her in the wheelchair. I was out the door so quickly that my own head was spinning: I rushed to pull the car up to the front door. Oh how fresh that air was when I hit the outside! I waited for them to come out. I was standing outside the car when I saw Charmaine being wheeled through the doors with that big ole' Raggedy Ann sitting in her lap. Dr. Hope pushed her; they were engaged in conversation.

As they neared the car, Charmaine showed me the doll letting me know how funny that must appear to folks to see that big doll sitting in her lap. My thoughts immediately flew to, "If only you knew…" as I helped her into the front seat of the car. Once buckled in, she placed the doll in the back seat put on her sunglasses for the ride home.

I told Charmaine that if she wanted a drink, we could stop and pick it up on our way. She asked for coke, so I swung by the store and picked up a few things which included a Redbox movie. She sat in the car with the doors locked. I was as quick as I could be, and I returned to find her fast asleep.

CHAPTER 23 THE SLUMBER PARTY

Once in Charmaine's home, I helped her to her room went to the kitchen to look for a glass for ice. When I returned, she was curled up on her bed. She motioned to a chair. She suggested that I pull it up closer if I wanted to, make myself at home. I noticed that everything was put to order at home, with no evidence of a mess or things being askew. That was reassuring. Given that Anna had been out for a ride, JR had appeared for the surgery, I half expected that the others may have been raising hell the night before.

Charmaine stated she was having some pain. She said it was difficult to be still. She wanted to get up, wanted to be in bed at the same time. She felt restless. I asked if she wanted something to eat. There were moments that I wondered if an Alter would appear to take the pain from her. I was ready for just about anything except Zoe. JR had let me know that Zoe was now locked in her room. I was glad about that as I was not up for Zoe. Charmaine did not need the activity her appearance would provoke.

After a bit I was able to convince Charmaine to eat. She thought she could fix herself an egg sandwich, but I was not convinced that she should. I made myself at home in the kitchen. After searching the cabinets I assembled the needed equipment. Though it involved a bit of banging around, I succeeded in preparing her a hot meal. I thought to myself jokingly, wonder what the code is for this with the insurance company?

She was very appreciative and said, "Well darn, to think my therapist is now providing room service." We both chuckled about that as I sat back down with my coke and joined her with a sandwich for myself. We prepared to watch a movie as I let her know to not get used to the room service.

Charmaine got comfortable, propped up in the bed. I had my feet up on the end of it, sitting close to her. The pain medicine seemed to be taking hold. We watched the movie together as she nodded off and on comfortably. There were times I saw her startle. Sometimes she would moan softly. There were moments where she was completely alert and involved in the movie.

She seemed to be glad she was not alone, somehow safer with a presence there beside her, for that I was glad. By the end of the movie, Charmaine was fast asleep. She looked peaceful. I brought out my laptop and documented the day's events. It was then I heard a soft voice murmuring, and realized Charmaine was talking in her sleep... a childlike voice, "S-th pwotected us fwom da bad Zoe again wight JR? her is dood to us wight?"

There was soft singing, followed by a quick movement, as if she had been disturbed in her sleep. Charmaine suddenly sat straight up in her bed. She immediately started talking. She scared the crap out of me. I was tipped back on two legs of the chair when it happened. I almost fell over she startled me so badly. I felt like I was in a movie of the zombies or something only Charmaine's arms were not sticking straight out. It was not Charmaine talking to me.

"Dr. Showalter. I am so pleased to see you taking such wonderful care of our Charmaine; I trust you are making yourself at home here, and that JR did not embarrass us all at lovely Dr. Hope's office. I want to let you know that I am happy to report that Zoe remains in lock down. She will not be jumping out again. I have been so very worried about you and Charmaine; I wanted to take this time to thank you. I realize that you saw the baby in the office and were probably concerned. I apologize for not having informed you, but there were at one time, many babies. Several are still here.

In the sketch you have studied for so long, perhaps you failed to see I am holding one of the babies close to me there. Oh dear you have had to absorb so much as a therapist with us, haven't you? Well now, I want you to know, there were many babies in the hallway, most have now gone, only Boo Boo and Charie are left. That precious child Boo Boo, who has no voice, that I nurture and hold so dear to me, and precious Charie, who brings such love and laughter to us. Rest now Dr. Showalter, and know that we trust you too. Charmaine trusts you with her life. I wanted to make sure you make yourself at home here. Please know how much you are appreciated. Close your eyes dear, just rest and make yourself at home. It has been a long day. Please be sure Dr. Hope knows of our appreciation. Even JR thinks she is a remarkable woman, and you know how JR is."

I sat wide eyed as I listened to Deseree; my eyes locked with hers until she finished. She reached over patted the side of my cheek insisting that I rest. As soon as she did that, she laid back down her head on the pillow, closing her eyes. I continued to stare at her as she turned on her side, facing me. She was sound asleep. I could feel my heart beating in my chest. I was still trying to get over the shock of her suddenly sitting straight up. I sure was glad it was me not Dr. Hope that it happened to.

I have no idea how long I sat watching her sleep. Was I looking at Charmaine, or Deseree, Charie, Boo Boo, Anna, Buck, the baby, JR? A combination of all that were at peace there at home, knowing they were safe. Has Deseree come to thank me, to tell me they trusted me, to let me know I had nothing to worry about with Zoe? Had she come to tell me I am not the brightest bulb in the lamb since I obviously missed a baby in the sketch? I was completely trusted? I have no idea. I just know there was no feeling like it in the world as I sat there. Slow down heart, just sit there breathe, those were the messages I was sending to my brain. I am very glad I did not tip the chair backwards, that much I do know.

I had not known I was asleep until I felt a hand on mine. A voice waking me saying, "Doc, Doc, I think I hear the door." It was Charmaine's voice. I opened my eyes sat straight up in my chair. It took a moment to reorient myself to my surroundings, to the right then of it.

I half way staggered to the door. There I found dear Dr. Hope. She had hot coffees in her hand a smile on her face. Oh goodness I must have gone out like a light. I looked at my fully refreshed friend standing there welcomed her in. She whispered in my ear, "You look like hell my friend, here's coffee."

We both walked to Charmaine's bedroom only to find her sitting on the side of the bed looking anxious. I think she had forgotten about Dr. Hope coming to relieve me. She greeted Dr. Hope warmly then asked her what in the world was she doing there in the middle of the night. We both laughed, reminding her that Dr. Hope was staying the night with her.

Charmaine tried to stand up but was uneasy on her feet. She sat back down, letting us know she had to go to the bathroom. "Why in the world would you come to stay the night Dr. Hope?" After I walked Charmaine to the bathroom I returned to the bedroom with that great cup of coffee as I expressed my gratitude to Dr. Hope. I sat on the side of the bed offering her my easy chair. We sat visiting about the night.

I quietly told her about the visit from Deseree while Charmaine slept. We were deep in conversation when Charmaine appeared at the bathroom door asking for a hand to her bed.

She was holding her abdomen looking distressed as she told Dr. Hope she was having a lot of pain after using the bathroom. Dr. Hope got up immediately assisted her back to the bed. She quickly gave her a pain pill. She assured Charmaine that she was doing fine. The repairs would take time to heal. She might be sore for several days. She urged her not to panic. While she explained to Charmaine once again, what to expect, Charmaine relaxed back into the pillows. Dr. Hope suggested a heating pad only to hear that Charmaine only had a hot water bottle. We found it as Charmaine went on a story about it being red to indicate hot/heat/warmth. I think it was the after effects of sedation, but it was quite the story and she quite the storyteller.

She looked at me as I took a sip of my coffee asking if I was going to share it with her. Dr. Hope laughed letting her know she had brought her a cup in the event that she was awake at this awful hour. Charmaine was touched by her generosity saying, "Well, you don't think I'm goin to sleep through my first grown up slumber party with two Docs do ya?" We thought that was very funny indeed, our own slumber party hosted by Charmaine, in the middle of the night, complete with coffee.

So there we sat, a brilliant physician, Charmaine, in her bed, and me on the side of the bed. We were just three women relaxing as we talked. We were just there, together in a room drinking coffee in the middle of the night. Charmaine had lost the argument; one of us would be there around the clock this first night.

I left for home letting them both know that I would drop in with coffee in the morning light. I did just that. The next morning I arrived to find them both at the kitchen table waiting for me. Charmaine was still in the clothes from the night before, Dr. Hope in jeans and a scrub shirt that looked like she had it worn in from years of use, soft, blue, comfortable.

I could tell when I handed out the coffee they had established a comfortable rapport in their time together. They were comfortable with each other. They had obviously been talking a lot in the night. Charmaine's thoughts were clearer, her balance good, her pain well managed.

Charmaine acknowledged that she had only a fuzzy recall of the surgery day. She said she had been amazed to wake several times, seeing one or the other of us there beside her bed. She wanted to pinch herself to see if she was dreaming. It was hard to imagine that we were standing by her with such care and compassion.

Charmaine looked at us both with tears in her eyes and asked "Why are you being so good to me? No one ever has before." Tears rolled down her cheeks. We told her that it was because she was worth it. What had been done to her before did not make her a bad person. She had never deserved the treatment she had experienced. Together we stressed that was then, this was now to her.

It was a great morning visit. Her surgery was now over. It was a successful outcome for her. After -care for Charmaine thankfully went without incident. It seemed she would be alright with both of us returning to our work schedules, leaving her alone with instructions to call if she needed to. We finally had to let her know, that she had thanked us more than enough. We encouraged her instead to tell us one more silly story to get our day off to a good start before we left.

We determined I would make a home visit for a session later in the week so that she would not have to drive to the office. She needed to take special care to not strain herself as she healed. Dr. Hope gave her strong restrictions on no lifting, no straining, no housework, ad infinitum, making sure she "got it" before we left. We would coordinate her follow-up appointment with Dr. Hope in the next few days.

We knew that Charmaine was a fighter, a hard headed woman with steely resolve so we went over it more than once. She was to call Dr. Hope check in with her. She was to call me if she had concerns, anxiety, or if stressors got up.

Interesting that Charmaine did not inquire about Alters or the times she did not remember since the surgery. I was glad that she didn't. There would be plenty of time for that later. Her presence was calm; her smile was genuinely filled with gratitude. Her energy was low from the surgery along with the after effects of the sedation. Add to that pain medicine, but that was to be expected. She planned to spend the day in bed resting. We both thought that a good idea.

Charmaine said she thought she might just get out her coloring books to relax by coloring but for me not to worry, it was "Charmaine speaking" not anyone else. With that I laughed hugging her as we both were leaving.

Dr. Hope and I walked to our cars, thanked each other for sharing the care vigil, for leaning into each other to provide care of a wonderful woman. We both had full days in front of us; we were off in a shot so as to not be late to our offices.

As I drove, I found myself visualizing Charmaine lying in bed coloring pictures watching one of the movies we left. This was the beginning of her being whole again, not just mentally and emotionally, but also physically.

I swung by the house for a quick shower a change of clothes. Soon I was absorbed in the stories of other patients. Before I knew it, the day was over. I was home with my feet up, relaxing before I realized I had not heard from Charmaine all day. In many ways that was good as well.

The next day I was walking into the office as the phone rang. It was Charmaine. Her voice sounded strained as she told me she had once again found the doors unlocked. Her back was killing her. She had awoken from a sound sleep with mud all over her sheets. She said, other than that, her day had been uneventful except for a phone call from her kids letting her know that they had been arguing with the ex-husband. The kids were ready to come home. They missed her. She had gotten off the phone so mad at him she could spit. Once again remembering why she divorced him. She was glad her kids had called. Once off the phone with her x, she had tried to calm herself down with a cup of coffee and some toast.

As she spoke I could hear the pain in her voice. I had to wonder if she had figured out that Buck probably snuck out to play in the dirt or uproot the flowers in the dark. Once again leaving the doors unlocked as his signature "got ya." Once she mentioned the children, she dismissed the entire issue of mud all over the bed. I however did not.

I listened to Charmaine, while pulling the sketch out of the desk drawer. I stared at it as she vented her frustration with the increased pain "down there" and in her back now. Amazingly, I had never noticed Deseree holding a baby before in that sketch. I could bet I had looked at it a thousand times.

Finally the phone went silent. I could tell that Charmaine was ready for me to say or do something. I calmly reminded her that Buck was often triggered by her anger at her ex. Perhaps Buck had snuck past Bart at the doorway. Buck may have been tearing up the flower beds again. That would account for her back hurting, which would cause increased pain from the surgery. "Remember Dr. Hope said no strenuous activity." Charmaine laughed for the first time saying that "Well to be truthful, if he was here, Buck might have learned some new cuss words from me Doc, cos' I was fit to be tied after I got off that phone with my kids."

As I slowed her down, I validated her anger. She walked outside with the phone in her hand sure enough; her flowers in that nicely kept garden was once again torn all to pieces. She was telling me all about it when I heard the door open. My next client had arrived. I told her I would call her back later. I suggested she try the red hot water bottle on her abdomen while taking it easy. I ended the call by reminding her she was still on the mend.

She apologized for her rant, thanked me for answering the call. She seemed to feel more in control by the time she hung up, saying she might have to "whup Bucks young ass", now that her garden needed to be fixed all over again. I smiled as I said so long to her. As I walked out to greet my next client I had the visual she had described.

Charmaine was moving at a quick pace in her understanding and acceptance of DID. At times it was still hard to comprehend that she would find remnants of the Alters and still being stunned by it. Maybe I would react the same way if I were in her shoes. At least she was safe. It seemed she needed to find a way to let Buck know she was listening, in order for him to stop this silly, defiant attention seeking behavior. I was sure that the detective mom in her would be figuring this out between now and our next session.

She had come so far. My brain exploded with the thoughts of where we first began. From the mirror of realities, the bike ride with JR, Charie in the corner Boo Boo on my pant leg, Zoe with that letter opener, Tina's antics, and Laylee her desire for freedom and free love. I thought about Charmaine in her mind's hallway, with the many doors. Charmaine was determined to understand her life while taking control of her destiny and her world. I was just along for the ride, to add clarification as the guardian of this journey.

Yes, I did put in a lot of extra off hours with Charmaine. To facilitate her growth, watching this unfold while seeing the progression in Charmaine as she learned more and more about how to handle her life was so rewarding. One day we would get to the trauma that caused all of this. Hopefully Charmaine would be able to handle that too. I knew that clients with Dissociative Identity Disorder suffered horrific abuse at the hands of evil or mean spirited people. She would need to grow in her understanding of this concept as we moved forward.

Charmaine's journal

Home at last and I have watched that video over and over. At least I know that it is real now. Once I know what something is then I know how to fight. I sat and looked at my copy of the drawing of me and the Alters. I see names that Doc has not told me about. I wonder if I can match any of these to the journal writings done by the Alters. One of them hates me. I can feel it.

I know it sounds kind of crazy...oh my I am laughing with tears down my face at that statement...but it actually feels comforting to know I have a mother figure that loves me considering I never had a mother that loved me before. Ok I can kinda live with some of this but parts of it scare me especially the Laylee part and the one that hates me.

Ok, gonna do my usual. Make a list of pros and cons. Well one pro is they make me more efficient as

I have someone for different things. Oh my I am almost hysterically crying and laughing at that. And where does Charie fit in? Maybe she is the child I never was. I guess I am going to have to sit down and read that book seriously on DID now so I can understand why I have so many different ages.

My head is spinning and I think I need to sleep. Maybe I will wake up feeling better. Yes, I believe there are Alters within me...now what?

THE ALTERS

"Round table time everyone" Deseree calls down the hallway. They all know that means to come to the meeting area in the hallway where they can all talk together.

Deseree hears grumbling from a few quarters but slowly JR, Charie, Tina, Buck, Jennie, Anna, Zoe, and Boo Boo all appear and take their places at the table. Charie crawls up on JR's lap who shifts her over to one leg so he can cross the other one.

Boo Boo appears in her little cotton gown holding a big doll that drags the ground. The doll is almost as tall as she is. Deseree says "Laylee will not be with us and the baby is asleep, so we can all talk now.

First I want you to understand that the movies and the pictures that Dr. Showalter took were only to help Charmaine know that they were all there. They were not to hurt her like the other pictures."

JR looks up and says "you ever have me out in that dang dress again and you will have to catch me because I will take us all for a ride." Deseree turned and apologized to JR saying it was necessary for Charmaine to see.

Charie leaned her head against JR's chest and with thumb in mouth says "me no wike picthures" and Deseree reaches over and pats her face and says "honey these are good pictures. The bad people Doc said to tell you are all gone just like those bad boy dolls she stomped on in the office."

Deseree and JR looked at each other and nodded. They had been keeping a check on those perverts and the last one had just passed away. Served them all right they both were thinking. They had a folder to show Charmaine at the right time with all the obituaries.

Charie's eyes got big when she heard Deseree sai the bad people were gone and she said "dey is?" Deseree said "yes, baby they are."

Boo Boo was the only one silent and she just leaned against the side of Deseree, who kept patting her.

Zoe started screaming at them all "well I do not care. I hate her HATE HER HATE HER. I hope she dies" and Deseree took Zoe's hand and said "look at me Zoe. You keep this up and you will be like Laylee, locked up in the room" Zoe pulled away and just sat there sullen looking with arms crossed.

Deseree asked her would she like to talk to Dr. Showalter all by herself some time and Zoe looked up and said "just me??" Deseree said "Just you Zoe and no one else." And for the first time, Zoe smiled.

Deseree went on to say "One day Charmaine may be able to come in here and sit at the table with us" and Charie sat up and said "WEALLY?" with huge child like eyes and Deseree answered yes. Zoe said she hoped so as she had things to say to that bitch.

The others asked could they talk to the Doc alone too and Deseree told them she was sure it could be arranged and each one could have their own day to talk.

JR turned to Zoe and said "girlie you better remember I am watching you and I will rearrange your back side you hurt Charmaine again. Do you hear me?"

Deseree told Zoe that if she ever hurt Charmaine again, she would not get her turn to talk to the

Doctor. Zoe just nodded and sat there thinking with a small smile.

JR asked Deseree why she just did not lock her up like Laylee and Deseree said "I truly believe she is angry because she thinks Charmaine let those people do bad things and if she can be made to understand, she will be like the rest of them there all for the good of Charmaine." JR just nodded but was not totally convinced.

Charmaine's Journal

I woke up this morning to find a chunk cut out of my hair. Thank God my hair is thick enough that I can hide it. And I found a scratch across my wrist and written in the journal is this:

I could have hurt u bad if I had wanted to bitch. I hate u. u let them hurt us.

And under it was this and I think this might be that JR.

I told u girlie that I was watching u. don't make me hurt u.

Who did I let hurt them? And why do they think I LET them? Well all I can say right now is I am thankful for JR watching over me and Deseree.

I better get a push on as I have a session today with Doc and she wants to talk some more about the video. A hot shower sounds good.

THE ALTERS

JR throws the towel on the floor and rummages for his cammies and tee shirt and boots. As usual, he wraps his chest to make it flat. After dressing, he goes out to the garage, takes the stuff off his motorcycle and he takes off for Showalter. Laughing to himself he thinks "this ought to get her"

As soon as he pulls up to the office, he pushes Charmaine out and she rushes in thinking she is late and does not even realize that she came on a motorcycle. She rushes into the office and........

Charmaine's journal

Oh what a session. I was late and Doc was waiting on me. We talked about the video some more and once again watched it and I told her I knew beyond a shadow of a doubt that I was DID.

I showed her the journal with that one ugly comment and asked her who hated me so and she told me it was Zoe. I said "why does she blame me for being hurt?" Doc explained that sometimes Alters felt like the host person being me...should have stopped them.

I said I did not understand because I was not aware that they were there and I still did not understand stop who???? Stop them from doing what????

Doc reminded me that she felt I had been horribly abused and when I asked her why I did not know, she told me it was because the Alters know. I said but who was supposed to have done this. I do not know anyone that did it.

Doc told me that Zoe had come out in a rage in the office and I saw she had a cut on her lip. She also said Zoe cut me trying to hurt me. She told me how JR saved her from Zoe and that Zoe was filled with so much anger that it was almost impossible to control her. I wanted to cry when I saw. This last session was horrible for I could not stand the thought that my body was used to hurt Doc. What does she hate me so?????

I feel like I am losing my mind again. What if I just turn on someone or one of the kids???? Why can't I control this? I have to learn how to control it. I guess I will read those damn books.

THE ALTERS

No one inside was paying much attention as Charmaine was in session. Zoe waited inside, her anger building and watched for a moment to make a break. It came perfect when Charie was talking to Bart. When she zoomed through the door, she did it so quickly and so violently. The moment that Zoe saw Doc, she started swearing like a sailor.

"That filthy bitch, fuck her, fuck you, son of a bitch... I will kill her." and she reached quickly and grabbed the letter opener off of the Doc's desk and started sawing on Charmaine's arm.

Zoe meant to hurt the Doc as well as Charmaine. She was fighting with all her might as she tried to saw a hole in her wrist. She even swung at the Doc and nicked her face. She also landed a fist to her eye bruising it. It happened so quickly that JR was caught off guard. Suddenly, he barreled past Bart as he threw Zoe back into the hallway at the same time. He quickly and strongly pulled his arms from Doc.

JR could see the concern on Doc's face and immediately said "Showalter, it's ok. It's JR" and the relief flooded Doc's face. JR told Doc that Bart and Deseree had Zoe now and were locking her in.

When the Doc tried to tell JR that she wanted to make Zoe understand Charmaine was not at fault, JR said "That is the same thing Deseree said but we will have to do this a different way. Maybe a little time locked up might make her cooperate more."

"Damn Doc looks bad. She can fight like a street fighter but Zoe was hurting her. I just do not know if Doc can help Zoe or not. Maybe we just need to kill Zoe off and that will be the end." JR told Deseree.

"JR" Deseree said. "If we kill Zoe off, we kill ourselves. We all live in the same body" as she patted his arm. He dropped his head and sat there nodding yes.

Charmaine's Diary

I woke up to the phone ringing. It is Doc and she asked me to come in tomorrow morning and bring my journal with me. She has not seen it in a few days and I have not shown her the blood stains or the angry writing. And boy the bar sounds are high today. Dang it, if that is you all talking why can I not understand you????

I sat here thinking about all the different Alters and yes, all the parts of me. Doc asked me had I ever noticed that when asked how I was or similar questions, I would respond "WE are doing fine" or "we had a rough day." She says many people with DID do that unconsciously.

I have this visual of my head being like a big condo full of rooms with all these people living in there. Maybe they even have satellite and computer service. Oh gosh yes I know I am being silly but if I do not find some humor I really will be nuts.

I assured Doc that I would be there in the morning and planned on a quiet evening at home. We hung up and I got all my stuff together on my desk and decided to take a shower and get ready

THE ALTERS

Tina had finally gotten permission to be out for a while. She had met someone but had not told anyone. She wanted to go out to eat and he was taking her to a nice restaurant that overlooked the water. Tina took special care to dress up really pretty and wore that satin dress with the big glass earrings that she loved.

She loved dressing up and she especially loved wearing high heels. The others teased her about wearing so much makeup but she loved makeup and she loved wearing fishnet stockings and long dangly earrings.

Tina had a date with this man called Tom at 8 and she knew that Deseree and the others would be laid back and quiet and so she could go out and nothing would be said. She opened the front door so that she could see him arrive and planned on slipping out the door and going to the car.

After Tom picked her up, she slid into his car. It was a beauty. She loved leather interiors and going to fancy places. He reached out and took her hand and said that he was looking forward to dinner and dancing.

Tina was so excited. She had bought this new cologne and hoped he liked it. He opened doors for her and held her chair just like a real gentleman. After he ordered for both of them, they sat close and talked and looked out on the water.

Tina seemed to have only eyes for Tom as they casually necked and so was not paying attention to anyone else in the restaurant. Tina was a teenager but looked older and not very experienced. She began to realize she was getting feelings she had not felt before and they felt good. They were off in a secluded area that was not as lit up as other areas of the restaurant.

She was so shocked when that dang Doc walked up and said "Charmaine? Oh crap she was going to be in trouble. That Doc made her go to the restroom and then she started calling for Deseree and suddenly Tina felt herself pulled inside the hallway and was standing by Bart.

She could hear Deseree talking to Doc and could hear Doc telling Deseree that while Tina was not as wild as Laylee that right now with so much turmoil that they did not need another Alter out that was being affectionate with a man.

Doc called the taxi and waited until Deseree was in it headed home and went in and told the man that Tina was called off for a family emergency and would be gone for a month.

As soon as Deseree walked in the house, she called Anna to come out. Anna loved to draw and was very serious and very well behaved and she knew things would be ok while she talked to Tina.

She promised Buck that after she was done talking to Tina that he could come out and read the three wheeler magazines that Charmaine's oldest son had. She hoped that would calm him. He was angry all the time because he felt no one listened to him.

Tina was standing nervously by Bart and Deseree looked at her and said "to the table Tina" and Deseree turned and walked into the hallway and called JR to come too and Jennie. Tina just followed with her head held down.

Once they all sat down, Deseree told Tina that they had talked about the need to keep things safe for Charmaine right now while she was accepting the fact that she really had Alters. She asked Tina "why were you kissing and all with that man in the restaurant? You know that upsets Charmaine especially if that man goes up to her in the day time and tries to do the same."

Tina said "I was just trying to have some fun. I never get to have any fun. I am not Laylee. I would never go all the way. I just like to kiss and pet a little. There is nothing wrong with that."

JR leaned over the table and told Tina to look at him and said "I am a man Tina and when a woman dresses like that all dressed up and flirtified, it gets a man's hormones going. You may not go all the way but the man will not know that. How will you feel then if he tries to jump on Charmaine when she is out or even Charie?"

Tina dropped her head and said "I guess I did not think that far." Deseree told her she was disappointed in her and now did not know if she could trust her or not. She told Tina that she was not locking her in but that Bart was told to never let her past without JR or Deseree's permission.

She looked at Tina and said "anything that happens to Charmaine happens to us too. For the safety of us all and the happiness of this hallway, we have to all work together and it is bad enough that

Laylee is like she is and Zoe wants to hurt Charmaine. I cannot have you jeopardizing Charmaine like that Tina."

Tina said she would not do anything without telling them again. Huge tears floated in her eyes and cascade down her cheeks. Now she felt so torn because she did not want to hurt Charmaine but kissing that man made her feel good things in private places.

Deseree told JR that he could go as she wanted to talk to the "girls." After JR left, Deseree said she thought it was time they talked about sex. She explained to them that because of the horrific abuse,

Charmaine could not stand to be touched and may never be able to have sex.

Deseree asked them did they realize that when they did things like Tina did with that man and they feel sexual feelings between their legs and places, that Charmaine, Charie, all of them were being exposed to that.

"We are here to help Charmaine, not bring harm to her. What you did today Tina was not only dangerous but could have left Charmaine waking up to those emotional feelings that she was feeling and it could send her to the cubby for days and days because of the fear.

So, I want you all to think about that. Our job is not to go out and party or have sex or have a boy friend. Look what Laylee did to her and what she has gone through."

When she looked at Jennie and Tina, both had their heads down and told Deseree they would never do anything like that again.

CHAPTER 24 WALKING OUT OF HELL

Warning from DRSES: This chapter may be triggering

Often as a therapist, we were taught the best lessons by those we provide a safe place for. We have learned so much by just listening. Our goal is to provide the tools to empower those we sit with, as we establish trust with them.

I had realized that Charmaine had become one of my best teachers. I had no idea the lessons would be matched by the pain I would experience as she entered my office for the session on one particular day. It was a day that will forever be etched in my memory: a day that no one could truly prepare for.

I sat absorbed in paperwork, talking to a client by phone that was scheduled to come in for a late appointment. She had just informed me that she had to cancel as a result of being ill with the flu. I listened to her talk: her voice strained, expressing her distress at having to miss the days' session. She needed desperately to talk, but felt so miserable she just had to stay in bed. I was thankful in many ways: I was particularly appreciative that she would not spread her germs by coming in when she felt so poorly. I felt bad for her, knowing that she wanted to follow up on her last session. After hanging up, I used the spare time to throw myself into paperwork.

I did not hear the door open, or Charmaine's footsteps as she entered. Deep in thought, I was writing case notes. Charmaine was standing quietly in the doorway. When she spoke; her voice startled me a little bit. I looked up to see her in there with a very intent smile on her face. "Hello Doc, you look busy." I had noticed she was a bit early as I glanced at my watch. I smiled welcomed her as I sat there still holding my pen. It looked like Charmaine was coming in with something on her mind. She had an agenda for our session, I found myself thinking. I looked forward to learning what it was. She had really invested in her own well-being. She had been working hard between sessions. Her journal writings were serving her well.

We had long established an open, "go with it", whatever it is a relationship working model in sessions. I believe that was the cornerstone that allowed her to grow and heal within. Charmaine interrupted my thoughts. There was something she needed us to do today, she said. I needed to be open to it she said even stronger. I listened as she continued to speak. I had not moved, my pen was still poised in my hand. She was standing at the desk. That was a first.

Charmaine looked at me, then sat in her chair and took a deep breath. She launched into what was on her mind. She looked me straight in the eye letting me know that she wanted to direct this session by taking me into the hallway of her brain; into the rooms of the Alters. She had to get to a specific room in the hallway. She stressed that I had to go with her. She told me that she would direct everything, each sight, each step with me at her side. She let me know she thought she was brave enough, strong enough, and she was ready right then, right there.

Charmaine maintained direct eye contact as she spoke. There was no hesitation, no doubt in what she was saying. As I sat listening, I realized she was telling me that she wanted to "take me into the realm of her mind, the world of DID" through guided imagery; the worst of the worst that we had yet to get to. She was very clear that she would be in control if I was willing to go there with her.

I had no real idea what we would venture into, yet I knew I had never seen this woman so utterly focused. A look of steel willed determination was on her face. I did know however that whatever was going to happen would be life changing for her. I had no idea that it would also change my life as a professional. As with so many turning points in therapy, the client's trust in our working relationship gave them the courage to approach un-trod territory. This appeared to be the case with Charmaine on this day. She was ready to take a giant leap forward.

I was not breathing fully as I worked to grasp the implications of what my client was requesting. Absorbing her words, her look, her intensity, I could feel my own body tense, my breath change. I realized that her trust in me as a professional had never been stronger. The call to be my best had never been more important than in this moment. I prayed silently for guidance to be present as her guardian, keeping us both from harm as I shielded myself for what was to come.

I was quickly trying to process whether I thought she was ready and was she strong enough? Would the Alters jump out and have one "hellified fit" over this. Was I strong enough to bear witness to what I had long suspected had triggered her DID. The abuse that had long been there within her, would it now come out? I questioned many things in a few seconds. I knew that I was looking at a woman who had come a long way in her therapy, one who was determined to do what was needed on her healing journey. I was equally determined to do whatever it took, to be there for her. She was staring intently at me for the answer.

This was the ultimate guided visualization I would ever experience. I had used this technique often with my clients. Seldom however, had a client walked in so determined, with a plan, wanting to lead me. Rarely if ever had a client wanted to direct the journey with such intensity and focus. Yet now, here was my client wanting to use it with me. The questions that filled my mind in those short seconds flooded my senses. I had to respond. This is where we had come to, where it all began.

She said she was ready. She had a strong compulsion to search out what was in the room at the end of the hallway in her head. The Alters had actually saved her life through the years. She too knew that there were still details that she had long blocked, details that had probably saved her sanity. She was ready now; she wanted to bring them out into the light. She needed, in this moment, to get to the very bottom of it. She was prepared to find the last of the puzzle pieces, and get the job done.

Charmaine stared at me intently, wanting to know if I would do this. Could we do this together? She motioned to my chair near her wanting to know, would I please come and sit down. I asked Charmaine to allow me to look at my appointment book first as I knew this would require extra time. She waited, never taking her eyes off of me.

I think she wondered if I would agree to her plan for this session. Knowing her so well, I am certain she had slept little, had thought this out for days; planning how she would present this to me. I worked hard to maintain my "therapist" face. My head was busy processing all she had said. I was considering how safe this session would be. Was she really ready? Was I? She was anxious, she was determined. She was not about to accept a delay or take no for an answer. I also knew that.

Quickly I realized that the next appointment had belonged to the client I had been on the phone with. The rest of the day was now freed up. I shared that with Charmaine. It was then that I moved from behind the desk, picking up my pad and pen. Charmaine immediately said; "No pens Doc, just YOU, no paper, just YOU, I want you to experience all of this with me."

As I moved around the desk, I kept wondering what exactly Charmaine had in mind for us during this session. At the same time I knew in my "gut", through many years of practice, it was going to be intense. She continued to look directly at me in a way that I was not accustomed to. She had given this a lot of thought. It was an important moment for her in her therapy. It would become a pivotal moment in her life as well based on the ongoing work we had been doing.

I could feel the energy in her; in the room. As I was about to take a seat she stopped me. Charmaine then indicated she needed to adjust the chairs first.

As I watched, Charmaine moved the chairs from their usual places that we had sat in on so many occasions. Rather than sitting across from each other, she placed the chairs side by side, as if we were sitting together on a plane or a train. She then directed me to my seat by patting the chair with her hand.

As I took my seat, she let me know that I was going to be accompanying her; into the hallway of her mind... into the place where the Alters lived. She would be going into this "room" that she had long feared, but knew that she had to enter. I was to be her guardian, to be with her there, as she did this. She said it would be like "walking out of hell" by the time we were done. She reached for my hand.

I looked at her, recognized that Charmaine was finally prepared to allow me entry into the very essence of the horrors she had experienced as a young child. The traumas that I suspected had created the Alters to step in when she could not cope. These very Alters that have saved her life through time that reside in her brain where she had described as a hallway. I was not sure how she planned to do this.

She went on to explain that she had been planning this for some time. That she and the Alters had been talking in the notebook I had given her. She said that it had taken her time to accept that the Alters were real, a very real part of her. Now she had come to accept this as fact.

She looked at me "Doc, this will be like those visualization things you do with me to help me relax. Only we will be going into my hallway, I think it is going to be what hell is, not some gentle relaxing place." Charmaine went on to tell me that she knew that the Alter "Boo Boo" was behind that last door. The little one who could not or did not speak had a story to tell. This was the only way that she could truly understand it all. She could not do this alone. That was the reason Charmaine said was that we had to do this together. I had to experience it with her. Charmaine explained that with me beside her, she felt she was strong enough to go down that hallway to be able to enter that last door. Hopefully she would emerge intact.

As I drew a deep breath I exhaled slowly. It hit me full force what we were entering into. I prayed for guidance, for her to have the strength that she would need. I looked with great admiration at this woman I had come to know so well. Her courage was astounding. At the same time, I could not help but reflect on Deseree's remarks about the Alters "bursting forward" under perceived threat of harm. I thought about JR emerging in Dr. Hope's office. I knew I would have to be mindful of this as Charmaine was approaching the most horrible of blocked memories, perhaps the origin of her DID.

She instructed me to take her hand, and close my eyes It dawned on me that my main door was unlocked. I did not want her to be interrupted by a mail delivery, walk-ins or any intrusions during this session. I had to interrupt her. I told her that I fully understood that this was going to be a time that we needed to be undisturbed. I needed to roll the phones to the answering service, and lock the doors. I also wanted to put a sign on the door for the mailman to leave the mail on the porch. She was frustrated, yet understood. She became a bit tearful as she thanked me for honoring her by recognizing the importance of what she was about to do.

As I went through the lobby to lock the door, Charmaine went into the bathroom. She returned with 2 bottles of water plus a box of Kleenex. Funny I had not noticed that neither was on the desk, as I usually have a supply on hand. The role reversal was amusing.

I found it interesting as I reflect back on the situation; we seemed to be preparing for something larger than ourselves. I had no idea of the magnitude of Charmaine's will to take me into that hallway and the brilliance of the visualization to come.

As we each sat down again, I felt compelled to let Charmaine know that I would do all that I could to keep her safe. I also wanted to make it clear that if I felt that she was becoming unsettled to a point of harm, or an Alter came out enraged, we would have to attend to that in the moment. I told her that I planned to let her lead this walk her way. I wanted her to let me know how and when to best assist her; but that as a therapist. I had to put her safety along with mine as the first priority.

I reinforced that my role was to be that of a guardian to and for her during this. I wanted to be what she needed in any way that was possible for the best outcome. I asked permission to video tape our session for us to view later before we began. She agreed, stipulating that the viewing was only for the two of us. That video was never shared, has since been destroyed. We had a ritual of cleansing with a fire in its destruction.

Once we had set the boundaries, started the video, Charmaine took my hand. She asked that I close my eyes. We began with Charmaine telling me that I was to "visualize the hallway" that we had talked about for so long. She instructed me to keep hold of her hand at all times.

It was funny to me in the beginning as I realized that she sounded like me, albeit the drawl. Charmaine had learned well over the months. She described to me in vivid detail how I was to relax, to breathe deeply as I followed her lead into the hallway. She was in complete control of this journey.

At first I was skeptical I must admit; after all I was the therapist. How in the hell am I going into this clients' brain? Really? Yet it became quite easy. It was amazingly colorful to be honest, in 3D, as I sat there, with my hand in hers. Two people, sitting side by side, were walking down a long hallway with doors on each side.

Let me be clearer; physically we were sitting side by side in my office. However once she took my hand in hers she began to talk, describe in graphic detail each step; we were transported, metaphysically to the hallway she had connected to inside her brain. The hallway appeared very long, hollow sounding with each step. Our goal was the door that entered the room of little silent "Boo Boo" the Alter.

As I visualized what Charmaine was telling me, I remembered her prior descriptions of so many events in her life. I thought about the Alters, the doors that were on each side of this long hallway. Apparently there was a room for each Alter there.

Charmaine had drawn a picture once showing me what the hallway looked like. Under the arch at the entrance, is where the gatekeeper stayed. Having seen this picture, it was very easy to visualize myself in that hallway. Entering the hallway, we had to get past the gatekeeper known as Bart. The hallway was wide. At the very, very end of the hallway was a white door.

This was the cubby that Charmaine was known to hide in when she was most frightened. The safe space she went to where she was able to find solace. I recalled from sessions her talking about running as fast and as hard as she could to get to her cubby. As she described it, I began to see it. I felt her hand tighten in mine as we entered the sacred brain of

Charmaine. My body tensed. I knew I was going where no one had ever gone before, including ME.

As Charmaine described "Bart" the gatekeeper; I realized that the description "Charie" had given was on the mark. It made me smile to visualize little Charie charming her way out of the hallway with Bart. I would describe him as a very "John Wayne" guy. He was tough gruff, at the same time, tender with little Charie.

As I sat there, eyes closed, Charmaine's hand in mine, I listened to her speak; "Ok, we are going to walk slowly because some rooms are still occupied. The room I want is at the end of the hallway on the right side. It is Boo Boo's room. Try to walk softly we don't want anyone to come out, make no noise on the floors if you can help it Doc... ok?" Charmaine walked slowly. I noticed the softness of her voice, feeling her tenseness as well.

I remembered the time I sat in the chair not so very many months back. I had felt a tug on my pant leg, only to realize that it was the Alter Boo Boo who did not speak. I recalled those profoundly sad eyes looking up at me. The fact that she could not speak indicated to me that Charmaine's abuse had started at a very early age.

Charmaine continued talking as we walked. She told me who lived behind each door. She talked quietly as she explained that some Alters were still behind the doors. Some of the others had taken their "baggage" leaving, no longer being needed, no longer in the hallway. They were gone now forever, she stated.

I asked Charmaine what she meant by "some of the rooms were empty now?" She softly explained that one day she had been able to feel herself in the hallway with the others. She said that Deseree had told her that each room contained memories that played a loop, similar to the loop on an old projector. Charmaine said she asked Deseree why it played over and over and over. She was told simply "because that is how it works." A profound statement if ever there was one. "Because that is how it works" (Alter)

Thank you Deseree, I thought. A light bulb went on in my own head. Yes, just like trauma, it is a loop. A loop that plays over and over; until it is worked through, until it is resolved. When it stops or the loop broken, the healing can begin. Charmaine's Alter Deseree through talk therapy had unlocked one of the best kept secrets. Charmaine finally understood why the memories stayed with her. She had not resolved the underlying issues, her trauma, and her grief.

She told me as she tightened her grip on my hand that she remembered when all the rooms were "occupied." She quietly let me know that when something scared her, she would retreat as fast as possible to her cubby at the end of the long hallway. Now she was remembering doors slamming shut as she ran past them. She said this made her adrenaline rush even more. Things were beginning to make sense to her, pieces of the puzzle were snapping into place it seemed.

I was amazed as I also remembered the movie called the Green Mile, where the warden took the hand of his prisoner and immediately became a part of his experience his pain, his truth. This type of soul work is akin to some of the haunting realities of connections that had been made or have been written about through time.

All of sudden Charmaine slammed her hand down hard on the arm of the leather chair. I sat bolt straight up in my chair, eyes wide open. I had not realized that she did that to emphasize the sound of the doors slamming as she passed each one running for safety in the hallway as she was speaking. I'm sure she was startled by my startled reaction as my grip tightening on her hand as well.

It was then I realized how deeply I had participated in the visualization. I felt my pulse quicken as I tried to settle myself. It took a moment to re-establish my focus on the sound of her voice. Charmaine smiled and told me that was how she felt for years and could not understand why. My startle at the sound was compared to her life as she knew it for years. I could not fathom that ongoing angst.

She used to describe it to me as if being in an underground facility with automatic doors that closed behind her each time she passed through one. She called them her security doors. Little did she realize that was exactly what they were in her mind. Perspective can be stronger than reality for some. The slamming doors were Alters protecting her as she raced toward the cubby. While she would be in her "cubby space", one of the Alters would come out managing her day to day life, or hour, or night. She had retreated, was unaware of anything going on. I was listening with all my senses.

She went on to explain to me that the rooms emptied after she had learned why the Alter came. When Charmaine was able to accept what traumas had occurred that created the Alters in the first place, she said they would be freed to leave. She had discovered this in our work together.

A few Alters she had actually talked with her in their rooms. They were gone soon after. Some, she told me just seemed to disappear over time. She finally understood that it was because she did not need them anymore. Charmaine thought that was what had happened to Jennie and Buck. Even Buck with all his rage had left her after she discovered the reason for his rage.

Charmaine explained that as she learned how to better manage her life, taking over the jobs they used to do for her. With excitement in her voice, she said "Doc that is the key. If people like me can take each Alter and find out why they are there and what their purpose is, then they can work on the reason until they no longer need that Alter to help them." She sounded like she was giving me the secret to the universe and in a way, I think she was.

She said she had discovered that all Alters came for a reason to help her survive. Charmaine gave a good example saying that JR was the protector for her. When she felt weak or scared, his total job was to protect her while keeping her safe. She had decided that was why her mind had created a male: someone who was very strong.

My God, she had come a long way in this therapeutic relationship. She had been constantly working her journey. I had to laugh when she patted my arm asking if I was ready to go on. It was as if she was inquiring if I had recuperated enough from the slamming of the doors. She asked if I needed more time to catch my breath perhaps, after all I was rather new to the sound she had heard for so long.

I assured her I had caught my breath, blood was circulating once again in my fingers. I was ready if she was. Continue she did, right where we left off. This was, and remains one extraordinary hallway; one that left me with no words, more than once.

I had to ask Charmaine if she knew what was behind the many doors there in that hall, and while I knew they were the rooms of Alters, I wondered if she knew who was behind what door and what each room looked like.

I was impressed when Charmaine was able to tell me in even greater detail that each room held live memories, personal memories that were the live action of why and what made that Alter come alive in her both for her or against her. She said the rooms looked like rooms from her childhood, the bedroom, a hallway, the bathroom, even the living room.

Charmaine spoke about the Alters the hallway, the loops that kept running, and then she hit on her blocked memories. She wanted to share what she had learned about them. The memories were all bad. When the horror was too much for her, her brain had created an Alter only she did not know it at the time.

The Alter(s) were there as a result of that bad and painful memory she had discovered through therapy, journal entries and reading. When anything that resembled that memory happened, or she had an overwhelming feeling familiar to that trauma, the Alter came out and took charge. I fought the urge to speak, to remind her of perceived threats as she spoke about fear.

Charmaine was talking in a whisper. She went deeper and deeper, in ways that only a person, who has lived through hell, can speak of with such eloquence. Charmaine then described the Alter known as Laylee; an Alter whom I had spent time with in the past.

She told me about Laylee taking her behind her door in the hallway. I was amazed at her calmness. Charmaine stopped talking and let go of my hand while she explained to me her visits with Laylee. I told Charmaine I remembered my time with Laylee. I recounted the last time she had appeared. As I began to ask her a question, she cut her eyes at me indicating I was to listen. I had to laugh. She told me I talked too much. I was not listening. "Hush" was the word and the look said it as well. It was time for me to let her do the walk. She could not take a break at that point to analyze the journey. Later she would answer questions.

Talk about role reversal, I thought to myself. I do believe I had been served Charmaine style notice. Bravo Charmaine! That session was a major breakthrough for Charmaine. Certainly it was a significant breakthrough for me also. I had never had an opportunity like this before in therapy. After my visual clue to "hush", Charmaine picked up on Laylee.

Apparently Laylee allowed Charmaine to enter her room. Charmaine had found the courage to meet her face to face. Believe me when I tell you, it took a lot of courage for that encounter. Laylee had hard feelings towards Charmaine. She was another Alter who used to cut Charmaine's arms to try to stop the pain.

Charmaine knew that Laylee hated her. Laylee would leave her messages in blood, calling her horrible names. She was also very promiscuous. She knew that Charmaine hated that too. It took a very courageous Charmaine to be willing to enter that room alone with Laylee. Charmaine said that little did she know at the time that Deseree and JR were close by listening in.

Entering that room, acknowledging the pain, learning through the journal writings and their messages, allowed Charmaine to understand the depth of the pain her Alter Laylee stored. It was only then Charmaine had grasped the roles of the Alters and why they were there.

Repeated traumas caused Charmaine to disassociate, forcing the brain to create Alters to cope. The ones that were no longer needed would be those ones that she had worked through or were no longer needed. Some Alters disappeared Deseree had told me. Charmaine never even knew they were there or why they were there in the first place. According to Deseree there had been many more Alters than I met. Many more than Charmaine was ever aware of as they never let themselves be known in the journals or notes. Charmaine had tightened her grip once again on my hand as she got back to Laylee. Laylee was a teenager. She came at a time when Charmaine was still young and being abused. Laylee knew what was going on, was to some degree willingly participating. In fact Laylee loved her sexuality, having sex, the nightlife along with hot cars and good times. However, she caused great guilt remorse, feelings of shame in Charmaine. This was quite an intense discovery for Charmaine, the woman who never wanted to be with another man as long as she lived.

Charmaine was able to talk about the "round table talks" held in the hallway. She had discovered all who would meet with Deseree who led those discussions. The Alters that tried to harm her would often be locked in their rooms or watched closely by JR and Bart. Charmaine had now recognized Deseree was the mother figure. She would not tolerate any mistreatment of Charmaine if she could stop it. Deseree often told the Alters that they were there to protect Charmaine, not to hurt her.

I asked Charmaine how it was that she now knew all of this. How she knew that they were gone, how it came to be that we were here together, today, on this walk. She told me that when Laylee told her that she,

[Charmaine] had been brutally raped repeatedly victimized and tortured as a child she had at first denied it and was ready to fight with Laylee. But, when Laylee told her that this abuse continued on until Laylee left home at 17 that triggered something inside of Charmaine. The memory began to return to her as did all the guilt and shame.

Charmaine said she turned to run away because she could not handle such horrid memories. She said it was then that Deseree appeared in the room. It was as if magically Deseree was there with Laylee and Charmaine as she was feeling overwhelmed to put her arms around her. Deseree validated everything Laylee had just told her by saying, "It is true child. I am here to hold you, but it is true and you are going to have to hear this." Charmaine said she looked up at Deseree, her internal mother, pleading with her wanting to know how this could have happened to her. Deseree said that she had no answers as to why it was done to her, but that she had created a family within that protected her.

Charmaine said she broke down crying herself to exhaustion at that point. She was later told that Deseree had held her, lying limp in her arms, until Charmaine was able to face the truth realizing that she was finally safe. After Charmaine was able to regain some composure, she said that she turned to Deseree looking her in the eye. "But Laylee hates me and cuts me, goes out with men and does all sorts of wicked things I would never ever do."

Charmaine went on to tell me that it was at that moment that Deseree gently escorted her to a chair in the corner of Laylee's room. Deseree then firmly told Laylee to sit down beside Charmaine and explain why she hated Charmaine so much. It was then that Laylee was able to break the loop that had been playing for so long. She was able to help Charmaine remember and understand. Laylee's need to cut Charmaine to get her attention, and to punish her ended.

Charmaine asked me as she looked into my eyes, "Doc, do you remember when I told you I was hearing those muffled sounds, like people talking in the distance? Well those were the round table discussions. As I learned about all the Alters and what they were doing, I also learned they each have their own room. Once I learned to listen better, one day I actually did hear them. Laylee must have known I could hear. She started talking directly to me; she told me how she hated me because I never made them stop. I asked her who? She told me "you know."

Charmaine told me that they (Alters) within the hallway had an intense discussion that day, with Deseree keeping things calm. Laylee finally made Charmaine understand that she had come when one of the men from Charmaine's father's work place had started molesting her. Charmaine was a teenager sexual feelings were new to her. The earlier abuse was not connected to Charmaine in a sexual way but a violent way. Charmaine said that when Laylee started talking about this, she felt her face flush from the memory, fear and shame.

The internal battle of the brain, body, and spirit was amplified as Charmaine could not accept the truth. "I told her she was a liar because I was never molested, abused or beaten. I did not remember being molested. Laylee looked at me, and for the first time, I saw the sadness in her eyes. She said "That is because it is my memory Charmaine, not yours. I took your place every time." Charmaine went on to say "Doc, it was then I realized that each Alter has a memory of something that happened to me. Something so wrong that I just went away to my cubby and the Alter(s) took my place, and that each horrible memory played over and over for them too. They came to rescue me every time I got scared. But, Laylee, who was angry with me, would also punish me. She is the reason for the blood in my journal."

Charmaine's revelations, continual flow of information was astounding. As she continued flooding me with all this news it took my breath away. The room felt hot, there was no air moving. Several times I felt like I could not keep up with the Alters, their writings, the hallway conversations. Charmaine's ability to find and maintain her train of thoughts with such courage was astonishing. I knew that I had to keep up, stay the course. This was the hell that she had referred to. It indeed was hell; this was also an example of extreme courage.

When I asked Charmaine why we were doing this on that particular day, she looked at me calmly and said "Because this is the day it was intended. The Alters said it was time. Deseree agreed. She let me know that many of the Alters were gone, but that there were some still here." I asked her if was Charie and JR were still here. She said, "Yes, Boo Boo is here, and a couple of others."

So I had my answer, it was "intended to be this day." This is the day that we would do this. I buckled my spiritual seat belt, asked Creator to give this woman the strength that she would need to proceed forward. I would and did need the strength and wisdom to be her passenger.

Charmaine had come to an awakening of her complicated traumatic past. She had come to a realization of the truth by hearing from her inner Alters. One was the internal mother, Deseree. Laylee had helped also, lending Charmaine another view. Even with all that was going on, Charmaine did not retreat to her cubby. I saw this as a very good sign.

She looked at me with teary eyes and asked how someone could feel pleasure when being abused. I gently explained that some things we have no control over. She was a young woman, still developing. Her body was reacting to the hormones surging, to stimulate, to life at the time. I also explained that it did not mean she enjoyed what the man did. Her naive body had experienced a physical reaction perhaps, or it might have been enjoyable for her. That we would never really know for sure as she was not present then, it was an Alter.

As I listened to Charmaine, she continued to tell me that at first she felt overwhelmed by what Laylee had told her. She hated what she heard, but she was not petrified. She had not wanted to run away. Interesting to note, now that she was hearing it, the memories were more accessible to her. She felt as though the memories had been in a dim fog from a very distant past. She felt the fog was lifting.

She talked quietly about the depth of the sadness she felt as a result of all her Alter Laylee had to endure on her behalf. Charmaine tried to explain that she felt a shadowy familiarity with the story Laylee told. Charmaine knew in her heart that she had heard the truth. Charmaine said she had worked hard, in earnest, to explain to Laylee that she did not hate her. She was so sorry that she did not stop it but she did not know how.

The expression on Charmaine's face showed pronounced pain. She stated that she had cried a lot that day. She said that our work in therapy, and her new understanding of the Alters had brought forward some very painful sad feelings unlike she had ever experienced. She felt she was crying not only for herself but for those who stepped in to take her place. Those who suffered when she was unable to stand the horror or the pain in her own life were the ones who also suffered in her mind now.

It seemed Charmaine was weeping for her whole lost life. To hear her talk so openly about her acceptance of DID, and all that she had learned was amazing. Her grief was for a lost life, trauma, and pain. Her grief now was also for the Alters that had jumped in when she disassociated retreating to the cubby at the end of the hallway of her brain.

I explained to Charmaine that denial is a very strong force. It serves as a powerful defense mechanism. The belief that horrid things happen to other people, in horrible families, is one way we protect ourselves from our own reality. When we convince ourselves that this could not have happened in our own family, we live in a constant state of denial. Her Alters held both her pain, and her truth. They also held the keys to her opening a door for her walk, stronger as a survivor to thriver.

Charmaine said that she felt her entire life had been a series of lies. The Alters covered for her. I told her that this happened to many abused children. When they became adults, they struggled with many unknown demons. So many children who suffered sexual trauma have gone through this same experience. With secrets, blocked or repressed memories. This often led to depression or complicated grief, not feeling safe in their lives.

Charmaine adamantly told me that there could be no denying that anymore. She knew everything was coming into focus. It had to be true. These Alters had saved her life in many situations. She felt she probably would have been dead long ago had they not taken over.

Charmaine said she had spent her whole life thinking that no one could or would do such terrible things to her. She had spent her life thinking everything was her fault; that she was just too sensitive, or that she had imagined things taken out of context, or been influenced by movies. Therefore those dim memories that waxed and waned within her surely were not true.

Yet, they sadly had happened to her. They were true memories. I felt more was to be revealed to her in this hallway. That it was becoming more real with each step we took together. She had certainly come a long way from the person who came to see me for reasons her physician stated as "grief" of parents who had died.

Charmaine looked at me quizzically wanting to if my questions were all done for now as she needed to get down this hallway before she lost her bravery. Biting my lip, so as to not smile; I assured her that I would hold further questions, for later. I dared not suggest that she had also engaged in the conversation we had just had.

On many levels she was spot on in regards to my engaging her... was I delaying what my heart knew was yet to come? Perhaps I was. We shall see. As she spoke with such conviction, she bowed her head. I felt her take my hand, her grip tightening.

With my raspy but low slow voice, I then asked her to tell me what she was seeing in the hallway now. I knew this walk was vital. This was it, I knew we were about to begin again. We were knee deep in it until it was over. I needed her to use descriptors. I wanted her to activate all her senses, even if it was she who was leading.

Charmaine looked at me, and then closed her eyes, I again closed mine. I realized I had dug my feet into the carpet. At times, I felt I was literally walking step by step as she walked. I stopped still as she talked. I mentally looked around the hallway in my mind's eye, nothing on the walls only white paint. Nothing on the floors, no carpet, no plants, no tables just a hallway. My body was in the hyper - vigilant mode I was expecting something unpredictable.

She walked slowly, yet with purpose. I noticed that her breathing pattern would change as she talked, depending on what room we were standing by. She told me at one point that she did not want them all to go away. She was talking about the Alters, now that she knew about them, she felt like she would be losing her family. I asked her if she knew who was left of the Alters. She stopped walking, shushed me saying "Remember, we are on a mission Doc. Pretend we are breaking into a building." She smiled and we started walking again.

I recognized that my asking questions indicated my own nervousness coupled with the need to know everything so that I could help her through this. I also realized that I was doing it to try to keep Charmaine calm, probably myself too.

As I listened, I could hear her breath change. It was as if Charmaine was speaking from a distance, although she was right beside me. As she continued walking, the visual was painfully clear. We were both close to witnessing something appalling at the same time. She continued talking even though she had stopped walking. I recognized that we were standing at a door that was open.

Charmaine had pulled her hand from mine. I opened my eyes to see if she was ok. I glanced toward Charmaine to see that she was sitting there with tears on her face, her eyes closed. She was gently moving her hand over something in front of her that was obviously in the hallway. I quietly asked her what she was touching. She said it was the door to Laylee's room.

She let me know that she remembered the time when the man was raping her. It was grisly, she had reached a point that she could not take anymore. That was when Laylee came out as she ran down the hallway to her cubby screaming. Laylee took the pain for her, became her. Laylee suffered because Charmaine could not cope with being abused by men. Charmaine did not know it at the time, but now felt responsible for using Laylee that way. It made her profoundly sad.

Charmaine choked back sobs as she explained her thoughts of what that man did to Laylee. She said the thoughts and images tore her heart out. Between sobs and blowing her nose, Charmaine also shared that Deseree had seared it into her brain as she also told her to remember that Laylee was part of her. So whatever happened to the Alters has happened to Charmaine.

I asked Charmaine if she had more memories of what the room had held. She did, they were faint ones that brought no real pain to her. She said that she knew Laylee had come to protect her. Laylee was also on edge when not angry that Charmaine could not/did

not protect her. "I swear Doc, I did not know, I just did not know, I have no memory except what she told me. That is when it came back to me." Charmaine bowed
her head, as the tears fell quietly while she squeezed my hand as she spoke.

Charmaine said she cried when talking to Laylee as she kept telling her how sorry she was for everything that had happened. She wished she could undo it. She said that then Laylee reached out to touch her. She first jerked back thinking Laylee was going to hit her, but then she saw a tear in the corner of Laylee's eye. Laylee put her hand on Charmaine's face as she told her all she ever wanted was Charmaine to understand that she had stood in for all the pain each and every time. Charmaine had thanked Laylee.

The acknowledgement along with the thank-you was all that Laylee needed to break the tape, to cut it loose. That said that was all she needed to be able to leave. Charmaine asked her what she meant by "leave." Laylee answered that it was time for her to go, that Charmaine no longer needed her. Charmaine said she cried out "No no, don't go." Laylee appeared to walk through the wall of the room quietly was gone. There were no more journal entries after that.

Charmaine said it took her a while to realize that this was how it should be...for her to let go. She said that at first, it felt like she had lost her dearest friend. She whispered to me that she did not want any of the others to leave. She did not want to be left alone. She did not want to feel abandoned. "Why couldn't they stay as long as we all worked together?"

All of a sudden I realized that Charmaine was trying to free herself from my ever tightening grip on her hand. I had not realized that while standing in that hallway bearing witness to this part of the story, I had tightened my grip on her hand. I suppose I had started to cause her a bit of pain, or tingling. I quietly apologized to Charmaine for hurting her hand. I asked that she continue. She did not seem to mind as she shook her hand a bit, and then returned it to mine. The office felt sweltering as she picked up where she left off.

I found it hard to imagine what this woman had endured in her lifetime. It is even more amazing that she has managed to come out of it, raise her kids primarily alone. Now she had the courage to walk this hallway.

It was terribly hard to hear the depths of pain that Charmaine was dealing with. At the same time; it was the most powerful thing to hear her talk about. Facing her Alter Laylee, she was talking about the reality of her past, and understanding. Charmaine was finally, truly "getting it", the reason the Alter(s) were there.

Once again, closing our eyes, I could see the doors more clearly than ever before as her voice softly started describing the hallway again. She talked about the warm glow in the hallway. The walls were a soft yellow. There were no pictures, no mementos, nothing, just a long hallway with doors on each side. Somehow it felt to me like I was looking through a fish eye lens. It was a very long way to the white door at the end of the hall where Charmaine felt safe. The cubby she had spoken of so often.

I suddenly felt like the cubby was further away than when we began. This type of soul journey with another, takes tremendous trust, incredible strength and endurance on the part of both client/therapist. A willingness on the part of the guardian to be led into another's world at their speed, remaining presentable to guide; yet not direct or influence what is being seen, heard, remembered or experienced. It is difficult to convey in writing what this experience is like. Charmaine said it is like watching a movie feeling thinking like you are in it. She was right.

As I listened, Charmaine continued in a voice that I had come to know well. One thing that continued to intrigue me was the ability to be IN her brain in the "hallway in her brain" with her. I was not sitting outside watching her. Rather we were sharing one visual. She described every detail. It was as if I too were seeing it all through her eyes. Visualization is a tool I use often in therapy, even with those suffering intense pain and trauma. This time, Charmaine was using it with me in a way that to this day makes me a strong advocate for guided imagery.

Charmaine explained that she had learned that each room in the hallway held its own memories, pains, and stories. Sometimes it was one playing over and over. Sometimes it was several memories playing back to back, over and over. In order to let the Alter return to her, she had to be willing to hear the story.

She had to be willing to cope with it, own it and accept it as her own. She had to know that it had happened learning to trust that it was then, not now. They were memories of experiences, not current threats.

Charmaine felt that once she heard each Alters' story, and understood that these experiences could not harm her now, she could let the Alter go. She had read the books I had given her. She knew that integration into one holistic self could happen.

With her southern drawl she said to me, "Doc are you ready now, are you with me, I need you to stay with me here ok?" I assured her I was with her. I closed my eyes concentrating on my breath, noting hers as I placed myself on the solid ground of the hallway floor. I listened for what was to come next.

Charmaine continued on about Laylee being gone from her sight now. I asked her if she could still see into Laylee's room, although she was gone. Charmaine quickly told me no. There was no longer a need. No Laylee, no need for a further look behind the door to the room for Laylee.

I notice how quiet it feels. The energy in the room feels different somehow. Charmaine is very quiet, as though she is walking us past something or near something that she was yet unable or unwilling to voice. I honored her silence. After a brief silence, she spoke again quietly, so quietly.

Charmaine whispered that we are going by rooms, with Alters in them. She said that later she will explain why the other Alters are gone. How some left even though she had not met them. It was as if they knew without words that she no longer needed them. But, she explained, today was about Boo Boo that was important.

I sat still listening to the sound of our breathing. Waiting for Charmaine to let me know where and what we were facing in the hallway. It was the silent moments in the hallway that heightened the suspense. As a guardian, you are not quite sure what was next. Wondering waiting; keeping the silence that is the task at hand. We wait a bit longer, as I wonder what she is seeing or thinking.

Charmaine tells me it is time to walk. She squeezed my hand as I notice her eyes were closed and her body rigid. The silence in the hallway is deafening, in the office; is palpable. I too close my eyes I am walking, noticing the doors the silence, and the heat. If there are Alters I cannot help but wonder why it is so very quiet. Maybe they know we are there? They are fearful or do not want to come out or are anxious? I notice that a few of the doors are closed after we have passed several opened ones.

Charmaine has already explained the empty rooms to me but has said nothing about the rooms with closed doors. I wonder why. I have already surmised that the rooms with closed doors still hold Alters. I wonder which doors are JR's, Charie's, or even the matronly Deseree...

She let me know that she does know for sure that JR, Desire and Charlie are all are behind the doors there. That little Boo Boo is behind the door near her cubby down the hall. That is where we are going. Now I have to wonder if Charmaine was in my head. She seemed to voice that just as I had wondered about the very same Alters. Interesting how sometimes questions can be answered before they are even asked. Charmaine is determined that we are going there. This is the day that it was intended. She has to do this. She is determined to do it her own way.

The names of the existing Alters she told me as easily as if telling me her own name. I believe she has come to know them very well. She has accepted them; they are becoming integrated into her whole being. Charmaine spoke softly during this time as if not wanting to disrupt the Alters. She told me that she had to get to, go into Boo Boo's room. She had to get this done. She had to deal with it. I notice that while she is still moving forward, her steps seem heavy. I can feel the uneasiness, the anxiety so thick you could cut it with a knife.

In her journal were notes. It is the only way Boo Boo has to communicate. It is through writings or touch. Boo Boo has never uttered a word, not when she has been out; not when she was in the office. Charmaine said that she has found notes in her medicine cabinet, notes on her desk, notes written in lipstick on the mirror that are childlike in appearance saying things like _"pweese save ME",_ in bold print.

The Alter Deseree, has always attempted to keep little Boo Boo in the hallway, has always tried to protect her. The same holds true with JR and Bart. It seems that both have a soft spot for her along with the little kids. They allow her out to color in coloring books or to play. Charmaine reported many times that she had found things at home, coloring books or her dolls on the floor. Charmaine began to tell me about the childish notes.

Boo Boo is always very sad. She has been known to carry a big stuffed doll upside down by its foot. I have seen this huge doll in Charmaine's bedroom in the "child's corner" as she always called it. It is not the same one that Anna carries. I never thought of that before. I think that Anna's big ole ass doll is way too big for Boo Boo to carry. Boo Boo carried her special doll the day she came into my office. I remembered how shocked Charmaine was to find it there after Boo Boo left.

Imagine the Alter Boo Boo as she holds her doll, twisting her hair with one hand, wanting to lean against someone for nurturing: Boo Boo who wants to be gently touched or lightly touched on the hand or shoulder. I found myself forgetting I was with an adult woman. I only noticed Boo Boo. She had such sad eyes. She was in so much pain. She was frightened and silent. Yet, she had been leaving notes implorations begging someone to save her. Now Charmaine was unwavering, wanting to get behind that door to her. She felt compelled, although she did not know exactly what she would find once inside the door.

Horror had created Charmaine's Alters. Now Charmaine was ready to integrate them into herself differently than ever before imagined. I felt a great trepidation as we continued this walk down the long hallway. Even I wondered if what was behind that door was going to be as disturbing as I feared it would be. This was where it had all begun, with this little precious child. Was Charmaine ready? Was I?

We both were right to have feared the worst as we continued to walk the hallway. At times Charmaine asked that I squeeze her hand to help give her strength. I asked her to tell me everything she was seeing: were there any smells, any photos on the walls, textures, feelings in her gut, any sounds. I would reassure her again of her courage, her bravery in this walk. I often would tell her that she was doing great. I reminded her frequently that I was with her and right beside her with each step she took.

Charmaine began talking about Charie, letting me know we had just passed her room. She said that Charie did not seem to be sexually or emotionally abused. Charmaine said she desperately hoped that was the case. I quickly opened my eyes and noticed that, although Charmaine had her head back and eyes closed, she was smiling as she talked. As she thought of Charie, she was recalling her as happy, loving, playful and funny.

As we stood in the hallway, again it became silent. I continued to think of how far we had come in this relationship through the therapeutic work she had done. She had mastered guided imagery, the ability to focus to direct me in this journey. She was brilliantly taking me into the core of her life and mind.

Her ability to take me into her brain, into her world of Alters was astonishing.

I noticed the grip on my hand getting tighter as Charmaine's body became tense and rigid. I knew we were walking again down the hallway. We were getting closer to the cubby, which meant we were getting closer to Boo Boo's room. I knew that because it was the door nearest the cubby of safety that she had fled to over the years.

Charmaine said in a tense voice, "Doc, I am getting scared now... please do not leave me. We have to stop a minute or walk slower for just a minute ok?" I could hear the panic in her voice. She was expressing genuine fear as I noticed her grip tighter in my hand. I glanced at her. Her eyes were clenched shut. I knew she was close to where she was determined to go. I assured her I was right with her, encouraged her to take her time, she could do this. Charmaine said that she could "feel" that this was the worst room of all. This room held all that was left to know.

I took my other hand placed it on her arm, asked quietly, "Do you know what is behind that door Charmaine?" Her reply came in short sentences. One time when she was running to her cubby in her mind, trying desperately to seek solace , she ran past that door. It was in the process of being closed but not before she got a peak of what was inside.

Charmaine was now visibly shaking. Silent tears ran down her cheeks. She continued to squeeze my hand. Charmaine opened her eyes briefly seeing that that I had my eyes opened. She said "Doc, you are not in the hallway. I need you in there." I apologized and told her that when I heard the pain in her voice, I had to look and see if she was ok.

I took her hand once more leaned closer toward her so that our shoulders were even touching. I asked Charmaine to please describe in as much detail as possible what she saw before the door closed that day. What she smelled, what she tasted, what she felt, what she witnessed, colors, sounds, sights, smells, everything. I promised her I would keep her safe from harm. I would be right with her each moment, each step.

Charmaine took a deep breath. She said the room was absolute evil. It was in the living room when she was little. There were people. "People all over the place, I knew them. They were all grownups. They were all sitting around in a circle, and it smelled nauseating."

She continued with tears streaking her face, her voice trembling she said, "And the worst part is I saw me, I am little, I was there naked on the couch and my parents and those people that were there were laughing and drinking, and doing disgusting things... and." I again opened my eyes as Charmaine's voice trailed off. I told her that she was safe, she was ok. I reinforced the importance of remembering that nothing in those rooms could hurt her again.

I felt the burn in my heart. We were standing outside the door of Boo Boo's room in hell. My God, this woman has discovered the original source of her trauma. The life that lies behind that door was the root of cumulative trauma. That is where she was about to enter. It involved her parents their social circle of friends. She was describing it so vividly that I felt, smelled, saw what she was saying in my visualization of this room.

Charmaine would uncover the ultimate betrayal of trust. The horrific abuse of a little child now grown into a woman was about to be uncovered. A grown woman sitting beside me, as she was preparing to confront such horror that she had blocked for decades was about to come face to face with the perpetrators. We sat quietly in an office physically where the air was still. In that same time we both had been transported to a hallway that is in her brain. She had finally gathered the strength to enter the hell of her past.

Her mind allowed her to create a hallway with a safe cubby at the end. The Alters took care of the horrors that she really knew deep inside but could not andle. The dim fog she now talks about is lifting granting her the courage of a survivor in her pursuit to integrate her life into wholeness. She wanted her life back.

I realize it does not matter that I can no longer feel my hand. I have no need to speak. She will speak when it is time. It is fine to stand in the hallway as she gathers what she needs to do what she must now. I am with her completely. From time to time I use my arm to apply pressure to her elbow to let her know I am right beside her, she is safe. "Doc, see this door, this is the door, and right down there is my cubby.

Please stay with me; I'm going to turn the knob ok? Are you ready?" I let her know I was ready, I was with her, and I wanted her to tell me everything she sees as she sees it. Everything she smells and touches. Again I whisper to her. Describe the things on the walls, the people, what they are saying, doing, who they are. I want her to speak her feelings as she has them. What are the sounds? Is there, music, crying, laughing, anything and everything; tell me as it is happening. We will do this together but she has to keep talking. There is no going back now, this is what she came to do on this day as she said "it was intended" she was ready.

Charmaine nods her head. I watch as she reaches one arm up, turning a doorknob to the right. She swings the door open. I feel her stop dead in her tracks. I tell her to keep telling me what she sees. She leans towards me whispers with a quivery voice, "Doc I am so glad that I don't have those accidents on myself anymore. Cos' if I did, it would be now. I'd be having one right here."

Charmaine then leans into me. Her body shaking, she seems to go limp from what she was seeing. I open my eyes quickly to assess the situation. I ask her if she was sure she wants to go forward. I reminded her that she does not have to do this if she is not ready. I knew even as I said it, there was no going back... it was something I had to say, yet as soon as I said it, I regretted it.

Charmaine's eyes snapped open as she looked at me. "YES, I have to do this now, I JUST HAVE TO." I placed my arm on her arm quietly and said, "Ok, I've got you Charmaine. Yes, you can do this; we will do this together then." Charmaine said that she felt sick. She thought she might know what was to come, but just opening the door has made her want to throw up. She needed a moment to just be still. I too felt I knew what was to come. Looking back I had no idea truthfully of the scope of ugliness and repulsion we were walking into.

Charmaine asked me not to center this book on the terrors, the hell of abuse that happened or more on the journey out of hell. I can assure you that what she saw in that room was horrific beyond words. To this day I wonder how such a sweet woman or anyone would/could survive it all. At the same time, I know now it was because of the Alters because of the creativity of the brain that allowed her to live through it all.

As Charmaine gathered her strength, I continued to provide a supportive presence. I prompted her to take me through this; step by step as she talked. I told Charmaine once again that she was safe. As hard as this is, it is a memory now. It is not real in real time, it is a memory. I kept telling her that she would come out of this intact. I again leaned into Charmaine telling her to "Use all of your senses. Charmaine, remember these are memories, Boo Boo's memory; it is not real right now. You are safe."

With that Charmaine pushed the door wide open. We looked into something that I have never seen before. Something that she had effectively blocked for most of her life. I felt myself suck air into my lungs from the jolt of her descriptions. I only hoped that she did not hear it. I squeezed her hand indicating I was there. I would walk with her. She explained that she wanted me to wait at the door. She would tell me everything as "those there in the room" could not see us. Charmaine knew she had to walk into this room alone for Boo Boo and for herself.

As I released her hand, she stopped me. She wanted me to keep hold of her hand even though she was walking in alone. Her breathing was fast as she spoke. She described in detail the people in the room. There was furniture in the inner hallway after entering the door, the priceless artwork on the walls. She described beautiful ornate expensive rugs on the floor. She described the people as they were dressed, in finery for the evening. They were esteemed leaders in the community; many were members of her family's church. She knew some of them by name. There was laughter, gaiety, and drinking. The smell of whisky filled the room. Some of the people were in groups and others were walking around chatting.

Charmaine spoke quietly to me as her eyes were darting under her eyelids. She continued to scan the room. I found myself bouncing on my toes trying to peek in past the door. I wanted to make sure that she was ok. Her hand tightened on mine as she leaned in a bit to whisper, "The stench of liquor has made my stomach flip, oh how terrible this is. I guess this is why I don't like to drink. The smell in here is making me want to gag."

I found I was using a "double squeeze" pump of the hand to indicate I heard her. I was with her. It was my way of not interrupting her description of what was happening. It seemed to be working well.

She had told me before we opened the door that she did not want me to let go of her hand, but that she was leaving me at the door. That was tricky. We were separated, but joined. I would just have to go with her on this. She was doing an excellent job describing the scene. Her pain was indescribable. When she was able she would loosen her grip a bit. She had the force of a body builder when she would grab hold again. As she walked deeper into the room, her grip got tighter and tighter. My fingers were tingling as they began to get numb from the pressure.

I could feel tears burning my eyes as I witnessed her trauma. Her story was emerging in living color. I was going through so many emotions myself. I was working hard to be aware of the state of mind that Charmaine was in; attempting to absorb all that she was seeing second by second of her telling me. At times I would open my eyes to get a true visual of her. Once again I closed my eyes as I returned to the doorway of Boo Boo's room. I truly believe I could have kept my eyes open staying in the hallway as it was so visual, the linkage had been made.

I leaned in closer in order to hear her because she was talking very softly. I was hearing her words through whispers as though she did not want to draw attention to either of us being there. She would tell me: "Look, there are people all around. My stomach is churning. Can you smell the stench? It's... I think it's that sex smell... I might have to throw up doc."

I appreciated that she was fully there. I knew there would be no backing out. She was sure that I was in fact there with her. I remained silent, recognizing that she was talking about the smell of semen that she now smells from time to time. We had discussed her reaction to the smell of semen in therapy. She originally found that out through washing clothes. At times there would be a smell that kept triggering reactions that she could not pinpoint. She would have violent reactions that ending with vomiting at that particular smell.

Having one son that is a teenager, I was sure that it was from his hand towels. She had discovered the smell and reactions when washing his clothing. It finally dawned on her what he was doing; she was appalled that she was getting the smell of semen. He is at the height of hormonal changes; no other males were in the house. I had worked hard to normalize that with her, yet she found it disgusting.

She learned through sessions that the association was probably being triggered from sexual abuse. Now she is saying she smells that same smell in the room with all these well groomed well established adults. She whispers to me "Oh dear God Doc, I smell that awful smell. Almost like being in an old locker room, where the old smells stay there, only this is the smell of sex. I know it is. Remember me telling you about the clothes and that smell, well it's the same smell but 100 times worse... can't you smell it Doc"...

I was unprepared when she told me where this room was. As she tightened even more the body builders grip on my hand she sat bolt up in her chair. "Lord have mercy Doc ...This is the living room from my childhood. The people sitting in there are people who are supposed to be some church Bridge group only they're not. They are evil Doc. I know these people.

I can hear the astonishment in her voice. I can tell that she is totally shocked by this revelation. Charmaine pulls my hand toward hers whispering that she is walking past some them quietly now. Then she proceeds to tell me what she is seeing.

She begins to describe the party that is going on in Boo Boo's room. The living room of her childhood since her birth, it seems. Adults she knew as a child. Some are kissing, and touching, and have their pants unzipped, down to their knees for others. Women are there that she knows with their dresses "hiked up" around their waists. She describes it so vividly that I can see it myself. Thankfully I am not able to smell the smells that she is describing. With the look on her face, I do not doubt that she is having tremendous sensory flashbacks from her childhood.

I can tell that Charmaine's pulse is racing. She is panting. I swear at times I can see her heart beating against her shirt. She tells me she can now hear little Charie in the background saying "Stop. Stop. Dey dot sticks. Dey dot shticks in dem pants. Dey hut u." She then paused for a minute trying to digest what she had said. I realized that I was not breathing in that instant either. What did Charie see that we did not? I am watching Charmaine so close I can see her artery beat in her neck. I can feel her pulse in the grip she has on my hand. She is gasping for air. As we both open our eyes we stare at each other. It is not lost on Charmaine, or me, that we both have tears on our faces. We both have just heard the same words.

We both need a moment to regain our composure. Charmaine cannot stop now. We have come too far to turn back now. She must continue now. It is crucial that she walks through this hell. She must not stop at this point. She is leading this she is now seeing it in full color. She now knows what happened to her as an innocent small child.

Charmaine leans back and closes her eyes tightly after grabbing my hand. She whispers with urgency that she has really got to find Charie and Boo Boo. She has a steel resolve that she must save the little ones. I find that my heart is aching for her, for her childhood and her life. I can only be the guardian of this woman in pain. This walk is Charmaine's. It was time to continue further into the room with my hand in hers.

I remembered the child's words even as she said them. The words and the drawings by Charie in the journal came back to me. The sweet little precocious Charie who loved to play in my corner of the office, how I hoped she would not be found in that room. I was remembering how adamant the Alter Charie was about those dolls I had. I could still see her face, the expressions when she talked about the "sticks in da pants dat hurt you." The same dolls I had to put in the trash then sit the can outside the office when Charie visited. Charlie had tremendous upset about the bad people doing bad things. I was brought out of that thought when Charmaine next spoke from the room...

Charmaine said "But this is Boo Boo's room. Why is Charie in here? I cannot see her anywhere." I realized immediately that Charmaine was looking around the room. As she was looking, she grabbed my arm, and whispered. "MY God Doc... look!" She then told me that there in that room; quite visible she was seeing two men with erections as women were performing oral sex on them.

Charmaine's look said what her words are saying. She was aghast at what she was seeing, just could not believe what she is describing. No longer were her eyes shut. They were wide open. She is repulsed at what she is experiencing. Charmaine describes the sights the smells, then leans in to me as she says, "The look in their eyes is glazed over. Like pure evil, with drool coming out of their mouths."

Charmaine went from talking in whispers with profound anguish, to talking as if she were reporting a boring weather broadcast on the six o'clock news. At times she showed complete detachment and at other times she vacillated between shock, the horror and the detachment as she walked through that room. It was horror personified involving a child of perhaps 3-5 that was naked in a room swirling with self-indulgent adults.

These were people known to the community. The same folks that a little child should have been able to trust with her life, her innocence and safety; but they were involving her in their debauchery as were her parents. They were the hosts of this sordid gathering, in her own home.

I had opened my eyes. I started to doubt if she could really continue with this. I saw that Charmaine had her eyes open as well. She was looking directly at me. I knew that Charmaine was filtering so many emotions, so many revelations at once. I was watching to see if she can handle them all. Charmaine let me know the people in the room are members of a bridge club that her parents are in. The others there she recognized as church members from long ago. Again she tells me of the smells, the repulsion, and the disgust she was experiencing.

Charmaine took a deep breath, her shoulders pulled back, she looked straight ahead. Suddenly I feel her energy shift to calm determination ready to continue on. The walk is back on again. She quietly stated, "I'm ok Doc. I am ok. Let's finish this. It's important to me and it has to be, just has to be done." I looked at her, did a quick assessment based on her eyes, her skin color, her breathing. I nodded my head indicating "OK, continue"... We settled back in our chairs and she closed her eyes.

I did believe she was good to continue although I had to wonder what other terrors were ahead. I had determined I could easily stay with her in this hallway and be completely with her; while at the same time, I was keeping one eye on her to monitor her closely. Charmaine had learned through all of this that she dealt with outrage in her life through a very detached lens. She was a classic textbook style of many who have been diagnosed with DID in many ways. We continued to walk through what she later referred to as hell personified. She reentered that room behind the door of little Boo Boo. She told me that she saw herself as a young girl (Boo Boo) sitting naked, her arms and legs pulled up tightly to her chest. She saw herself; wide eyed, petrified beyond belief, with the scum of the earth adults as they drank, performed sexual acts completely ignoring her. I was appalled.

Through talk therapy, EMDR, visualization, and trauma resolution techniques, Charmaine had come to recognize her own signs of fear, trauma and her own coping mechanisms. She was able to describe what she was seeing in this child Alter known as Boo who did not speak. She recognized the trauma in the eyes of that innocent victim of 5 years old.

"OH DEAR GOD NO!." I leaned toward her asking her to share with me what she is seeing. "Tell me what is happening now." With a gasp, Charmaine says, "One of the men just walked over to Boo Boo and said it is time. He ...he just come to the couch and grabbed Boo Boo; he is pulling her onto the floor now. Oh Doc, Boo Boo is shaking so badly. She's trembling; the poor little thing is shaking and naked. She has bruises all over. She's so scared. Oh no, she has peed all over the floor."

With a voice filled with new discovery betrayal and shock, Charmaine says "But Wait...this child is me. I have dug my heels in the floor and am crying and screaming and pulling against him... I am trying to get away... and others are watching and... and...and..." Charmaine continued. Some of the others in the room drew near. One of them moved in slapped her hard across the face, making her fall hard to the ground. She hit her little head so hard as she fell it bounced on the floor. The others had started putting their hands all over her. "The smells...oh my God the smells! I see my Mother sitting in a chair with a drink in her hand across the room. She's just sitting there. They did nothing to help me."

As Charmaine watches what is happening in the room, she is telling me the intrinsic details. Her eyes are wide open, fixed on nothing in particular but being in that room as she says she can see her eyes begin to roll back in her head as a man rams his penis in her anus. Charmaine is barely breathing as she whispers, her hand in mind. I know that as I looked down but no longer have feeling in any fingers from her grip. She tells me the little child looks as though she has lost consciousness as her head slumped to the side, her body limp. As she speaks, tears are falling on her face. She has a death grip on my hand. She has her eyes wide open as seeing this for the first time, in real time.

I too was having trouble breathing. As she was walking me through her trauma, I double squeezed Charmaine's hand to let her know I was right beside her. I heard myself speak to Charmaine. Letting her know that she was safe and this was a memory, it was the fog lifting: I said she was there for a purpose, reminding her that those people could never harm her again. I adjusted my breathing to accommodate for what the description of this child's trauma was doing to me. I shielded myself from its impact. Realizing that this is exactly where it all began, where Boo Boo came in and where the other Alters were born; from such hedonistic behaviors, vile acts against an innocent child.

We were silent for a bit. I attempted to get Charmaine's attention. The silence had gone on too long. Charmaine finally felt my squeeze against her hand. Moments later it was as if she too realized that Boo Boo evolved once she lost consciousness in that horrid traumatic event. It was at that time that I believe Charmaine was able to hear my words. We took several deep breaths together; calming breaths, meant to reclaim our balance.

This was an exercise we had done often. One that was familiar to Charmaine. She opened her eyes and looked at me, mouthing the words "thank you" to me. Quietly I urged Charmaine to continue, to move through this moment. She told me that she saw a pathetic little girl, whose eyes were now staring dead in space. The smell of semen, urine and blood were filling her nostrils as she looked on.

I heard her breath making ragged sounds. I opened my eyes again to look at her. She squeezed my hand and said "I'm ok Doc." She proceeded to tell me how she had heard raucous laughter, heavy breathing, and absolutely no sounds at all from the child. She said she saw both her parents. They were having a grand time. They were drunk with no care or regard for the little sexually abused child that belonged to them. Most everyone there was drunk on alcohol. She thought that she recognized the man who had raped the child. There was blood on the floor where Boo Boo was.

Charmaine shifted in the chair as I opened my eyes to see her looking at me. She had miserably sad eyes. She lowered her head. As if she was thinking out loud, she quietly said that she now knew that it was Boo Boo who went through this abuse rather than her. She began to remember all the times she had screamed hollered, cried and had been beaten. Charmaine then said, she understood things clearly now: it was because of Boo Boo that she had no memories of what had happened to her as a small child.

Charmaine took my hand once more. She told she had to finish this. "I HAVE TO!." she said. Once again she closed her eyes as she started talking. She described Boo Boo, not herself. She was exploring what was striking her the most; talking about the times of such horror, abuse and everything that was going on. While all this pain was inflicted on this little child, she never made a sound, never uttered a word.

Charmaine repeatedly stated that Boo Boo's eyes looked dead. She gazed off to a place where there were no people and never made as much as a whimper. I had to wonder if she was seeing herself for the first time, and remembered the bruising, the pain, the fears or if she was still talking about Boo Boo. I could tell connections were being made. It was a painful reality.

She continued to lead me through the room, quietly describing the things that were happening in parlors, in hallways, on sofas and couches. She described the drinking, sex, laughter, and smells, in vivid detail. She detested the high style paintings, the rugs, and fancy décor. Under the auspices of a weekly bridge gathering of church friends; it was a time of drunkenness and sexual exploitation of the child by the host couple's associates.

She used words like "unthinkable, people taking turns, all kissing together, doing things I have never heard of, and making noises like animals." She spoke of the Doctor carrying Boo Boo to the couch as we stood and watched. How he laid her there naked with all the adults laughing and partying.

Charmaine said she wanted to go to her and cover her. She was afraid to touch her. Afraid that touching her might hurt her, or frighten her. Charmaine was disgusted; she said the men kept lusting after her limp little body lying there so pitiful, hurt and so very vulnerable.

I noticed that Charmaine had turned herself in the chair as if looking over her shoulder. She said we were walking again. It was then that Charmaine looked back again and told me to look over my shoulder at Boo Boo. She told me Boo Boo was limp from the horrible brutality, and taking on so much on her behalf, she had not really remembered this having occurred until now. Charmaine had expressed deep pain and sorrow.

Charmaine told me that Boo Boo was filthy from being on the floor, there was blood now caked on her precious little body. She was cold. Her eyes were pleading for someone to save her, to get her out of there. Yet all those people were just drinking and partying like she did not exist.

She did not know if Boo Boo was asleep or unconscious from pain, she only knew that this was horrendous, and she was ready to leave. I double squeezed her hand tightly and told her whenever she was ready. For her to be sure she had done all she had come for.

Charmaine turned around in her chair, squeezing my hand she said, in a whisper, "I'm ready to go Doc" and nodded her head up and down. We were walking out of hell it seemed. Charmaine raised her hand like she was closing the door with the knob and I knew we were heading back toward the archway. She had done what she come to do, no need for her to flee to her cubby anymore, we were on our way.

Later Charmaine said she could not help but look at her parents and wonder why they ever had her, if only to abuse her and allow others to harm her this way.

One thing is certain, Charmaine's parents at one time were the upper class by the descriptions she was giving of her home, the furnishings and the well-to-do people they associated with.

Their death had not left her with an inheritance. She was a woman of little means, which told me that not only had she been severely emotionally, physically and tragically abused; she had also been left with nothing from these people who exploited her.

I was glad they were dead and could not hurt her anymore. It was as if I was being read the script of a bad porn movie, or a horror film gone wrong. No one to go after or prosecute; the victim so very harmed by it all that she had no emotional energy left as she witnessed it firsthand. She was the orator of a series of events. She spoke as someone who was totally detached from the series of criminal and emotional damage done to her as a little child.

At that moment, it felt as though I would explode with outrage. My client was unemotional in the telling secondary to her DID. She was not there at the moment: she was only sharing the script, the story. She had yet to process the pain. She wanted to get through the room, out of the hallway to someplace she could once again breathe.

There were moments of great emotional response from the pain of long ago, but most of her upset was directed toward the Alters. How had they been able, and willing to do this for her? The Alters had suffered, in her behalf. Yet, as she witnessed and reported this, there was an odd sense of detachment in the telling: it was as though she cared more for the Alters than she could care for herself.

On some level she had experienced this through the Alters. It was me who was seeing it all for the first time, I had to remember. To some degree I had to remain objective through it all. Sometimes it was a real challenge to remain an advocate, to remain so neutral, when your own mind is reeling in outrage; knowing that the people who did such horrendous acts are no longer alive to be punished for something so wrong.

Staying present continues to be a most valued asset in dealing with trauma. Whether new, recurring, or delayed onset; this was a reminder of the value of being present and meeting a client where they are. At times like this, it indeed tests a person on all levels as you bear witness to such horror and tragedy. Such acts of perversion and travesty against innocents are hard to digest or to understand, yet alone process.

I'm certain that it was not lost on Charmaine the many times she felt my hand shake as I held on to her, nor the many tears I shed as I quietly listened to all that she was sharing in such graphic detail. It was difficult to keep our steps in sync as we walked that walk.

I recognized that there were times when she probably questioned why I was having an emotional reaction; those times that made my heart beat against my chest when she was not feeling anything at all. She had only to tell the story, often in a monotone voice with no expression. In her mind, this had happened a long time ago, it was over and done, it was not her memory. She had detached so long ago, it was hard to own the events, even though they had happened to her over and over.

We would spend more time on that issue at a later date. The important thing was the work she was doing now and my emotions were not the issue nor the problem. Privately, I wept for the many children that had suffered in similar circumstances. Some who will never even know why their lives are so complex and troubled. I have never been more proud of a person and their courage, than I was of Charmaine as she sought to understand all that had happened to her.

All of a sudden Charmaine's body tensed. She let go of my hand and faced me. "My God Doc, she cannot go away like Laylee, she is just a baby. The loop is still running. I have to save her, that is what those messages in my journal have been saying, that is why her eyes were pleading with me. I have to save Boo Boo from that hell. I have to go back and get her Doc. That is Boo Boo's memory, it is a constant loop Doc. It will just keep playing and playing, with those bastards over and over forever and forever if I do not go back and get her, do you understand that? They are doing what they were doing when we first opened the door and now they are repeating it over and over. DO YOU HEAR ME??? I HAVE TO SAVE HER. I cannot let that happen. I will not let that happen, I am going back to get Boo Boo."

Together we turned around once more. Charmaine told me to stay there right there in the hallway as she ran back to the door and reached her hand up to turn the knob. Before doing so, she turned and looked me in the eye and said. "Doc, you have to wait there, I have to do this by myself. I will be back. I'm alright, but I have to save Boo Boo." With that announcement, as I watched, Charmaine reached up and turned the knob on the door and went into hell alone to save the little Alter known as Boo Boo.

I waited. The silence was deafening. I did not say a word. I just waited as I bowed my head. I found myself looking around. Without realizing it I had started to very slowly stroll back toward the archway in my mind's eye, when all of a sudden I heard Charmaine's soft voice.

I was never a very good as a bystander anyway. I figured I could pace a little until she had done what she needed to do. The urgency in her voice was not lost on me. "Doc, hold out your hands quick"... without thinking I extended my arms in the air. Charmaine quickly said, "Here I want you to hold Boo Boo, I'll be right back! Hold her now. Cuddle her tight to you."

I looked at my arms, and brought them up to my chest as if I had a child in them. I then looked at Charmaine who had by then turned and was running back to Boo Boo's room.

I stood for the longest time as though holding Boo Boo close to my chest. I found I was rocking gently, this invisible Alter who to me was quite real since I had actually been with Charmaine when Boo Boo had been present in the office. I had been in that place, behind the door, as Charmaine vividly described the child, and what she endured.

This was not a hard stretch; to imagine that I was holding this fragile and tremendously abused little child. And yes, I wept once again as I sat silently rocking in my seat, hoping this gave comfort to that part of Charmaine. All of a sudden I heard a loud explosion. I whirled around and look back down the hallway. I see Charmaine running for all she is worth. Billowing smoke was pouring out of Boo Boo's room. Charmaine is yelling "RUN DOC...RUN" ...

As we got to the entrance to the hallway, we stopped and looked back at all the smoke, the blazing fire. We heard more explosions. I asked Charmaine what in the hell she did. She looked at me with eyes wide saying, "I sent the room to hell where it belongs. I set the place on fire. I went back in ... I poured all that alcohol all over them. I threw matches on them all and lit napkins in liquor bottles and I blew the place up Doc."

I just looked at her. I was trying to regain my own composure. She almost scared me to death. As I tried to grasp what she was telling me, I could swear I smelled smoke. I could sense the tension in my body. Charmaine felt victorious. She was jubilant.

I calmly managed to ask her to tell me again exactly what she had done. It was only then I looked down to see if Boo Boo was alright. I realized that Boo Boo was in reality, not in my arms. That is how real this walk through hell had gotten.

Charmaine hugged me and said "Open your eyes Doc, we're out." She proceeded to tell me that she had returned to the last room, to that scene of hell, and had kicked, hollered, screamed, but had been able to get Boo Boo out. She let them all know what she thought. Torching the room had caused the explosion. She was proud of herself. She had done it.

With that done, she ran down that hall as fast as she could. We had walked out of hell. When she realized Boo Boo was no longer in my arms, Charmaine started crying and said "I saved her Doc. I did it... I saved her." Charmaine just sat there with her hands clasped to her chest as she cried. "I did not want her to disappear. I wanted to hug her and tell her I love her."

I looked at her and asked her if she did not realize that she had gone back to do what no one had done for her back then. She had gone back and saved herself.

Sitting side by side in those chairs, Charmaine almost crumpled as she cried "I did it. I saved me. I saved me." I started to extend my hand to comfort her, when she suddenly sat straight up, with tears streaming down her face said "I did it, didn't I Doc. I really did it."

Charmaine looked at me, and asked me if that meant all the rooms were empty now. I told her that in a perfect world the answer would be yes, but that I felt sure there were still a very small number of essential Alters that were there. Only time would tell. I explained to her that integration within, for her, was probably happening more than she knew. I knew it was not integration that she wanted. She just wanted them all to work in harmony.

Charmaine was now feeling the depth of her own reality, past and present. She did not know that she had beautifully, skillfully executed her very own intervention: though clinical in nature, she had decided when and how. Such intense emotional re-exposure to traumatic events; revisiting her past was necessary, but fraught with peril. I had to rely on my experience with this client, and the emotional state that she was in when we did this walk, to monitor both her and me. Observing her physical and mental state(s) was critical. I knew it was truly soul work. And work it did.

She had indeed walked down that long hall, into the hell that was behind that last door. The trauma had been cumulative, and yes, she unearthed it at its core. She was seeing most of it for the first time as she witnessed it through the eyes of the adult she was; looking at the child she had been. There is always a risk of secondary or vicarious trauma in the telling or reliving of it. It was traumatizing, it was hell. We had to deal with that. We would complete the work that still needed to be done later on in the sessions. Her lost childhood had to be mourned, not only for her, but the Alters as well.

As we sat there, in the safety of my office, I felt overwhelmed with emotion. I felt great pride in this client, and filled with awe. The emotions still needed to be held tightly within me as I watched Charmaine.

Her body language reflected the emotions that had before been so distant. She now owned fully all that she had seen and felt in the presence of Boo Boo.

I too felt exhausted, my own body, mind, and spirit feeling the effects of hearing, seeing, feeling such brutality, horror and pain. Those scenes would stay with me longer than I thought. It was not my story, not my life, not mine to concentrate on. I only knew I was feeling the shift from wanting to throw up, to wanting to be sure that she was alright.

I did not want her leaving the office until we had time to debrief on what had happened; to bring to light the positive emotions there; and release the negative ones. I asked her to sit and talk with me about the walk, about the Alters. We laughed at some of the memories, while she cried at others. We talked until I could tell the tension had left her body. Resolve had settled in. She was fully aware of how the Alters came about. How they had served her, and why they had left.

This woman had managed to do what years and years of intense therapy alone only hope to accomplish. Goals had been set. The questions had been asked, denial worked through and debated: a plan was initiated. It had been to some degree "flying by the seat of my pants" and yet somehow, it was scripted and well thought out. Charmaine had made the decision on that day. She had planned it, explained its importance, and announced her intention to do it when she entered my office on that day.

She had a well thought out plan to convince me that she could lead this walk through this hell. I suspected she had rehearsed it over and again. She had spent hours on how to present it to me while secretly wondering if I would allow it to happen on her terms and in her time. I glanced at my watch.

I realized we had been in that hallway more than three hours. Until then, I'd had no idea how much time had passed. I asked Charmaine if she knew how long we had been there. Her reply was, "Well hell Doc, I don't know, I think about 30 minutes or so?"

We had both lost track of time during the walk through hell. I found that in many ways, it seemed both a short amount of time and an event that was endless. As we continued to process the journey, I was struck by the deep well of emotions that Charmaine was now able to express. Her tears fell freely as she recounted the sorrow and pain of the Alter Boo Boo. She now could recall the very real experiences that she had been subjected to as an innocent child.

As she spoke now from such a deep place of grief and sorrow, it seemed she was able to realize that the miracle lay in the fact that she had lived through it. She was amazed that she had managed to raise her own children with love, given that her Alters were born of such tragic circumstances.

We talked about the brain as her creative force that had in fact saved her life. The hallway she visualized held those doors and pathways. The Alters "took over" during times of severe stress, perceived, and very real, threats that she could not, did not, have the ability to cope with.

Charmaine now understood this better than I did. I understood in a way that I never had before. I had grown as a therapist that day in ways that I had not learned through education, seminars or the technical trainings. As we sat together, we had both lost track of time and space.

I also realized that not many could ever truly understand the depths of going with someone into the innermost sanctuary of their mind, and spirit: into the very core of their being. It takes such tremendous trust and courage. Charmaine had mustered all that and more to face her past, its violence, and her demons. The ability she had to describe in such a visual way what that hallway was like and the horrors in that room amaze me still.

We both felt as if someone had simultaneously pulled the same plug from both of us, as exhaustion set in. Before I could say a word, Charmaine said it best, "Doc, I feel so drained I just do not know how I will put one foot in front of the other to get in the car and get home." I wanted to tell her I was feeling the same way, but the therapist in me would not allow it, although I'm sure I showed it in my face. I too felt weak from the walk through hell.

Charmaine, though spent, was calm, smiling easier, exuding pride in her accomplishment. As we ended our session, I asked if she would like me to smudge her with sage once we were outside, to cleanse and purify all that she had been through. Hopefully it would give her enough energy to get home.

Although exhausted, she looked lighter in many ways; the worry gone from her face, the fear gone from her eyes. Hope seemed to create an aura around her. I lit the sage in a bowl and its smoke encircled her on that dark night of healing. She walked the walk......

I was just the guardian and it was intended to be that way on that day.

Charmaine let me know that she thought that was a fitting end to all we had been through. While she did not think our work together was finished, one thing was certain, she had learned a lot about choices. Her choice was to heal herself. She had to find all the strength and power within herself to reclaim her life.

As she turned and walked down the stairs to her car, I noticed the change in her posture. I found myself smiling as I recognized JR's swagger. He turned to salute me once Charmaine had opened the car door. Somehow, I had known that he would still be around. As exhausted as Charmaine was, I had half figured that he would be driving them home.

I had just known in my heart that certain Alters would remain until Charmaine no longer needed them and the security of having JR was one reason I had half expected JR to still be here. I knew that even though Charmaine was feeling stronger, she still liked knowing that JR was there to protect her.

Sometimes total integration does not always happen but rather total cooperation. And wondered if this was what was happening to Charmaine now.

Charmaine's journal- Walking Out of Hell

I always remembered always hearing doors slam when I ran to my cubby. I always wondered what they were. And sometimes I would be sitting doing nothing or be in a group of people and hear those doors slam or hear the bar sound talking but never knew what it was. Then one day, after Doc had talked to me about having Alters, it dawned on me that the rooms were the Alters. I am very sensory and have a great visual capacity which grew under Doc's guidance. She used visualization a lot and so visualizing the hallway and the rooms inside the hallway became easier and easier.

One day, I could hear someone talking and I kept saying "who are you?" like asking out into space "anyone out there?" But the strange thing was, this time I got an answer and it was "I am Laylee. What do you want dahlin?" I shivered because no one was in the room with me but someone answered me. Could it really be an Alter? I was so scared that I ran to my cubby and that is the last I remembered.

I don't know how long it has been...days I think. It dawned on me that when I ran to my cubby that some of the doors were open. Hmmm I wonder what that means?? As I look at my journal, I keep finding entries that say in childlike writing:

"Please help me. Please save me."

"Please someone save me."

Over and over I find these notes. One time I even found them in my bathroom on the mirror in childish scrawling. I found myself crying when I saw those for I could tell by the notes that someone was in trouble or was in bad pain. But how do I help them??

It has been a week since I heard the voice tell me it was Laylee. Who was Laylee? I remembered that name. I suddenly felt sick as I remembered Laylee. I thought she was locked up. She was the one that took me to that town where Doc had to come save me. Ok, if Laylee was out I wanted to talk to her. So I called out so softly as I did not want anyone to hear me.

"Laylee? Are you there?" Laylee answered and I almost fell out of my chair. Again she said "What do you want dahlin?" Finally, nervously, I said "I want to talk to you." And Laylee told me to come on in. I told her that I did not know how and she told me to go lay down on the bed this time and close my eyes and head to my cubby. That she would meet me there.

I thought what the hell and got up and headed to the bed. The only way I will know is to do it. If I tell Doc this, she will commit me for sure. Lying down, I did what I always did and started down the hallway to my cubby and there in the hallway stood Laylee who looked just like the drawings. She said "hello shuga. What you want?" I found myself staring with my jaw slack. Finally, I asked her to tell me about them in the hallway. And that is when I learned how the hallway worked.

I found we were sitting at a table in the hallway. I asked her why and she said "this is where we have round table talks". I asked her to please tell me about the rooms and how they got there. Laylee told me that each Alter came because of the ugly abuse and I was stunned and said "what abuse? I don't remember any abuse."

And Laylee told me that of course I did not remember as it was hers and the other Alters memories. The realization was more than I could take at that moment and I started wailing. Laylee told me how she and Zoe hated me because I did not make them stop and I told her how could I make someone stop when I don't remember it or know how? And that made me cry even worse. I felt like I had done something horrible to her.

Laylee showed me her room and in it was like a movie going on only it repeated and repeated. I felt my breath suck from me and leaned against the wall crying no no no. Suddenly someone was at my side holding me and it took me a few minutes to recognize Deseree from the pictures. She told me it was all true and that the Alters lived the nightmare over and over until I learned how to deal with it and then they could go and leave the hallway. I asked her to where and she said "Why, of course to the inside of you my precious Charmaine". I could not get it at first and said "Isn't this inside of me??" And Deseree said "no, this is the hallway where you have made us each a cubby"

Looking back into the room at the sexual acts going on, I wonder when did this all happen? I have no memory of it. At times Laylee looked like she was enjoying it and then other times she looked deeply hurt and in pain. I did not understand. ...I looked at Laylee and said "I am so very sorry. I am so sorry. I did not know and did not know to stop them Laylee." And I started crying because the full realization of what she said hit me so hard.

Laylee looked at me, hugged me and told me that was all she needed to know and turned and walked away from me and it looked like she was going through the wall of the room. I started crying "NO NO don't go please don't go" as I ran to the wall but nothing was there anymore. I beat my hands on the wall screaming *"Laylee, come back. Please come back"* as tears ran down my face. And when I turned around the movie was gone. Deseree said for me not to worry that Laylee was in me but right then I felt like I lost part of me and it scared me and hurt me. I could not stand it. I did not want to lose any of them.

After that, Deseree explained to me that some Alters were gone already as I learned to deal with things in therapy but that a few remained. I asked her who was sending me notes to help her and Deseree told me about Boo Boo and how she did not talk. I just nodded and told her I wanted to go to my cubby. I did not feel good. She led me down and even tucked me in and I went to sleep.

When I woke up, it seemed like days later. I sat there thinking and knew I wanted to take Doc in this hallway and was not sure how I could do it but I was going to try because there was one room I wanted to go into that I had avoided all this time. It was the door closest to my cubby at the end of the hallway. Today was a session day and I was eager to see Doc. I felt like the day had been dragging until time for my appointment and could not stay still because I felt like today was the day we would take care of that room. I finally left and drove around town just to pass the time until my session time. I had been thinking about this for a while. As I drove up to the office, I almost laughed when I thought about what I was going to suggest to Doc because I could see her face. I was going to use her own words on her just because she would get it.

It was time for her to open her mind and her visualize so that she could see that hallway. I knew that if anyone saw me now they would think I was losing it cause I was riding in my car and giggling my head off at the idea of visualization and Doc when I said those words to her. Doc was pretty open and willing to try new things though. When I got to the office, I could tell no clients were there as hers was the only car. I walked on into the building and to her office. The door was open and so I stepped into the door frame. She was busy writing at her desk. I knew I was a few minutes early, so I just stood there and watched.

Suddenly she looked up and saw me and stopped writing. I heard her say "Gosh Charmaine, you startled me. I was so focused on what I was doing. You are early but come on in." I could feel the excitement brewing in me as I knew what I wanted to do. I walked inside and sat down in the big overstuffed chair and looked at her. She sat watching me with her pencil still poised to write and only silence lay between us. She raised an eyebrow with a quizzical and I finally told her that I wanted us to do something different today. Laying her pencil down, Doc looked at me and said "ok. What is it?" Taking a deep breath, I told her I wanted to take her into the hallway with me because there was a room I wanted to go into but I wanted her to go with me.

Still looking at me directly she asked me how I purposed to do that. Grinning, I said "the same way you have been telling me to go inside the hallway.

"Just close your eyes Charmaine and allow yourself to see inside the hallway and those that are there". Doc laid her pen down and started laughing and replied "oh great, now the grasshopper is using my own words on me". We decided that this was going to be a very intense appointment and we needed to know the afternoon was free and it was.

As she got up from her desk with her pad, I looked at her and said "No no. Getting you inside will be hard enough without you trying to write." She said she would agree if I allowed her to video tape and I told her that was fine. She had videotaped a lot of our sessions so I was not worried.

I was thankful she was willing to do this because I knew it was a little bit off the wall from what most therapists did. I told her I needed her to sit real close to me so that our legs and shoulders were touching to keep us connected. She just smiled and nodded. I was ready to smack that nod off her head but had to laugh.

Before we started, she made sure the sign was on the office door telling "session in progress-do not disturb" and returned to her seat. She looked at me, reached over and took my hand and leaned her head back on the back of the big chair and told me "ok, let's go". I smiled to myself because I was about to take Doc "where no man had gone before" and I started giggling at the thought. She opened one eye and said "I am waiting". I told her what went through my head and she even laughed and then we settled down to walking the hallway in my head.

The following is my talking as best as I can recall it and her asking questions. This is my memory and how I felt during the walk. I asked Doc was she ready to start and she nodded. I said "Ok, we are going through a big arched door like you see in the stucco houses and inside it is a long hallway. It is kind of like those doors you see in those movies with the underground labs with security doors that shut after each section. The hall is wide and there are multiple doors on each side".

She asked me how long was the hallway and I told her it was very long and there were many doors on each side and at the end was my cubby that I refer to in sessions that I ran to when scared. I asked her could she visualize it and she said yes. I told her that a guy called Bart stood guard at this door but that he would not hurt us. Doc told me she was already aware of Bart so all was good. As I leaned back into the chair,

I started talking very slowly as I used my mind's eye to visualize the hallway. "Ok, we are going to walk slowly cause a very few rooms are still occupied but the room I want is at the end of the hallway on the right side. It is Boo Boo's room. I think Boo Boo is maybe five years old."

Doc explained to me that she had seen Boo Boo and that Boo Boo always broke her heart as she looked like a war victim. I told her I just knew it was Boo Boo sending me messages for help. As we are "walking", I explained to her how these rooms used to be all occupied and every time I passed a door the door would slam shut and make a horrible sound like this

(And I smacked my hand on the other side of the big stuffed chair and Doc jumped) but that I usually was running down this hallway scared and so did not stop to see why.

In my head, it was doors of the hallway slamming shut like security doors. It took Laylee and Deseree to help me understand that Alters lived in these rooms and that the rooms contained film loops of the abuse. I knew some of these rooms had emptied out and the contents and the Alters that occupied them were gone but it had taken me until now to understand what made them empty. She asked how many doors and all I could tell her was "a lot".

We came to the first room on the left, I told her that this room was Laylee's room but Laylee was gone now and so was the stuff in the room. She asked me how I knew. I told her I would tell her later but that Laylee told me. I said that at first I was overwhelmed from Laylee because it was like a faint memory that I had always carried was coming into focus.

I remember crying that day …crying because the faint memories I had were really true. I thought I was just too sensitive and was taking on movies I had seen and that it was not true. Surely no one would do such horrible things to me. But, they had. I think Doc realized I was getting veered away from the walk and so she tightened her grip on my hand as I talked. She asked me what the room had looked like and I told her that it was a scene of some man from my father's work that was undressing me. And it was sex where Laylee sometimes appeared flirtatious and other times appeared to be unhappy and hurting. It was hard to understand at times.

I started describing the look on my face in that room and how suddenly I seemed to go limp as the man positioned himself over me and forced himself inside me. I knew that when I had reached a point I could not take anymore. I was told that it was then Laylee became me and she was the one being abused by the man. I did not go into great detail as I had already been through this room before and did not want to spend time talking about it. I understood why Laylee had come to live in my head. It was to protect me and like a ghost that could rest until this or that was done, she had remained captive in the hallway until I learned to deal with it.

I do not think Doc realized that she was gripping my hand so hard and I did not realize it at first as I became lost in the revealing of what I knew about the hallway inside my head. I stretched my fingers out to try to get her to relax the grip some and she did and said "sorry" softly. Doc asked me could I see all that in the room now and I told her no. The last time the room was alive, I was in there and saw it and that was the first time I understood what an Alter did.

I told Doc that once I could see and understand what had happened to me and why the Alter came, the Alter left and never returned. I felt like I lost part of me at that time but I knew intellectually that the door she walked out of was really a door into me as we merged into one. It was the emotional loss I would have to deal with later on.

The silence in the hallway is palpable as we continue walking. A few doors are closed and I told Doc that and she asked me why? I said because JR still lives in one, Charie lives in one, Deseree lives in one, Boo Boo (who is older than Charie) lives in that one on the end. I think there may be others too. It is Boo Boo's room that I need to go to as I keep finding notes from Boo Boo in my journal and torn off and stuck in places like in my medicine cabinet and the notes would say things like "please save me".

Boo Boo never talks. Boo Boo truly looks like and is a war victim Deseree told me as she went on to say that Boo Boo got the worst of the abuse as it came from that group who pretended to be such good upstanding members of society. It was then I learned that Deseree and JR had been tracking those people keeping records on them until they had learned that they had all died and they had their obituaries to show me one day soon.

As we continued walking down the hallway, I started talking about Charie and I told Doc that Charie did not seem to be abused. She was too happy and loving and playful and funny. I really think that Charie is the child I never got to be. She is also so innocent and so funny and when she talks, people actually think there is a child in the room. My oldest son, who is the only one of the three that know of my DID, actually favored JR and Charie of all the Alters.

I remember helping a friend who had split up with his wife and I was cleaning in the house to help him. He told me later that he kept hearing this child's voice and when he went and looked, it was me. I was washing the glass doors to the patio and he said the first thing he heard was "oh no. me not mean do that" in a child's voice and I would rub and rub the window with the rag. And then he heard this child giggling and looked again and I was standing there spraying Windex foam on the window and I was drawing pictures in the foam and laughing.

Something brought Charie out at his house. Perhaps it was that I trust this person and felt safe with him and so did Charie. After I finished helping clean and was about to leave, he told me about hearing the child and seeing me so child like. He said he was shocked at first and thought "I hear a small child" and started searching the house. He knows that I am DID and so he knew what it was. I was lucky in that this person accepted me as I am because many did not. I hated people knowing that I was different because some would always try to prove that I was "faking" and make comments. No one in their right mind would fake being DID.

I finally told one person that no one would want to live as I had been living with all the blank spots and ending up in places that did not know how I got there. But some people would get jealous if others showed attention and those jealous would try to prove me a fake. I learned to distance myself from those kinds of people.

As we kept walking, Doc told me that she had encountered Charie before and that Charie was precocious and made her laugh more than once. She asked me to describe Bart to her because she said that Charie always told her that Bart would let her sneak out to play. And she would say for Doc to "pwease no tell. Me get in twouble". I told her that Bart is this big burly guy who is very kind but Deseree has him to guard the door for Alters that hurt me would try to get out and Bart's job was to keep them in and all the others in unless she knew.

Doc asked me what Charie's room looked like and I said it looked like a room made for a very special child with dolls and a doll house and books and pretty dresses and a beautiful canopy bed made for a child. I told her that was the reason that I thought Charie was the child I never got to be...happy and full of love and life. Charie had this way of holding her arms out and opening and closing her little hands for a hug. This, I had determined was where my love of dolls came from and my love of children's toys.

I stopped for a minute and Doc asked me what was wrong. I told her that I was just listening because I had all my life heard what sounded like bar sounds...people talking but you would not understand a word they said and now the mumbling sound was much lower and occasionally I would catch phrases. I told her that the hallway was really quiet today and I guessed it was because I was walking her down the hallway.

The closer we got to Boo Boo's room, the slower my feet were moving. I was getting scared. I told Doc that this was the most horrific room and that I was terrified of it because one day I was running to my cubby and the door was just shutting and I saw inside. She asked me to describe what I saw at that moment and I told her it was a living room and there were people in there all grownups and they were sitting all around doing sex things. But what scared me was I saw Boo Boo sitting on the couch and she was so little and she had no clothes on and the people had this horrific look in their eyes. I can only describe it as evil.

When we got to Boo Boo's door, I could feel myself shaking inside and thought to myself that I was so glad that I no longer had accidents or I would have one now. I leaned against Doc's arm for a minute and she asked me was I ok. I told her yes but that I felt sick because I thought I knew what was on the other side of the door only I kept it hidden and standing there I could feel part of the horror. OMG, I want to run...damn I want to run. I think I am going to be sick. Whew, I am not sure I can do this. Doc told me "You know you do not have to go in now if you do not want to". I held her hand tightly and said "**I know but I have to...I just have to!**". Doc told me ok and said she was right here with me. She told me to tell her everything I saw, smelled, and heard and to use all my senses but to remember that I was not there anymore. I was watching from a distance.

I pushed the door open and started describing to her what I saw from the door. I described the people in there and where they were and what they were wearing and even the looks on their faces. They were all dressed almost like going to church. Some were grouped and some were walking around. I could smell the alcohol from the door way and felt my stomach *lurch. I said "I think this is why I do not like to drink". Doc had started using this double gentle squeeze to let me know she was hearing me she said so she did not have to interrupt me.*

I think I have a death grip on Doc's hand as we stand at the door. She wants to walk in with me but I tell her I must do this alone. But that I don't want her to let go of my hand and just squeeze if she hears me. There are people all around the room. I am not sure how many. My heart is racing and my stomach is churning for I smell that smell that makes me feel sick instantly. I learned through my therapy that the smell that makes me throw up is the smell of semen and I smell it in this room; semen, alcohol, tobacco and flesh smell I think.

This is the living room of my childhood and is filled with expensive ornately carved wooden chairs with a lot of sculpted and tufted padding and expensive statues and vases. On the floor are oriental rugs on top of the wood flooring.. And the people sitting in there are people who are supposed to be some church prayer group only they are not. They are evil I tell Doc.

I walk slowly through and around people. There are some who are kissing and touching and have pants unzipped and dresses hiked up. I hear Charie in the background saying "Stop. Stop. Dey dot sticks. They dot sticks in dey pant. They hut u." And I pause for a minute trying to digest what she said. I turn and look at Doc and she has the same look of shock on her face as I do. I think we both realize that maybe Charie was abused too.

Doc tells me of the drawings that Charie would do showing men with sticks coming out of their zippered pants where the male penis would be. I look around the room and quite visible are two men with erections while women are doing oral sex on them. And the look in their eyes is glazed over and looks like pure evil with drool coming off their mouths. I feel the blood rush to my face in total shock and embarrassment and I can barely breathe.

I learn later that I am talking in a very detached manner describing horrific scenes as if I were reciting the weather. I guess this was how I have dealt with all the horror. I saw me sitting on the couch naked and I am maybe four or five and my little arms and legs were pulled up to hide myself and the trauma in my eyes is beyond belief. I felt myself stumbling not only physically but also emotionally. I am choking back sobs. Doc keeps squeezing my hand as if to ask am I ok. I guess I had stopped talking. I squeezed back and then held tight as if she were a life line. I stand there almost in a daze watching. I don't know if I can explain what it is like to watch you being raped. I do not know if Doc will even understand that.

One of the players in the room says "It is time" and comes over to where I sit on the couch and pulls me down on the floor and I am shaking and start crying and screaming and one of them slaps me hard across the face. Others proceed to put their hands all over me. I see my eyes roll backwards and my head falls to the side as one jams his penis into my rectum. And as I watch from here, I see this writhing, screaming child suddenly change. Her head lifts back up but her eyes are blank almost and she just lays there letting them do what they want. One of the perverts actually tells her "There's the good girl." as they are raping her repeatedly.

And what I saw was Boo Boo emerging. I was told by Deseree that the reason Boo Boo came is because she would make no sounds. I had been beaten senseless because I would scream out in horror and Boo Boo could take it and never let out a whimper. As I look at Boo Boo, I see the pain and brutality of what is happening reflected in her eyes but she never makes a sound. As I continue to talk to Doc as I walk through the room, describing people and actions that were going on, I felt like I was reading from a script of the horror and had no feeling at all about what was happening at that moment. I felt like I was devoid of feelings and I could not understand it.

I could feel Doc's hand shake a time or two in my hand and knew she was feeling emotions but I had to try to finish the walk through. Then it would be over and Boo Boo could leave like Laylee did. I had to finish. I described in graphic detail all those people did to Boo Boo/me....all of it. It was beyond imagination and people were taking turns doing things to Boo Boo and those that were not were engaged with each other in brutal sex acts that included violence and yet their faces had these horrible evil smiles, drool dripping off their chins as their mouths screamed pure filth.

By the time we got to the door, other acts of brutality had taken place on Boo Boo and she was just laying limp and looked like she was passed out on the floor. She lay there like she was unconscious only her eyes were open pleading and she was dirty from the floor. Those people stood up and straightened their clothes and were smiling and drinking their drinks like at the beginning and one said "she will be ready again in a little while. I like it better when she fights".

I told Doc that was all and we walked out the door and I shut the door behind us thinking now Boo Boo would leave and the room would be empty. As we started back down the hallway, we got about halfway back down the hallway and something inside me clicked. Boo Boo did not leave the room and what the people were doing at the end was like what they did at the beginning. It was like Boo Boo's reel of memory was stuck and playing over and over. That is why she asked me to save her. It was about to happen again to Boo Boo. I could not let that happen.

I asked Doc to wait there for me in the hallway and let go of her hand. I told her I would be right back. I had to do something. I just had to. I ran down that hallway back to Boo Boo's room. I went back to get her and to bring her out of that room. I did not care if she stayed with me forever. I just could not leave her. I went back into that room and what I saw made me almost sick...such perversion and sickness and the smells made me double over but I knew I had to save her somehow. I just had to.

I was screaming at them and started kicking and pushing them off of Boo Boo and I picked her up and walked out the door way and back down the hallway and asked Doc to hold her arms out. She asked me why and I told her it was Boo Boo and I wanted her to hold her. Doc never flinched. She put her arms out and I laid Boo Boo in them and told her I would be right back.

I went back to the room and I got every bit of alcohol I could find in that room, poured it on people, all over the furniture, on the floor and as I walked out, I turned and lit a match book and threw it into the room. I ran back down the hallway yelling "Run! Run!" to Doc, she looked at me and was saying "What? What?" and about that time a loud "boom" sounded only it was really me slapping my hands on the leather chair arms.

Doc said it startled her so badly she sat straight up was, she calmly asked me "what did you do?" As she took my hand back, I told her about pouring the alcohol on them and the stuff in the room and lighting matches and throwing them on them and their screams and look as I walked out the door and slammed it shut. I told her that I just could not leave Boo Boo there. I had to save her. I did!!

I told Doc that I had saved her and showed her that someone loved her and cared about her. And I felt as if part of my life had just ended. I felt like I had failed. She was gone. NO NO NO!! I didn't save her as she was gone. And again I had another empty space. As I was telling Doc all of this, I could feel the emotion in my words and looked at Doc and could see the smile and the tears. She told me that I had done something that was a therapy technique and wanted to know did

I know that. I told her no, that all I knew was I had to save Boo Boo because she had begged too long for someone to save her and to love her and I could not let her down again.

This was the beginning of my learning about choices. I could have chosen to stay a victim or I could choose to save myself and become a survivor by taking action in my own life. I wish I could tell you all the Alters are gone but they are not. They are down to three. JR who came to be my protector and as long as I feel the need to be protected, I have a feeling he will be around.

One was Deseree who was the mother I never had and still need, Charie who was the child I never got to be and as I learn to let go and be that child, who knows...she too may disappear one day. Those that hurt and abuse you would do it again. And I believe Boo Boo remains within my heart as the warrior I have learned to be.

I told Doc that we were walking past Bart and out the big door and we were out of the hallway. Doc asked me if I knew why Boo Boo had come and why she had disappeared and I told her yes with tears in my eyes. She asked me why I was crying and I told her because I lost Boo Boo. I wanted to hold her and love her and she was gone. Doc tried to console me but at that moment I was inconsolable. I felt like a failure.

Me and my big ideas sure did not work. But, Doc kept talking and told me that yes they did work. She said Boo Boo would never feel that torture again and that I was so brave. And I cried again when she looked at me and said "Charmaine, you did what no one did for you years ago. You saved yourself." It took me a few minutes to digest that and then it hit me that yes, I did save her.

I wanted to see what Doc's feelings were about walking the hallway and she told me that she actually felt like she was there and that she felt the explosion and saw the determination on my face when I handed Boo Boo to her and went back to that room. Doc allowed herself to walk with me and to be part of this visualization and said she actually felt Boo Boo in her arms and saw her battered body and had tears in her eyes as she thought about what I had endured. And she looked at me and said "one more room not just empty but blown up and was gone forever".

Doc asked me if I wanted to unwind a few minutes and I said yes. We talked about Charie and all the other Alters. Doc asked me to describe Bart as she wanted to see if my description matched Charie's. I said he was a big hulking man but looked very gentle unless he was dealing with one like Zoe. Doc said "right on target" and smiled. After we had decided to tell my oldest son about the DID issue and Alters, he became my watcher and was always looking to protect me. But, the funny thing was that he must have just really liked the Alter Charie because he would go shopping and ask Charie to come out and go.

The journal told me that Charie would get in the scooters in the store and take off across the store heading for the toys with my son running behind her *trying to catch her. He told me himself that he learned to go first to was occupied while they got whatever they were there to pick up. My son also bought a stocking every year for Christmas for Charie and was always picking up coloring books and crayons and putting them in my room. Doc and I both laughed at the visual of my preppy looking son chasing Charie across Wal-Mart. And yet he always asked to take Charie to the store. We talked about the Alters a lot and then Doc said she was going to smudge me to release all the energies the walk had brought out. I told her fine. I loved when she did the sage and smudge stuff. It felt very cleansing.*

She said she wanted to listen to the tape that night and then wanted us to talk about it tomorrow. I told her that was fine. We both sat there talking a few more minutes about the hallway and I thanked her for walking with me and allowing herself to be in the "picture" as we talked and walked down that hallway, into that room and out of hell. I knew there would be more rooms to enter but I Also knew that the most horrific rooms had been entered and emptied and that gave me hope for my future.

I went home and that night, I slept like I had never slept befor Am I totally over DID? No, I was not but it no longer took my life and hid it from me. I am sure that JR, Deseree and Charie will be here as long as I need them. I probably will have Deseree as long as I need a mother in my life and will have Charie as long as the little girl in me is learning how to be a child and grow into adulthood. As far as JR, right now he makes me feel safe and none of these three does anything to disrupt my life. Sometimes I hear them tell me when I start to get shaky that it is ok. I hear the chant "it is ok. You can do it."

The journey is not over but we have come to the end of a chapter for the most horrific rooms have been entered and I came out, perhaps singed and bruised and battered a bit but I think stronger than ever before. And I am content to be united with all the other Alters and also to be working in unison with the three left. I could not bear to lose any more of me for that is how it feels; like pieces of me are dying and that hurts so badly.

Charmaine's Journal

I am lying here months after finishing the walk through hell and therapy and I realize that I no longer hear the sound of the doors in the hallway. I no longer hear Charie singing in the back of my head and I no longer know where my cubby is. It all seems to have disappeared. I also no longer heard the footsteps running down the hallway. I feel alone and a little shaky but yet at the same time, I feel like I have crossed that line that says I am whole.

While I believe that the Alters Charie, Deseree and JR may be gone, I notice that I still have parts of their essence in me. I find myself clapping my hands like Charie at delightful things. And I look at life through the innocence and joy of a child and yet I am the child....no longer Charie but Charie all grown up; I am Charmaine.

My oldest son says I make expressions just like JR with that raised eyebrow look or with my finger up in the air only not quite. So, this is what tells me that they have finally come home within my soul and are me instead of pieces floating in the universe.

And I have learned how to mother myself and comfort myself. I believe Doc called it "self soothing". I have learned when I get anxious and feel that fluttery feeling to do things that help me relax and keep me from subconsciously needing someone else to take care of things for me. I miss them. I missed the comfort of knowing they were there and of knowing that if something bad did happen, JR would handle it.

And yet, there are times I put on that old baseball cap of JR's and walk outside and sit on the porch and put on his shades and look at the world trying to see it from his side of the lens. As I think about JR and all he did for me, I realize that I did love myself greatly for if I did not, I would never have created a world of Alters to take care of me. And I love them all for all they did. I look at the pictures of them and pictures my son kept to show me how I looked when they were out and I am stunned at the difference.

I have always been alone except for my kids and they are now grown. And so when after the walk through hell and JR, Charie and Deseree were still there, I felt like I had a family and always felt like I was never alone. I have not learned to trust because of *being mistreated so but I have learned to be at peace and happy in my own little world where I paint, draw and do other art. Sometimes just for the fun of it, I call out one of their names and sing an old Red Rover tune...."Charie Charie..come out come out wherever you are. Please Send Charie right over" knowing full well that Charie will not appear. I pick the dolls up and look at them and smell them wondering if you can smell an Alter.*

And sometimes, when I fix something here at my little country cottage and one of my kids turns and asks me how I knew how to fix this or that, I just smile to myself knowing it was JR who held the key to that bit of mechanical knowledge. And when I sit on the old wooden swing in the back yard and gently push back and forth on it, I have sometimes wondered what it would have been like to have a mother that wanted and loved me and would push me in a swing. I would never know those things. I can only give those things to my sons and daughter and their children.

The sad thing about DID is that most of us are alone and lonely. People can be cruel because they do not understand. This is what I hope my story does for those with DID. I hope it helps those families who just do not get it to understand that we are real and so are the Alters and we need love not criticizing.

I miss them. I miss the comfort of knowing that they were there and knowing that if something bad happened JR would handle it. And yet, there are times I put on that old baseball cap of JR's and walk outside and sit on the porch and put on his shades and look at the world trying to see it from his side of the lens.

And sometimes the loneliness is palpable because what is different is not always accepted. I have learned to live alone with my art and my animals but that does not mean I do not ever think about what it would be like to have someone who loved me and cherished me. Being DID does not mean that we are not normal in our desires.

My one child that knows about the DID says that when each Alter came out, the way they talked (except Boo Boo) sounded different, facial expressions were very different, how they wore their hair differently, even how they walked differently and I now know it is true. Many will say it does not exist, some will say "oh I do that", and some will know what it is really like and will nod and think "oh, yes."

I am forever grateful for the fact that my friend led me to a therapist that worked outside the box and was willing to look at DID through a different lens. Many will say it does not exist, some will say "oh I do that", and some will know what it is really like and will nod and think...."oh...my ...yes." And I pray that my story gives them comfort to know that we can make it.

And my deepest desire is to let those suffering with DID and their families know that trying to heal and not near as bad as what you already endured. So, please do not be afraid. Just step out there and do the work to get better for it is possible.

Chapter 25 Afterthoughts

Writing this book has been another great challenge, turned opportunity in my life; one that has taken me back through the times spent with Charmaine, the discoveries of her Alters as they came to be known. Just when we think we have the answers, the questions seem to change. The landscapes of life are all different, always changing as we are once again reminded of the resiliency of the human spirit.

Throughout the years I have studied MPD and have seen its rise to popularity through the movies like Sybil and the Three Faces of Eve. I watched as talk shows seemed to bring the DSM to light with so many seeking the lime light. I had to wonder if this was truly real or not. I tried to be open to the possibilities, the very realness that many personalities could reside within one person and take over, or take control. I still had reservations based on what I too had seen on mainstream media through the years.

I had worked with a few people that I thought had actual manifestations of DID, however, I had never come to know them well enough over time to conclude that the diagnosis fit. Some elected to not continue therapy with me, often not keeping appointments, or just disappearing all together. One I vaguely remember referring to someone much more experienced than I during the early years of my career.

I had my own thoughts about DID. I have always been one to remain open. I am a believer in the magnificent power of the brain. It has the ability to save us when it seems we are lost or drowning in hurt or trauma. I thought I knew so much. In fact, I knew that I was a good, competent and knowledgeable therapist. I came to realize in my work with Charmaine that I had much to learn. Once again, my best teachers have been my clients.

It occurred to me, as if struck by lightning, late one night, as I sat in the dark outside on my lanai, writing furiously, that's what Charmaine's son had so long ago meant. I vividly recalled a session with Charmaine where she and her son were sitting in my office together.

Her son was telling me about a day he had left his Mother in the car as he went in a store. He returned to find the car locked windows up. Rather than his mother looking at him from inside the car; he was seeing a sweet, innocent childlike presence waving at him. As he gently knocked on the window and pointed at the door locks he said to her, "Honey, unlock the door for me." To his shock she grinned and said, "NO'.

I remember the looks exchanged between Charmaine and her son. Their grins, the unconditional love exchanged as he continued to share with me this story: his continued efforts to get her to unlock the doors as people walked by. He was animated as he described trying not to draw attention to himself, only to continually have her tell him "NO." As I listened, I could visualize the situation. I found myself wondering how I would react; what I would do under similar or the same set of circumstances!

He went on to say that he noticed her childlike mannerisms, the mischievous glimmer in her eyes. It didn't take but a hot second to realize he was not dealing with his Mother. He recognized quickly it was little Charie. All he could think of at the time was how in the world he was going to get in that car without drawing attention to her or himself.

I was right there in my mind with him! I could see it as I reflected on that story, on the love shared between a Mother and her accepting son. He let me know that at one point that he said, "Charie, let me in honey" she said... "Nuh uh, ou tell me no ope doors to NOBODY wight?" That young man must have been born with the patience and humor of a saint!

With that, we all laughed ourselves silly. Charmaine slapped his arm letting him know he had just let out the last of their secrets. Charmaine said she guessed she finally let him in the car. She did remember sitting there in the car asking him why in the world he brought her melted ice cream that day. Her son was laughing as he reminded her that it was frozen when he left the store, so it had to be her fault.

That is resiliency, and that is DID; real and uncensored. There was no great drama in shifts of who was out, times of change, as one would read about, or see in the media and talk on shows. It just was what it was, when it was.

Charmaine at the time only remembered the melted ice cream. She had no idea Charie had been there. She did however discover her dark hair a different color, her home in perfect order with good smelling baked goods or conversely, an utter wreck. She could wake up in her usual bed clothes or something that Laylee had worn out the night before. There would be crayons or writings in a journal, bandages on her wrists, or not. She often experienced the consequences, but without an understanding why.

The saving grace was that she showed up one day at the urging of her physician, a pastor, and a friend's suggestion, and plainly stated "I want to know if I am crazy."

From there, began one long twisted journey. That night, as I was near completion of this book, I felt as though I had been knocked out of my chair with a revelation. While I have indeed mulled around many thoughts, had studied, researched, and even questioned myself; it became crystal clear. This had been a soul journey. One of such depth and intensity that DID is as real as I am. In order to help someone walk through the maze of Dissociative Identity Disorder, we must be willing to accept them where they are.

The most difficult and most important thing for a person with DID, may just be that, of being believed. That is critical to the person with the diagnosis, the symptoms, the day to day living. Charmaine would tell me that honesty was the only thing she could control in her life. When someone did not believe her it cut her to the depths of her soul. I soon realized that what Charmaine wanted more than anything was to be believed, and so did the Alters.

The day I met the very first Alter, I realized that Charmaine was a person with Dissociative Identity Disorder. While I stood in amazement, as I watched the Alters, I knew in my heart that this person's identity had been fractured long ago. The hows and whys would be difficult to unearth. My job was to help her put the pieces back together.

There was no doubt in my mind, although there was enough for both of us in hers. She was very different from those we see on the Dr. Phil show; those we see seeking fortune and fame as the next new diagnosis around the corner, or who go into trances and do things that are just too strange for words.

She and her Alters were as real as you or I. When they burst out, or crept out of her brilliant mind, she was nowhere to be found, nor did she have any recall of them later on. Not until she came to understand it all and accept her own reality. This is where meeting and accepting someone as they are becomes as important as breath.

Those were the times that I had to adjust my own lens, for when she appeared as the little Charie, I saw a grown woman in the floor who seemed to appear small, to take on such innocent mannerisms, speech, gestures and actions that it could not have been staged.

There is no way anyone could have pulled that off even if they tried, nor would they want to. There were times I would have to shake my head and take a deep breath. Yet there was the reality that an innocent little girl was sitting in my floor, joyously happy, giving me information about others in the hallway that matched a sketch found in her home that she was unaware of.

Yes, this was a soul journey; a once in a lifetime opportunity for me. To be given the gift of such trust. To have been able to uncover the many mysteries Charmaine's life posed for her. It is my hope that others with DID, and those that love them, or work with them, may be empowered. From a woman with a tortured childhood; to an Alter who played in the floor; to JR who appeared taller, very masculine and forceful, calling me "Showalter;" they paraded before me. JR was so real that I did not notice that he had breasts, as I was so taken by his walk, his talk, his very presence. He was not Charmaine.

Years later, I learned that when JR left the house in his own clothing he wrapped the breasts with Ace bandages to make sure they were not obvious to the world. That was a revelation that only came to me in a letter from him after our therapy was long over. It hit me that with Charmaine there were so many obvious things that separated her and the diagnosis of DID from those who claim to be DID for whatever reasons. From things that Laylee did in her promiscuity, to Deseree with her matronly way she gathered the Alters and kept the house in such tidy order to that wonderful ride on JR's motorcycle that had been hidden so well that Charmaine did not even know she had one.

Those who are pretending to be DID, would never take their teeth out in public and hand them to someone, or let a therapist or stranger know that someone pooped on the porch. They would not ride through Wal-Mart on a cart with their son running after them as they giggled; as only a child can. This is real DID.

Many with this disorder hide from the public; they retreat from therapy or social events because they fear what may happen. They cannot predict the events in their lives, in fact they do not even know what happens when they experience black outs. I have heard some with DID express feelings that they do not have the love or support of friends and family who accept them as they are. Most will never know what they have suffered, or how they have been traumatized unless they piece together clues left by their Alters.

There lies the great tragedy, so many persons with DID are so alone in their pain, not knowing how to heal. This journey **Down the Hallway** is in real time and now gives another face to DID. A face to therapy that is open; accepting of the point where a client began her journey and her life. This has been her walk from fear through hell, to the top of the mountain as we are reminded of hope, integrity, and courage. It has been an exceptional honor to walk with Charmaine. I pray I have done her story justice.

As the months progressed, Charmaine slowly let go of the remaining Alters without even realizing it. She came to my office to tell me of the revelation she had that she no longer heard the doors slam in her hallway. No longer did she run down the hallway to safety. We completed our journey together as a client/therapist.

What she never realized as our time came to a close, was that as I looked at her I still saw expressions of Charie or Deseree, and even JR. I see their mannerisms and expressions. While they are no longer Alters that burst forward, they have fully become Charmaine. That is who they were all along: Charmaine carved into pieces through trauma and pain but still Charmaine.

Now the pieces are in place working as a whole. Trauma realized, processed, healing moving through life. Her life is fuller and richer. The walk through hell allowed her to gain control. Charmaine still has the humor, the innocence of Charie, the organizational skills and comforting nature of Deseree; the warrior spirit of JR and all the other Alters that made up who she is today. Only she no longer needs the hallway for them to live in.

"Life is one continuous dance through this great hoop called life. We can either live life sitting on the sidelines, afraid to wear a hole in our moccasins or we can dance until they fall off. The mocs can be replaced, or you can dance barefoot. Celebrate life in right way relations, ALL DAY all ways." [DRSES]

The Author:

Dr. Showalter is a Licensed Clinical Social Worker, Board Certified Diplomate, and an Ordained Minister of Metaphysics; a lifelong learner, now living on the Gulf coast of Florida. She has spent decades working in hospice care.

Dr. Showalter was born in Virginia, and served as a first responder during 9/11 at the Pentagon. She is certified in Mass Fatalities, trauma response, and EMDR.

A graduate of The American University, Virginia Commonwealth University and the University of Sedona, Dr. Showalter now speaks across the country to groups, communities, and businesses on a myriad of topics. Her most requested keynotes/ seminars are that of inspiration, motivation, hope, humor, loss, death and compassion fatigue for those in health and mental health professions.

Dr. Showalter received the esteemed National Heart of Hospice award for psycho-social-spiritual Caregiving from the National Hospice and Palliative Care Organization. She is listed in WHO"S WHO for lifetime achievement and is a member of NASW, ARC, NAPW, ADEC. She has been published numerous times in professional journals for her work on loss, death, and grief.

She is also the author of Healing Heartaches, Stories of Loss and Life and co-author of Chronic Pain; Hand in Hand. Dr. Showalter has worked with individuals across the life span, has learned from each individual and family that she walked beside.

She often states that she is "amazed at the resiliency of the human spirit." *Down The Hallway* is a book that has taken her from her wheel house of grief into another dimension. She has experienced levels of grief and trauma that were both complicated and unfamiliar with challenges that were opportunities. It was a journey with an ever changing landscape of one woman's fight to reclaim her life in her own way as she moved from fear to survival.

"It has been a remarkable journey, in real time and again in writing the story. I am honored to have been chosen to tell Charmaine's story while spreading awareness of another dimension of DID, real and uncensored." [DRSES}

info@drsherryeshowalter.com

www.authordrsherryeshowalter.com

Twitter @DRSES

Twitter @DownHallway

www.drseswordpress.com

www.facebook.com/DrShjerryEShowalter

www.youtube.com/DrSherryKeepinItReal

Made in United States
Orlando, FL
23 December 2022

27591329R00349